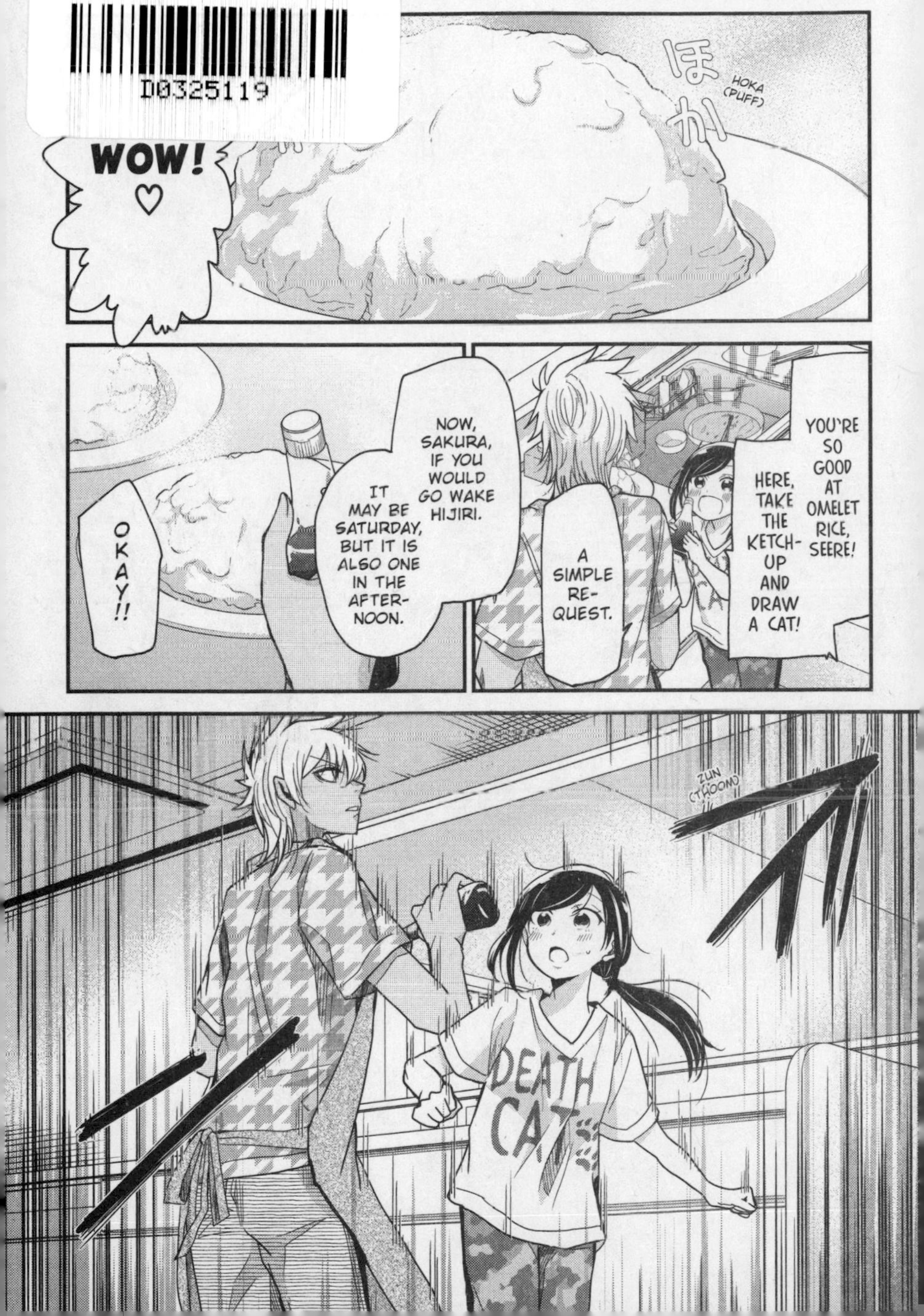
ほか
HOKA (PUFF)
WOW! ♥
YOU'RE SO GOOD AT OMELET RICE, SEERE!
HERE, TAKE THE KETCH-UP AND DRAW A CAT!
A SIMPLE RE-QUEST.
NOW, SAKURA, IF YOU WOULD GO WAKE HIJIRI.
IT MAY BE SATURDAY, BUT IT IS ALSO ONE IN THE AFTER-NOON.
OKAY!!
ZUN (THOOM)
DEATH CAT

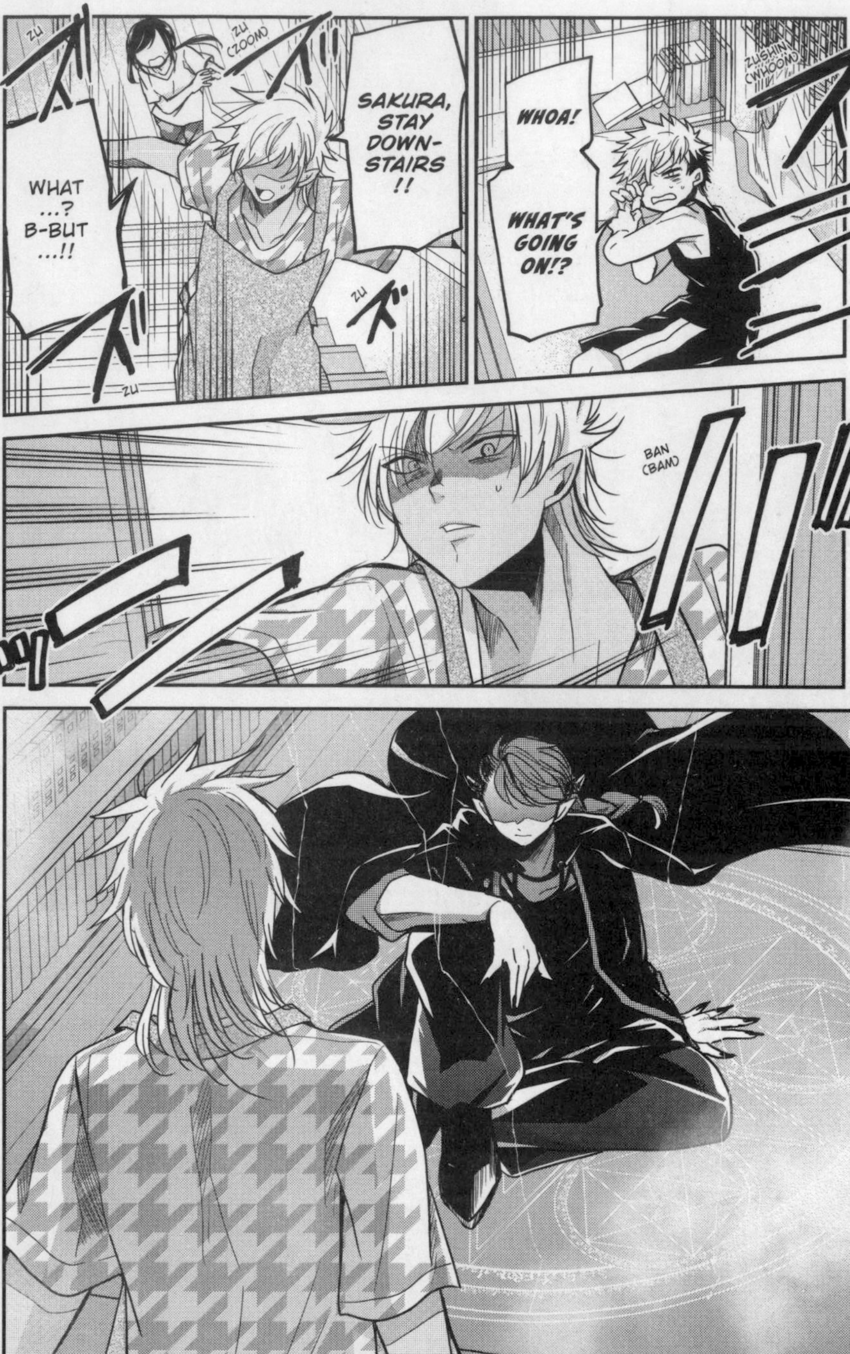
ZUSHIN (WHOOM)
WHOA!
WHAT'S GOING ON!?
ZU (ZOOM)
ZU
SAKURA, STAY DOWN-STAIRS!!
WHAT ...? B-BUT ...!!
ZU
ZU
BAN (BAM)

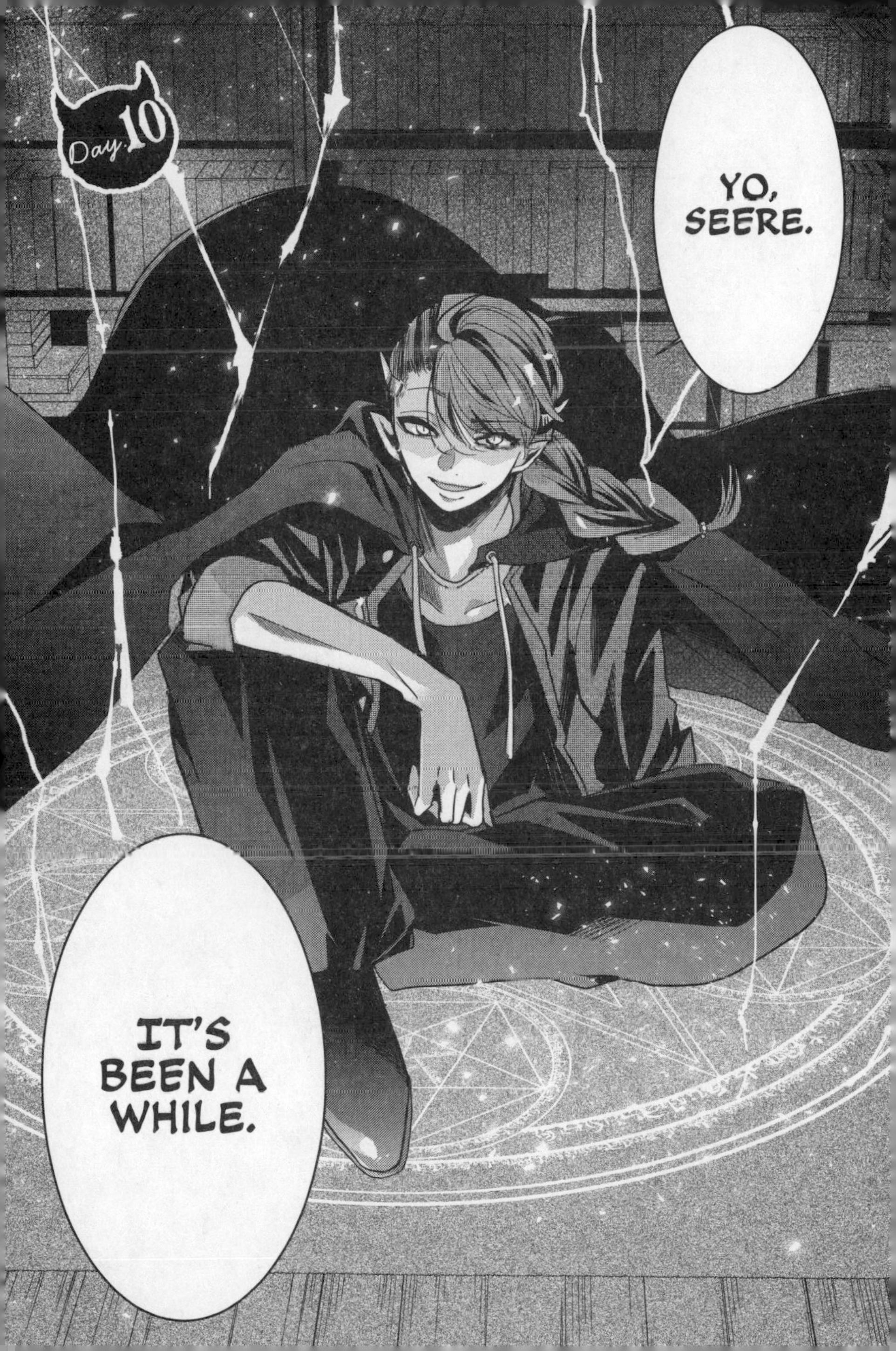
Day. 10
YO, SEERE.
IT'S BEEN A WHILE.

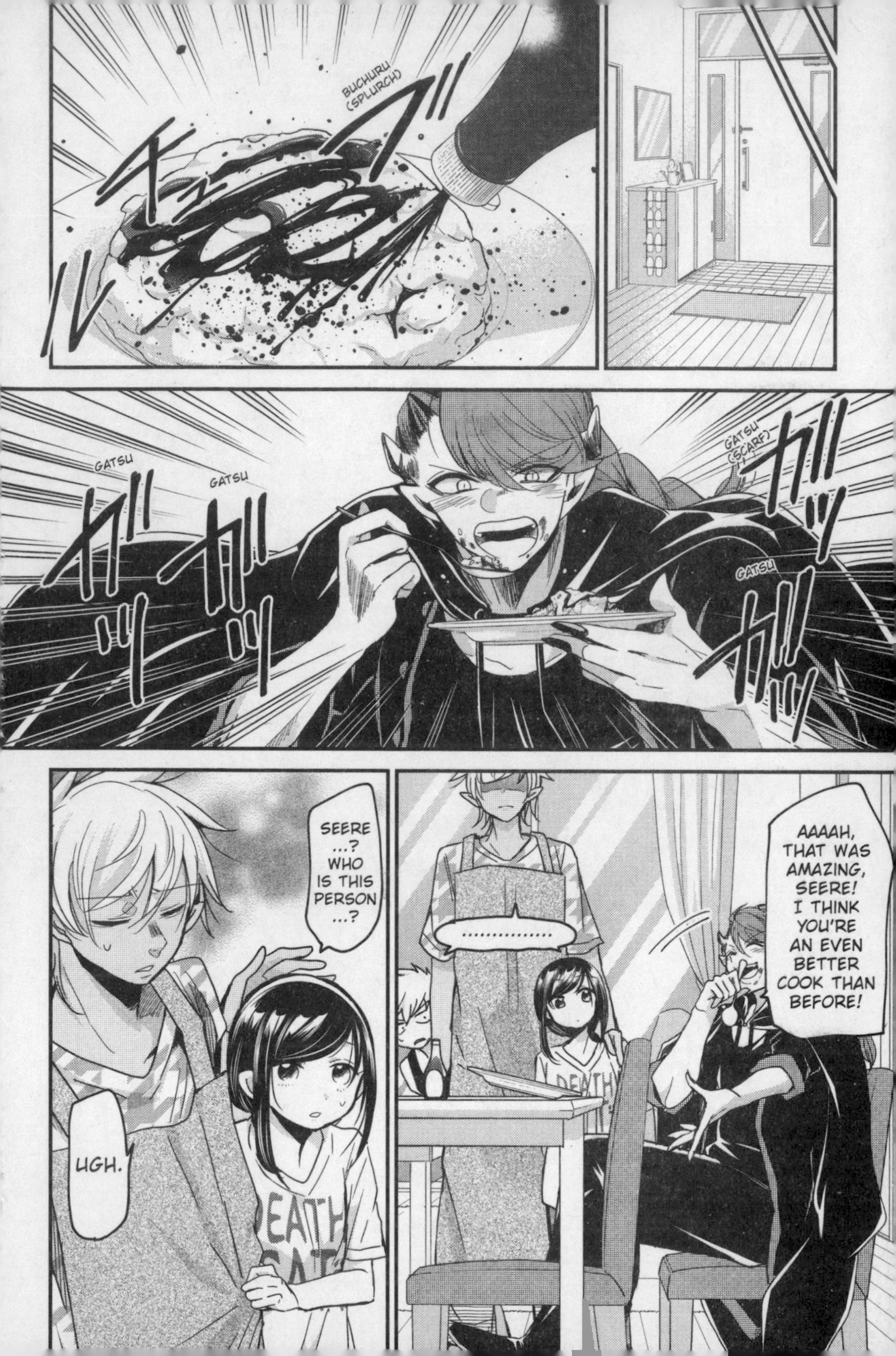
BUCHURU (SPLURCH)
GATSU (SCARF)
GATSU
GATSU
GATSU
AAAAH, THAT WAS AMAZING, SEERE! I THINK YOU'RE AN EVEN BETTER COOK THAN BEFORE!
...............
SEERE ...? WHO IS THIS PERSON ...?
UGH.

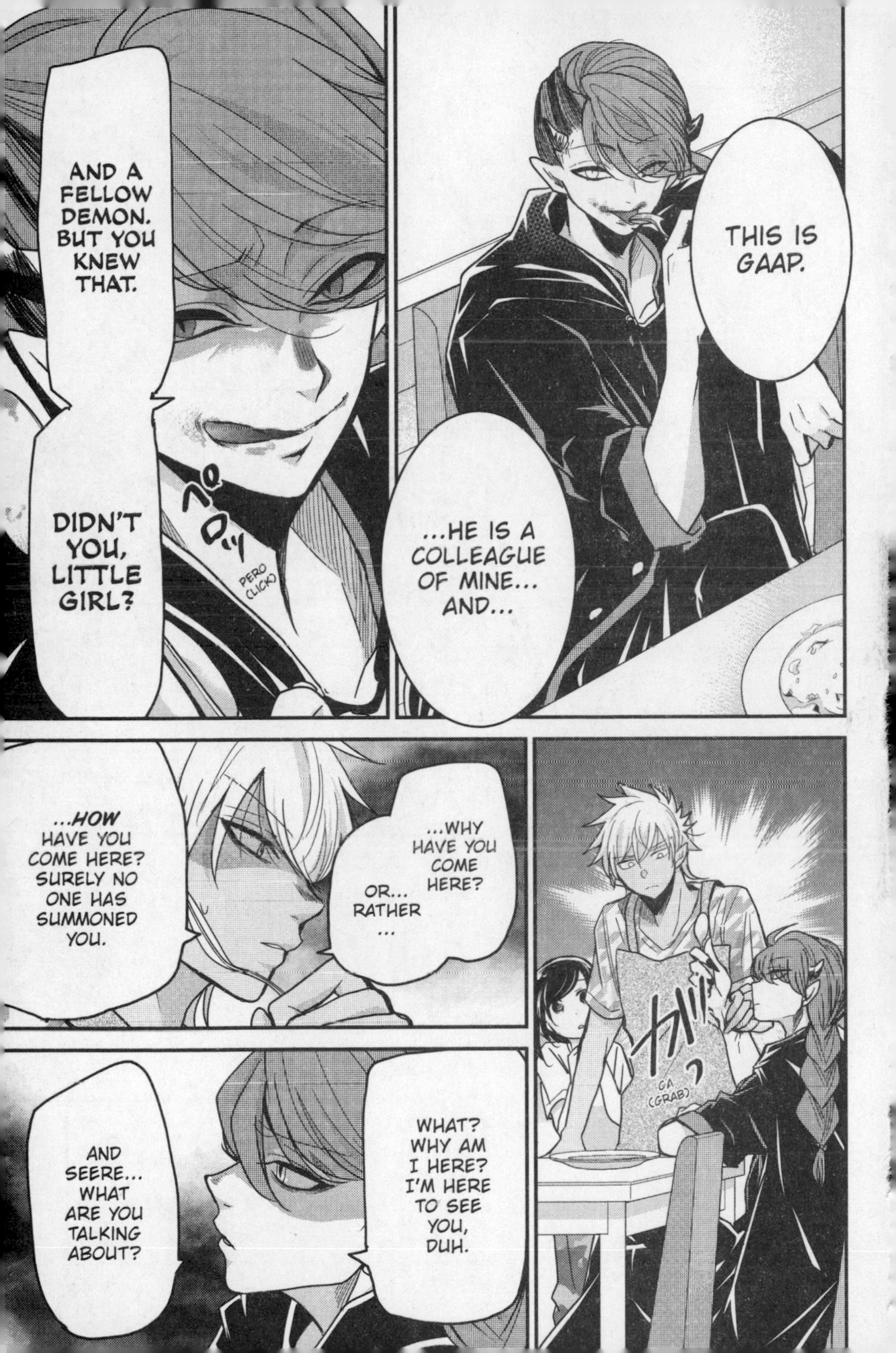
THIS IS GAAP.
...HE IS A COLLEAGUE OF MINE... AND...
AND A FELLOW DEMON. BUT YOU KNEW THAT.
ペロッ
PERO (LICK)
DIDN'T YOU, LITTLE GIRL?
ガッ
GA (GRAB)
...WHY HAVE YOU COME HERE?
OR... RATHER ...
...*HOW* HAVE YOU COME HERE? SURELY NO ONE HAS SUMMONED YOU.
WHAT? WHY AM I HERE? I'M HERE TO SEE YOU, DUH.
AND SEERE... WHAT ARE YOU TALKING ABOUT?

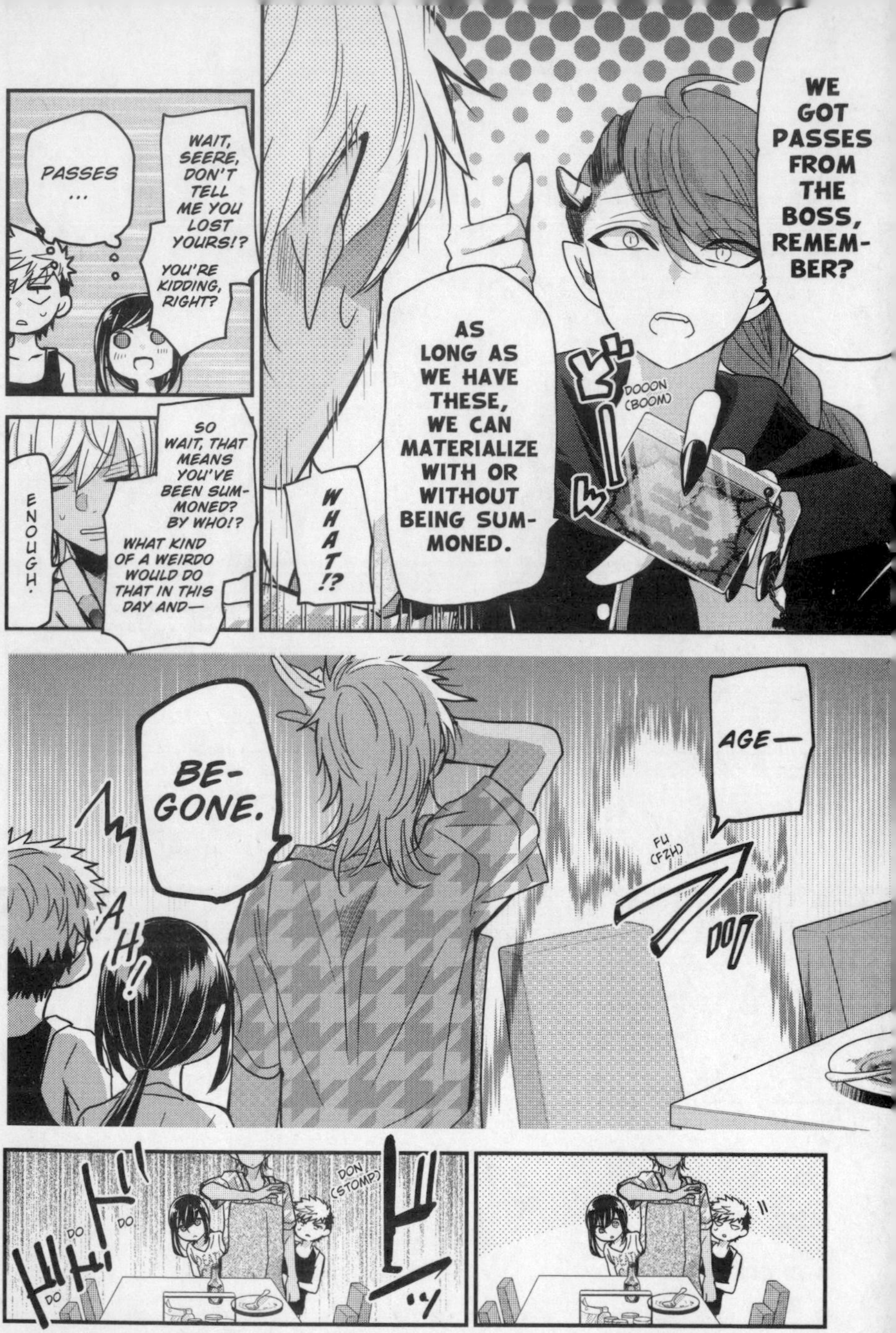
WE GOT PASSES FROM THE BOSS, REMEMBER?
AS LONG AS WE HAVE THESE, WE CAN MATERIALIZE WITH OR WITHOUT BEING SUMMONED.
DOOON (BOOM)
WHAT!?
WAIT, SEERE, DON'T TELL ME YOU LOST YOURS!?
YOU'RE KIDDING, RIGHT?
PASSES...
SO WAIT, THAT MEANS YOU'VE BEEN SUMMONED? BY WHO!?
WHAT KIND OF A WEIRDO WOULD DO THAT IN THIS DAY AND—
ENOUGH.
AGE—
FU (FZH)
BE-GONE.
AH!
DON (STOMP)
DO
DO
DO

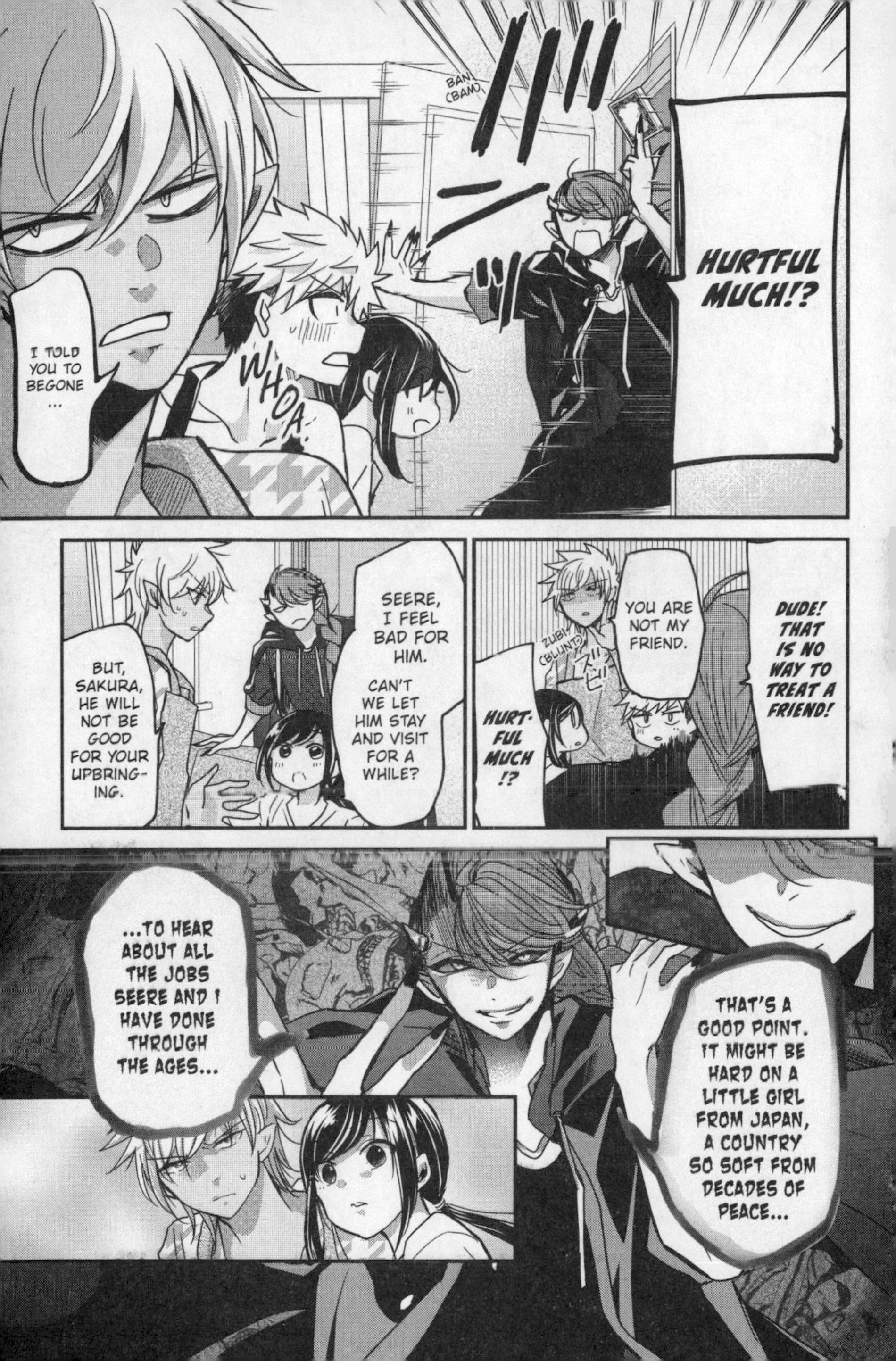
BAN (BAM)
HURTFUL MUCH!?
WHOA
I TOLD YOU TO BEGONE ...
DUDE! THAT IS NO WAY TO TREAT A FRIEND!
YOU ARE NOT MY FRIEND.
ZUBI (BLUNT)
HURT-FUL MUCH !?
SEERE, I FEEL BAD FOR HIM.
CAN'T WE LET HIM STAY AND VISIT FOR A WHILE?
BUT, SAKURA, HE WILL NOT BE GOOD FOR YOUR UPBRING-ING.
THAT'S A GOOD POINT. IT MIGHT BE HARD ON A LITTLE GIRL FROM JAPAN, A COUNTRY SO SOFT FROM DECADES OF PEACE...
...TO HEAR ABOUT ALL THE JOBS SEERE AND I HAVE DONE THROUGH THE AGES...

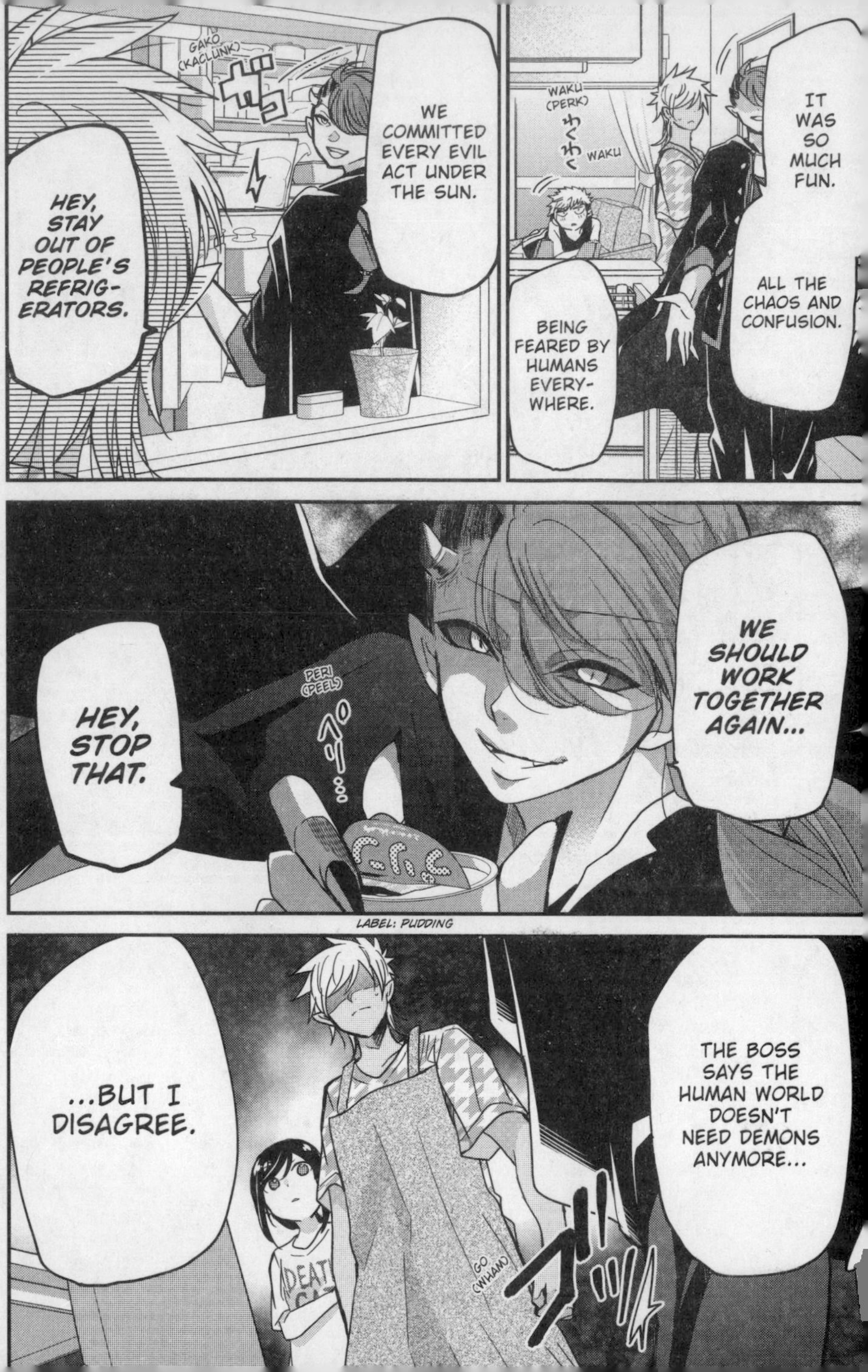
IT WAS SO MUCH FUN.
WAKU (PERK) WAKU
ALL THE CHAOS AND CONFUSION.
BEING FEARED BY HUMANS EVERYWHERE.
WE COMMITTED EVERY EVIL ACT UNDER THE SUN.
GAKO (KACLUNK)
HEY, STAY OUT OF PEOPLE'S REFRIGERATORS.
WE SHOULD WORK TOGETHER AGAIN...
PERI (PEEL)
HEY, STOP THAT.
LABEL: PUDDING
THE BOSS SAYS THE HUMAN WORLD DOESN'T NEED DEMONS ANYMORE...
GO (WHAM)
...BUT I DISAGREE.

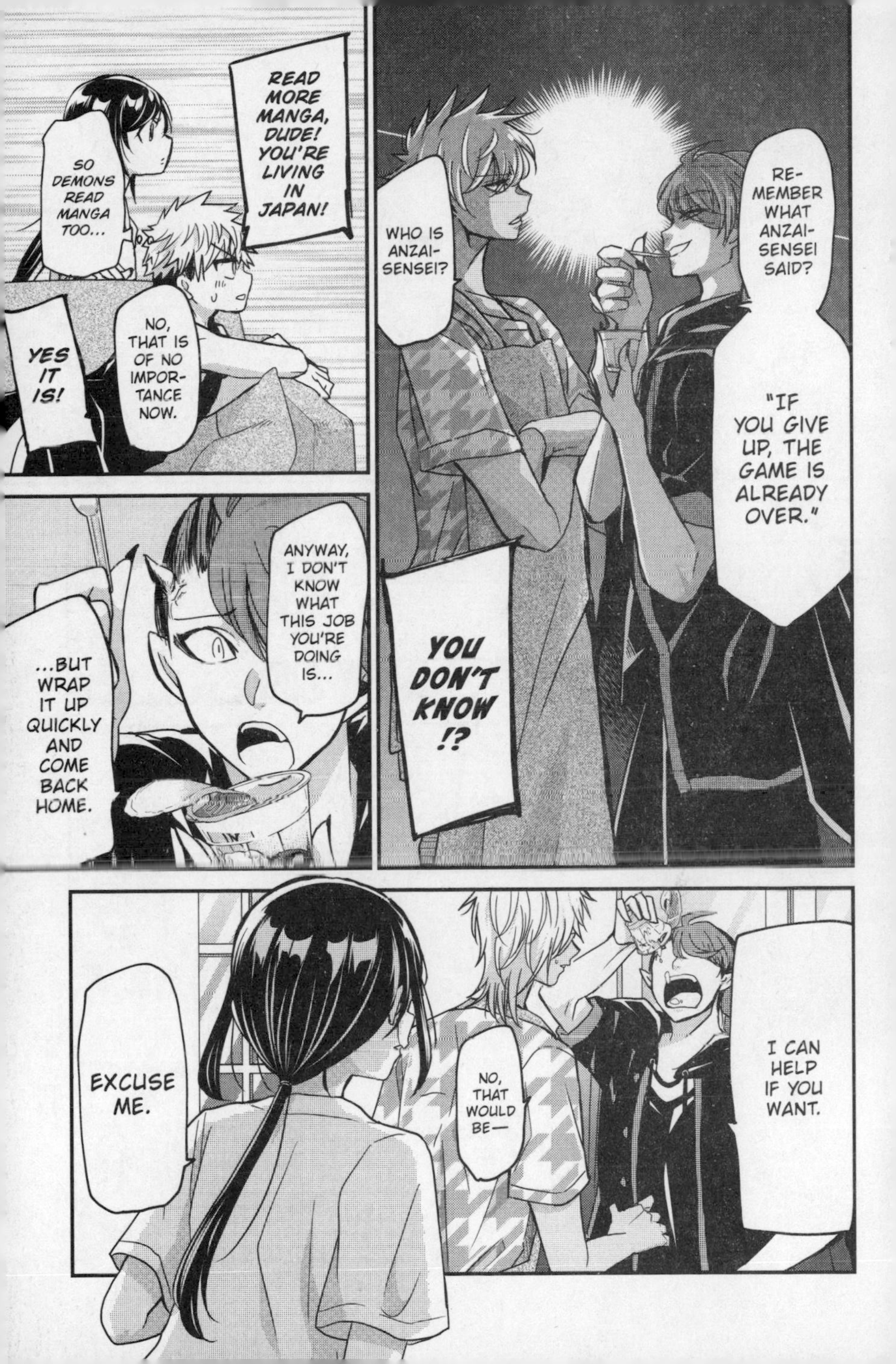
RE-MEMBER WHAT ANZAI-SENSEI SAID?
WHO IS ANZAI-SENSEI?
"IF YOU GIVE UP, THE GAME IS ALREADY OVER."
YOU DON'T KNOW!?
READ MORE MANGA, DUDE! YOU'RE LIVING IN JAPAN!
SO DEMONS READ MANGA TOO...
NO, THAT IS OF NO IMPORTANCE NOW.
YES IT IS!
ANYWAY, I DON'T KNOW WHAT THIS JOB YOU'RE DOING IS...
...BUT WRAP IT UP QUICKLY AND COME BACK HOME.
I CAN HELP IF YOU WANT.
NO, THAT WOULD BE—
EXCUSE ME.

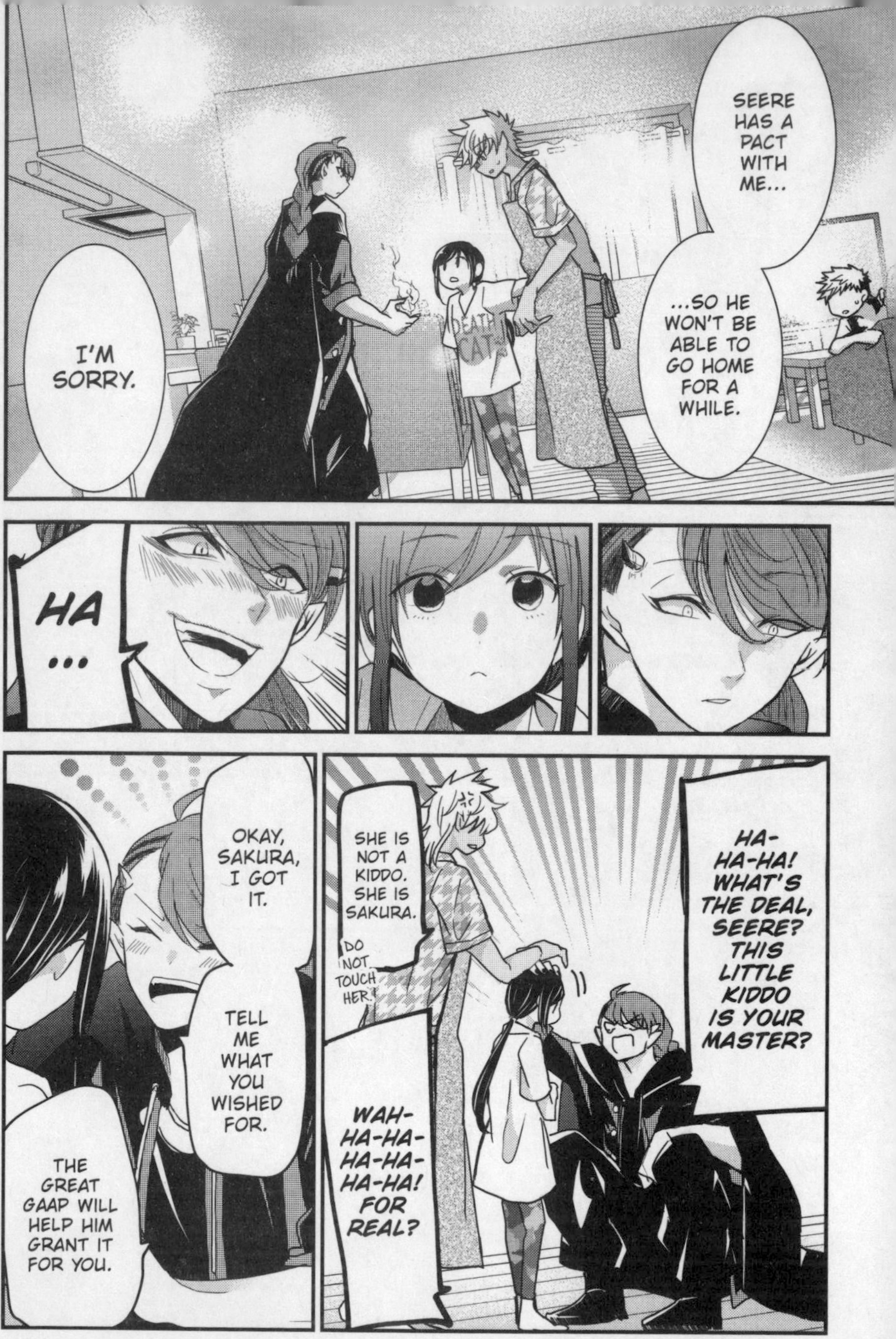
SEERE HAS A PACT WITH ME...
...SO HE WON'T BE ABLE TO GO HOME FOR A WHILE.
I'M SORRY.
HA ...
HA-HA-HA! WHAT'S THE DEAL, SEERE? THIS LITTLE KIDDO IS YOUR MASTER?
WAH-HA-HA-HA-HA-HA-HA! FOR REAL?
SHE IS NOT A KIDDO. SHE IS SAKURA.
DO NOT TOUCH HER.
OKAY, SAKURA, I GOT IT.
TELL ME WHAT YOU WISHED FOR.
THE GREAT GAAP WILL HELP HIM GRANT IT FOR YOU.

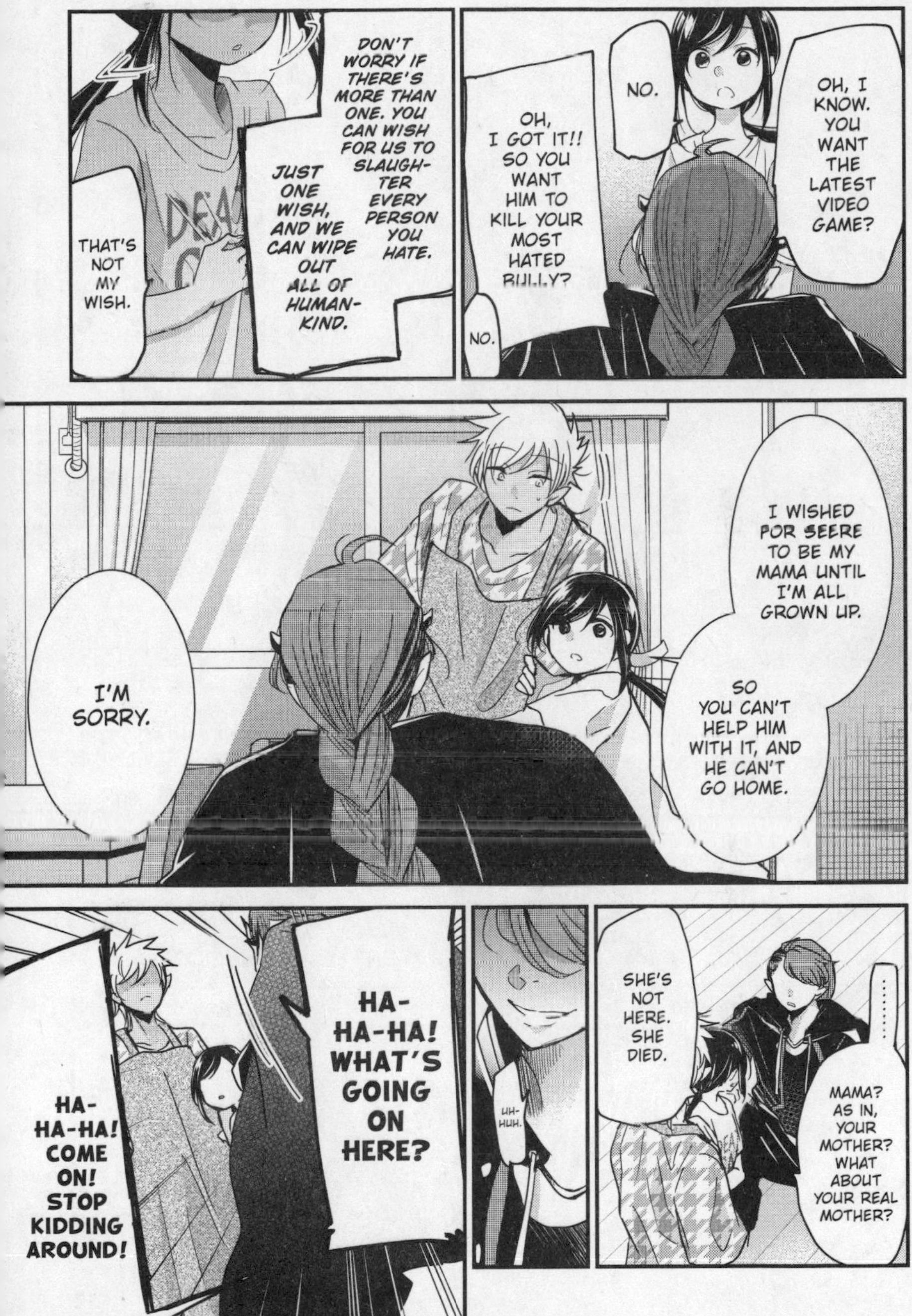
OH, I KNOW. YOU WANT THE LATEST VIDEO GAME?
NO.
OH, I GOT IT!! SO YOU WANT HIM TO KILL YOUR MOST HATED BULLY?
NO.
DON'T WORRY IF THERE'S MORE THAN ONE. YOU CAN WISH FOR US TO SLAUGHTER EVERY PERSON YOU HATE.
JUST ONE WISH, AND WE CAN WIPE OUT ALL OF HUMANKIND.
THAT'S NOT MY WISH.
I WISHED FOR SEERE TO BE MY MAMA UNTIL I'M ALL GROWN UP.
SO YOU CAN'T HELP HIM WITH IT, AND HE CAN'T GO HOME.
I'M SORRY.
......
MAMA? AS IN, YOUR MOTHER? WHAT ABOUT YOUR REAL MOTHER?
SHE'S NOT HERE. SHE DIED.
UH-HUH.
HA-HA-HA! WHAT'S GOING ON HERE?
HA-HA-HA! COME ON! STOP KIDDING AROUND!

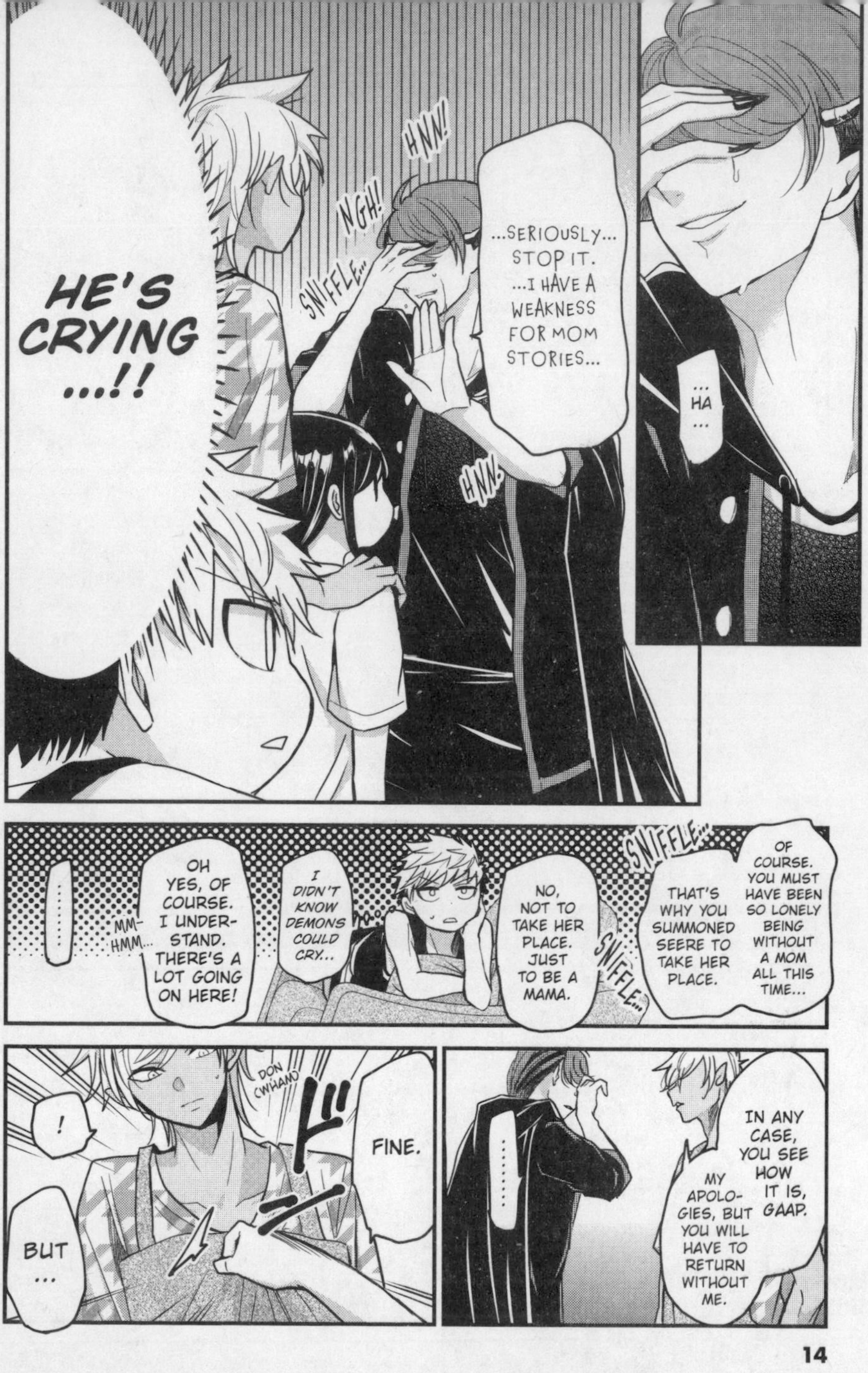
... HA ...
HNN!
NGH!
SNIFFLE...
...SERIOUSLY... STOP IT. ...I HAVE A WEAKNESS FOR MOM STORIES...
HNN.
HE'S CRYING ...!!
OF COURSE. YOU MUST HAVE BEEN SO LONELY BEING WITHOUT A MOM ALL THIS TIME...
THAT'S WHY YOU SUMMONED SEERE TO TAKE HER PLACE.
SNIFFLE...
SNIFFLE...
NO, NOT TO TAKE HER PLACE. JUST TO BE A MAMA.
I DIDN'T KNOW DEMONS COULD CRY...
OH YES, OF COURSE. I UNDERSTAND. THERE'S A LOT GOING ON HERE!
MM-HMM...
......
IN ANY CASE, YOU SEE HOW IT IS, GAAP.
MY APOLOGIES, BUT YOU WILL HAVE TO RETURN WITHOUT ME.
......
FINE.
DON (WHAM)
!
BUT ...

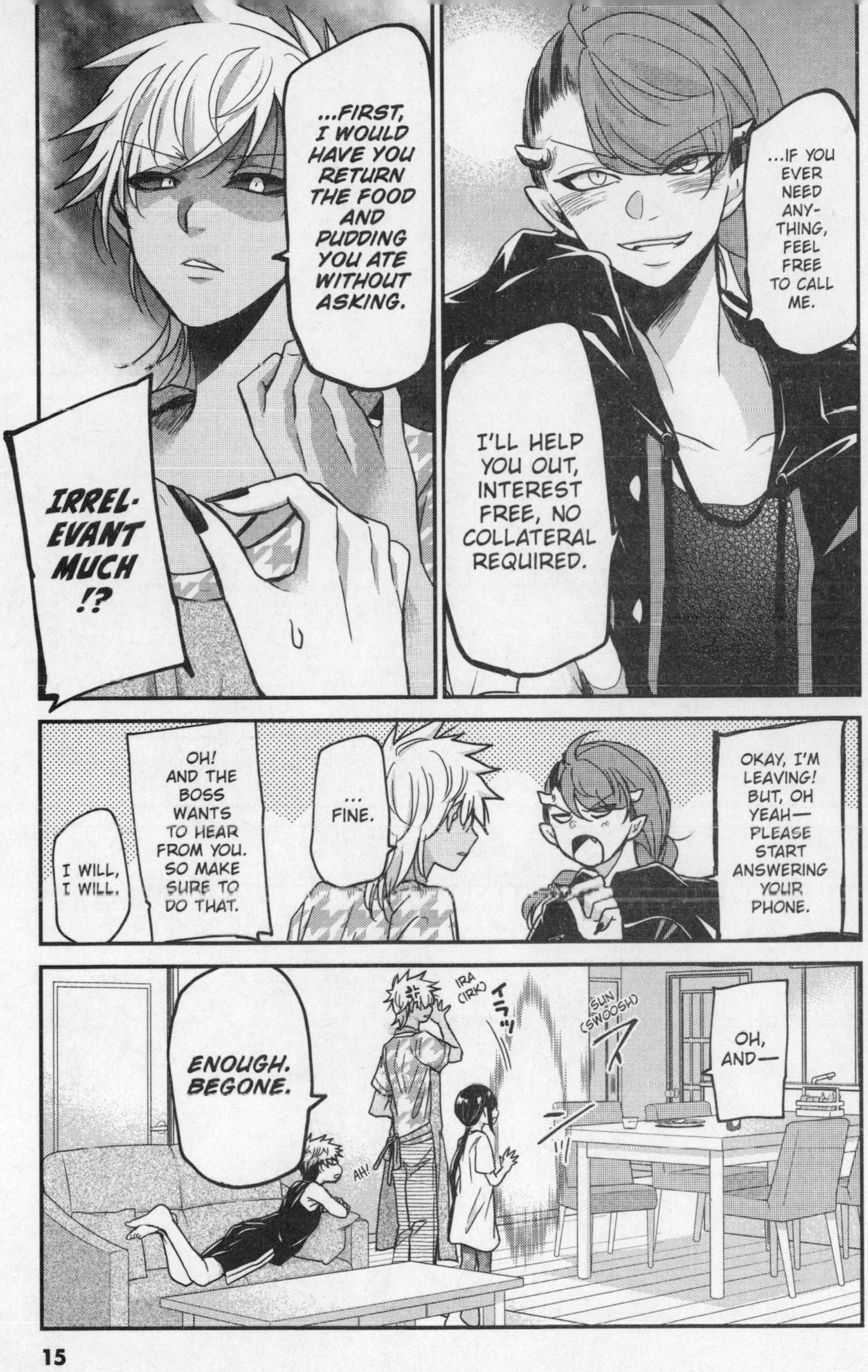
...IF YOU EVER NEED ANY-THING, FEEL FREE TO CALL ME.
I'LL HELP YOU OUT, INTEREST FREE, NO COLLATERAL REQUIRED.
...FIRST, I WOULD HAVE YOU RETURN THE FOOD AND PUDDING YOU ATE WITHOUT ASKING.
IRREL-EVANT MUCH !?
OKAY, I'M LEAVING! BUT, OH YEAH— PLEASE START ANSWERING YOUR PHONE.
... FINE.
OH! AND THE BOSS WANTS TO HEAR FROM YOU. SO MAKE SURE TO DO THAT.
I WILL, I WILL.
OH, AND—
SUN (SWOOSH)
IRA (IRK)
ENOUGH. BEGONE.
AH!

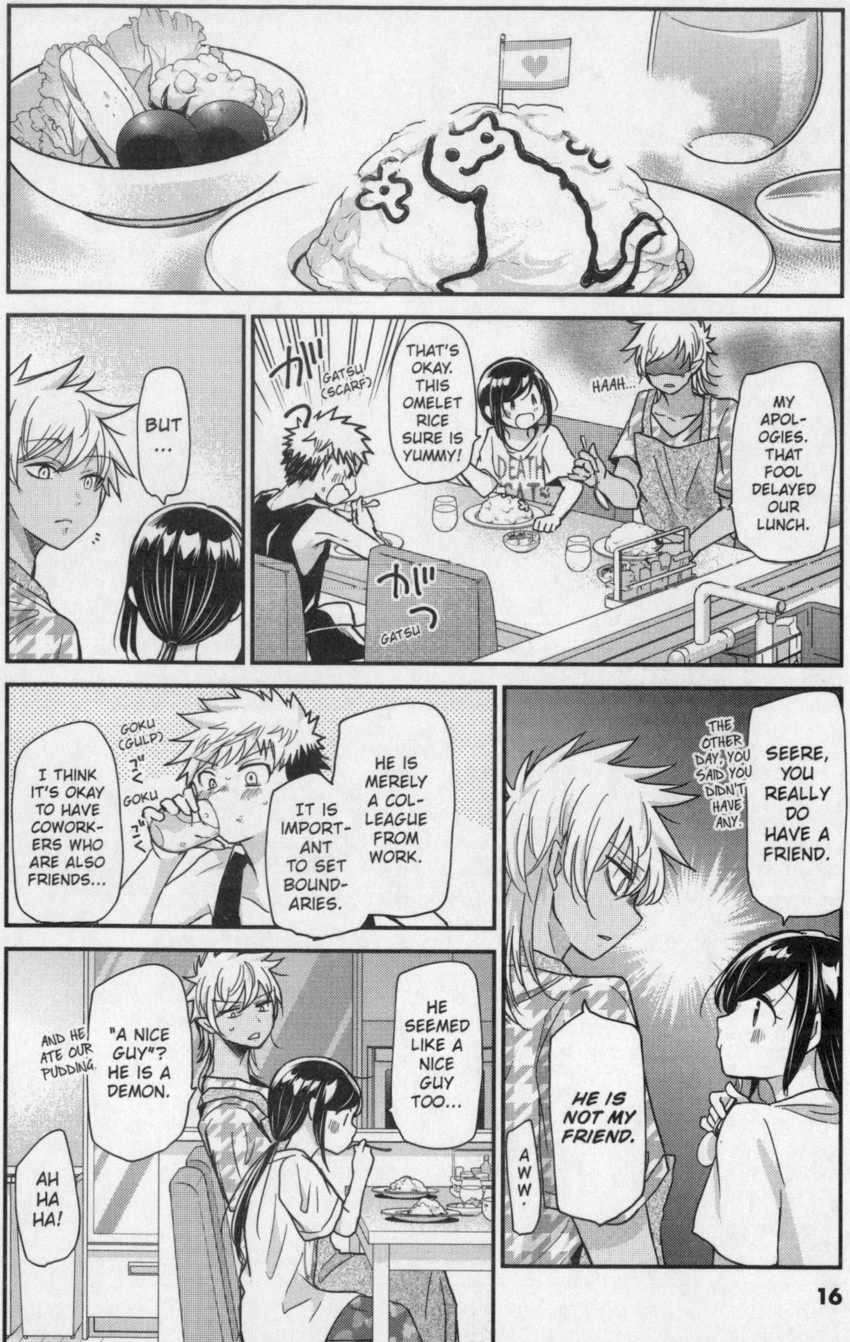
MY APOLOGIES. THAT FOOL DELAYED OUR LUNCH.
HAAH...
THAT'S OKAY. THIS OMELET RICE SURE IS YUMMY!
GATSU (SCARF)
GATSU
BUT...
SEERE, YOU REALLY DO HAVE A FRIEND.
THE OTHER DAY, YOU SAID YOU DIDN'T HAVE ANY.
HE IS NOT MY FRIEND.
AWW.
HE IS MERELY A COLLEAGUE FROM WORK.
IT IS IMPORTANT TO SET BOUNDARIES.
GOKU (GULP)
GOKU
I THINK IT'S OKAY TO HAVE COWORKERS WHO ARE ALSO FRIENDS...
HE SEEMED LIKE A NICE GUY TOO...
"A NICE GUY"? HE IS A DEMON.
AND HE ATE OUR PUDDING.
AH HA HA!

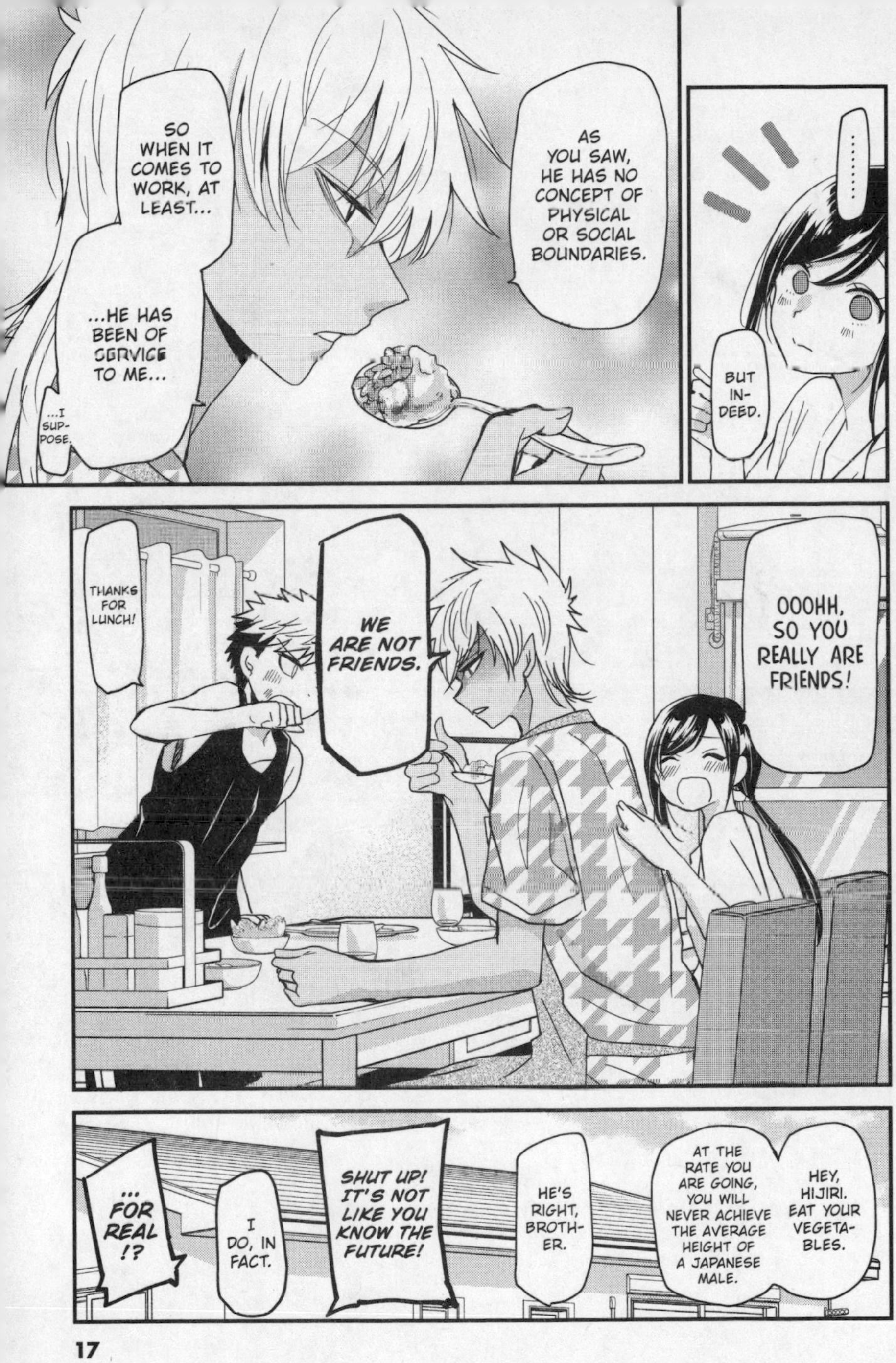
......
BUT INDEED.
AS YOU SAW, HE HAS NO CONCEPT OF PHYSICAL OR SOCIAL BOUNDARIES.
SO WHEN IT COMES TO WORK, AT LEAST...
...HE HAS BEEN OF SERVICE TO ME...
...I SUPPOSE.
OOOHH, SO YOU REALLY ARE FRIENDS!
WE ARE NOT FRIENDS.
THANKS FOR LUNCH!
HEY, HIJIRI. EAT YOUR VEGETABLES.
AT THE RATE YOU ARE GOING, YOU WILL NEVER ACHIEVE THE AVERAGE HEIGHT OF A JAPANESE MALE.
HE'S RIGHT, BROTHER.
SHUT UP! IT'S NOT LIKE YOU KNOW THE FUTURE!
I DO, IN FACT.
...FOR REAL!?

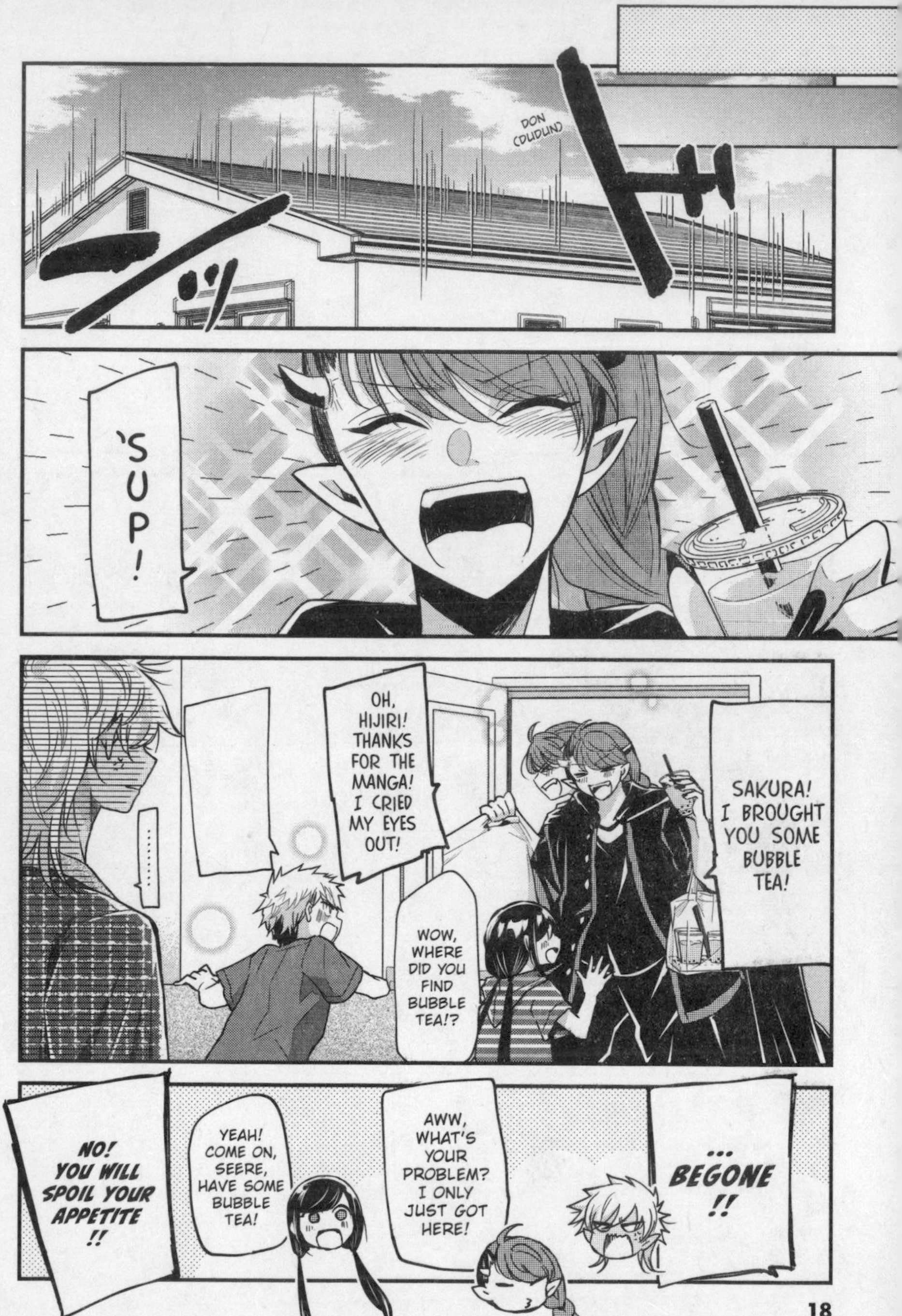
DON (DUDUN)
'SUP!
SAKURA! I BROUGHT YOU SOME BUBBLE TEA!
OH, HIJIRI! THANKS FOR THE MANGA! I CRIED MY EYES OUT!
WOW, WHERE DID YOU FIND BUBBLE TEA!?
......
...BEGONE!!
AWW, WHAT'S YOUR PROBLEM? I ONLY JUST GOT HERE!
YEAH! COME ON, SEERE, HAVE SOME BUBBLE TEA!
NO! YOU WILL SPOIL YOUR APPETITE!!

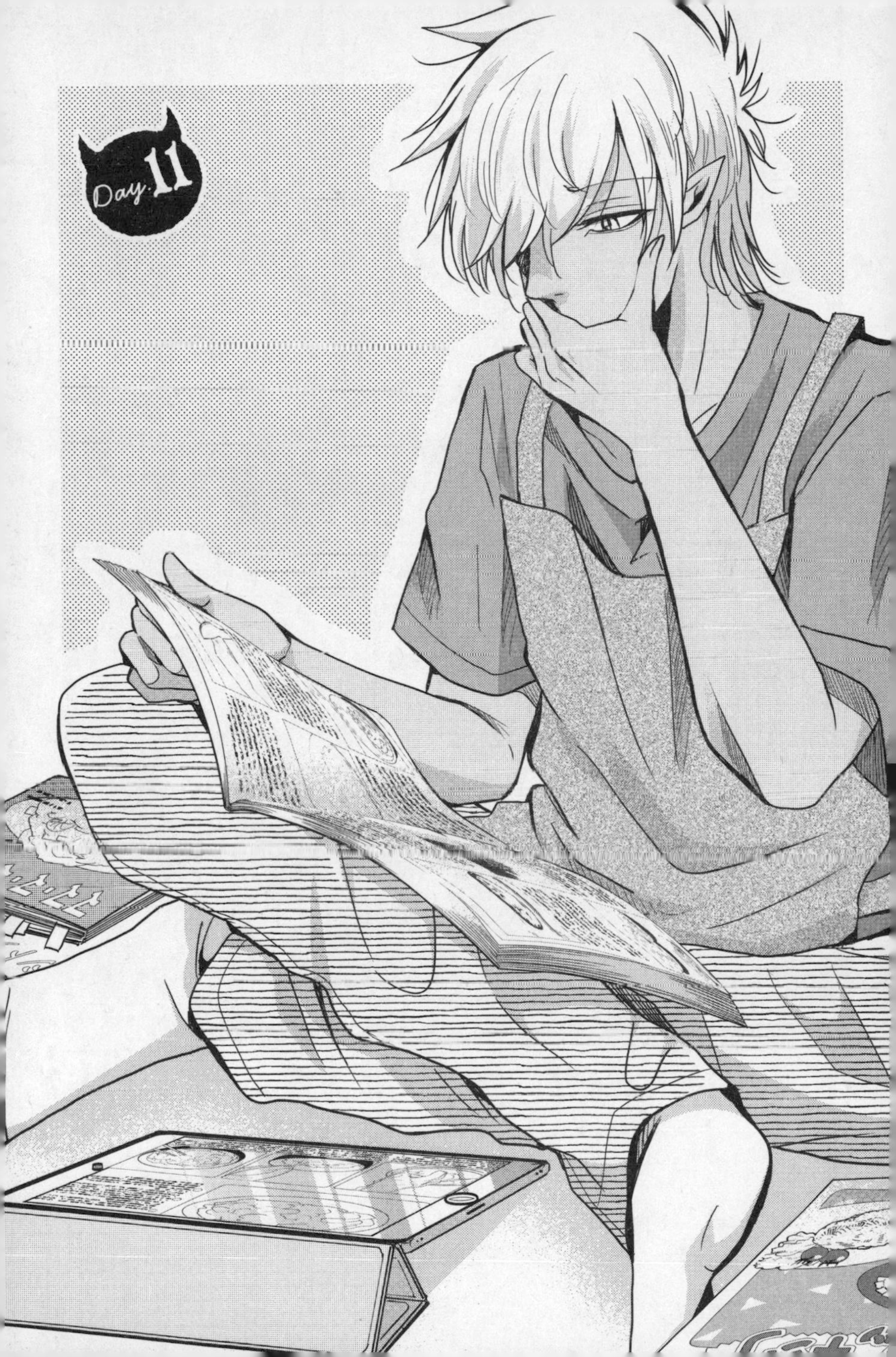
Day. 11

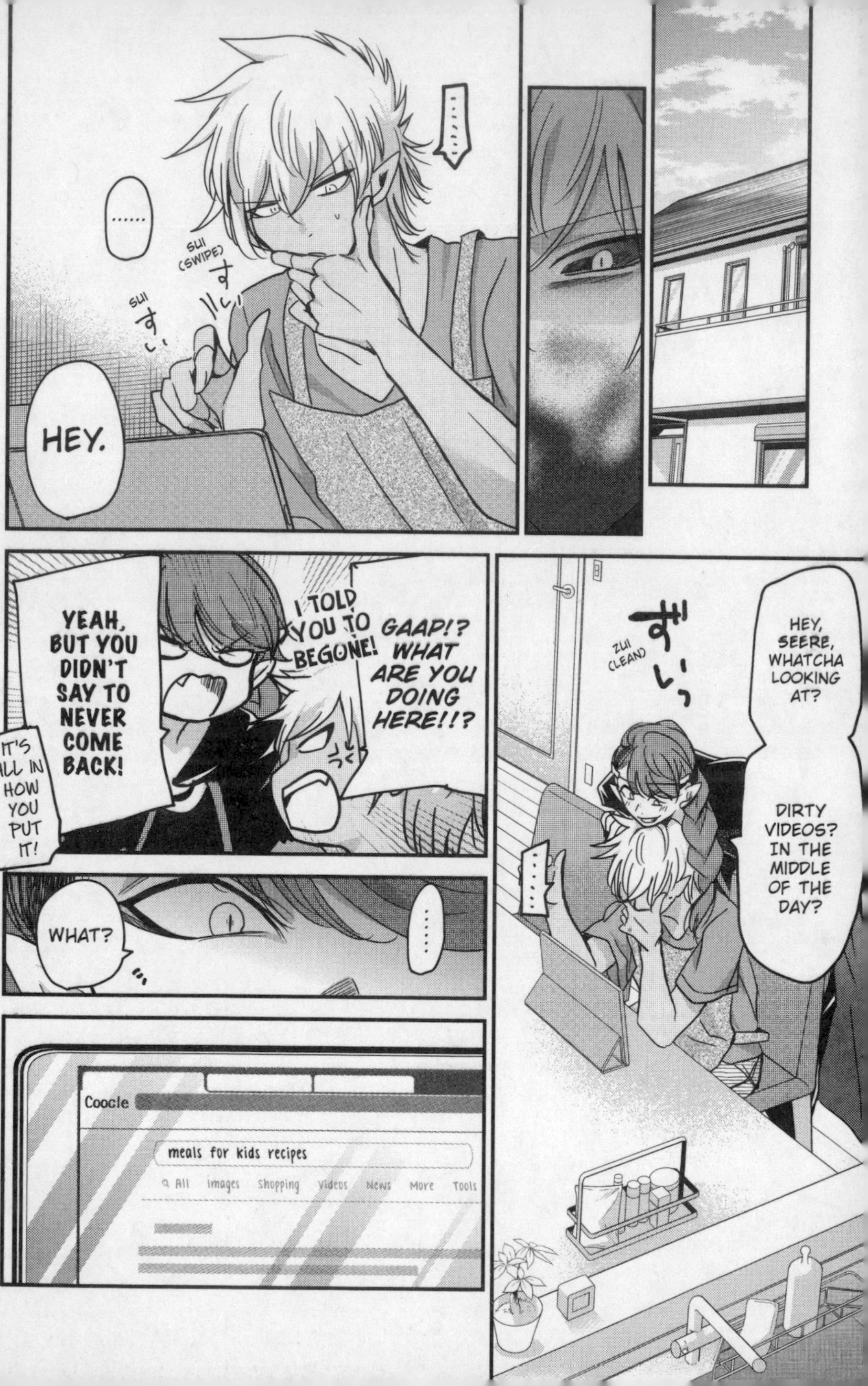
......!
......
SUI (SWIPE)
SUI
HEY.
ZUI (LEAN)
HEY, SEERE, WHATCHA LOOKING AT?
DIRTY VIDEOS? IN THE MIDDLE OF THE DAY?
......!
GAAP!? WHAT ARE YOU DOING HERE!!?
I TOLD YOU TO BEGONE!
YEAH, BUT YOU DIDN'T SAY TO NEVER COME BACK!
IT'S ALL IN HOW YOU PUT IT!
......
WHAT?
Coocle
meals for kids recipes
All Images Shopping Videos News More Tools

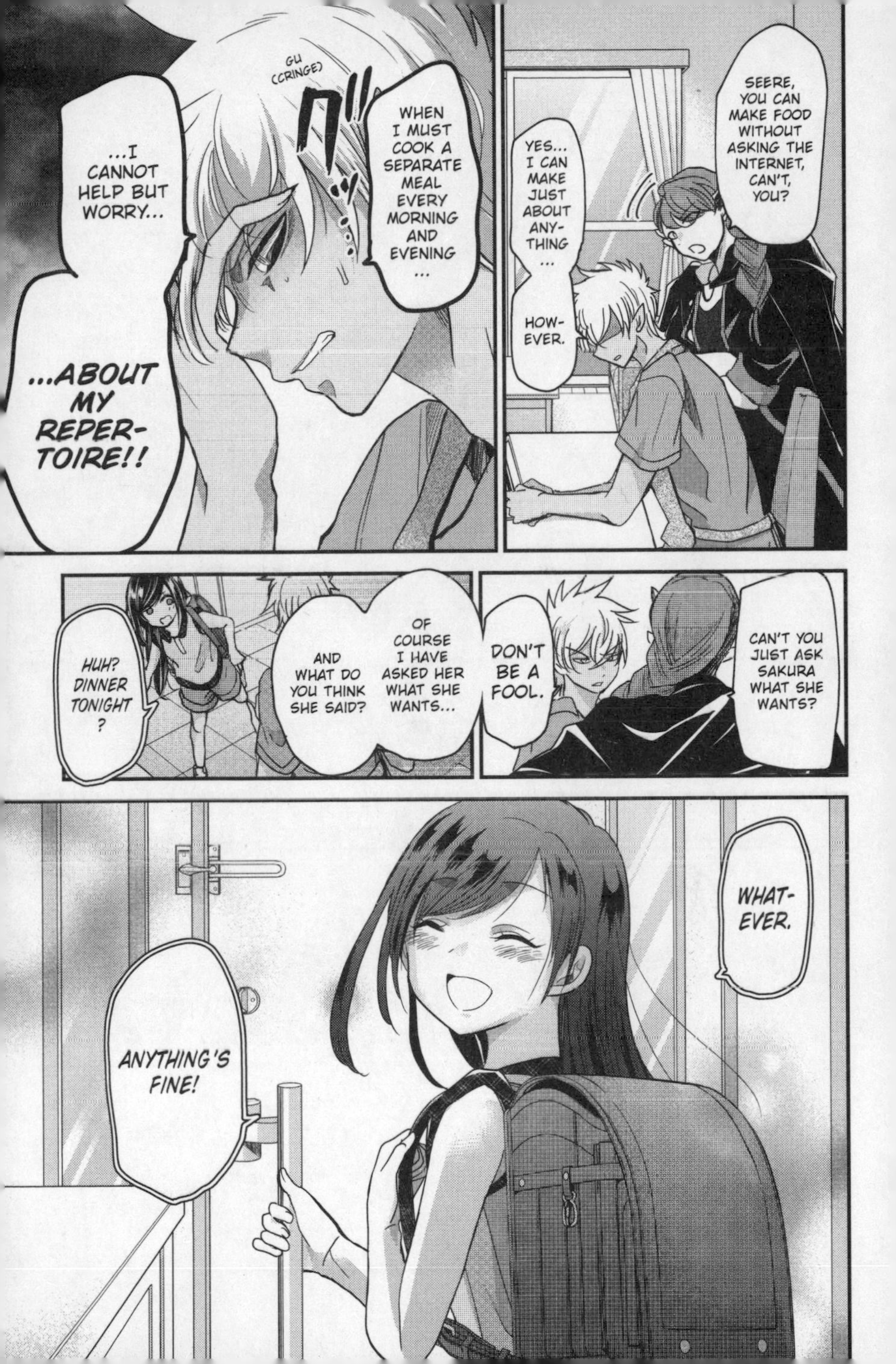
SEERE, YOU CAN MAKE FOOD WITHOUT ASKING THE INTERNET, CAN'T YOU?
YES... I CAN MAKE JUST ABOUT ANY-THING...
HOW-EVER.
GU (CRINGE)
WHEN I MUST COOK A SEPARATE MEAL EVERY MORNING AND EVENING...
...I CANNOT HELP BUT WORRY...
...ABOUT MY REPER-TOIRE!!
CAN'T YOU JUST ASK SAKURA WHAT SHE WANTS?
DON'T BE A FOOL.
OF COURSE I HAVE ASKED HER WHAT SHE WANTS...
AND WHAT DO YOU THINK SHE SAID?
HUH? DINNER TONIGHT?
WHAT-EVER.
ANYTHING'S FINE!

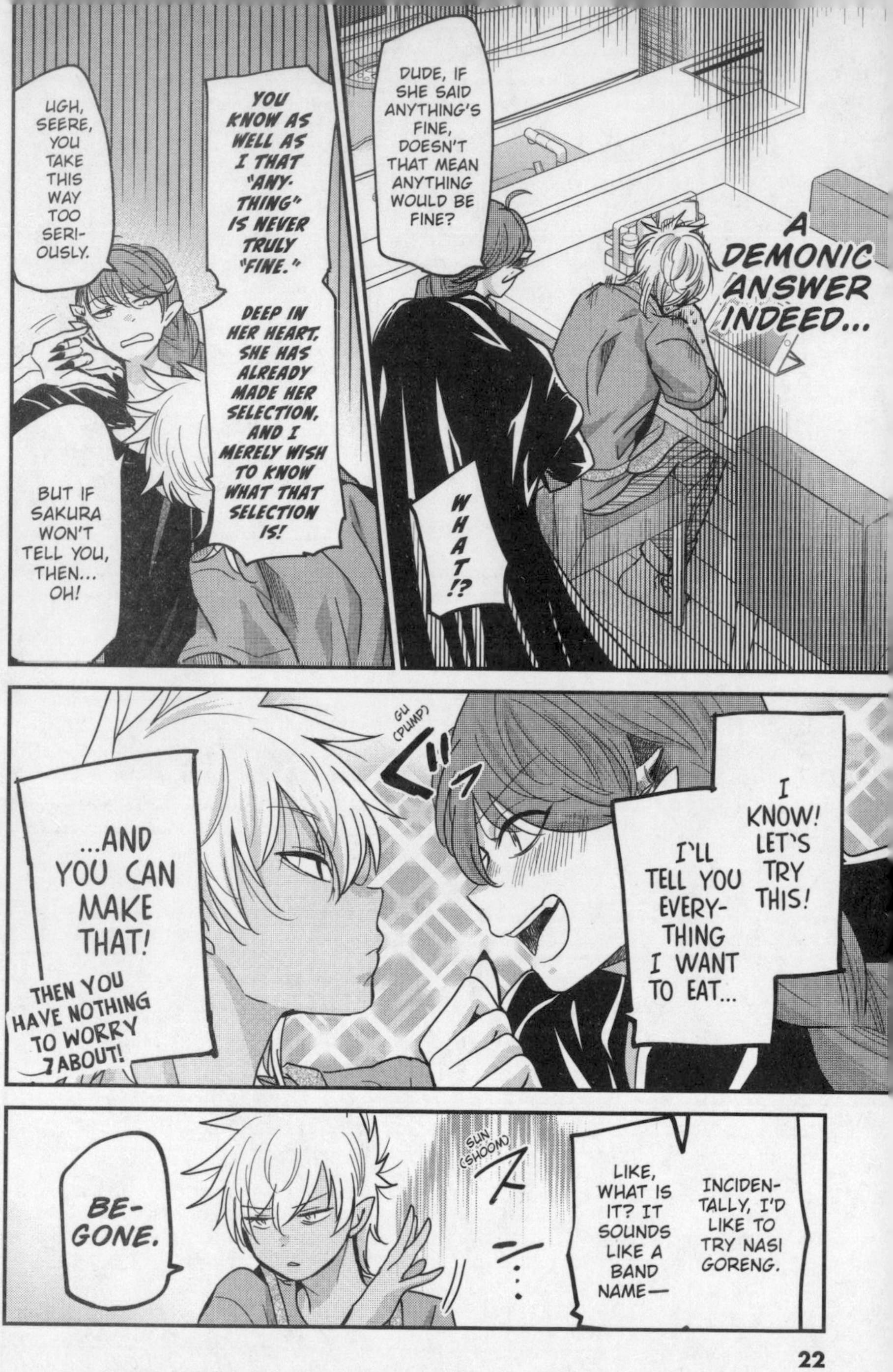
A DEMONIC ANSWER INDEED...
DUDE, IF SHE SAID ANYTHING'S FINE, DOESN'T THAT MEAN ANYTHING WOULD BE FINE?
WHAT!?
YOU KNOW AS WELL AS I THAT "ANY-THING" IS NEVER TRULY "FINE."
DEEP IN HER HEART, SHE HAS ALREADY MADE HER SELECTION, AND I MERELY WISH TO KNOW WHAT THAT SELECTION IS!
UGH, SEERE, YOU TAKE THIS WAY TOO SERI-OUSLY.
BUT IF SAKURA WON'T TELL YOU, THEN... OH!
GU (PUMP)
I KNOW! LET'S TRY THIS!
I'LL TELL YOU EVERY-THING I WANT TO EAT...
...AND YOU CAN MAKE THAT!
THEN YOU HAVE NOTHING TO WORRY ABOUT!
INCIDEN-TALLY, I'D LIKE TO TRY NASI GORENG.
LIKE, WHAT IS IT? IT SOUNDS LIKE A BAND NAME—
SUN (SHOOM)
BE-GONE.

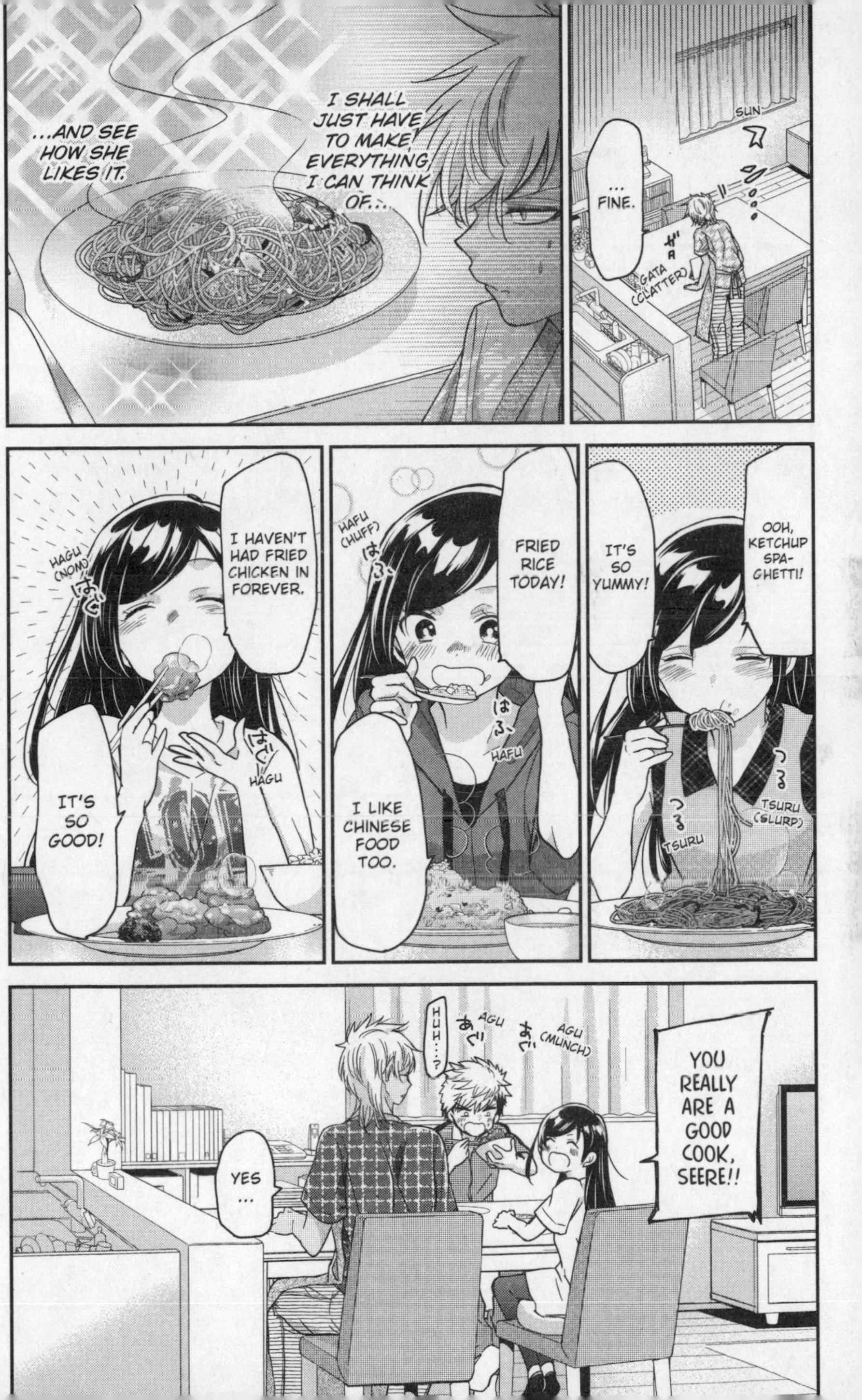
...FINE.
SUN
ガタ
GATA (CLATTER)
I SHALL JUST HAVE TO MAKE EVERYTHING I CAN THINK OF...
...AND SEE HOW SHE LIKES IT.
OOH, KETCHUP SPA-GHETTI!
IT'S SO YUMMY!
つる
TSURU (SLURP)
つる
TSURU
FRIED RICE TODAY!
HAFU (HUFF)
はふ
はふ
HAFU
I LIKE CHINESE FOOD TOO.
I HAVEN'T HAD FRIED CHICKEN IN FOREVER.
HAGU (NOM)
はぐ
はぐ
HAGU
IT'S SO GOOD!
YOU REALLY ARE A GOOD COOK, SEERE!!
あぐ
AGU (MUNCH)
あぐ
AGU
HUH...?
YES...

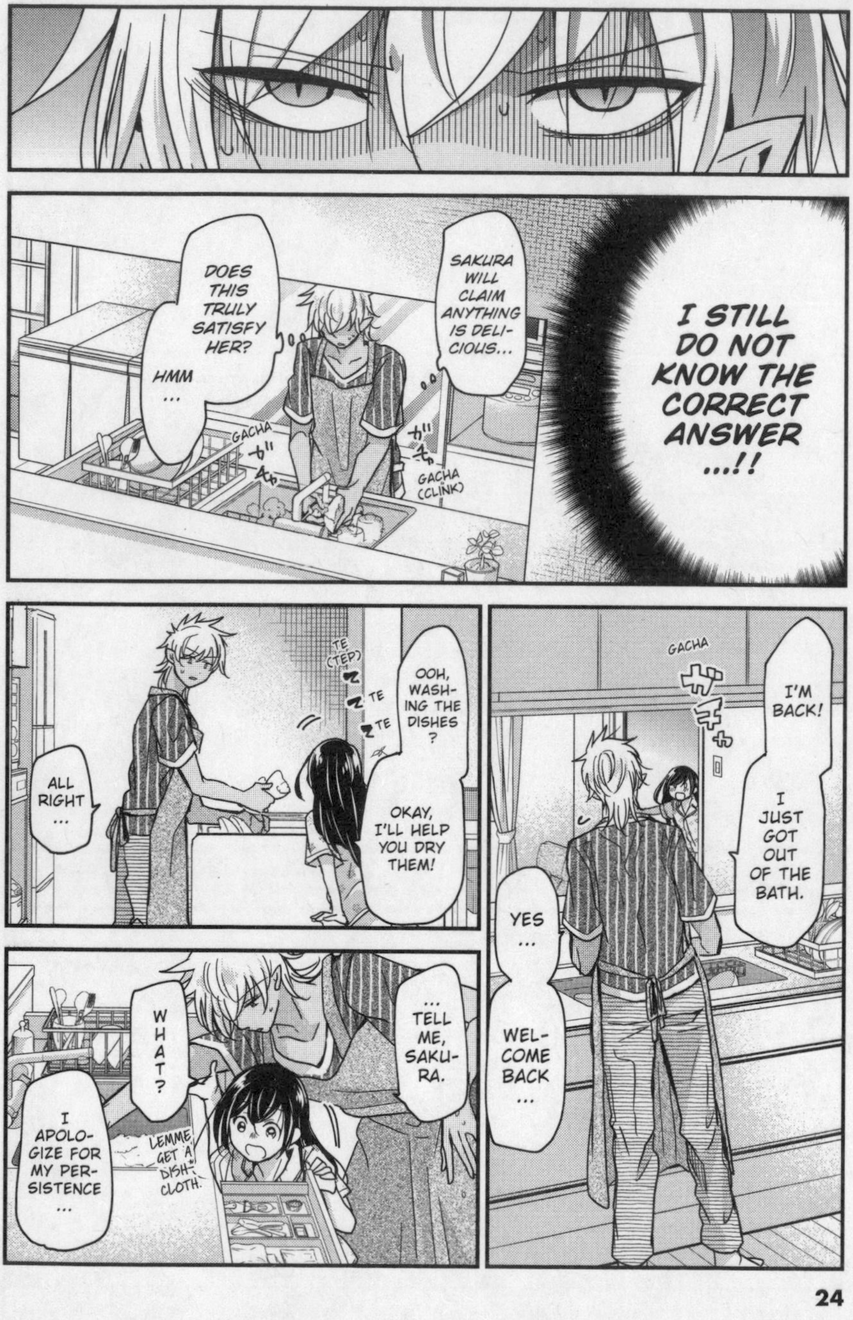
I STILL DO NOT KNOW THE CORRECT ANSWER ...!!
SAKURA WILL CLAIM ANYTHING IS DELICIOUS...
DOES THIS TRULY SATISFY HER?
HMM ...
GACHA
GACHA (CLINK)
GACHA
I'M BACK!
I JUST GOT OUT OF THE BATH.
YES ...
WELCOME BACK ...
TE (TEP)
TE
TE
OOH, WASHING THE DISHES?
OKAY, I'LL HELP YOU DRY THEM!
ALL RIGHT ...
... TELL ME, SAKURA.
WHAT?
LEMME GET A DISHCLOTH.
I APOLOGIZE FOR MY PERSISTENCE ...

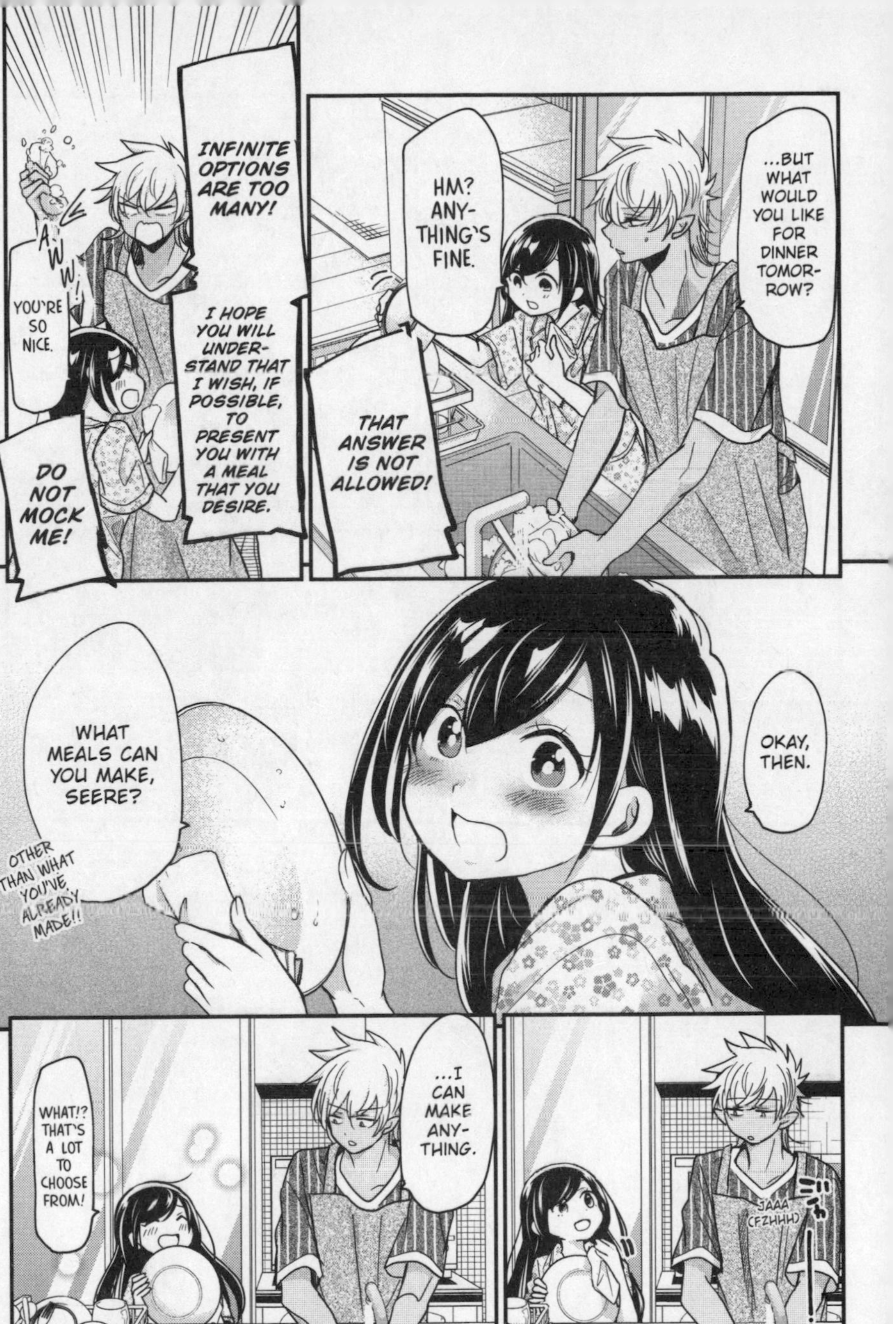

...BUT WHAT WOULD YOU LIKE FOR DINNER TOMORROW?
HM? ANY-THING'S FINE.
THAT ANSWER IS NOT ALLOWED!
INFINITE OPTIONS ARE TOO MANY!
I HOPE YOU WILL UNDER-STAND THAT I WISH, IF POSSIBLE, TO PRESENT YOU WITH A MEAL THAT YOU DESIRE.
AWW!
YOU'RE SO NICE.
DO NOT MOCK ME!
OKAY, THEN.
WHAT MEALS CAN YOU MAKE, SEERE?
OTHER THAN WHAT YOU'VE ALREADY MADE!!
JAAA (FZHHH)
......
...I CAN MAKE ANY-THING.
WHAT!? THAT'S A LOT TO CHOOSE FROM!

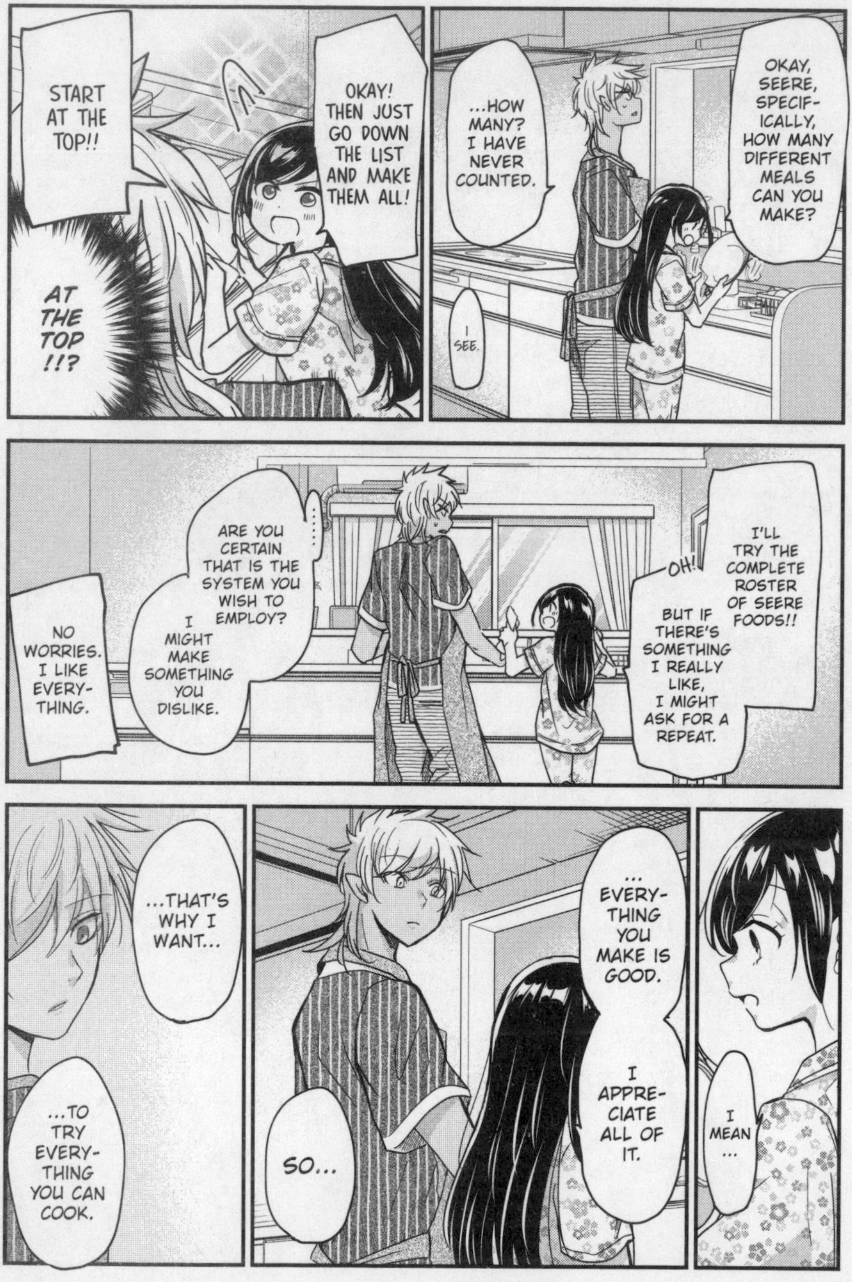

OKAY, SEERE, SPECIFICALLY, HOW MANY DIFFERENT MEALS CAN YOU MAKE?
...HOW MANY? I HAVE NEVER COUNTED.
I SEE.
OKAY! THEN JUST GO DOWN THE LIST AND MAKE THEM ALL!
START AT THE TOP!!
AT THE TOP!!?
I'LL TRY THE COMPLETE ROSTER OF SEERE FOODS!!
OH!
BUT IF THERE'S SOMETHING I REALLY LIKE, I MIGHT ASK FOR A REPEAT.
......
ARE YOU CERTAIN THAT IS THE SYSTEM YOU WISH TO EMPLOY?
I MIGHT MAKE SOMETHING YOU DISLIKE.
NO WORRIES. I LIKE EVERYTHING.
I MEAN...
...EVERYTHING YOU MAKE IS GOOD.
I APPRECIATE ALL OF IT.
SO...
...THAT'S WHY I WANT...
...TO TRY EVERYTHING YOU CAN COOK.

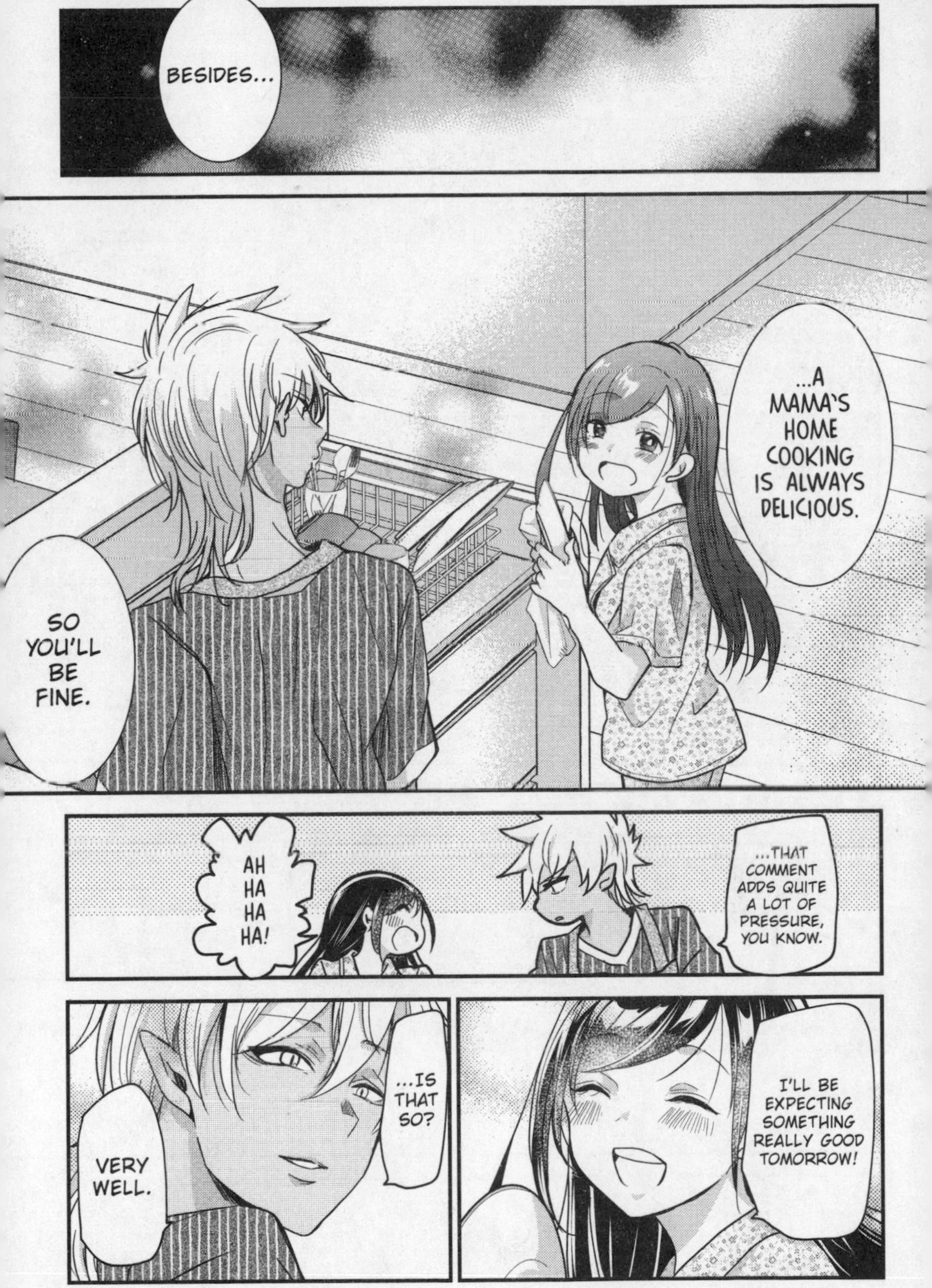
BESIDES...
...A MAMA'S HOME COOKING IS ALWAYS DELICIOUS.
SO YOU'LL BE FINE.
...THAT COMMENT ADDS QUITE A LOT OF PRESSURE, YOU KNOW.
AH HA HA HA!
I'LL BE EXPECTING SOMETHING REALLY GOOD TOMORROW!
...IS THAT SO?
VERY WELL.

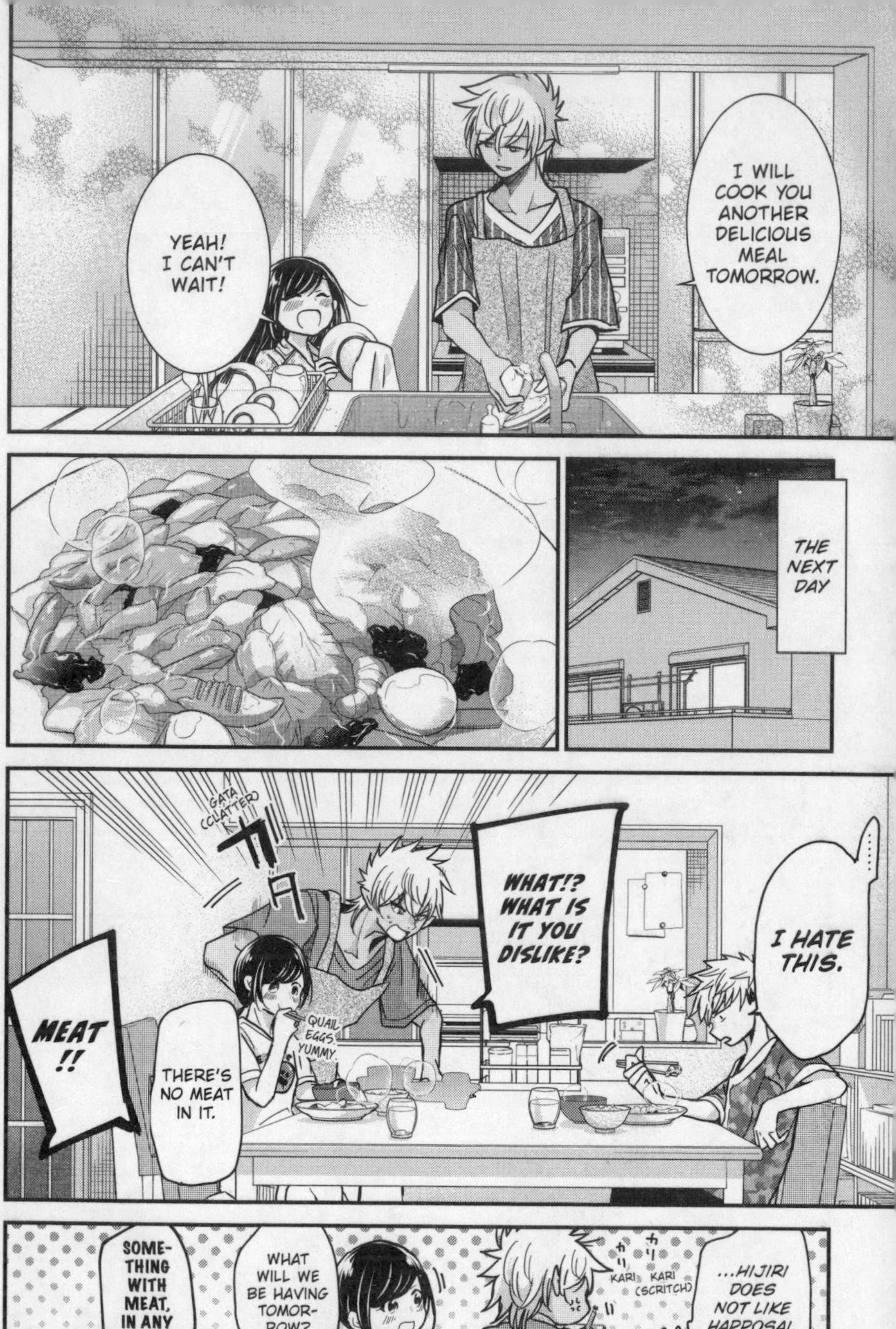
I WILL COOK YOU ANOTHER DELICIOUS MEAL TOMORROW.
YEAH! I CAN'T WAIT!
THE NEXT DAY
I HATE THIS.
WHAT!? WHAT IS IT YOU DISLIKE?
GATA (CLATTER)
THERE'S NO MEAT IN IT.
QUAIL EGGS. YUMMY.
MEAT!!
...HIJIRI DOES NOT LIKE HAPPOSAI.
KARI KARI (SCRITCH)
WHAT WILL WE BE HAVING TOMORROW?
SOMETHING WITH MEAT, IN ANY CASE.

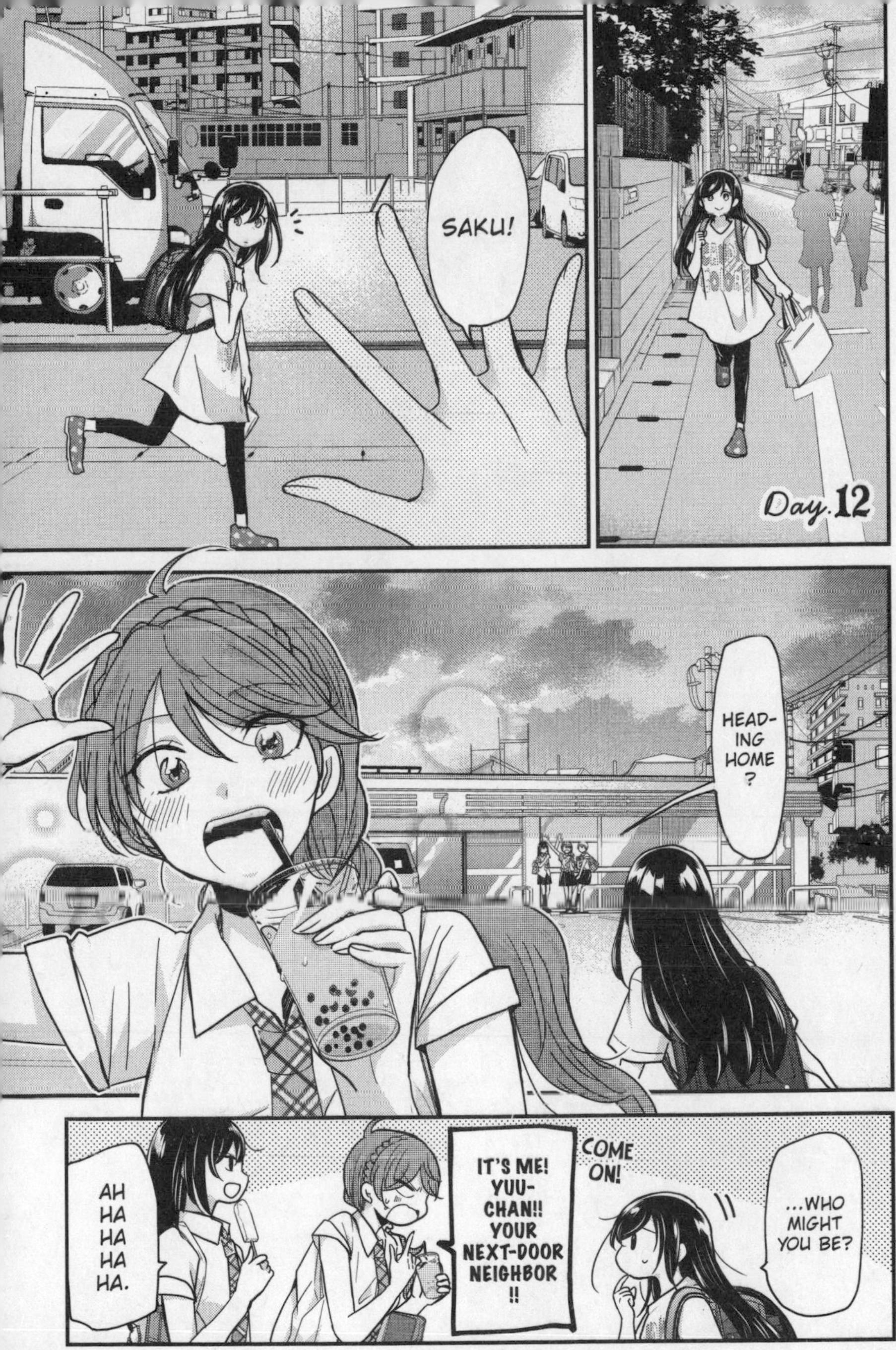
Day.12
SAKU!
HEAD-ING HOME?
...WHO MIGHT YOU BE?
COME ON!
IT'S ME! YUU-CHAN!! YOUR NEXT-DOOR NEIGHBOR!!
AH HA HA HA HA.

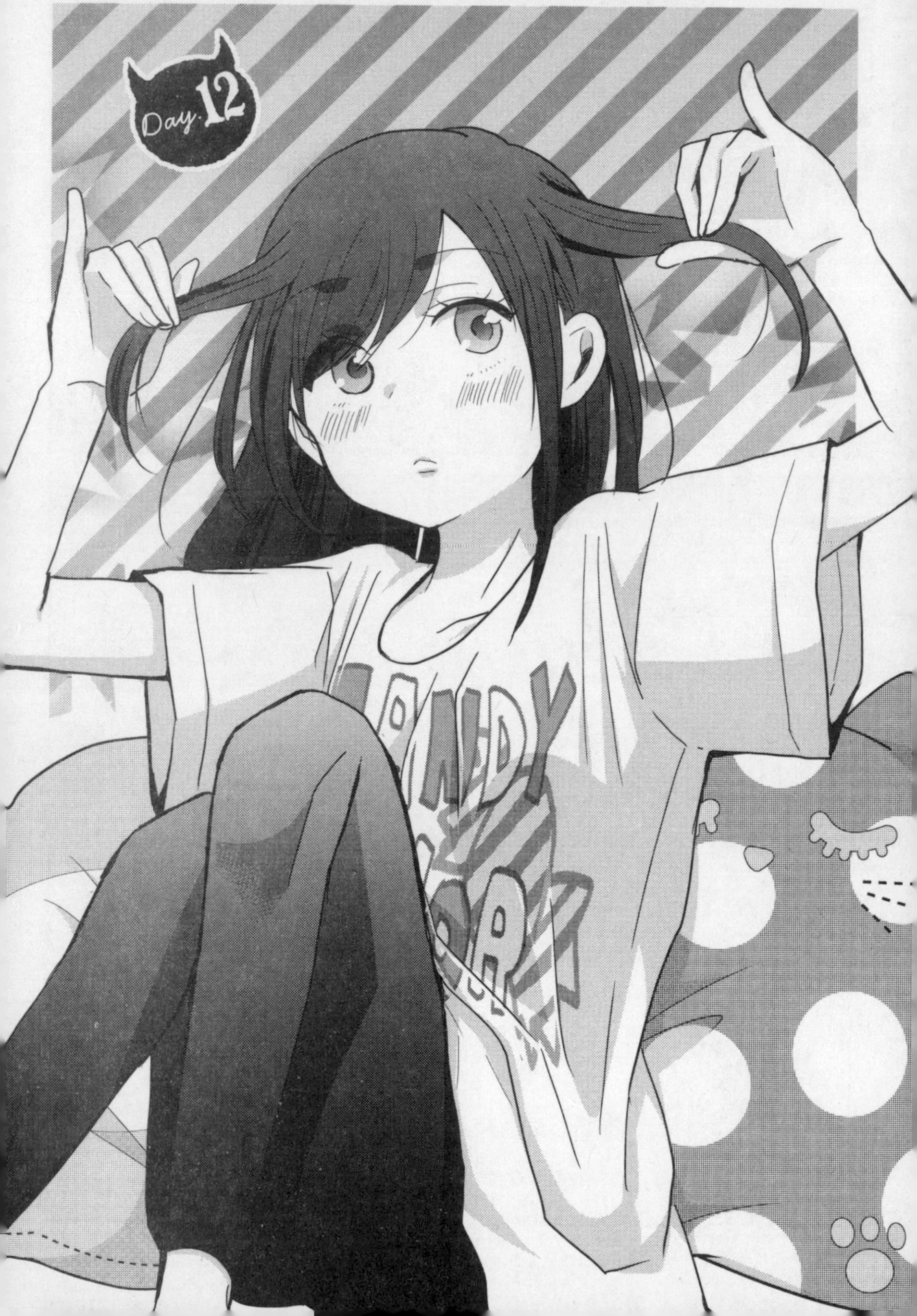
Day. 12

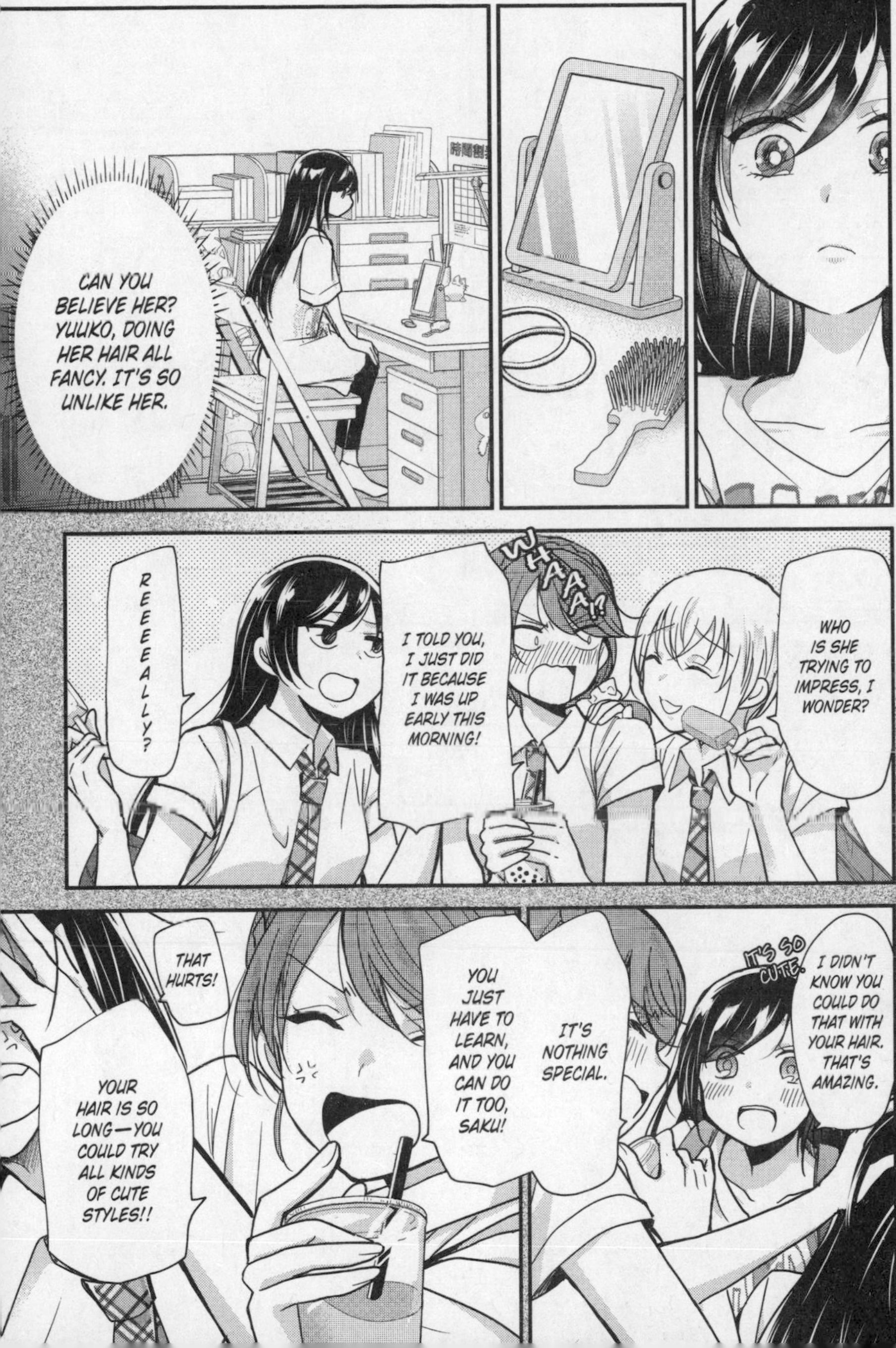
CAN YOU BELIEVE HER? YUUKO, DOING HER HAIR ALL FANCY. IT'S SO UNLIKE HER.
WHO IS SHE TRYING TO IMPRESS, I WONDER?
WHAAAA!?
I TOLD YOU, I JUST DID IT BECAUSE I WAS UP EARLY THIS MORNING!
REEEEEALLY?
IT'S SO CUTE.
I DIDN'T KNOW YOU COULD DO THAT WITH YOUR HAIR. THAT'S AMAZING.
IT'S NOTHING SPECIAL.
YOU JUST HAVE TO LEARN, AND YOU CAN DO IT TOO, SAKU!
THAT HURTS!
YOUR HAIR IS SO LONG—YOU COULD TRY ALL KINDS OF CUTE STYLES!!

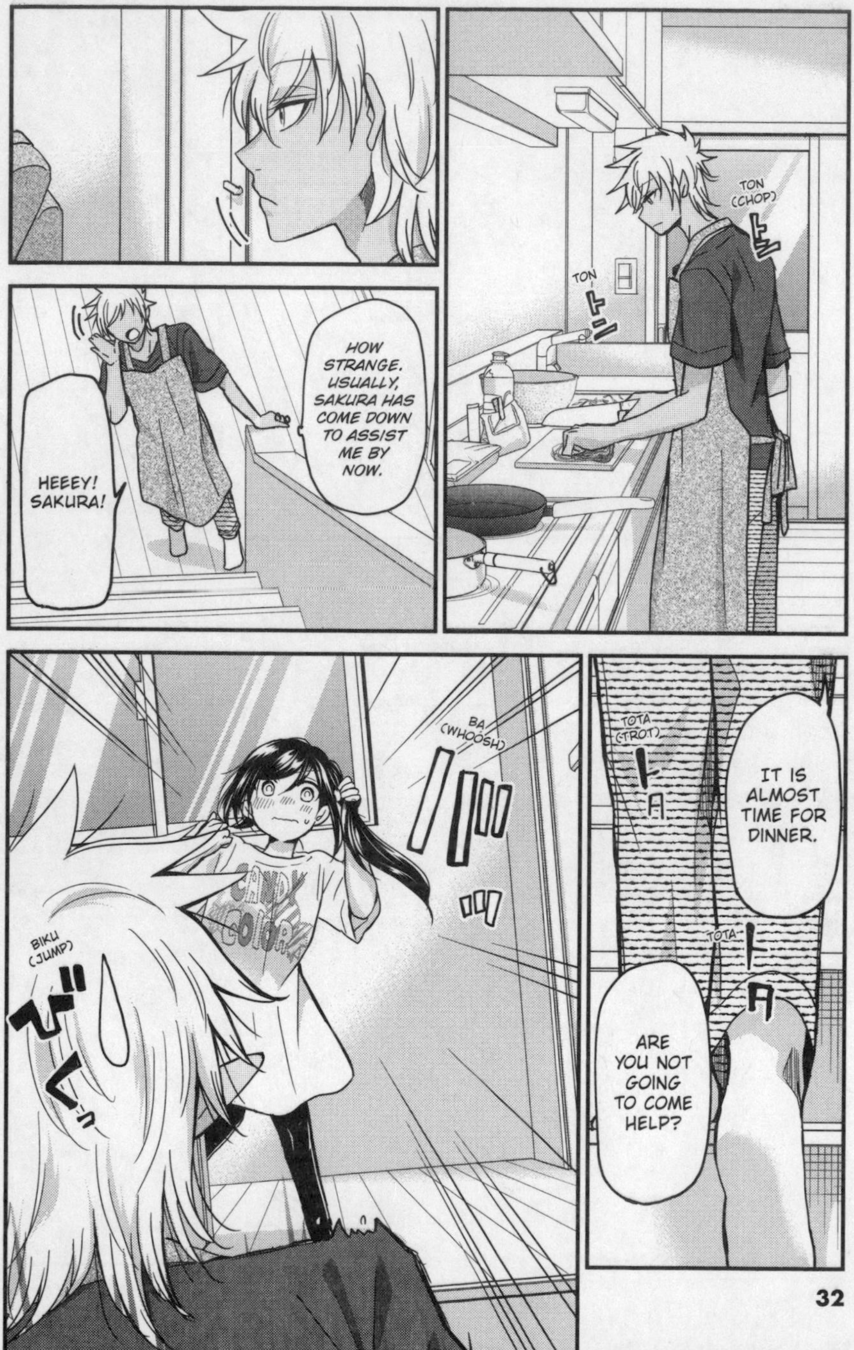
TON
(CHOP)
TON
HOW STRANGE. USUALLY, SAKURA HAS COME DOWN TO ASSIST ME BY NOW.
HEEEY! SAKURA!
TOTA
(TROT)
IT IS ALMOST TIME FOR DINNER.
TOTA
ARE YOU NOT GOING TO COME HELP?
BA
(WHOOSH)
BIKU
(JUMP)

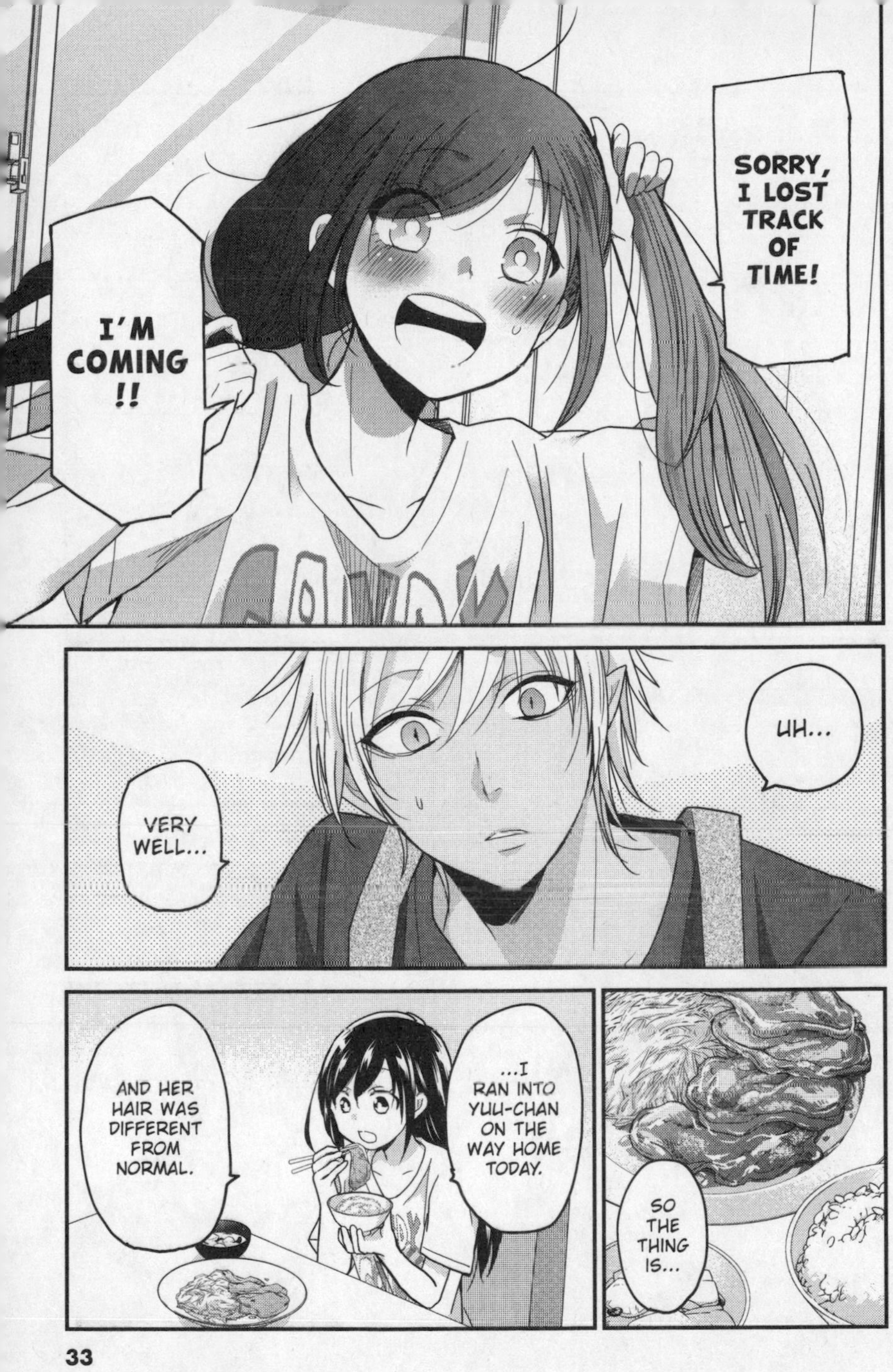
SORRY, I LOST TRACK OF TIME!
I'M COMING!!
UH...
VERY WELL...
SO THE THING IS...
...I RAN INTO YUU-CHAN ON THE WAY HOME TODAY.
AND HER HAIR WAS DIFFERENT FROM NORMAL.

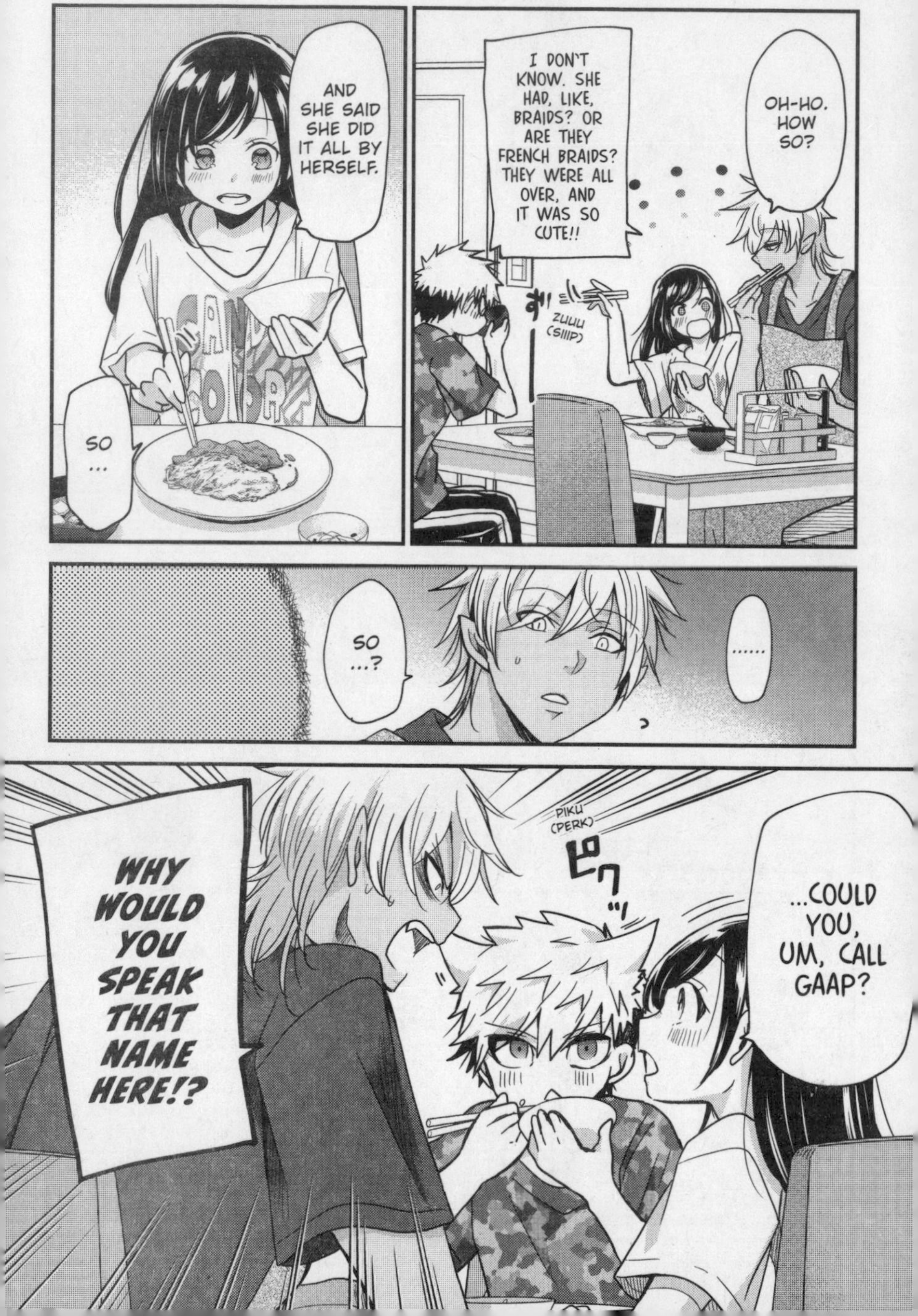
OH-HO. HOW SO?
I DON'T KNOW. SHE HAD, LIKE, BRAIDS? OR ARE THEY FRENCH BRAIDS? THEY WERE ALL OVER, AND IT WAS SO CUTE!!
ZUUU (SIIIP)
AND SHE SAID SHE DID IT ALL BY HERSELF.
SO ...
......
SO ...?
...COULD YOU, UM, CALL GAAP?
PIKU (PERK)
WHY WOULD YOU SPEAK THAT NAME HERE!?

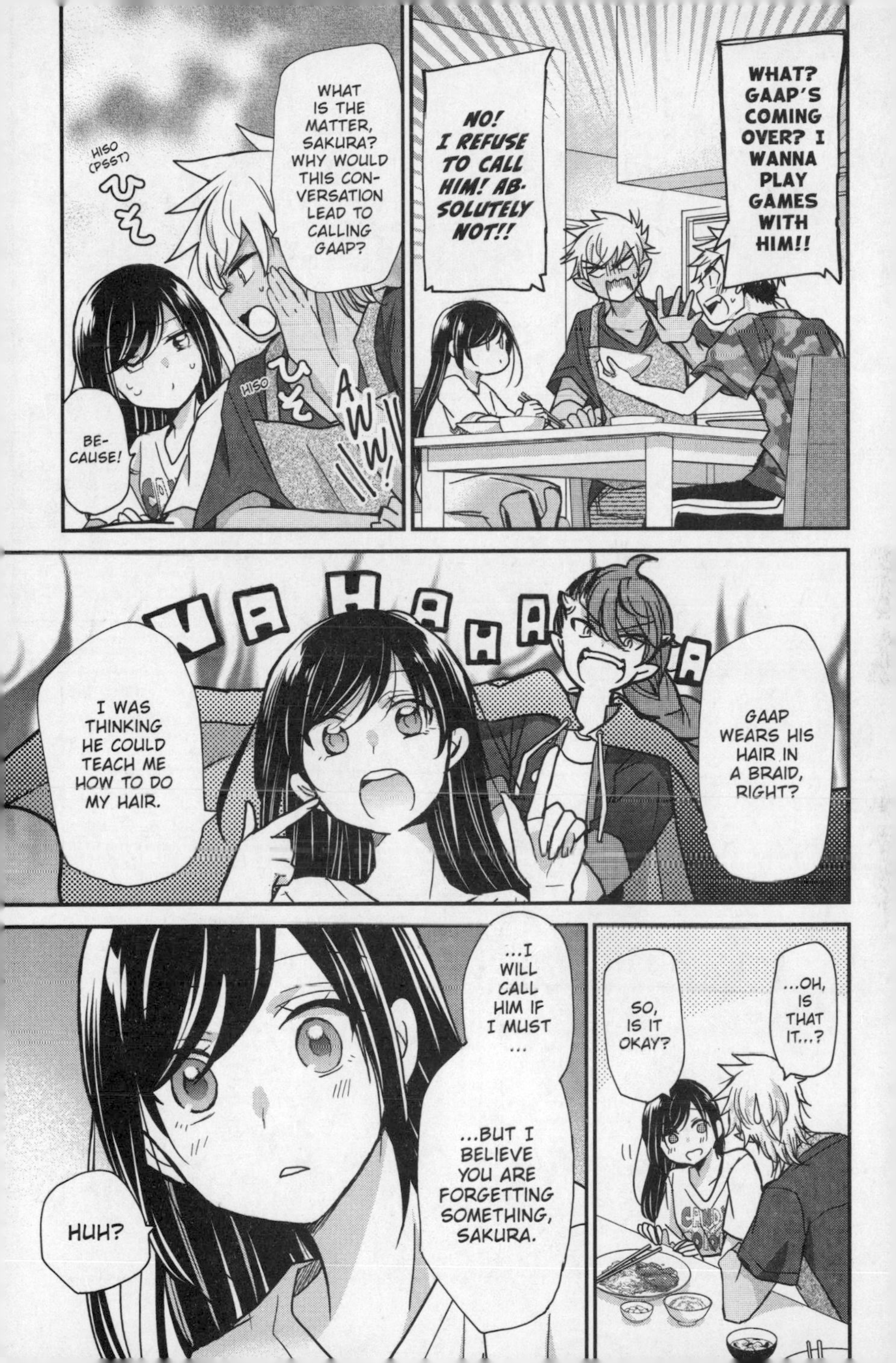
WHAT? GAAP'S COMING OVER? I WANNA PLAY GAMES WITH HIM!!
NO! I REFUSE TO CALL HIM! AB-SOLUTELY NOT!!
WHAT IS THE MATTER, SAKURA? WHY WOULD THIS CON-VERSATION LEAD TO CALLING GAAP?
HISO (PSST)
HISO
AWW
BE-CAUSE!
GAAP WEARS HIS HAIR IN A BRAID, RIGHT?
I WAS THINKING HE COULD TEACH ME HOW TO DO MY HAIR.
...OH, IS THAT IT...?
SO, IS IT OKAY?
...I WILL CALL HIM IF I MUST...
...BUT I BELIEVE YOU ARE FORGETTING SOMETHING, SAKURA.
HUH?

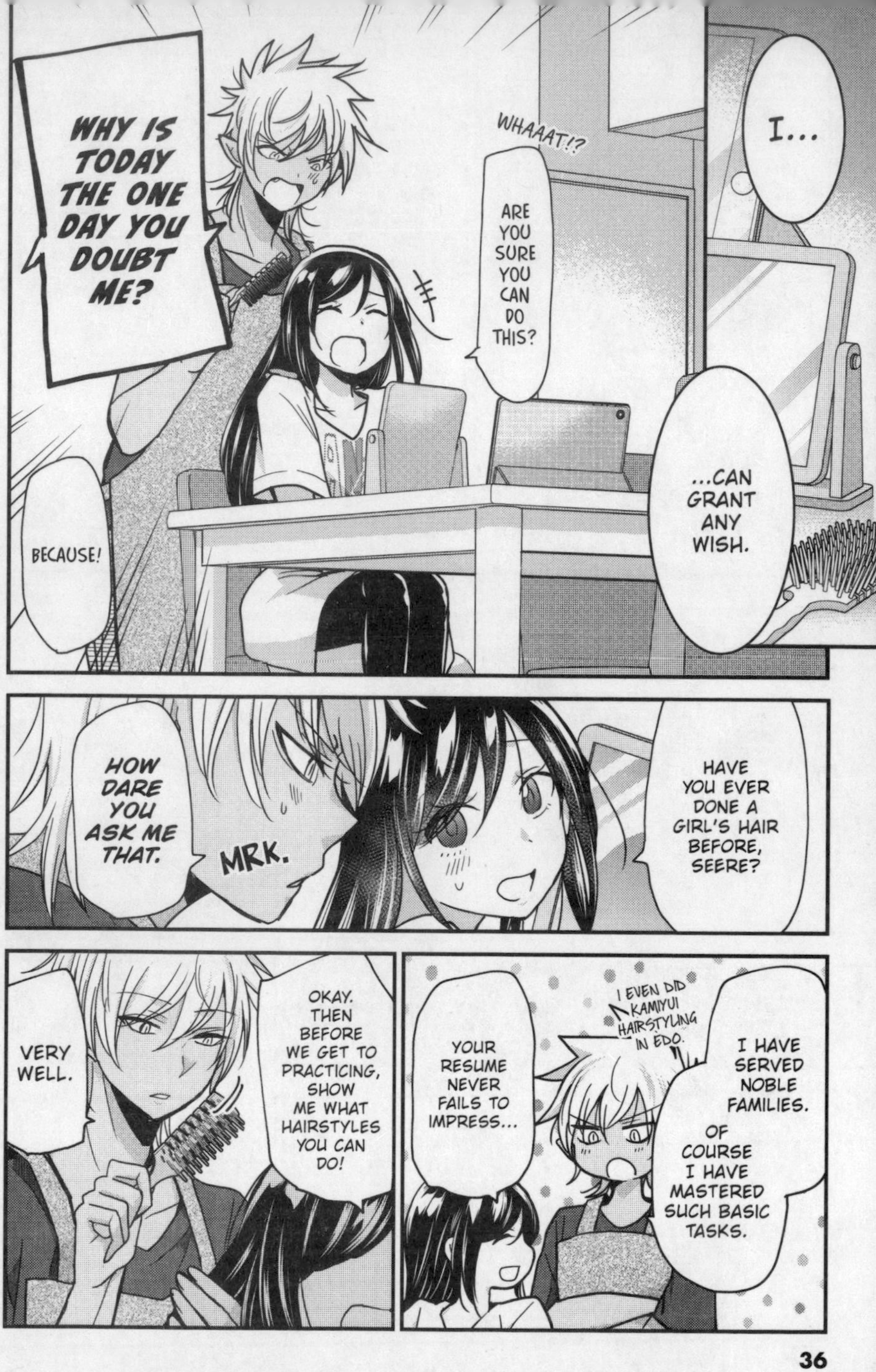
I...
...CAN GRANT ANY WISH.
WHAAAT!?
ARE YOU SURE YOU CAN DO THIS?
WHY IS TODAY THE ONE DAY YOU DOUBT ME?
BECAUSE!
HAVE YOU EVER DONE A GIRL'S HAIR BEFORE, SEERE?
MRK.
HOW DARE YOU ASK ME THAT.
I HAVE SERVED NOBLE FAMILIES.
OF COURSE I HAVE MASTERED SUCH BASIC TASKS.
I EVEN DID KAMIYUI HAIRSTYLING IN EDO.
YOUR RESUME NEVER FAILS TO IMPRESS...
OKAY. THEN BEFORE WE GET TO PRACTICING, SHOW ME WHAT HAIRSTYLES YOU CAN DO!
VERY WELL.

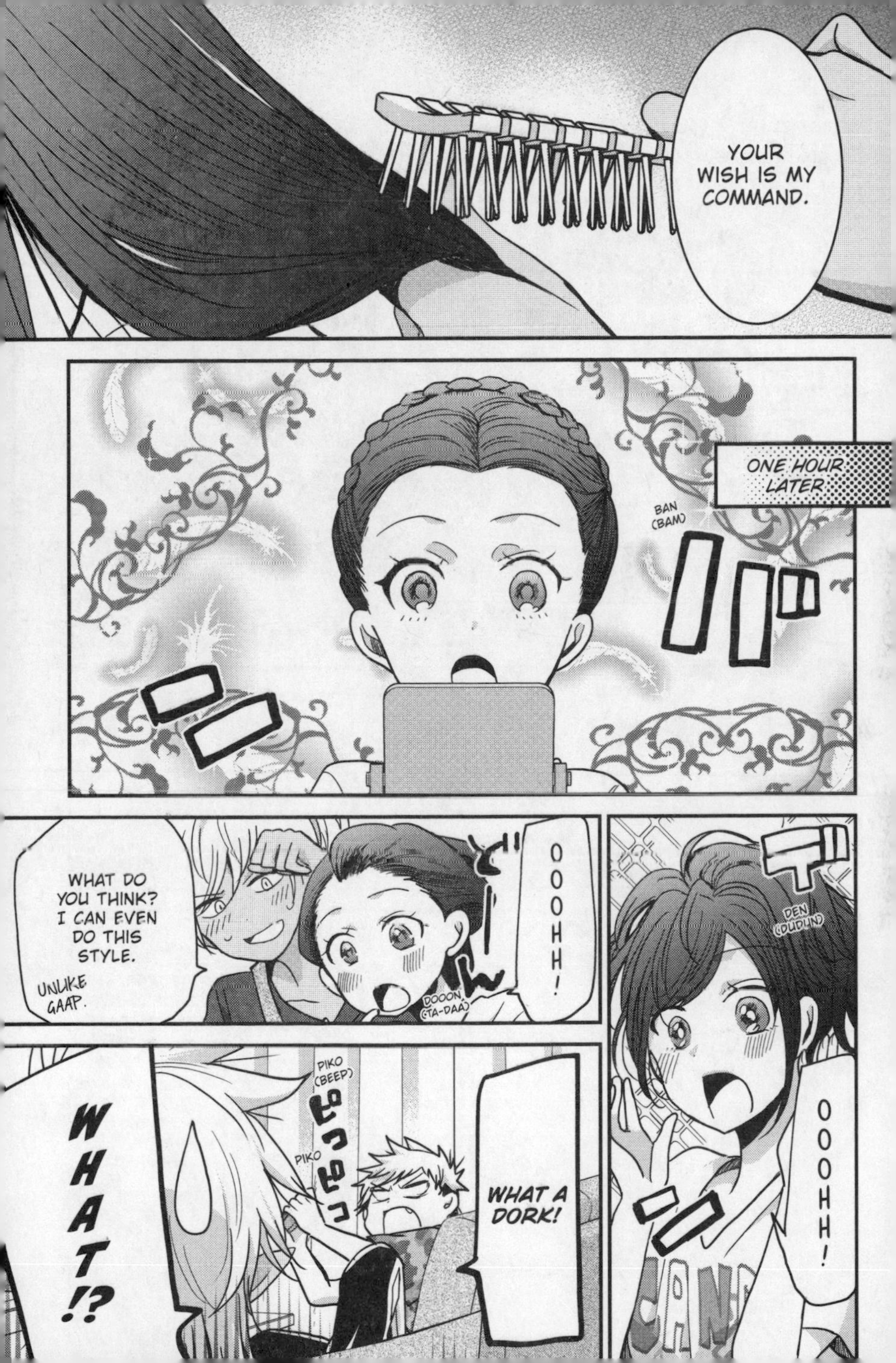

YOUR WISH IS MY COMMAND.
ONE HOUR LATER
BAN (BAM)
DEN (DUDUN)
OOOOHH!
OOOOHH!
DOOON (TA-DAA)
WHAT DO YOU THINK? I CAN EVEN DO THIS STYLE.
UNLIKE GAAP.
WHAT A DORK!
PIKO (BEEP)
PIKO
WHAT!?

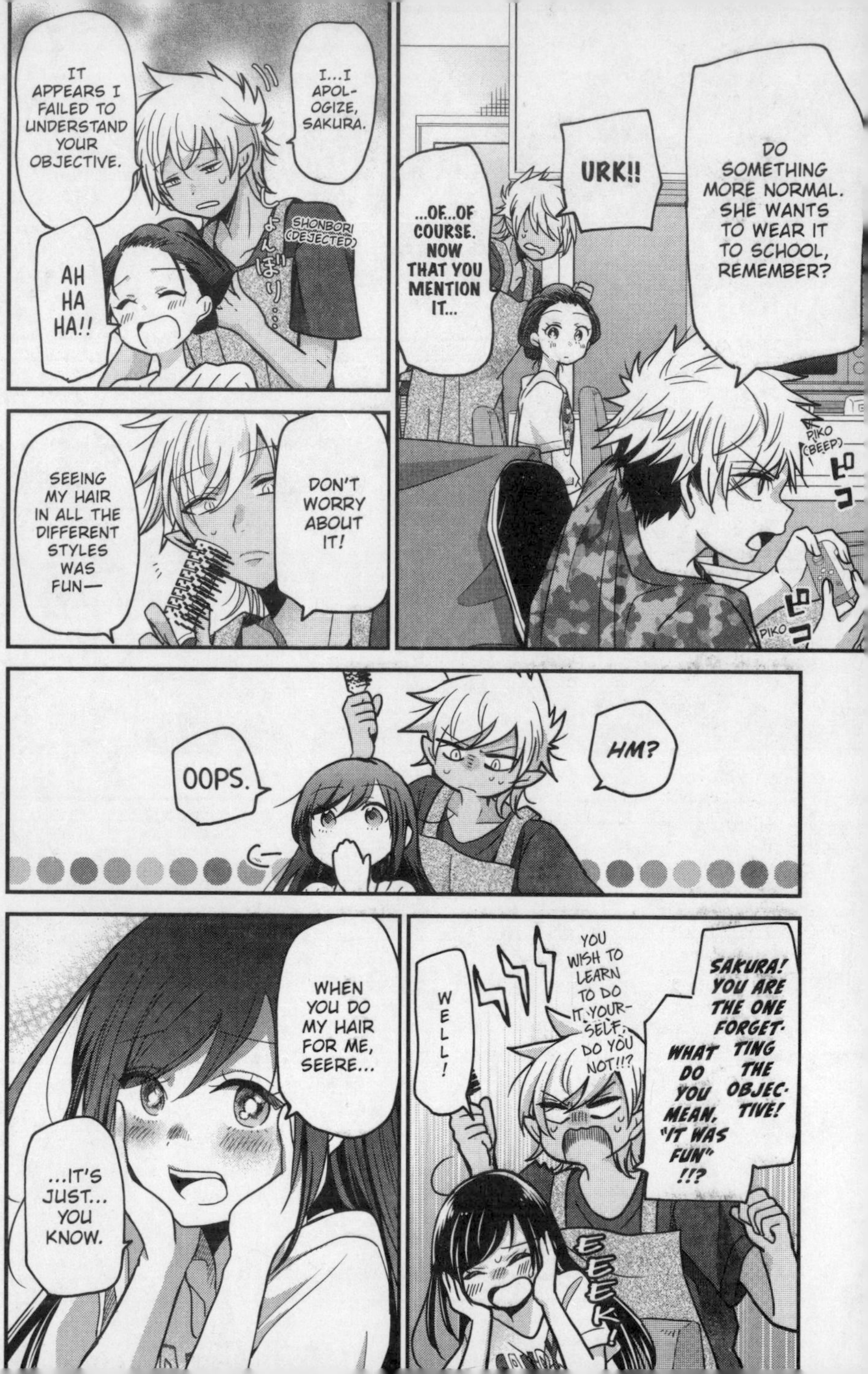
DO SOMETHING MORE NORMAL. SHE WANTS TO WEAR IT TO SCHOOL, REMEMBER?
PIKO (BEEP)
PIKO
URK!!
...OF...OF COURSE. NOW THAT YOU MENTION IT...
I...I APOLOGIZE, SAKURA.
IT APPEARS I FAILED TO UNDERSTAND YOUR OBJECTIVE.
SHONBORI (DEJECTED)
AH HA HA!!
DON'T WORRY ABOUT IT!
SEEING MY HAIR IN ALL THE DIFFERENT STYLES WAS FUN—
HM?
OOPS.
SAKURA! YOU ARE THE ONE FORGETTING THE OBJECTIVE! WHAT DO YOU MEAN, "IT WAS FUN" !!?
YOU WISH TO LEARN TO DO IT YOURSELF, DO YOU NOT!!?
WELL!
EEEEK
WHEN YOU DO MY HAIR FOR ME, SEERE...
...IT'S JUST... YOU KNOW.

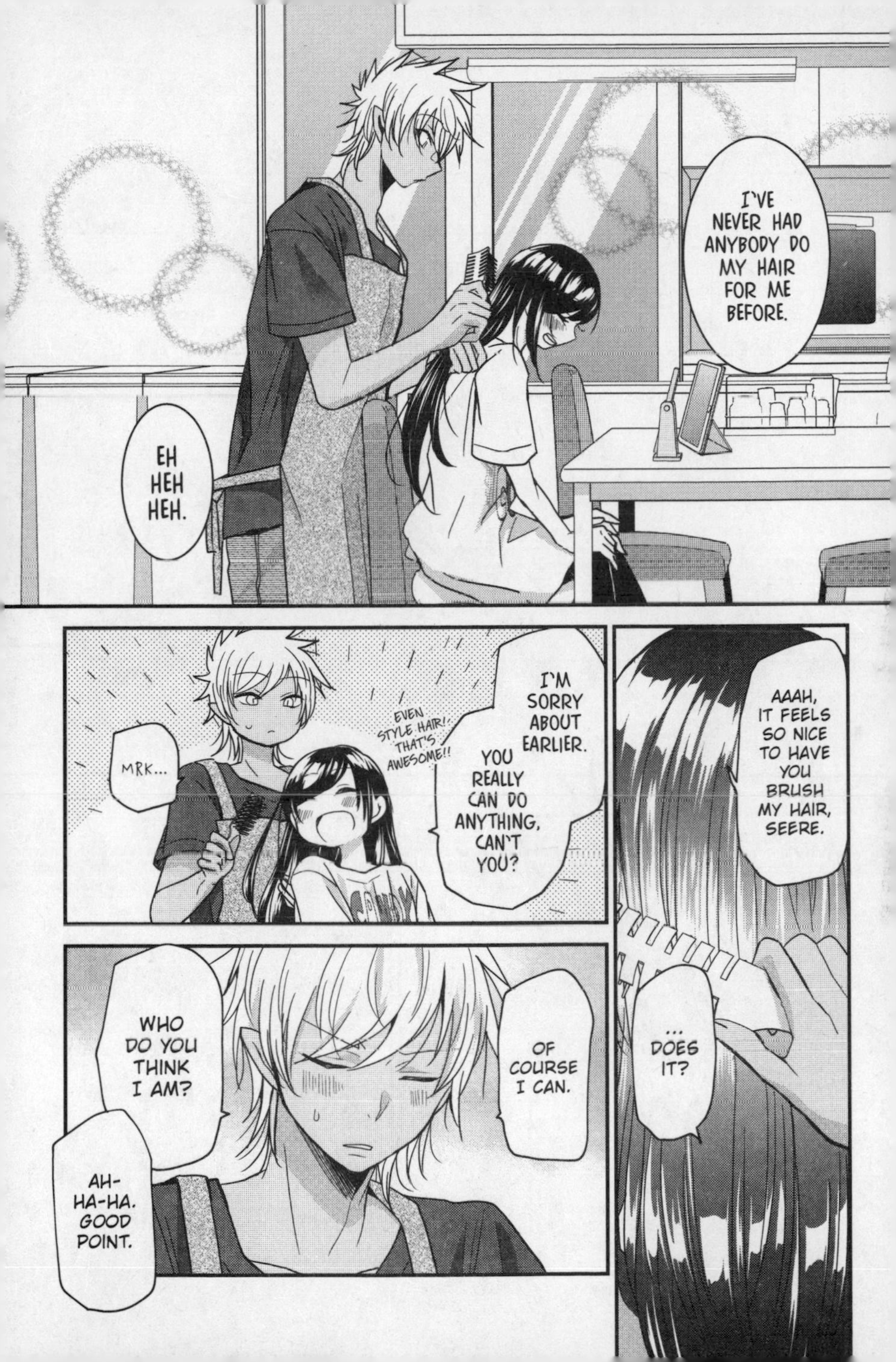
I'VE NEVER HAD ANYBODY DO MY HAIR FOR ME BEFORE.
EH HEH HEH.
AAAH, IT FEELS SO NICE TO HAVE YOU BRUSH MY HAIR, SEERE.
...DOES IT?
I'M SORRY ABOUT EARLIER.
YOU REALLY CAN DO ANYTHING, CAN'T YOU?
EVEN STYLE HAIR!! THAT'S AWESOME!!
MRK...
OF COURSE I CAN.
WHO DO YOU THINK I AM?
AH-HA-HA. GOOD POINT.

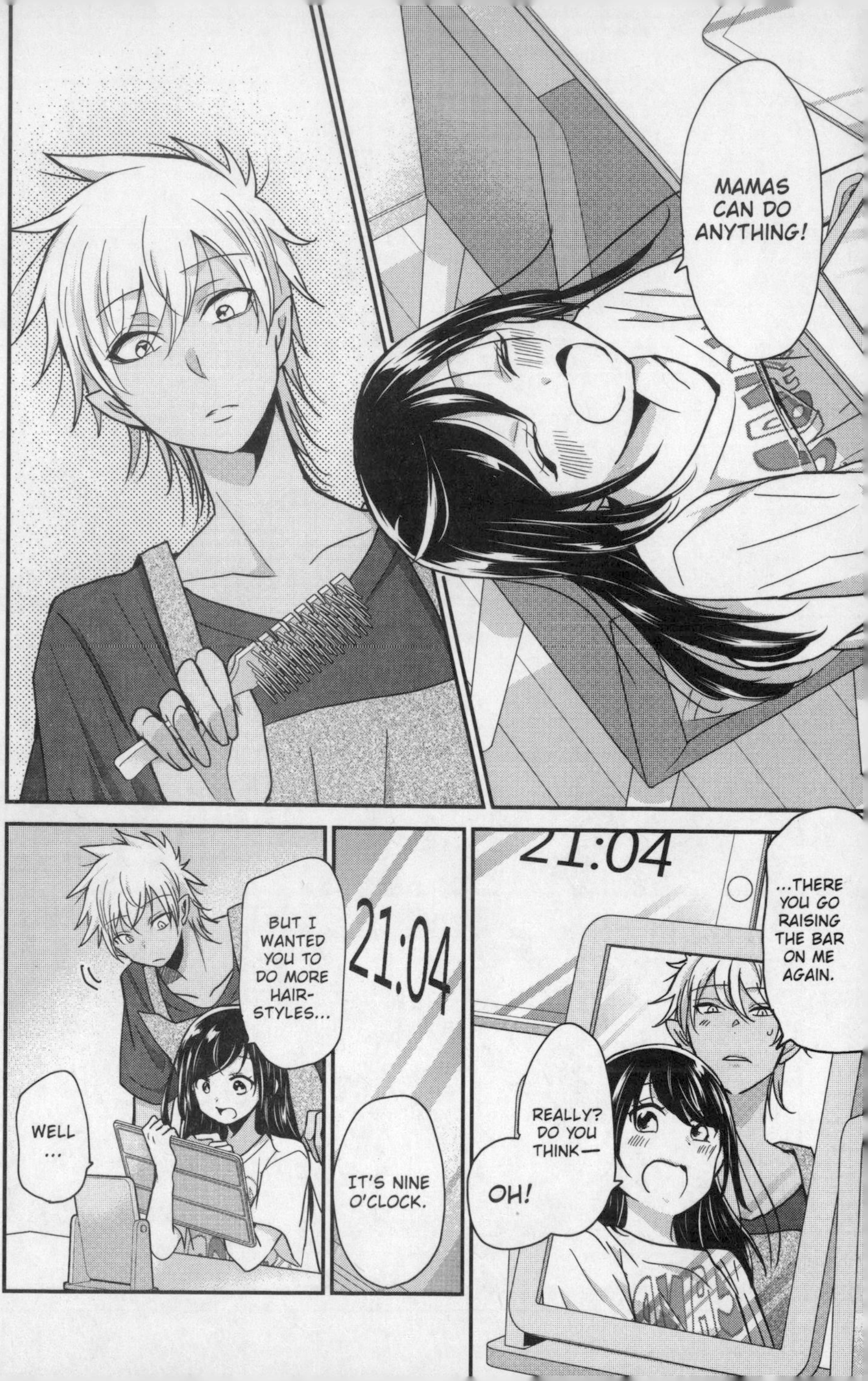
MAMAS CAN DO ANYTHING!
21:04
...THERE YOU GO RAISING THE BAR ON ME AGAIN.
REALLY? DO YOU THINK—
OH!
21:04
IT'S NINE O'CLOCK.
BUT I WANTED YOU TO DO MORE HAIR-STYLES...
WELL ...

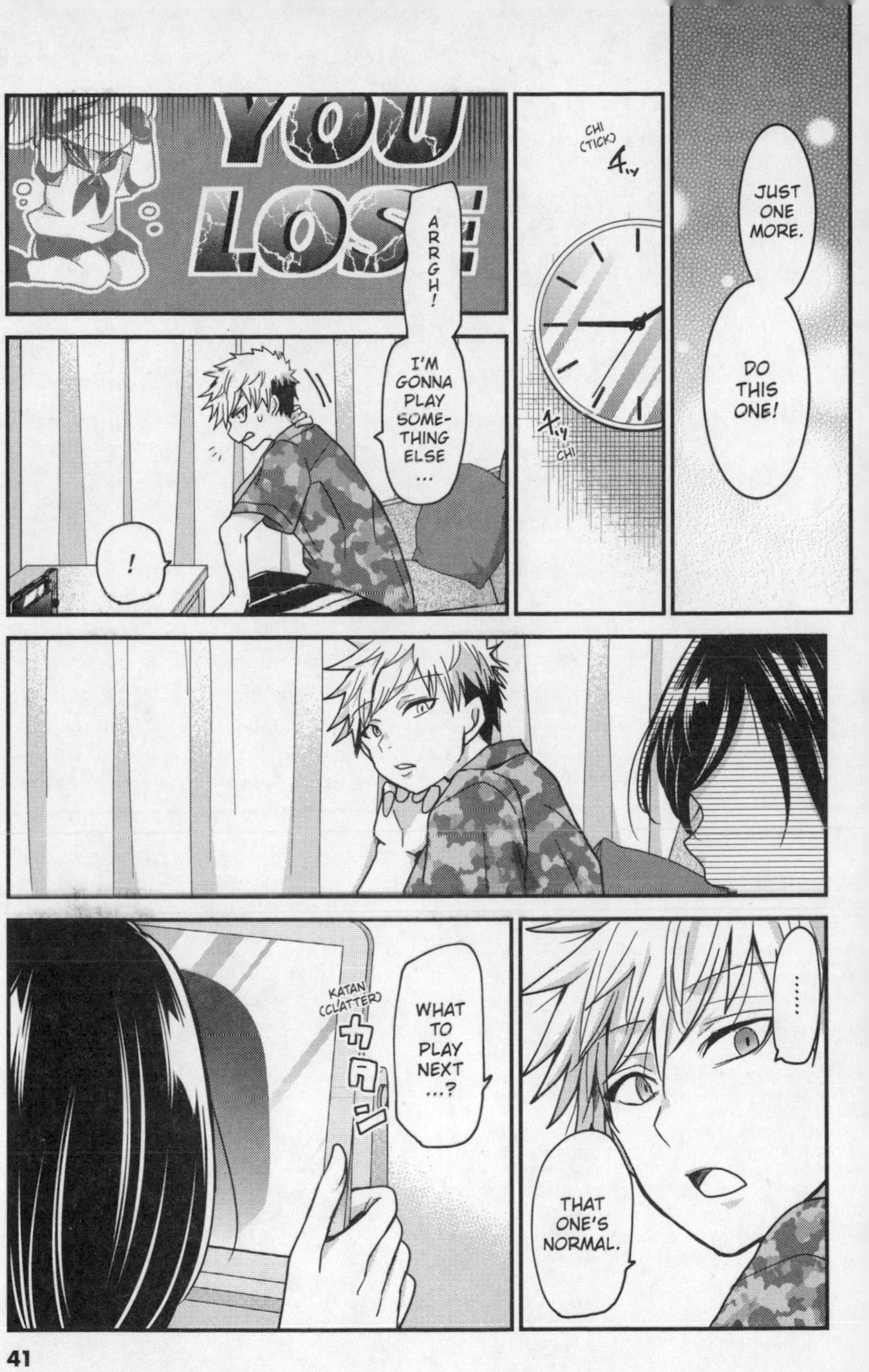
JUST ONE MORE.
DO THIS ONE!
CHI (TICK)
CHI
YOU LOSE
ARRGH!
I'M GONNA PLAY SOMETHING ELSE...
!
......
THAT ONE'S NORMAL.
WHAT TO PLAY NEXT...?
KATAN (CLATTER)

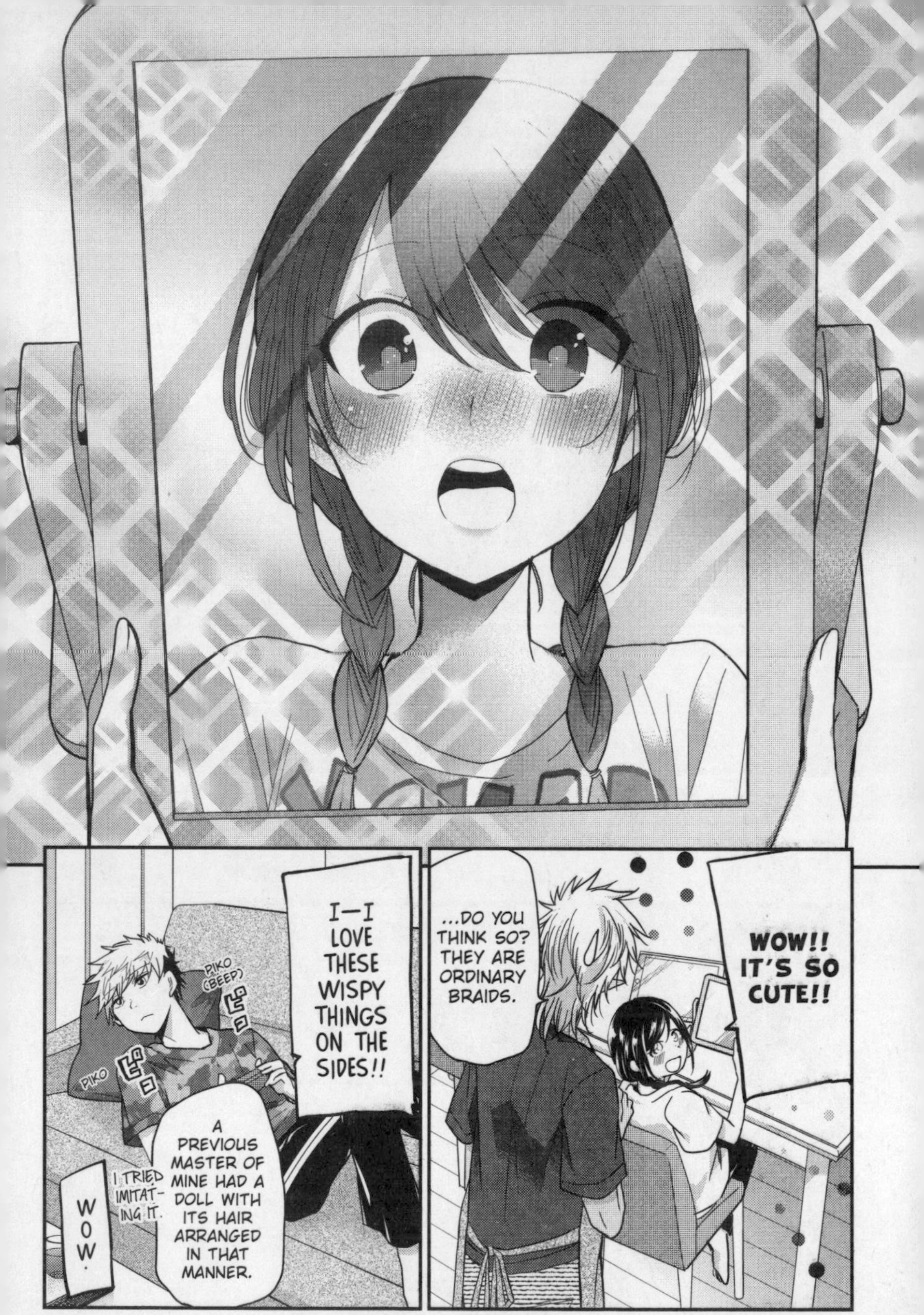
WOW!! IT'S SO CUTE!!
...DO YOU THINK SO? THEY ARE ORDINARY BRAIDS.
I—I LOVE THESE WISPY THINGS ON THE SIDES!!
PIKO (BEEP)
PIKO
A PREVIOUS MASTER OF MINE HAD A DOLL WITH ITS HAIR ARRANGED IN THAT MANNER.
I TRIED IMITATING IT.
WOW.

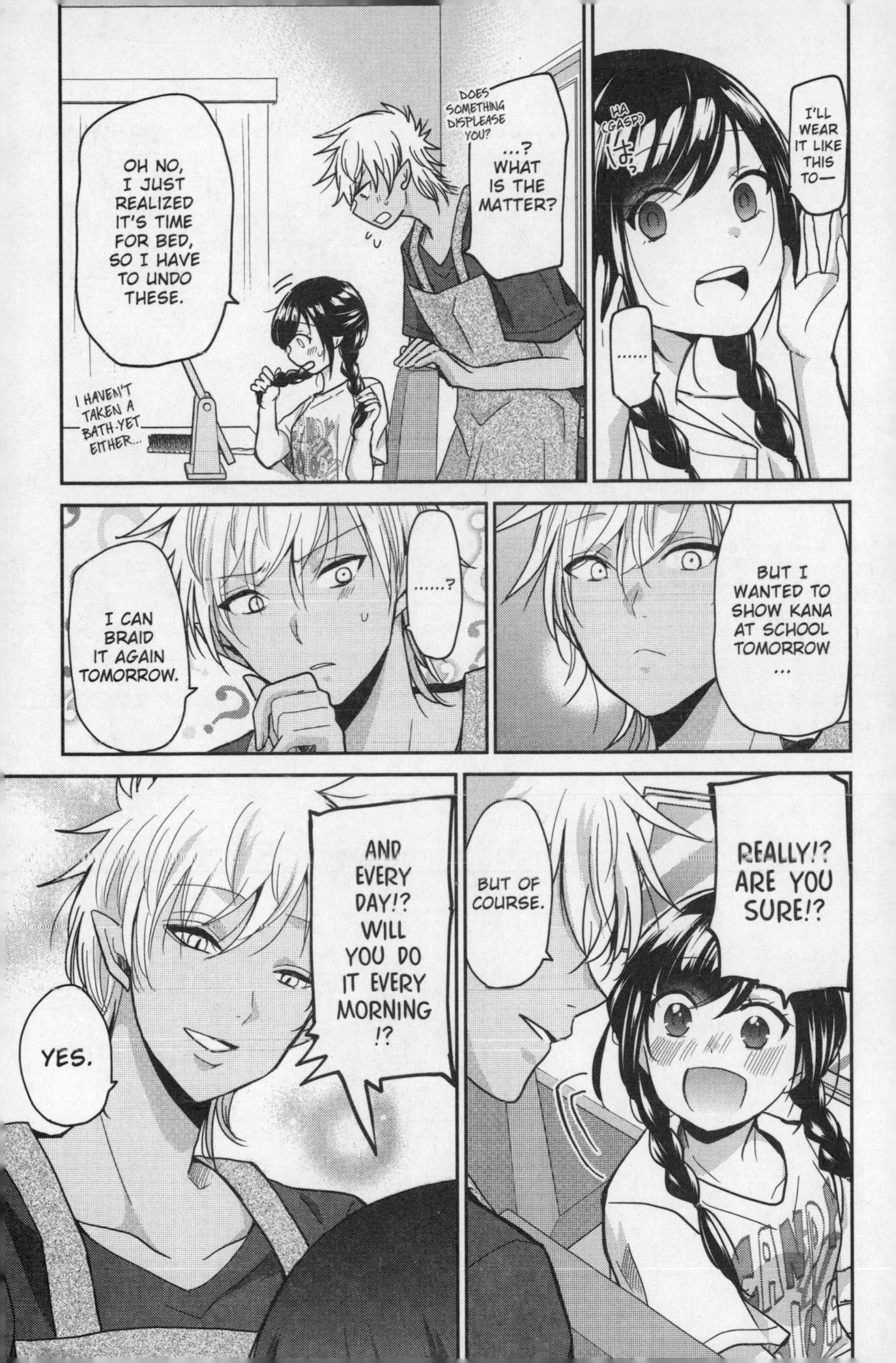
I'LL WEAR IT LIKE THIS TO—
HA (GASP)
......
...? WHAT IS THE MATTER?
DOES SOMETHING DISPLEASE YOU?
OH NO, I JUST REALIZED IT'S TIME FOR BED, SO I HAVE TO UNDO THESE.
I HAVEN'T TAKEN A BATH YET EITHER...
BUT I WANTED TO SHOW KANA AT SCHOOL TOMORROW ...
......?
I CAN BRAID IT AGAIN TOMORROW.
REALLY!? ARE YOU SURE!?
BUT OF COURSE.
AND EVERY DAY!? WILL YOU DO IT EVERY MORNING !?
YES.

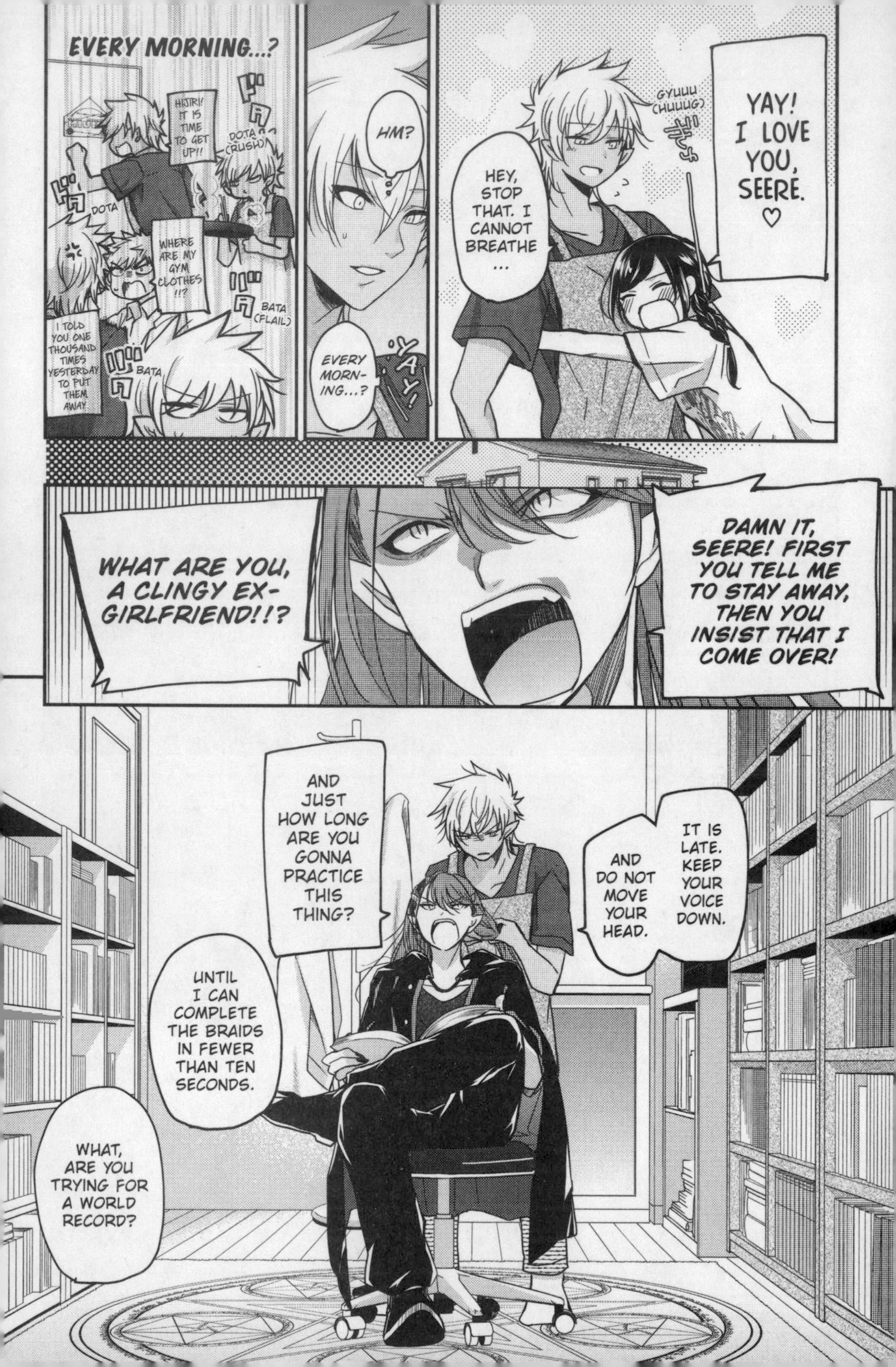
YAY! I LOVE YOU, SEERE. ♡
GYUUU (HUUUG)
HEY, STOP THAT. I CANNOT BREATHE ...
HM?
EVERY MORNING...?
YAY
EVERY MORNING...?
HIJIRI! IT IS TIME TO GET UP!!
DOTA (RUSH)
DOTA
WHERE ARE MY GYM CLOTHES!!?
BATA (FLAIL)
I TOLD YOU ONE THOUSAND TIMES YESTERDAY TO PUT THEM AWAY.
BATA
DAMN IT, SEERE! FIRST YOU TELL ME TO STAY AWAY, THEN YOU INSIST THAT I COME OVER!
WHAT ARE YOU, A CLINGY EX-GIRLFRIEND!!?
IT IS LATE. KEEP YOUR VOICE DOWN.
AND DO NOT MOVE YOUR HEAD.
AND JUST HOW LONG ARE YOU GONNA PRACTICE THIS THING?
UNTIL I CAN COMPLETE THE BRAIDS IN FEWER THAN TEN SECONDS.
WHAT, ARE YOU TRYING FOR A WORLD RECORD?

# Day. 13

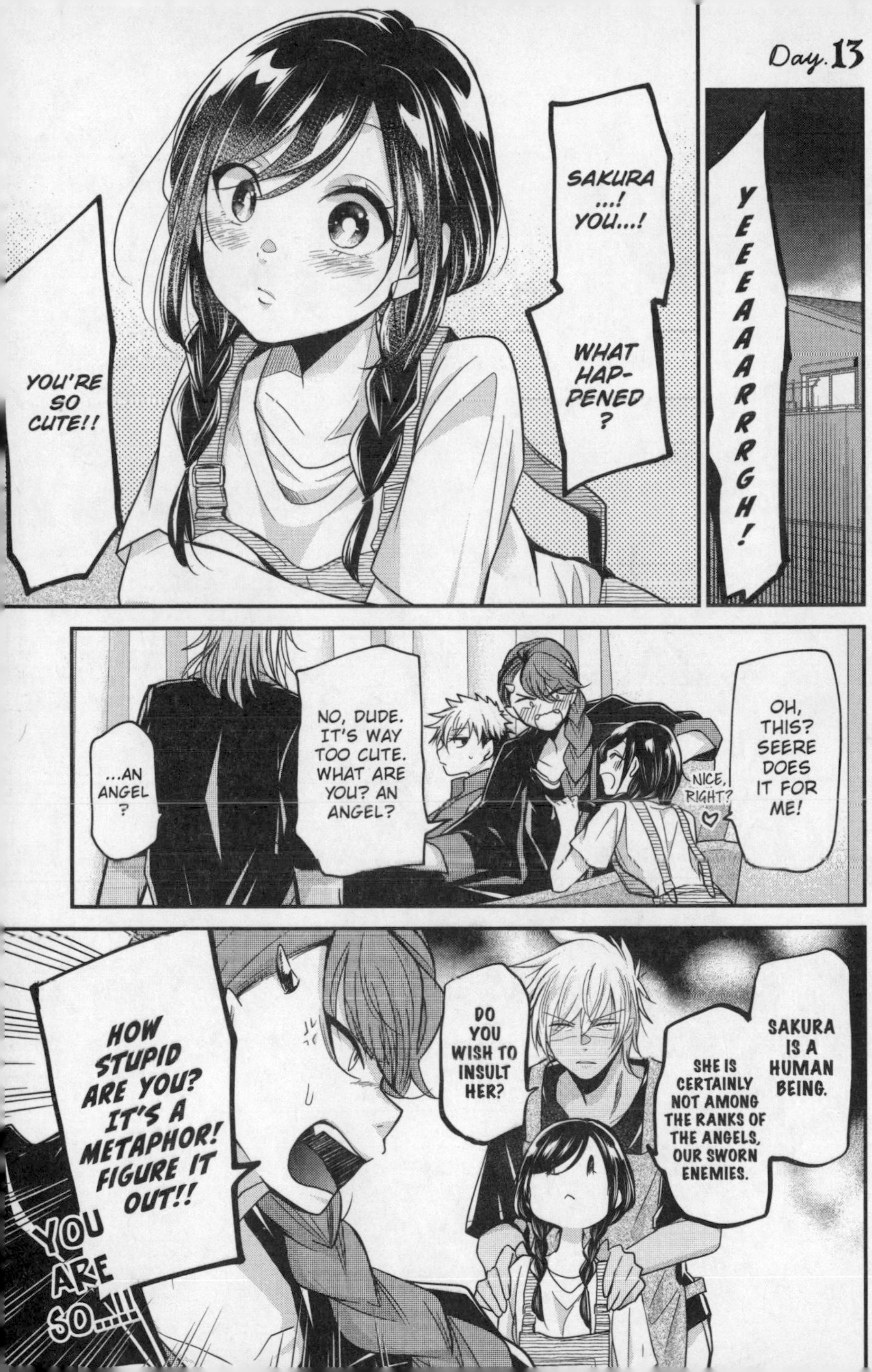
YEEEAAARRRGH!
SAKURA ...! YOU...!
WHAT HAPPENED?
YOU'RE SO CUTE!!
OH, THIS? SEERE DOES IT FOR ME!
NICE, RIGHT? ♥
NO, DUDE. IT'S WAY TOO CUTE. WHAT ARE YOU? AN ANGEL?
...AN ANGEL?
SAKURA IS A HUMAN BEING.
SHE IS CERTAINLY NOT AMONG THE RANKS OF THE ANGELS, OUR SWORN ENEMIES.
DO YOU WISH TO INSULT HER?
HOW STUPID ARE YOU? IT'S A METAPHOR! FIGURE IT OUT!!
YOU ARE SO...!!!

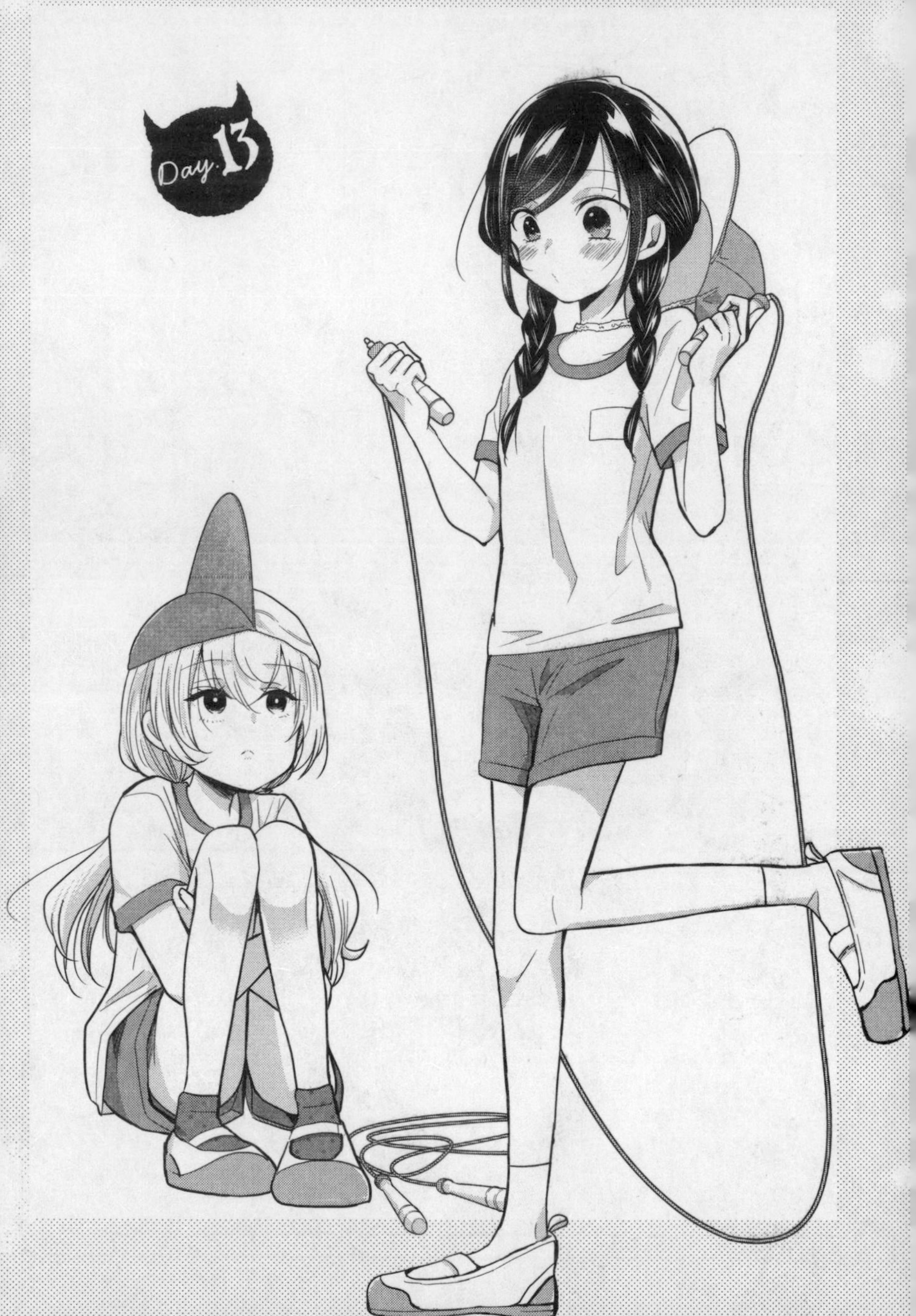
Day. 13

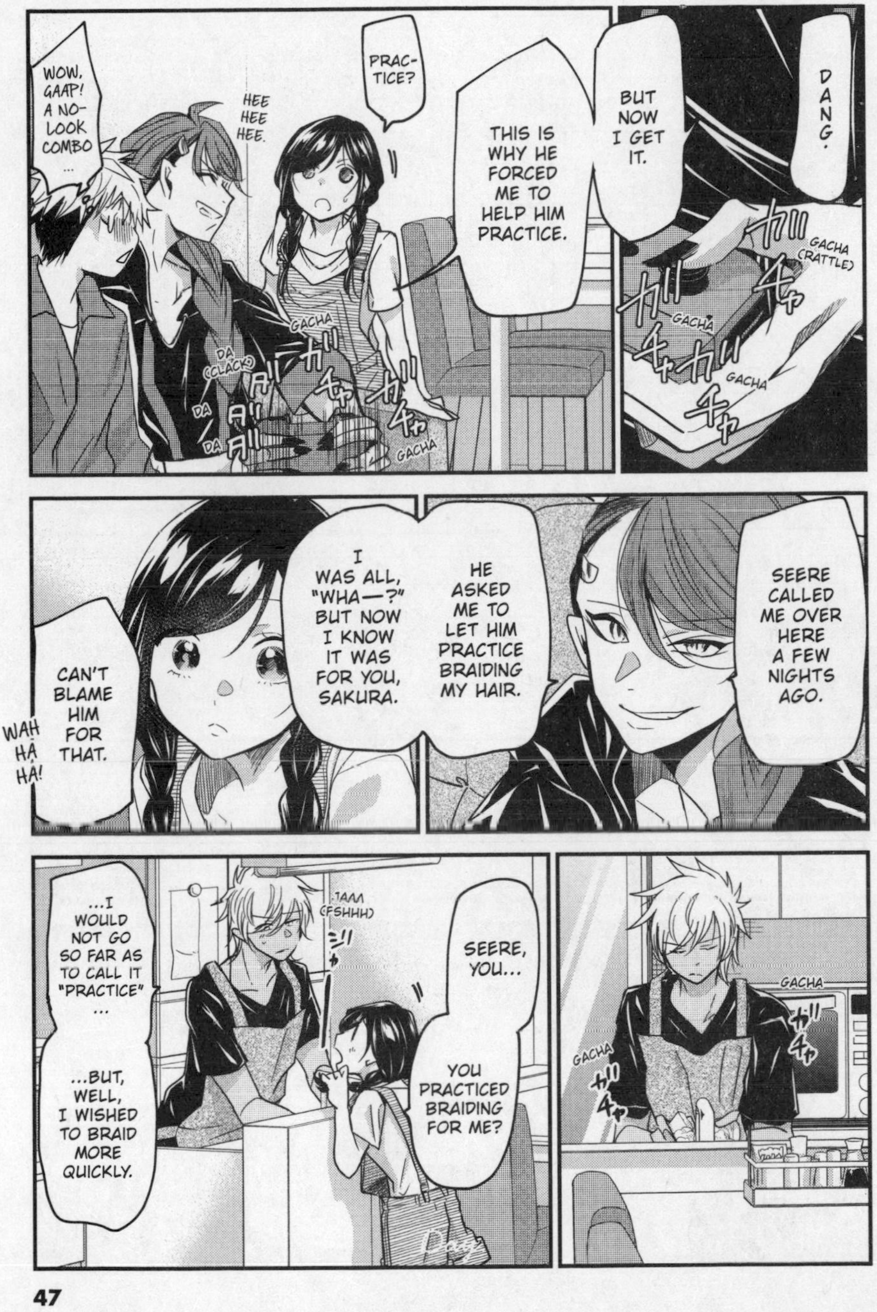
DANG.
GACHA (RATTLE)
GACHA
GACHA
BUT NOW I GET IT.
THIS IS WHY HE FORCED ME TO HELP HIM PRACTICE.
PRAC-TICE?
HEE HEE HEE.
WOW, GAAP! A NO-LOOK COMBO...
GACHA
DA (CLACK)
DA
DA
GACHA
SEERE CALLED ME OVER HERE A FEW NIGHTS AGO.
HE ASKED ME TO LET HIM PRACTICE BRAIDING MY HAIR.
I WAS ALL, "WHA—?" BUT NOW I KNOW IT WAS FOR YOU, SAKURA.
CAN'T BLAME HIM FOR THAT.
WAH HA HA!
GACHA
GACHA
SEERE, YOU...
YOU PRACTICED BRAIDING FOR ME?
JAAA (FSHHH)
...I WOULD NOT GO SO FAR AS TO CALL IT "PRACTICE"...
...BUT, WELL, I WISHED TO BRAID MORE QUICKLY.

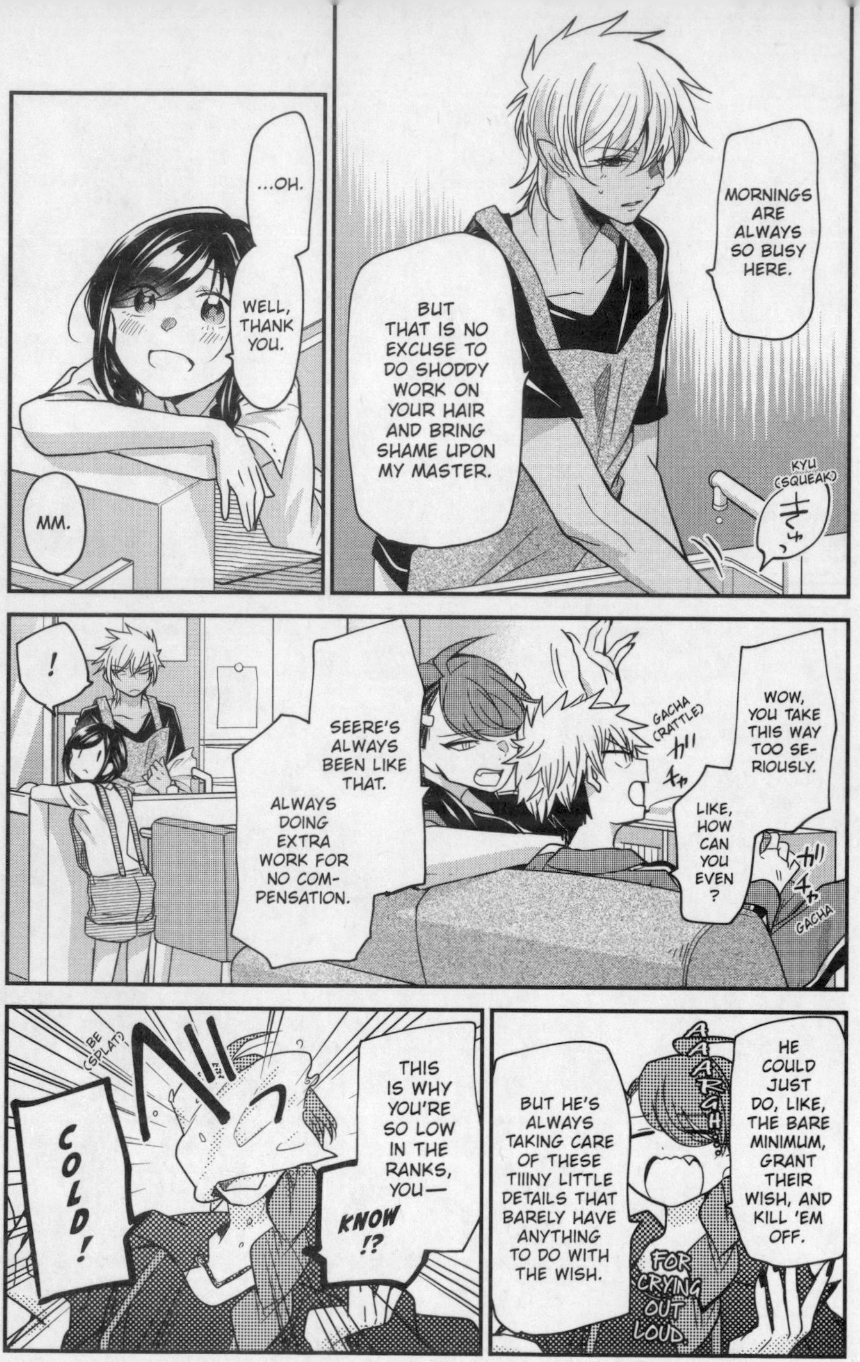
MORNINGS ARE ALWAYS SO BUSY HERE.
BUT THAT IS NO EXCUSE TO DO SHODDY WORK ON YOUR HAIR AND BRING SHAME UPON MY MASTER.
KYU (SQUEAK)
...OH.
WELL, THANK YOU.
MM.
WOW, YOU TAKE THIS WAY TOO SE-RIOUSLY.
GACHA (RATTLE)
LIKE, HOW CAN YOU EVEN ?
GACHA
SEERE'S ALWAYS BEEN LIKE THAT.
ALWAYS DOING EXTRA WORK FOR NO COM-PENSATION.
!
HE COULD JUST DO, LIKE, THE BARE MINIMUM, GRANT THEIR WISH, AND KILL 'EM OFF.
BUT HE'S ALWAYS TAKING CARE OF THESE TIIINY LITTLE DETAILS THAT BARELY HAVE ANYTHING TO DO WITH THE WISH.
AAAARGH
FOR CRYING OUT LOUD
THIS IS WHY YOU'RE SO LOW IN THE RANKS, YOU—
KNOW!?
BE (SPLAT)
COLD!

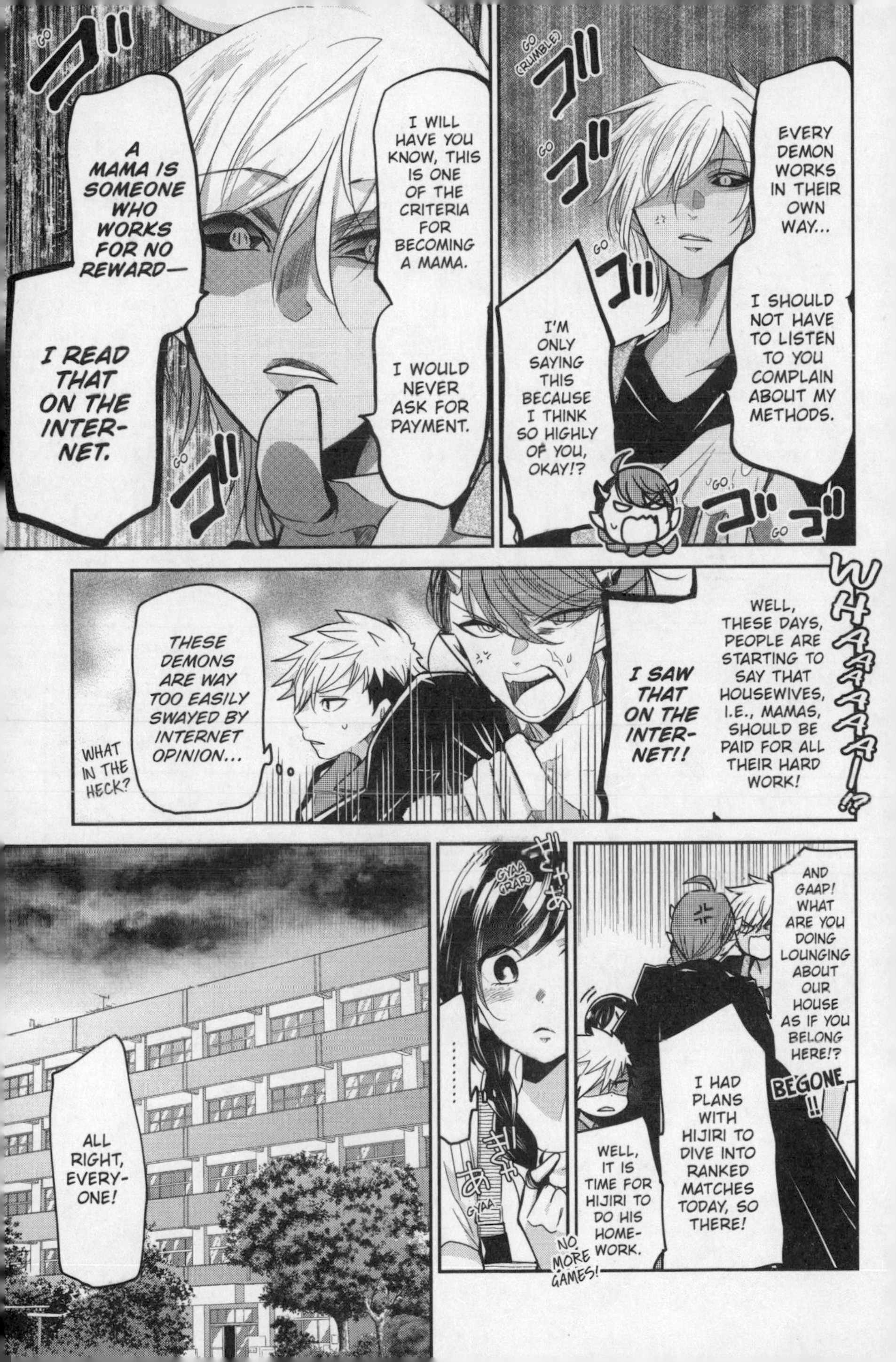
GO (RUMBLE)
GO
EVERY DEMON WORKS IN THEIR OWN WAY...
GO
I SHOULD NOT HAVE TO LISTEN TO YOU COMPLAIN ABOUT MY METHODS.
I'M ONLY SAYING THIS BECAUSE I THINK SO HIGHLY OF YOU, OKAY!?
GO
GO
GO
I WILL HAVE YOU KNOW, THIS IS ONE OF THE CRITERIA FOR BECOMING A MAMA.
I WOULD NEVER ASK FOR PAYMENT.
A MAMA IS SOMEONE WHO WORKS FOR NO REWARD—
I READ THAT ON THE INTERNET.
GO
WHAAAAAAA!!?
WELL, THESE DAYS, PEOPLE ARE STARTING TO SAY THAT HOUSEWIVES, I.E., MAMAS, SHOULD BE PAID FOR ALL THEIR HARD WORK!
I SAW THAT ON THE INTERNET!!
THESE DEMONS ARE WAY TOO EASILY SWAYED BY INTERNET OPINION...
WHAT IN THE HECK?
AND GAAP! WHAT ARE YOU DOING LOUNGING ABOUT OUR HOUSE AS IF YOU BELONG HERE!?
BEGONE!!
I HAD PLANS WITH HIJIRI TO DIVE INTO RANKED MATCHES TODAY, SO THERE!
GYAA (GRAR)
GYAA
......
WELL, IT IS TIME FOR HIJIRI TO DO HIS HOMEWORK.
NO MORE GAMES!
ALL RIGHT, EVERYONE!

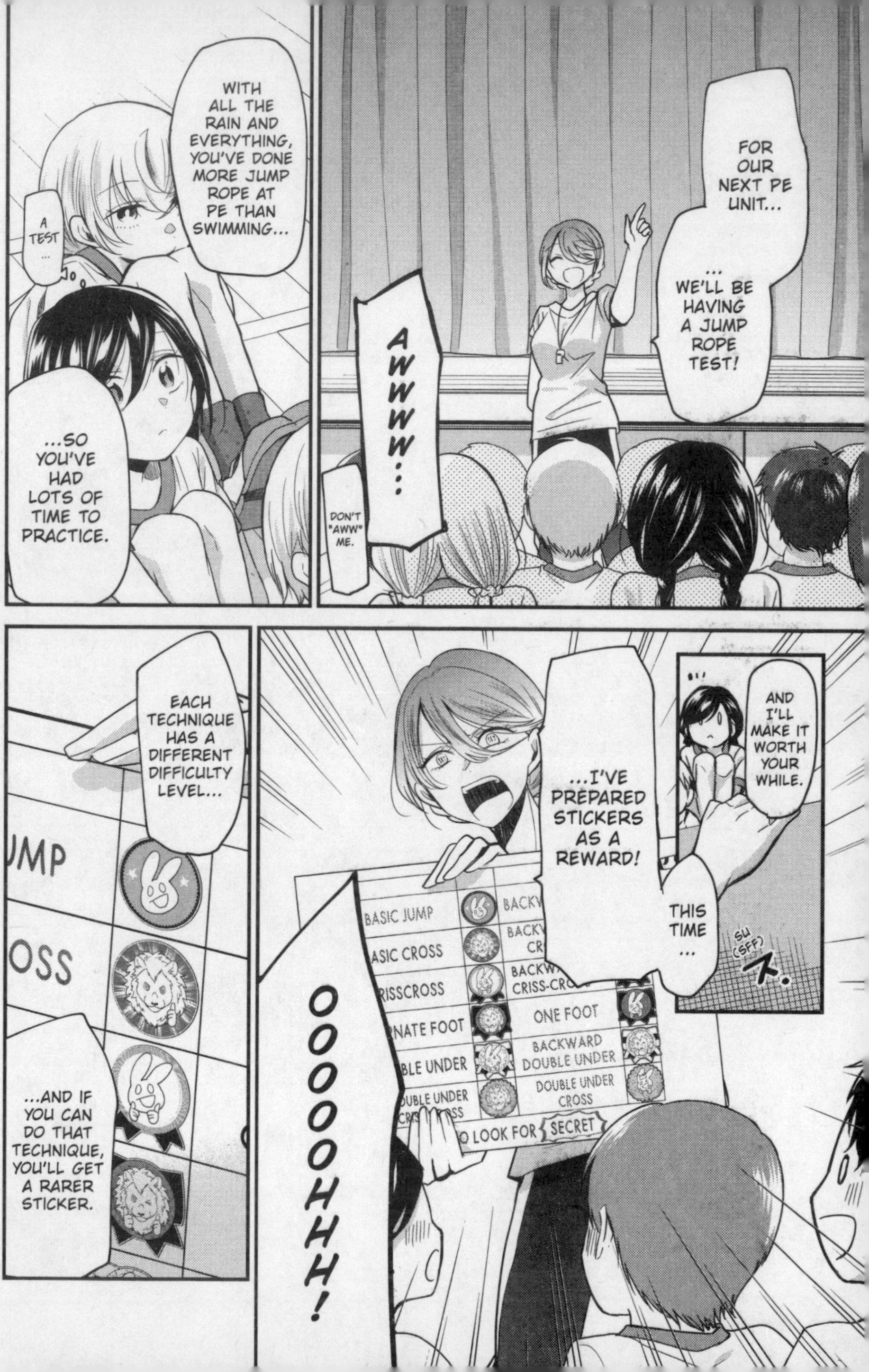
FOR OUR NEXT PE UNIT...
...WE'LL BE HAVING A JUMP ROPE TEST!
AWWWWW...
DON'T "AWW" ME.
A TEST...
WITH ALL THE RAIN AND EVERYTHING, YOU'VE DONE MORE JUMP ROPE AT PE THAN SWIMMING...
...SO YOU'VE HAD LOTS OF TIME TO PRACTICE.
AND I'LL MAKE IT WORTH YOUR WHILE.
SU (SFF)
THIS TIME...
...I'VE PREPARED STICKERS AS A REWARD!
BASIC JUMP
BASIC CROSS
ONE FOOT
BACKWARD DOUBLE UNDER
DOUBLE UNDER CROSS
SECRET
OOOOOOHHHH!
EACH TECHNIQUE HAS A DIFFERENT DIFFICULTY LEVEL...
...AND IF YOU CAN DO THAT TECHNIQUE, YOU'LL GET A RARER STICKER.

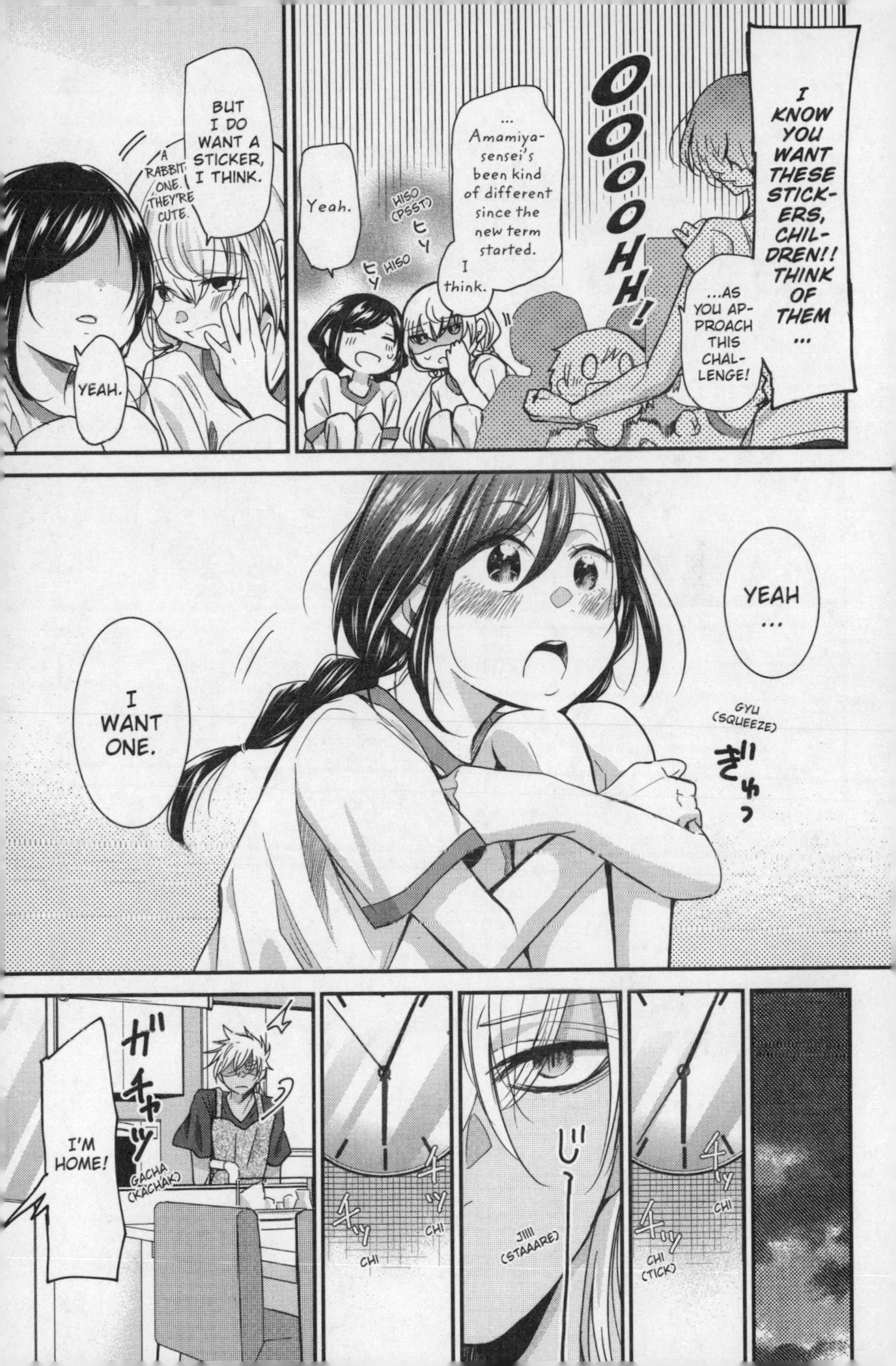
I KNOW YOU WANT THESE STICKERS, CHILDREN!! THINK OF THEM...
...AS YOU APPROACH THIS CHALLENGE!
OOOOOHH!
...Amamiya-sensei's been kind of different since the new term started.
I think.
HISO (PSST)
HISO
Yeah.
BUT I DO WANT A STICKER, I THINK.
A RABBIT ONE. THEY'RE CUTE.
YEAH.
YEAH...
GYU (SQUEEZE)
ぎゅっ
I WANT ONE.
CHI (TICK)
CHI
JIIII (STAAARE)
CHI
CHI
ガチャッ
GACHA (KACHAK)
I'M HOME!

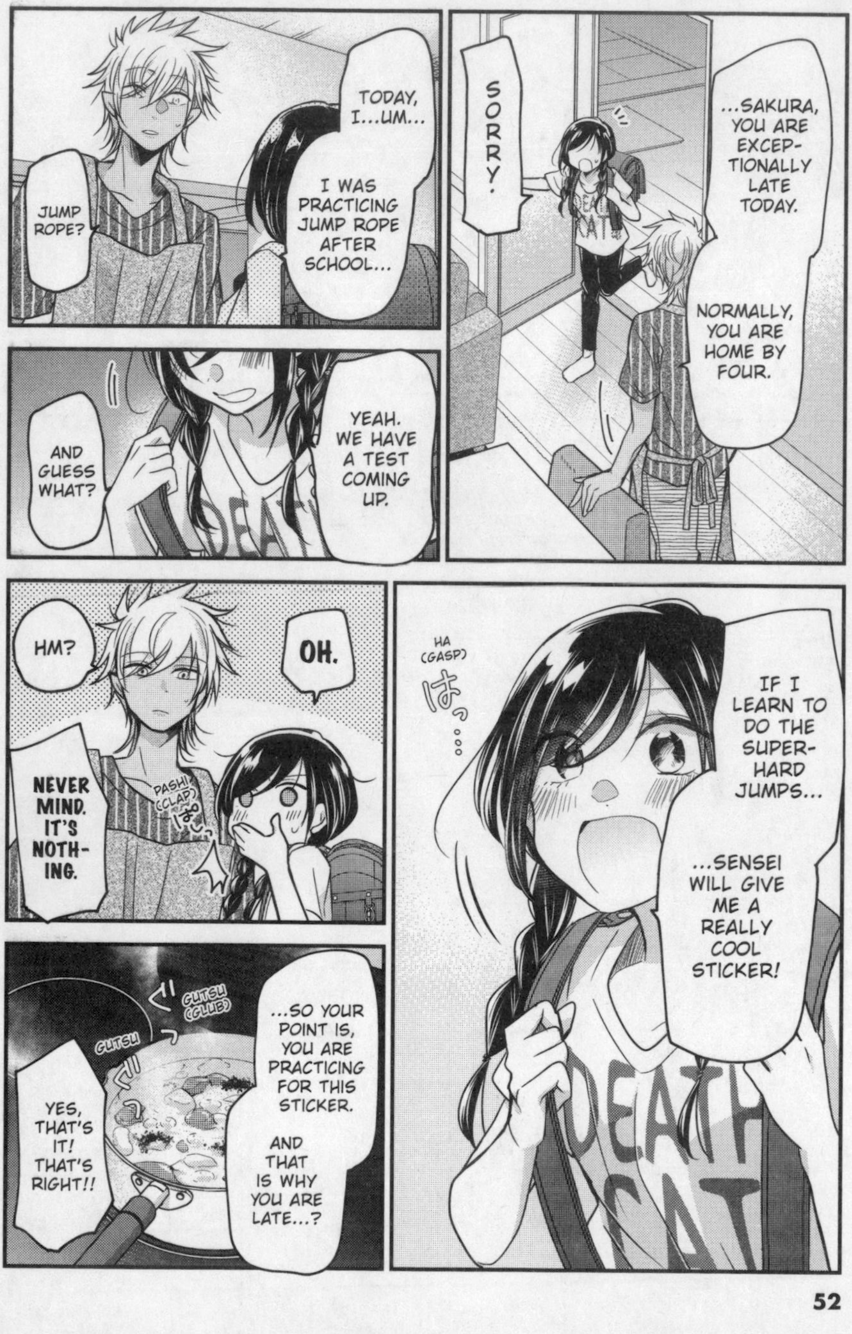

...SAKURA, YOU ARE EXCEPTIONALLY LATE TODAY.
NORMALLY, YOU ARE HOME BY FOUR.
SORRY.
TODAY, I...UM...
I WAS PRACTICING JUMP ROPE AFTER SCHOOL...
JUMP ROPE?
YEAH. WE HAVE A TEST COMING UP.
AND GUESS WHAT?
HA (GASP)
はっ…
IF I LEARN TO DO THE SUPER-HARD JUMPS...
...SENSEI WILL GIVE ME A REALLY COOL STICKER!
OH.
HM?
PASHI (CLAP)
ぱしっ
NEVER MIND. IT'S NOTHING.
GUTSU (GLUB)
GUTSU
...SO YOUR POINT IS, YOU ARE PRACTICING FOR THIS STICKER.
AND THAT IS WHY YOU ARE LATE...?
YES, THAT'S IT! THAT'S RIGHT!!

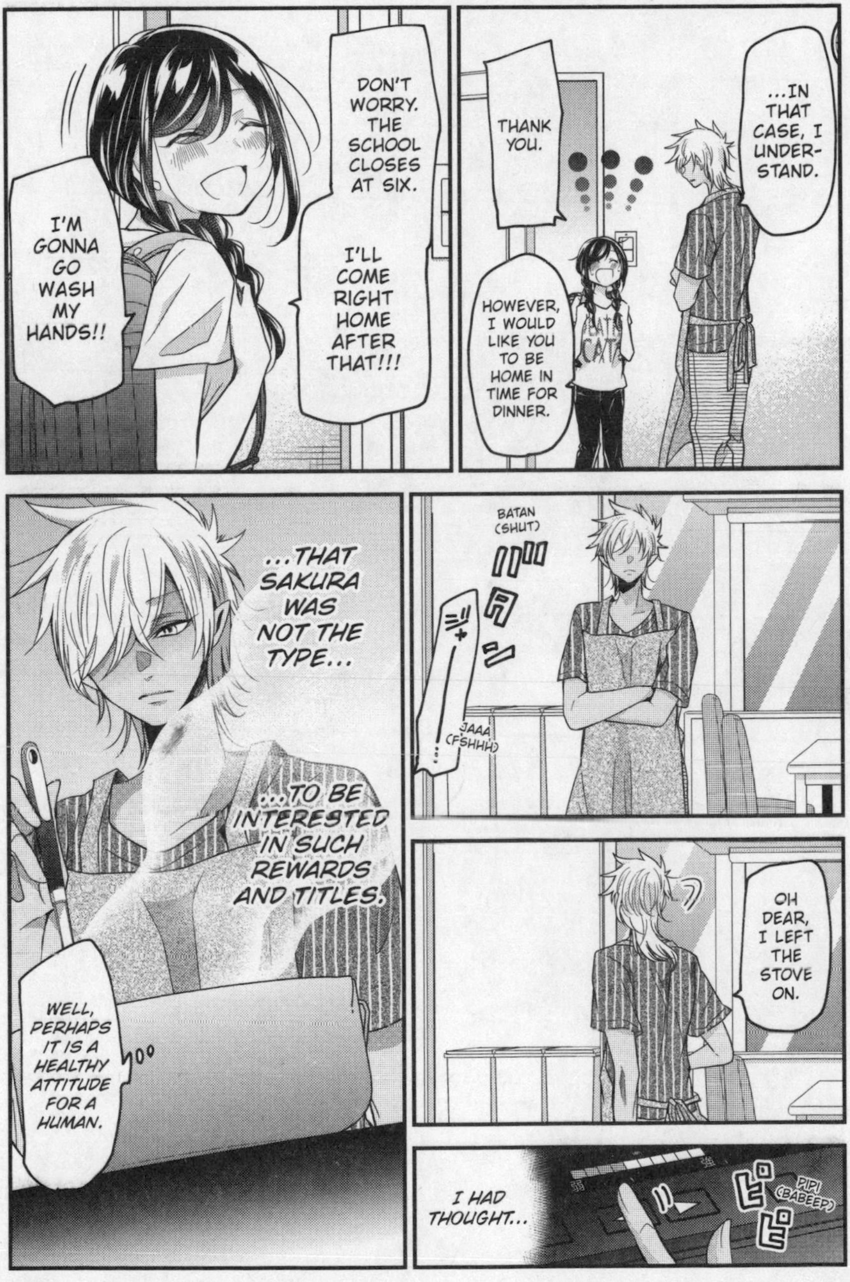
...IN THAT CASE, I UNDERSTAND.
HOWEVER, I WOULD LIKE YOU TO BE HOME IN TIME FOR DINNER.
THANK YOU.
DON'T WORRY. THE SCHOOL CLOSES AT SIX.
I'LL COME RIGHT HOME AFTER THAT!!!
I'M GONNA GO WASH MY HANDS!!
BATAN (SHUT)
JAAA (FSHHH)
OH DEAR, I LEFT THE STOVE ON.
PIPI (BABEEP)
I HAD THOUGHT...
...THAT SAKURA WAS NOT THE TYPE...
...TO BE INTERESTED IN SUCH REWARDS AND TITLES.
WELL, PERHAPS IT IS A HEALTHY ATTITUDE FOR A HUMAN.

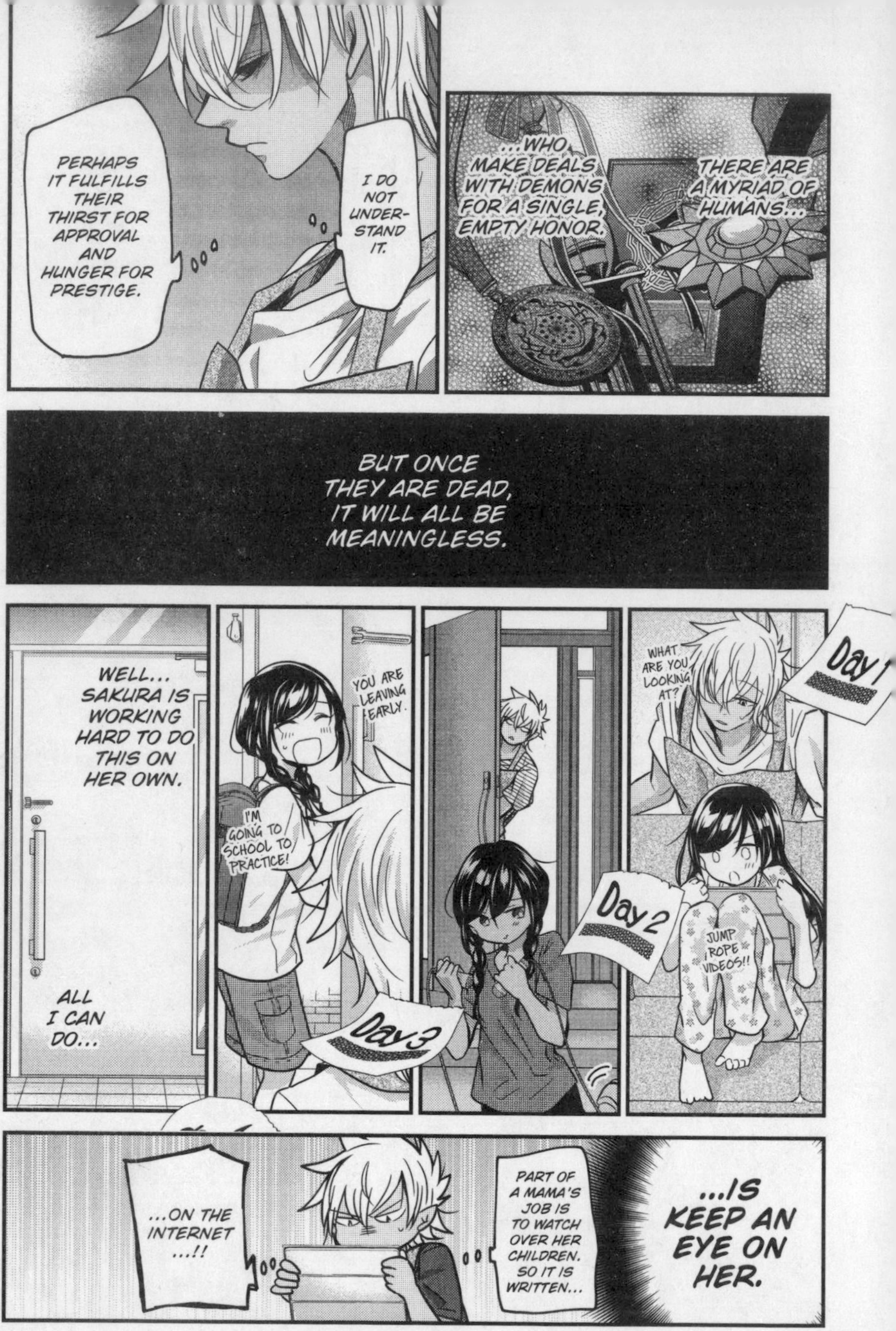
THERE ARE A MYRIAD OF HUMANS...
...WHO MAKE DEALS WITH DEMONS FOR A SINGLE, EMPTY HONOR.
I DO NOT UNDERSTAND IT.
PERHAPS IT FULFILLS THEIR THIRST FOR APPROVAL AND HUNGER FOR PRESTIGE.
BUT ONCE THEY ARE DEAD, IT WILL ALL BE MEANINGLESS.
Day 1
WHAT ARE YOU LOOKING AT?
JUMP ROPE VIDEOS!!
Day 2
YOU ARE LEAVING EARLY.
I'M GOING TO SCHOOL TO PRACTICE!
Day 3
WELL... SAKURA IS WORKING HARD TO DO THIS ON HER OWN.
ALL I CAN DO...
...IS KEEP AN EYE ON HER.
PART OF A MAMA'S JOB IS TO WATCH OVER HER CHILDREN. SO IT IS WRITTEN...
...ON THE INTERNET ...!!

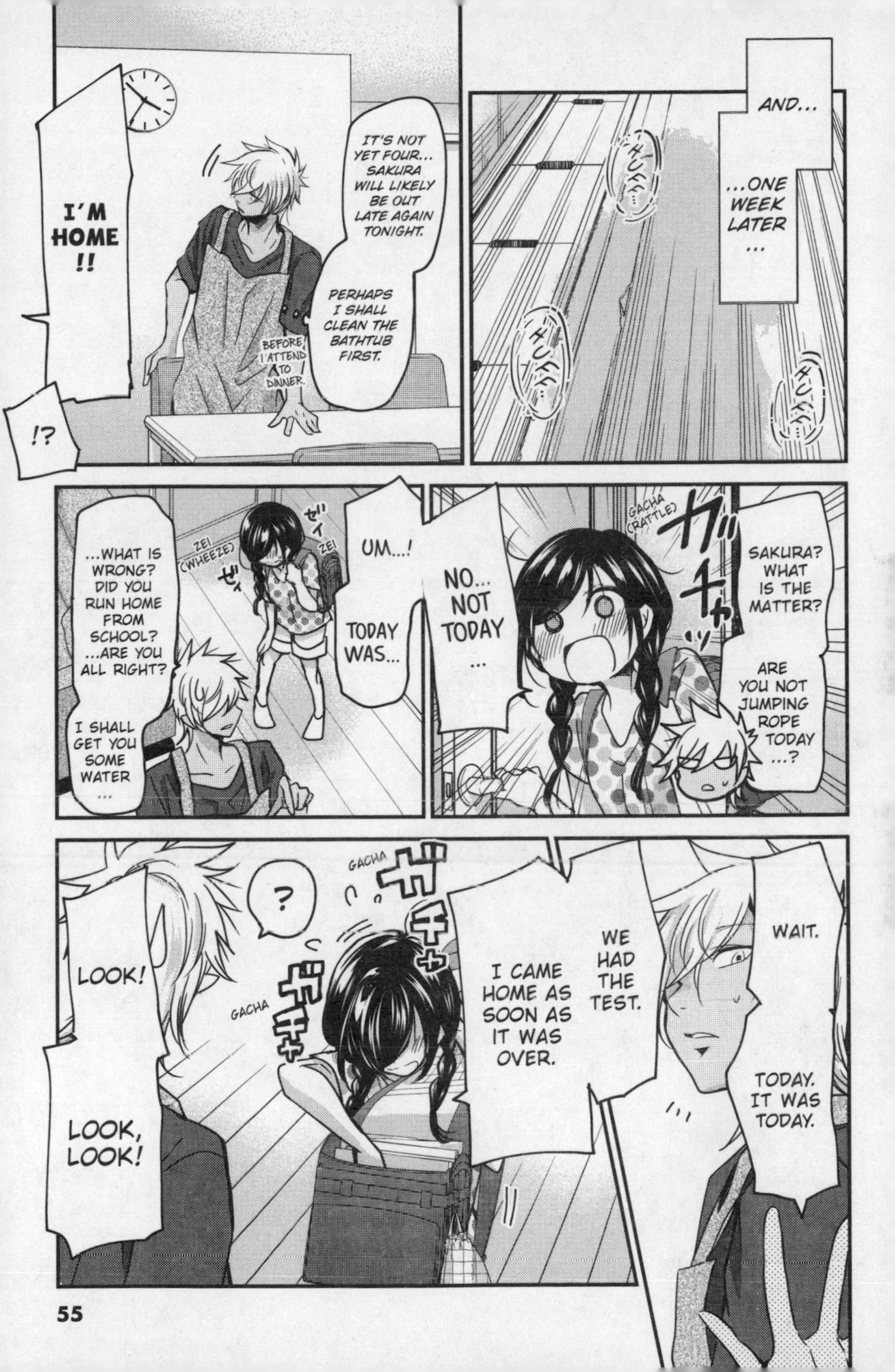
AND...
...ONE WEEK LATER...
HUFF...
HUFF...
HUFF...
IT'S NOT YET FOUR... SAKURA WILL LIKELY BE OUT LATE AGAIN TONIGHT.
PERHAPS I SHALL CLEAN THE BATHTUB FIRST.
BEFORE I ATTEND TO DINNER.
I'M HOME!!
!?
GACHA (RATTLE)
SAKURA? WHAT IS THE MATTER?
ARE YOU NOT JUMPING ROPE TODAY...?
NO... NOT TODAY...
UM...!
TODAY WAS...
ZEI ZEI (WHEEZE)
...WHAT IS WRONG? DID YOU RUN HOME FROM SCHOOL? ...ARE YOU ALL RIGHT?
I SHALL GET YOU SOME WATER...
WAIT.
TODAY. IT WAS TODAY.
WE HAD THE TEST.
I CAME HOME AS SOON AS IT WAS OVER.
GACHA
GACHA
?
LOOK!
LOOK, LOOK!

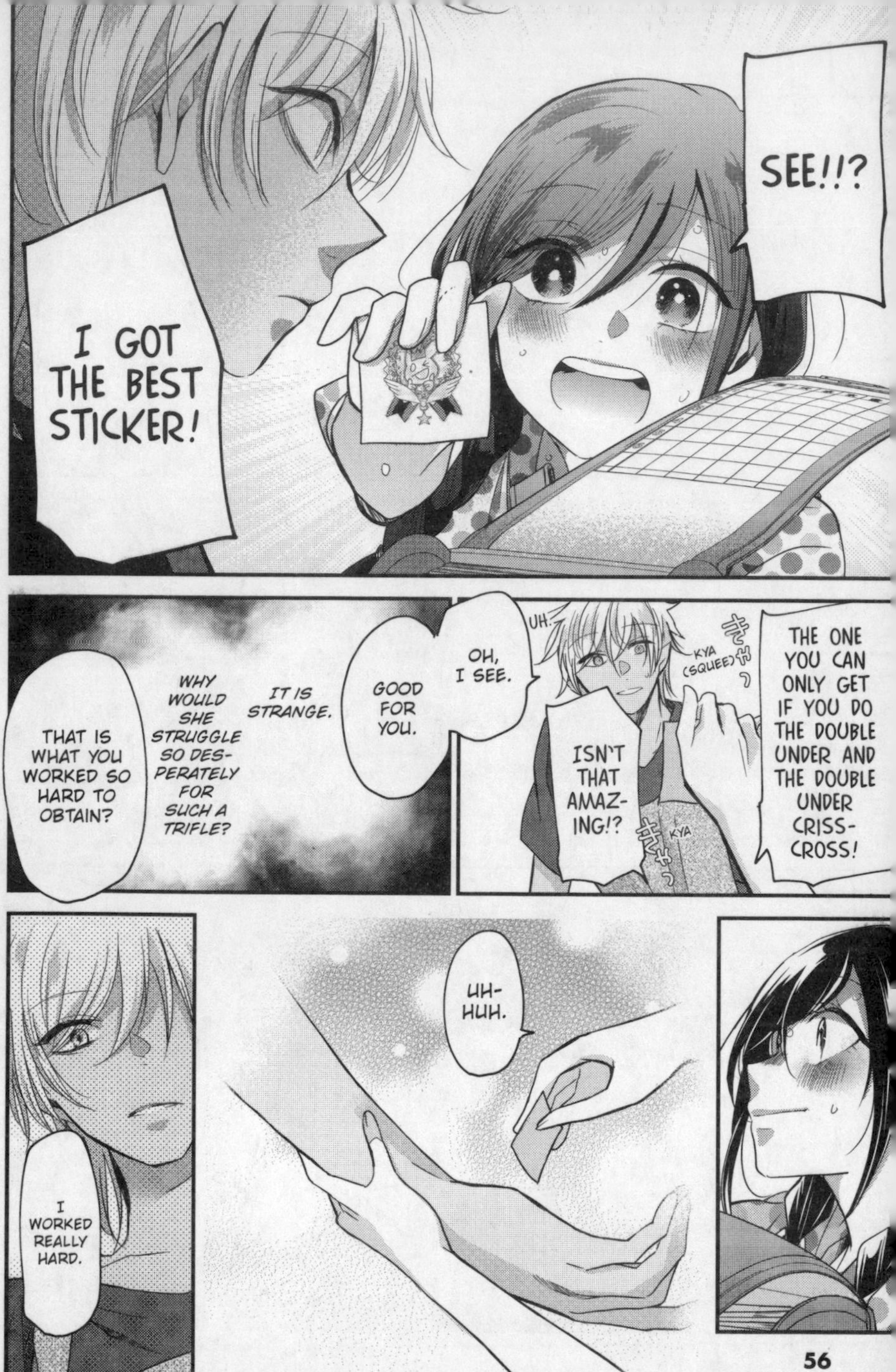
SEE!!?
I GOT THE BEST STICKER!
THE ONE YOU CAN ONLY GET IF YOU DO THE DOUBLE UNDER AND THE DOUBLE UNDER CRISS-CROSS!
きゃっ
KYA (SQUEE)
ISN'T THAT AMAZ-ING!?
きゃっ
KYA
UH.
OH, I SEE.
GOOD FOR YOU.
IT IS STRANGE.
WHY WOULD SHE STRUGGLE SO DES-PERATELY FOR SUCH A TRIFLE?
THAT IS WHAT YOU WORKED SO HARD TO OBTAIN?
UH-HUH.
I WORKED REALLY HARD.

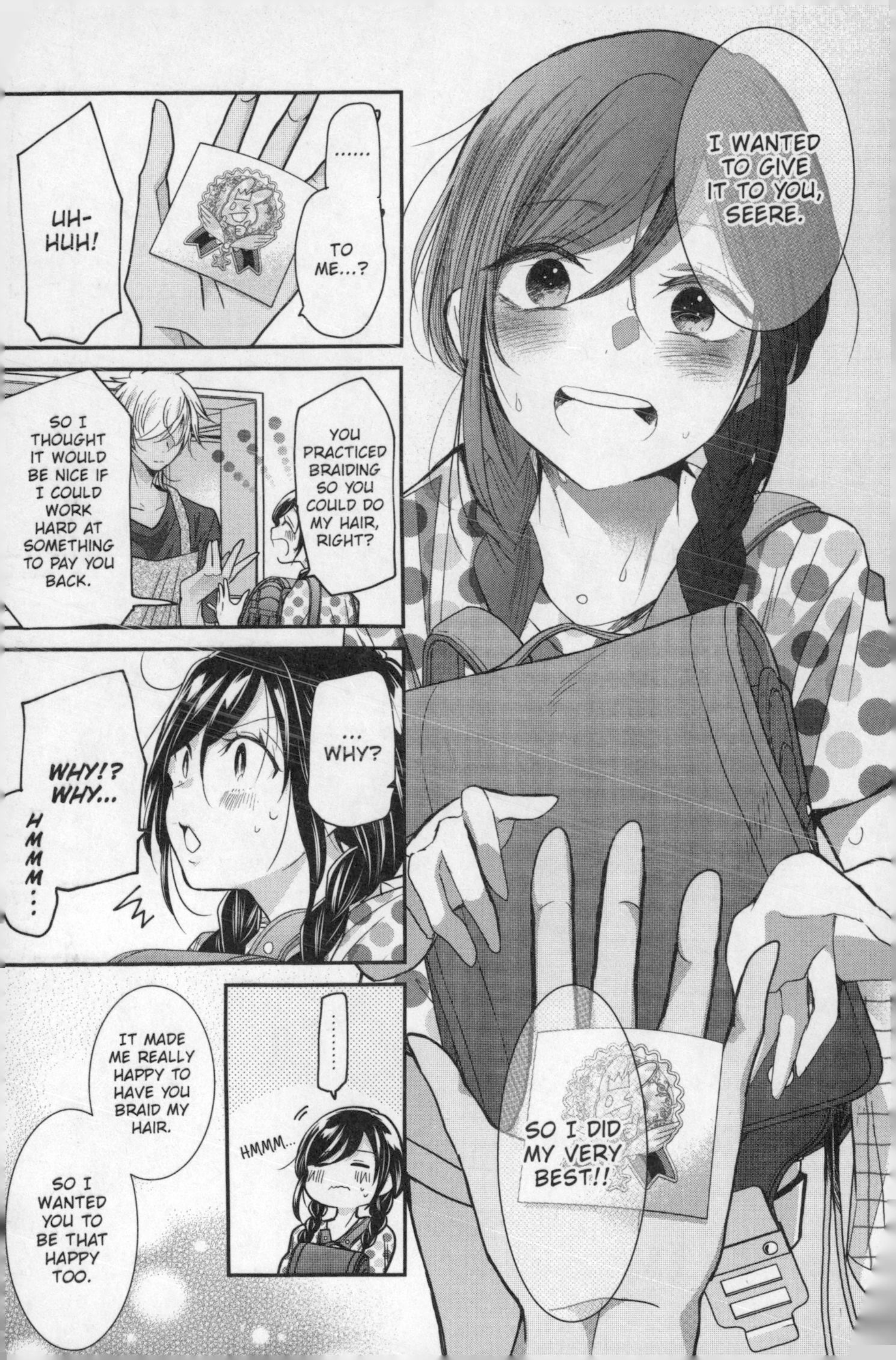
I WANTED TO GIVE IT TO YOU, SEERE.
......
TO ME...?
UH-HUH!
YOU PRACTICED BRAIDING SO YOU COULD DO MY HAIR, RIGHT?
SO I THOUGHT IT WOULD BE NICE IF I COULD WORK HARD AT SOMETHING TO PAY YOU BACK.
...WHY?
WHY!? WHY...
HMMM...
........
HMMM...
IT MADE ME REALLY HAPPY TO HAVE YOU BRAID MY HAIR.
SO I WANTED YOU TO BE THAT HAPPY TOO.
SO I DID MY VERY BEST!!

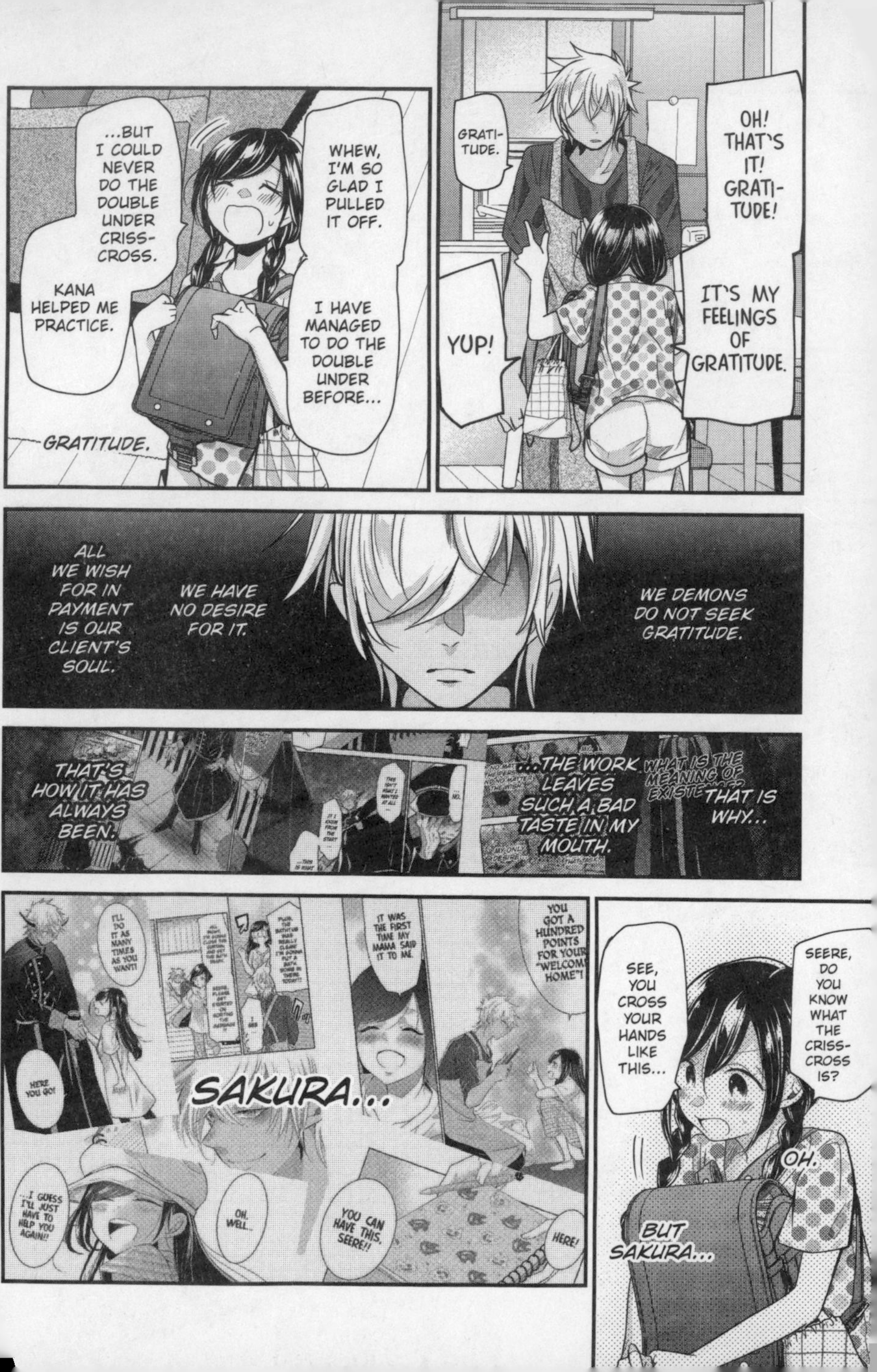
OH! THAT'S IT! GRATITUDE!
IT'S MY FEELINGS OF GRATITUDE.
GRATITUDE.
YUP!
WHEW, I'M SO GLAD I PULLED IT OFF.
I HAVE MANAGED TO DO THE DOUBLE UNDER BEFORE...
...BUT I COULD NEVER DO THE DOUBLE UNDER CRISS-CROSS.
KANA HELPED ME PRACTICE.
GRATITUDE.
WE DEMONS DO NOT SEEK GRATITUDE.
WE HAVE NO DESIRE FOR IT.
ALL WE WISH FOR IN PAYMENT IS OUR CLIENT'S SOUL.
THAT IS WHY...
...THE WORK LEAVES SUCH A BAD TASTE IN MY MOUTH.
THAT'S HOW IT HAS ALWAYS BEEN.
SEERE, DO YOU KNOW WHAT THE CRISS-CROSS IS?
SEE, YOU CROSS YOUR HANDS LIKE THIS...
OH.
BUT SAKURA...
YOU GOT A HUNDRED POINTS FOR YOUR "WELCOME HOME"!
IT WAS THE FIRST TIME MY MAMA SAID IT TO ME.
I'LL DO IT AS MANY TIMES AS YOU WANT!!
HERE YOU GO!
SAKURA...
HERE!
YOU CAN HAVE THIS, SEERE!!
OH, WELL...
...I GUESS I'LL JUST HAVE TO HELP YOU AGAIN!!

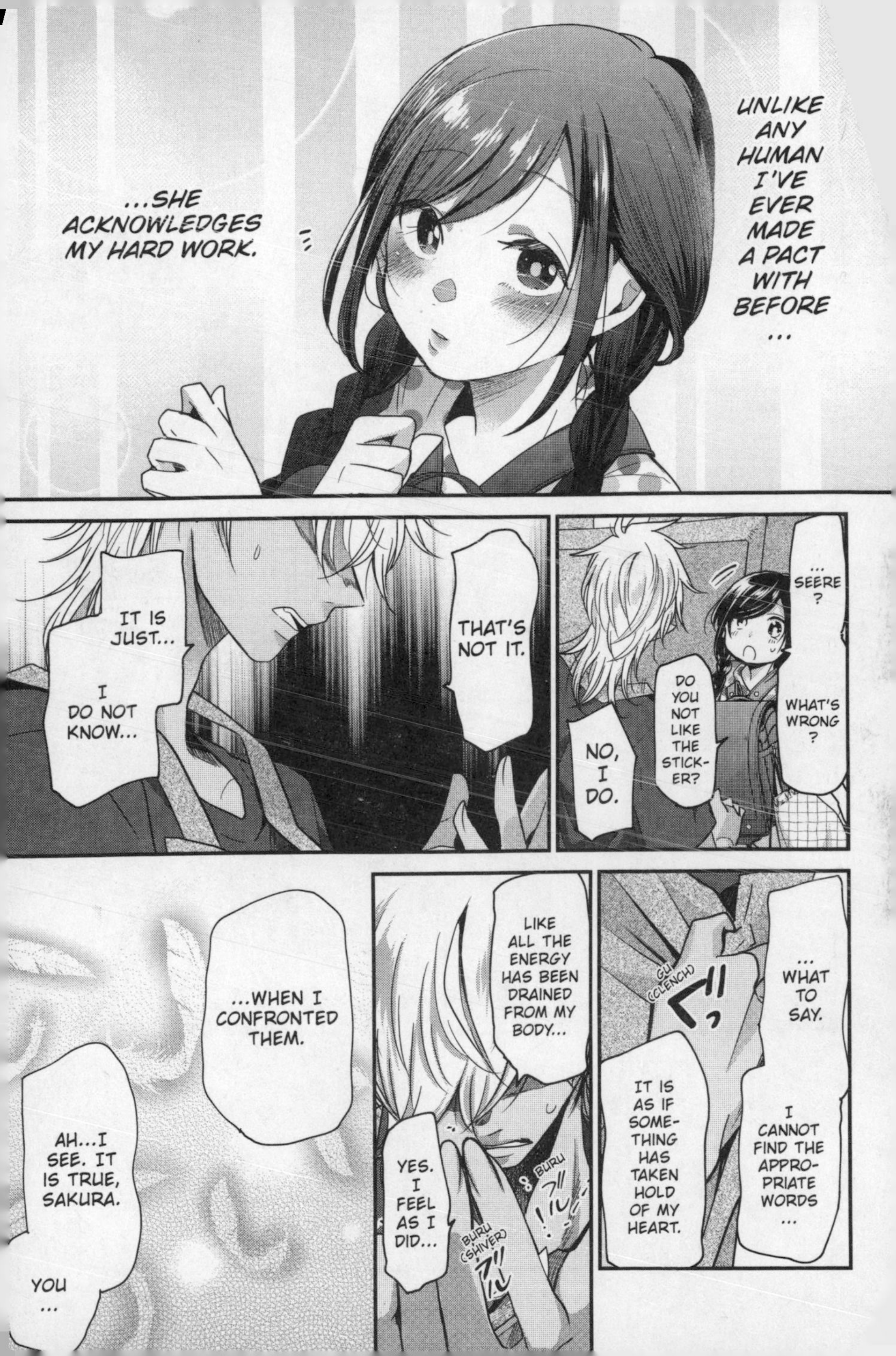
UNLIKE ANY HUMAN I'VE EVER MADE A PACT WITH BEFORE...
...SHE ACKNOWLEDGES MY HARD WORK.
...SEERE?
WHAT'S WRONG?
DO YOU NOT LIKE THE STICKER?
NO, I DO.
THAT'S NOT IT.
IT IS JUST...
I DO NOT KNOW...
...WHAT TO SAY.
GU (CLENCH)
I CANNOT FIND THE APPROPRIATE WORDS...
IT IS AS IF SOMETHING HAS TAKEN HOLD OF MY HEART.
LIKE ALL THE ENERGY HAS BEEN DRAINED FROM MY BODY...
BURU
BURU (SHIVER)
YES. I FEEL AS I DID...
...WHEN I CONFRONTED THEM.
AH...I SEE. IT IS TRUE, SAKURA.
YOU...

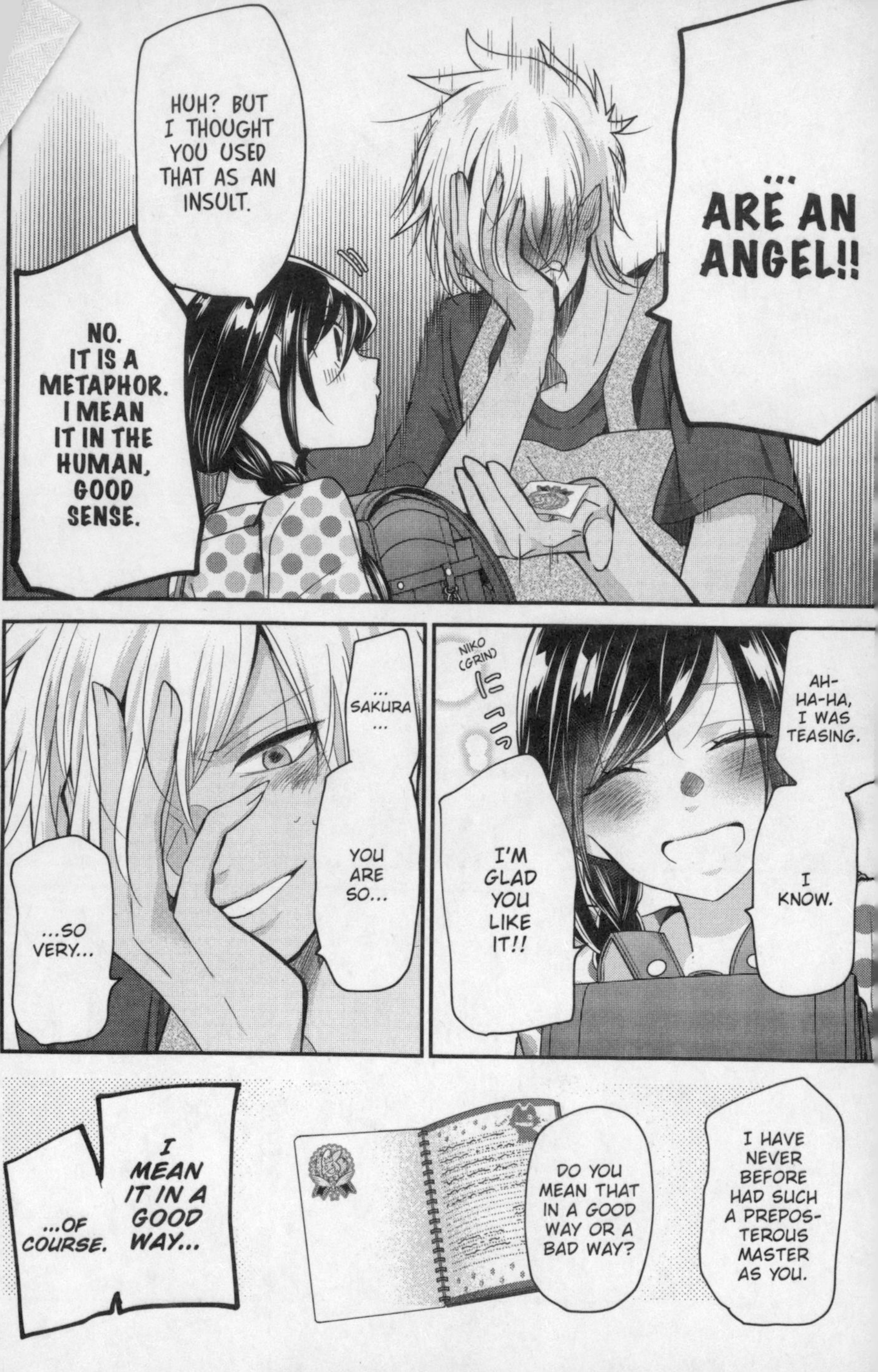
...ARE AN ANGEL!!
HUH? BUT I THOUGHT YOU USED THAT AS AN INSULT.
NO. IT IS A METAPHOR. I MEAN IT IN THE HUMAN, GOOD SENSE.
AH-HA-HA, I WAS TEASING.
I KNOW.
NIKO (GRIN)
I'M GLAD YOU LIKE IT!!
...SAKURA...
YOU ARE SO...
...SO VERY...
I HAVE NEVER BEFORE HAD SUCH A PREPOSTEROUS MASTER AS YOU.
DO YOU MEAN THAT IN A GOOD WAY OR A BAD WAY?
I MEAN IT IN A GOOD WAY...
...OF COURSE.

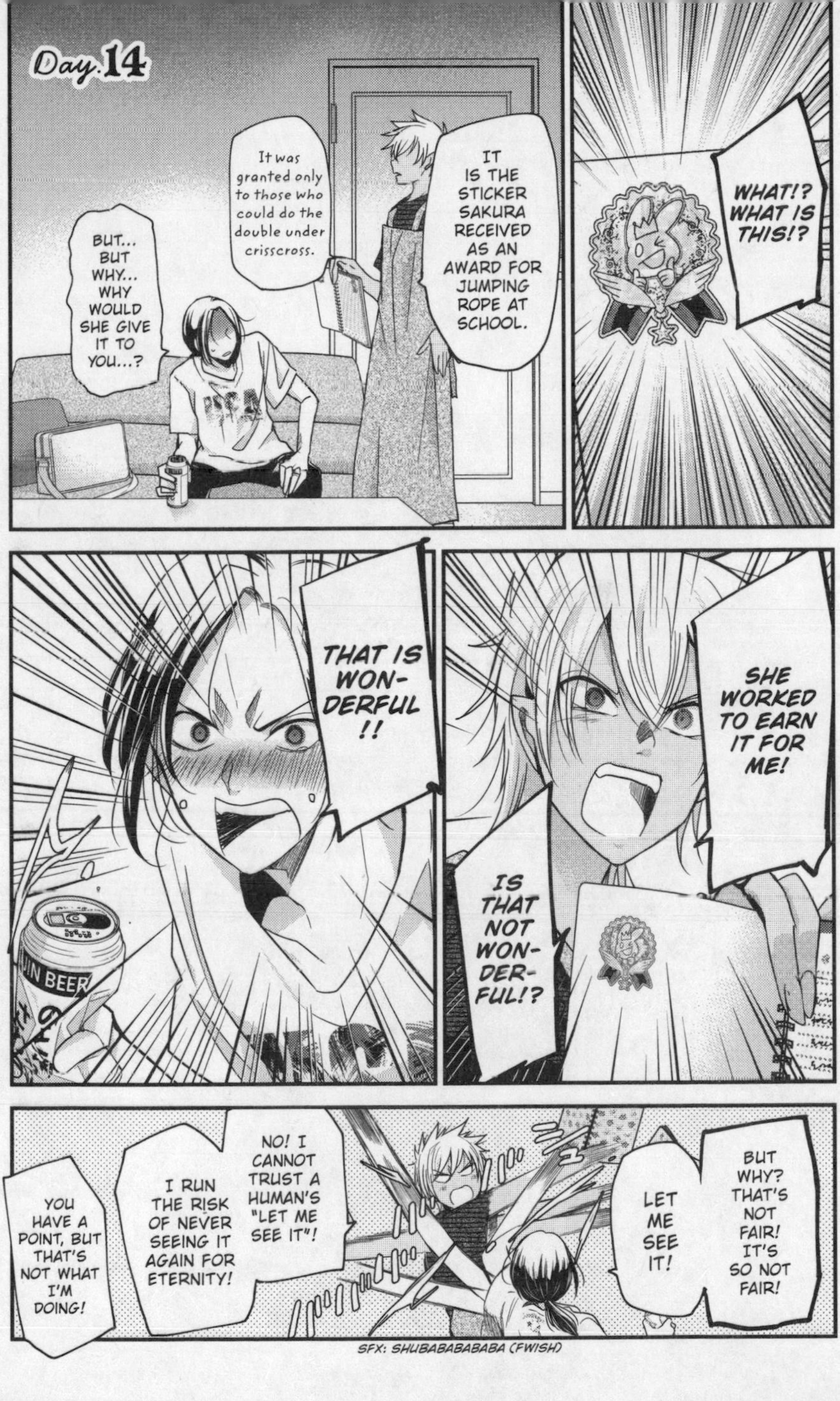
Day.14
WHAT!? WHAT IS THIS!?
IT IS THE STICKER SAKURA RECEIVED AS AN AWARD FOR JUMPING ROPE AT SCHOOL.
It was granted only to those who could do the double under crisscross.
BUT... BUT WHY... WHY WOULD SHE GIVE IT TO YOU...?
SHE WORKED TO EARN IT FOR ME!
IS THAT NOT WONDERFUL!?
THAT IS WONDERFUL!!
BUT WHY? THAT'S NOT FAIR! IT'S SO NOT FAIR!
LET ME SEE IT!
NO! I CANNOT TRUST A HUMAN'S "LET ME SEE IT"!
I RUN THE RISK OF NEVER SEEING IT AGAIN FOR ETERNITY!
YOU HAVE A POINT, BUT THAT'S NOT WHAT I'M DOING!
SFX: SHUBABABABABA (FWISH)

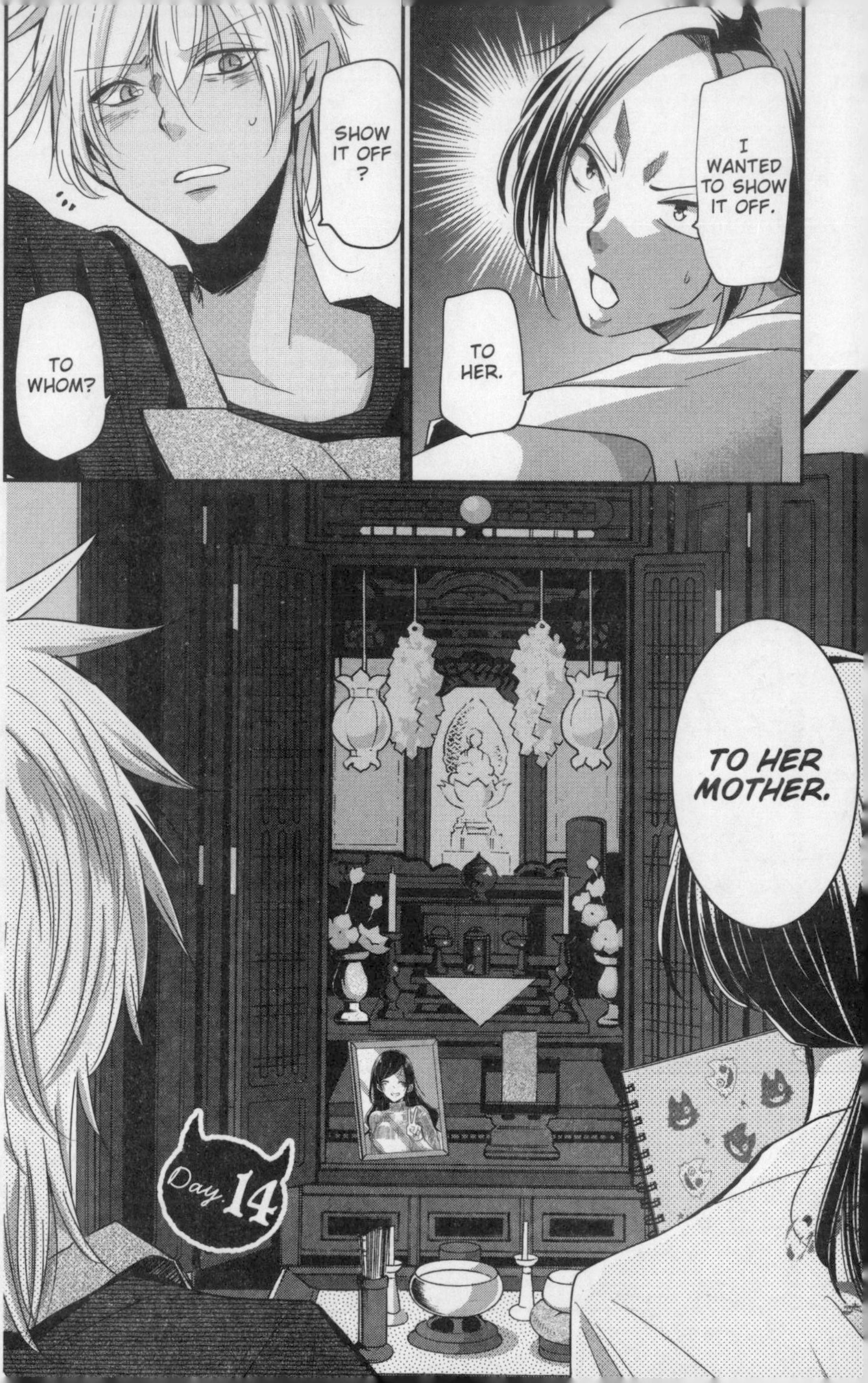
I WANTED TO SHOW IT OFF.
SHOW IT OFF?
...
TO HER.
TO WHOM?
TO HER MOTHER.
Day. 14

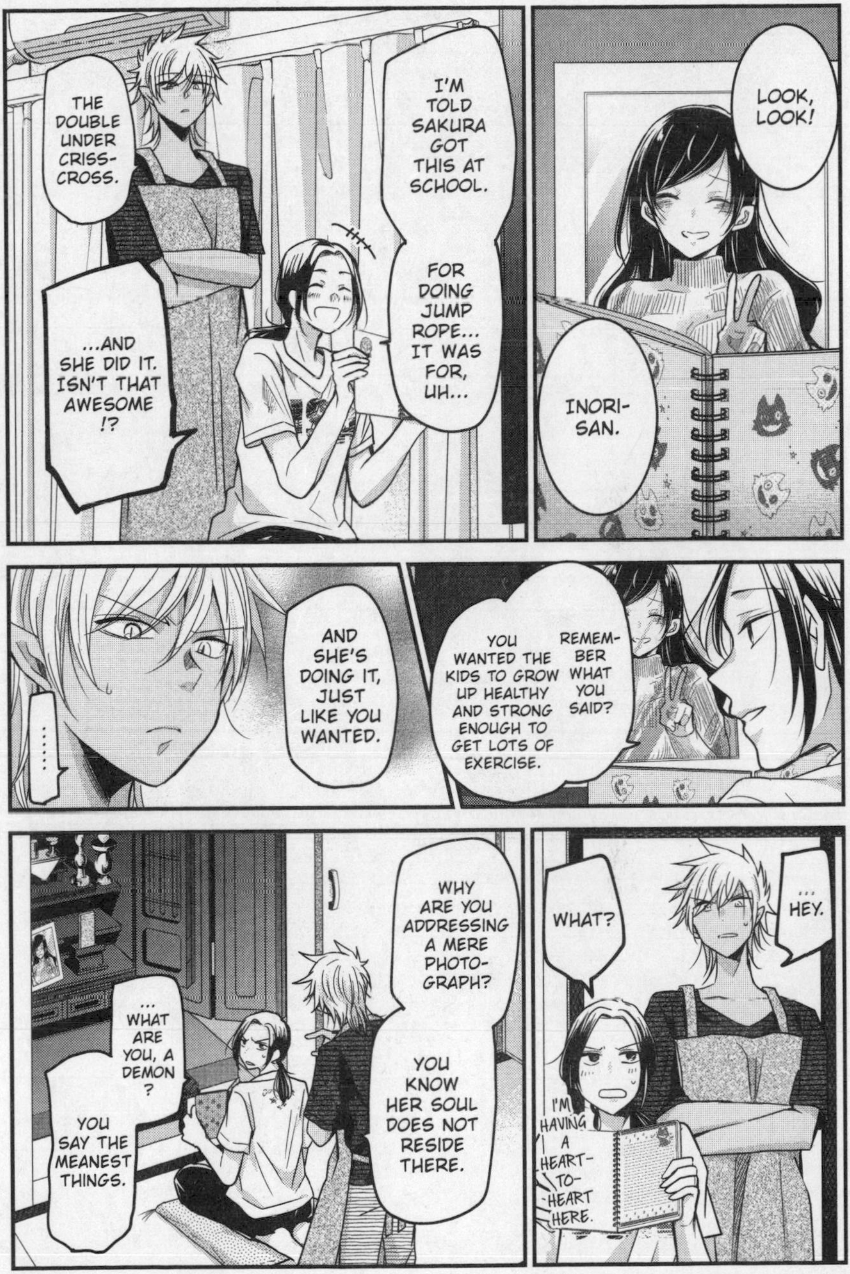
LOOK, LOOK!
INORI-SAN.
I'M TOLD SAKURA GOT THIS AT SCHOOL.
FOR DOING JUMP ROPE... IT WAS FOR, UH...
THE DOUBLE UNDER CRISS-CROSS.
...AND SHE DID IT. ISN'T THAT AWESOME!?
REMEMBER WHAT YOU SAID?
YOU WANTED THE KIDS TO GROW UP HEALTHY AND STRONG ENOUGH TO GET LOTS OF EXERCISE.
AND SHE'S DOING IT, JUST LIKE YOU WANTED.
......
...HEY.
WHAT?
I'M HAVING A HEART-TO-HEART HERE.
WHY ARE YOU ADDRESSING A MERE PHOTOGRAPH?
YOU KNOW HER SOUL DOES NOT RESIDE THERE.
...WHAT ARE YOU, A DEMON?
YOU SAY THE MEANEST THINGS.

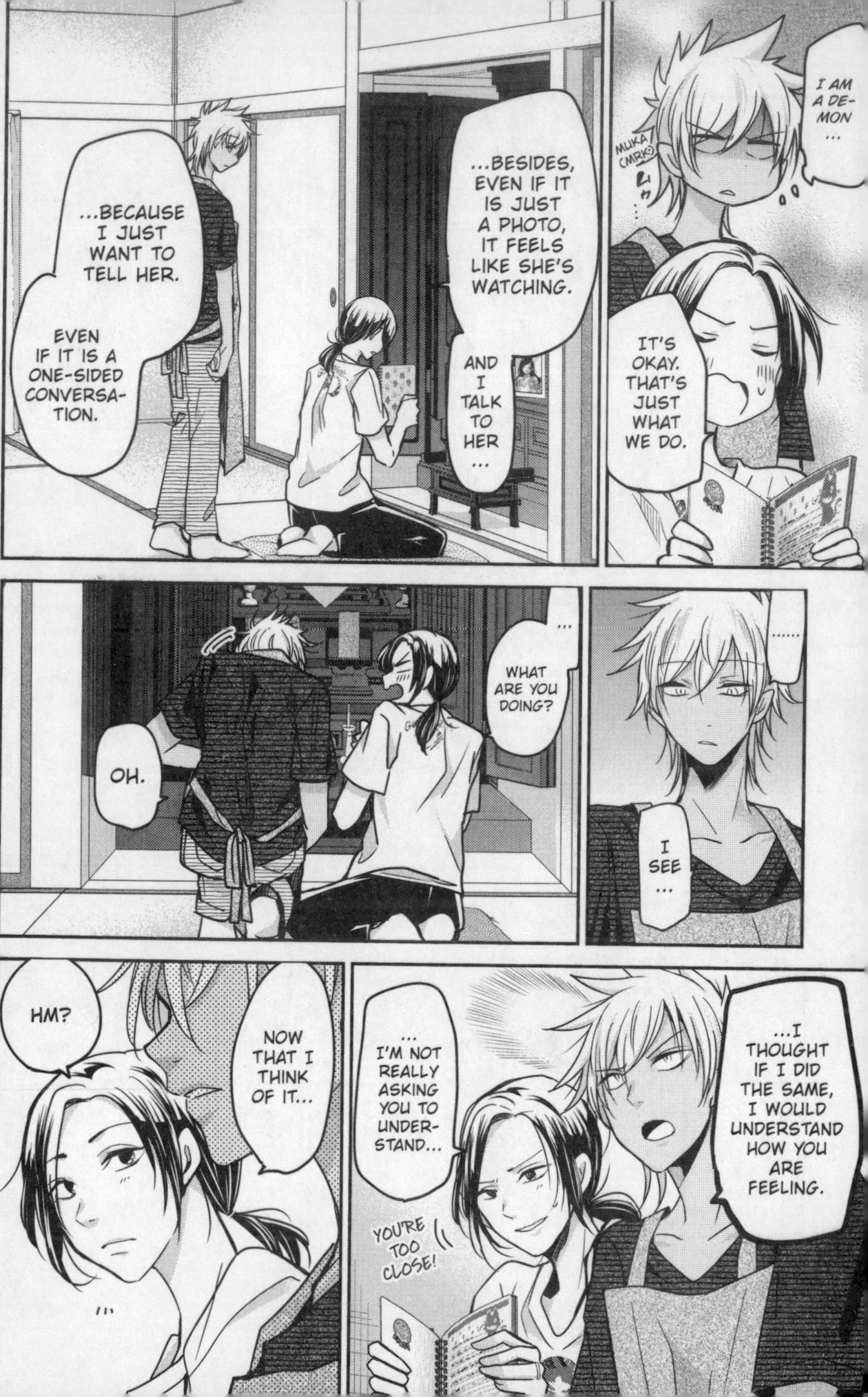
I AM A DEMON ...
MUKA (MRK)
IT'S OKAY. THAT'S JUST WHAT WE DO.
...BESIDES, EVEN IF IT IS JUST A PHOTO, IT FEELS LIKE SHE'S WATCHING.
AND I TALK TO HER ...
...BECAUSE I JUST WANT TO TELL HER.
EVEN IF IT IS A ONE-SIDED CONVERSATION.
......
I SEE ...
...
WHAT ARE YOU DOING?
OH.
...I THOUGHT IF I DID THE SAME, I WOULD UNDERSTAND HOW YOU ARE FEELING.
... I'M NOT REALLY ASKING YOU TO UNDERSTAND...
YOU'RE TOO CLOSE!
NOW THAT I THINK OF IT...
HM?

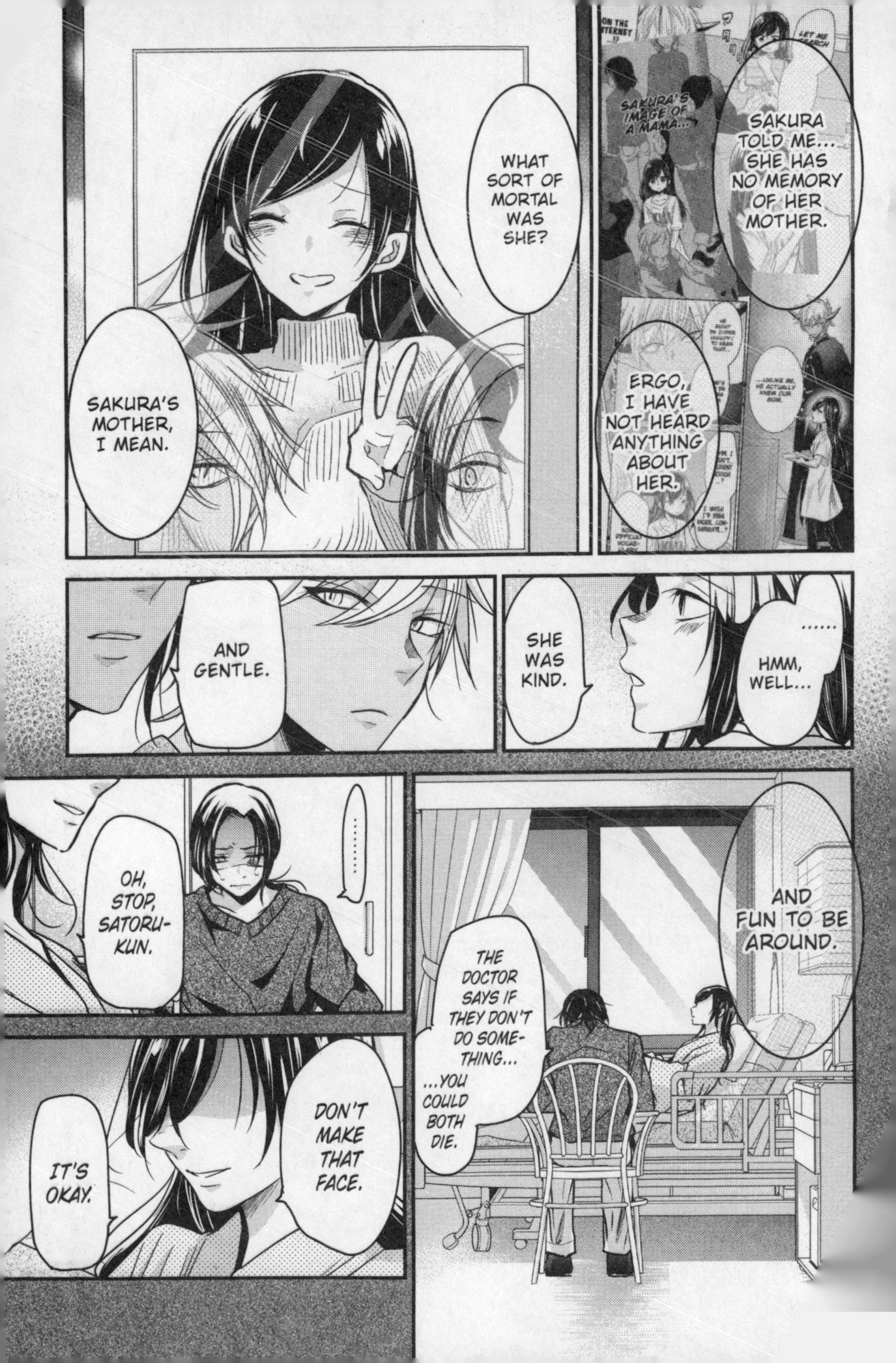
SAKURA TOLD ME... SHE HAS NO MEMORY OF HER MOTHER.
SAKURA'S IMAGE OF A MAMA...
ERGO, I HAVE NOT HEARD ANYTHING ABOUT HER.
...UNLIKE ME, HE ACTUALLY KNEW OUR MOM.
WHAT SORT OF MORTAL WAS SHE?
SAKURA'S MOTHER, I MEAN.
......
HMM, WELL...
SHE WAS KIND.
AND GENTLE.
AND FUN TO BE AROUND.
THE DOCTOR SAYS IF THEY DON'T DO SOME-THING...
...YOU COULD BOTH DIE.
......
OH, STOP, SATORU-KUN.
DON'T MAKE THAT FACE.
IT'S OKAY.

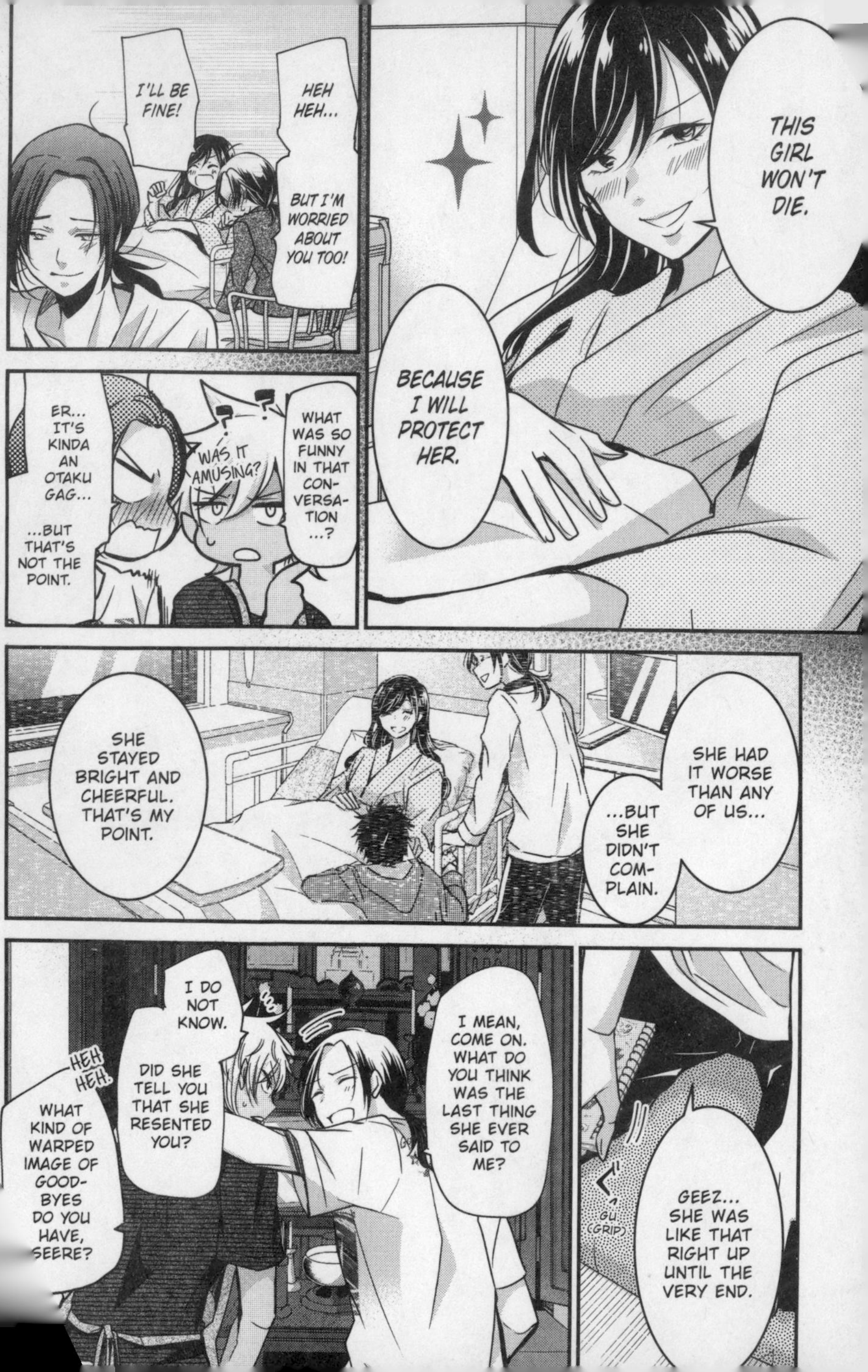
THIS GIRL WON'T DIE.
BECAUSE I WILL PROTECT HER.
HEH HEH... BUT I'M WORRIED ABOUT YOU TOO!
I'LL BE FINE!
WHAT WAS SO FUNNY IN THAT CONVERSATION...?
WAS IT AMUSING?
ER... IT'S KINDA AN OTAKU GAG...
...BUT THAT'S NOT THE POINT.
SHE HAD IT WORSE THAN ANY OF US...
...BUT SHE DIDN'T COMPLAIN.
SHE STAYED BRIGHT AND CHEERFUL. THAT'S MY POINT.
GU (GRIP)
GEEZ... SHE WAS LIKE THAT RIGHT UP UNTIL THE VERY END.
I MEAN, COME ON. WHAT DO YOU THINK WAS THE LAST THING SHE EVER SAID TO ME?
I DO NOT KNOW.
DID SHE TELL YOU THAT SHE RESENTED YOU?
HEH HEH.
WHAT KIND OF WARPED IMAGE OF GOOD-BYES DO YOU HAVE, SEERE?

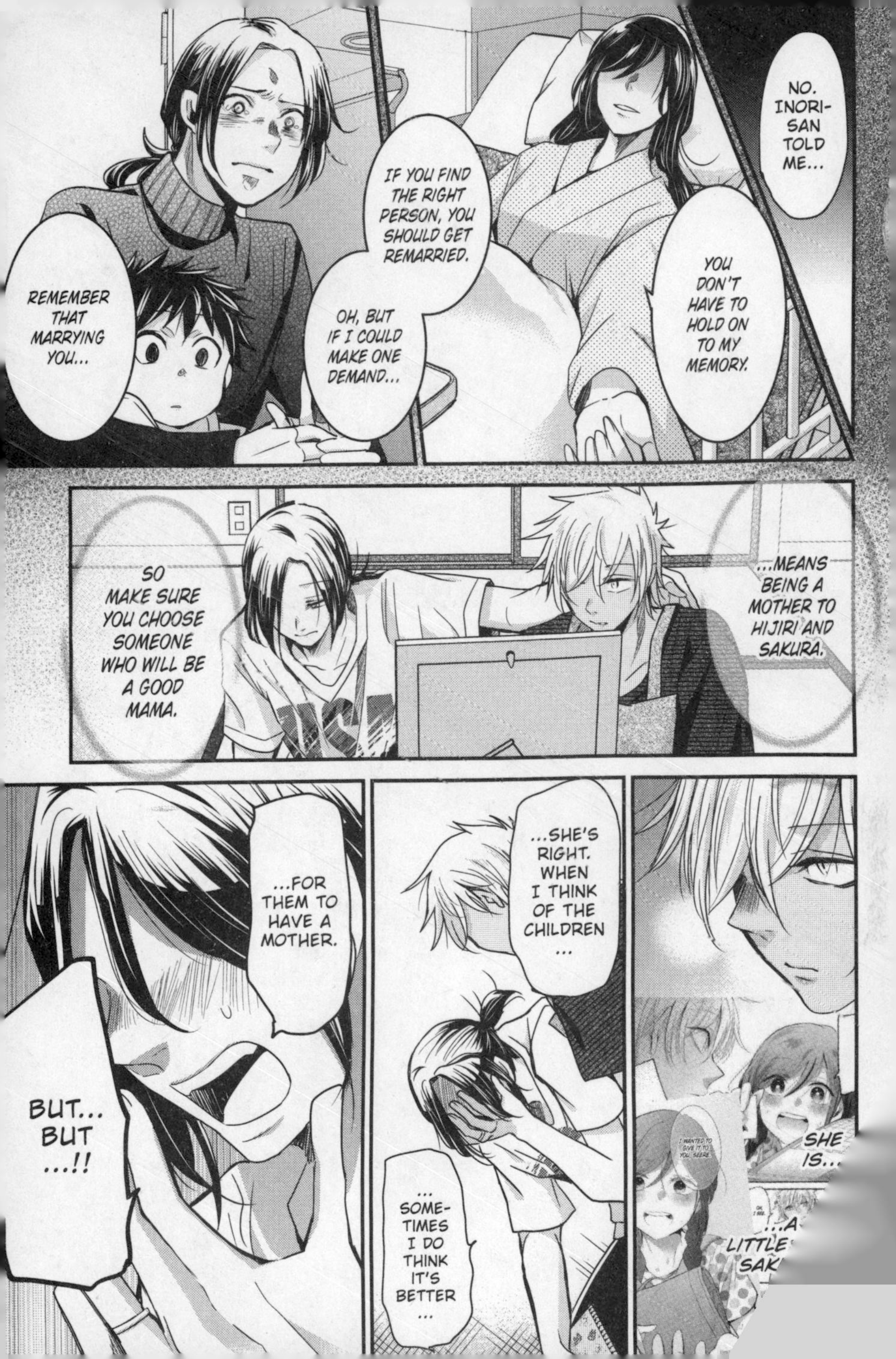
NO. INORI-SAN TOLD ME...
YOU DON'T HAVE TO HOLD ON TO MY MEMORY.
IF YOU FIND THE RIGHT PERSON, YOU SHOULD GET REMARRIED.
OH, BUT IF I COULD MAKE ONE DEMAND...
REMEMBER THAT MARRYING YOU...
...MEANS BEING A MOTHER TO HIJIRI AND SAKURA.
SO MAKE SURE YOU CHOOSE SOMEONE WHO WILL BE A GOOD MAMA.
SHE IS...
...A LITTLE SAK
...SHE'S RIGHT. WHEN I THINK OF THE CHILDREN...
...SOMETIMES I DO THINK IT'S BETTER...
...FOR THEM TO HAVE A MOTHER.
BUT... BUT ...!!

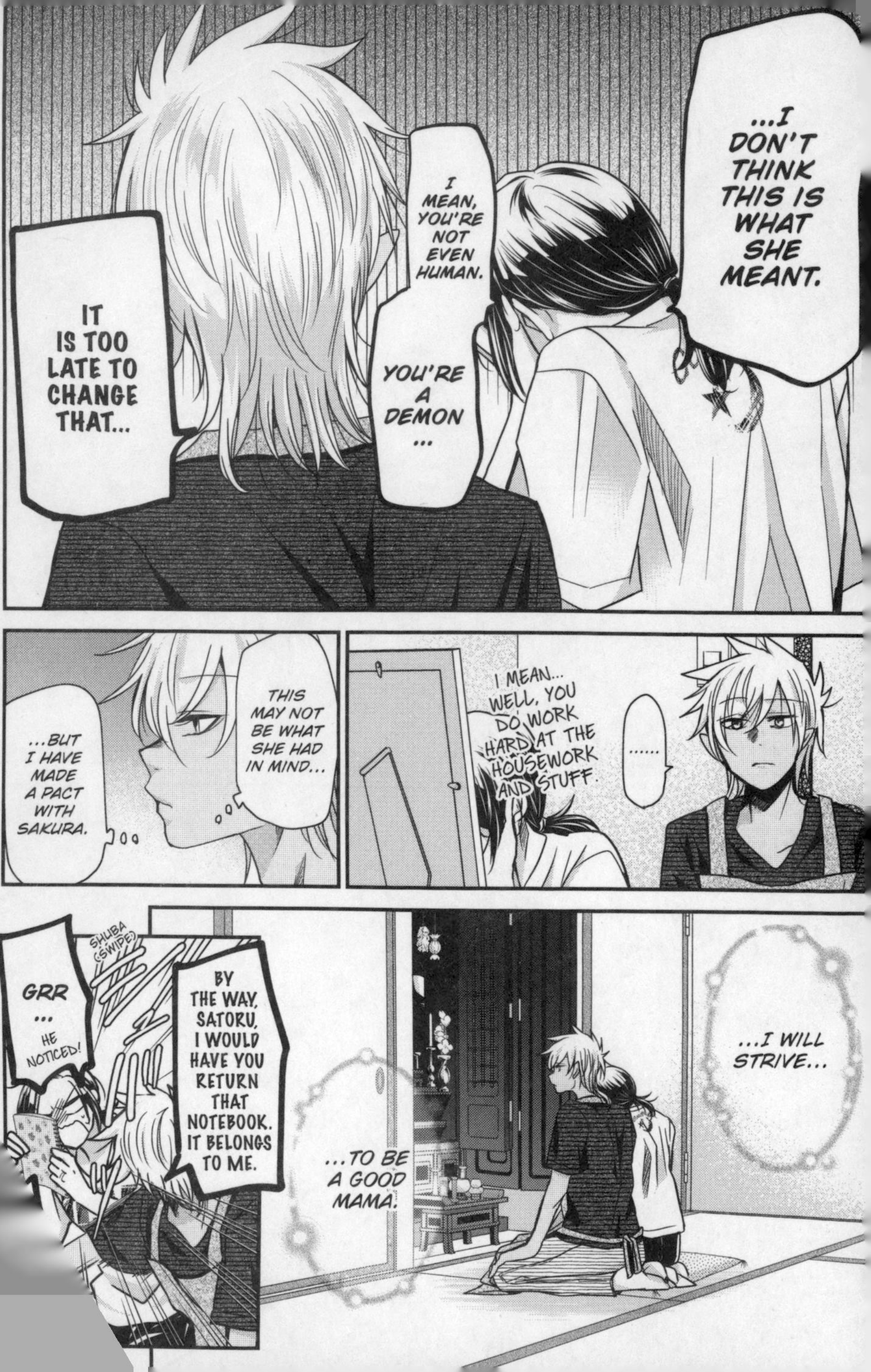
...I DON'T THINK THIS IS WHAT SHE MEANT.
I MEAN, YOU'RE NOT EVEN HUMAN.
YOU'RE A DEMON...
IT IS TOO LATE TO CHANGE THAT...
......
I MEAN... WELL, YOU DO WORK HARD AT THE HOUSEWORK AND STUFF.
THIS MAY NOT BE WHAT SHE HAD IN MIND...
...BUT I HAVE MADE A PACT WITH SAKURA.
...I WILL STRIVE...
...TO BE A GOOD MAMA.
BY THE WAY, SATORU, I WOULD HAVE YOU RETURN THAT NOTEBOOK. IT BELONGS TO ME.
SHUBA (SWIPE)
GRR...
HE NOTICED!

# Day. 15

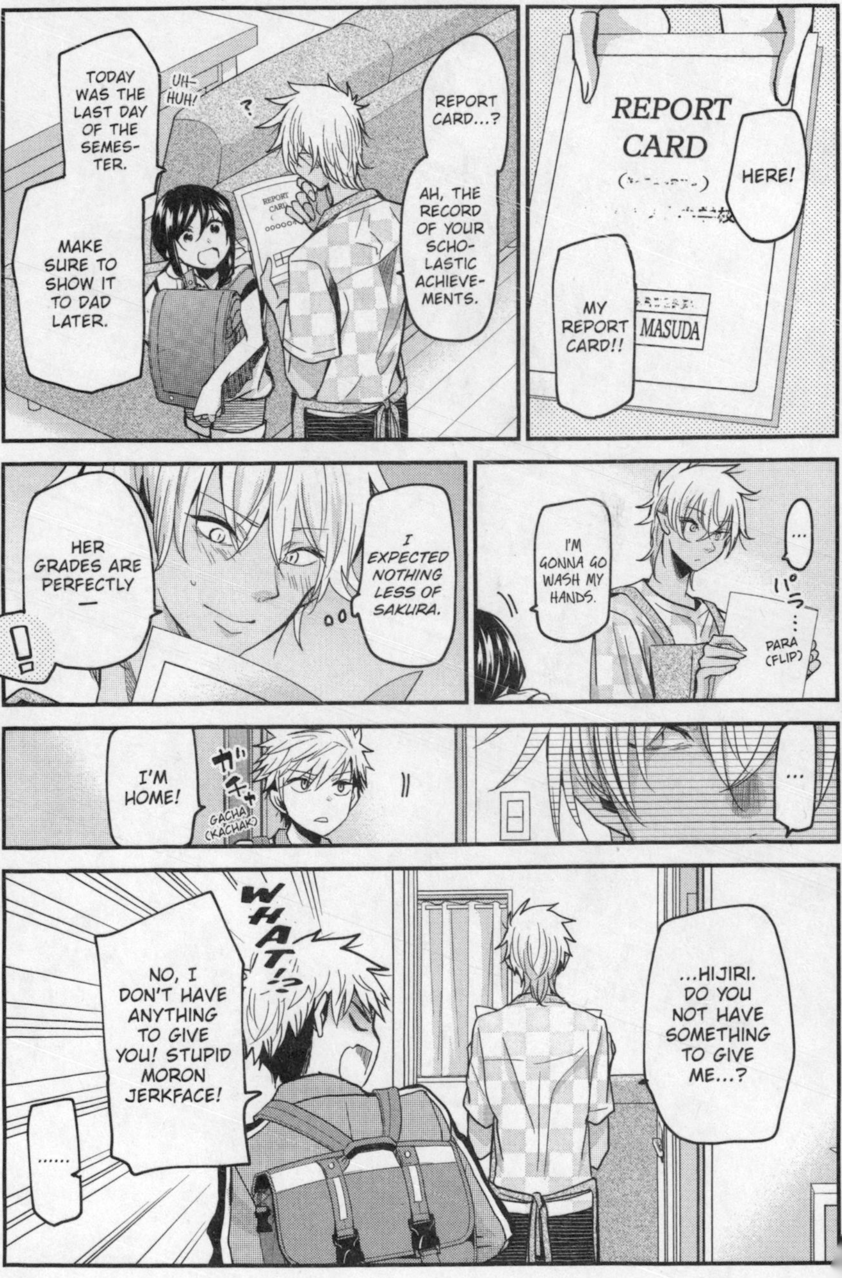

REPORT CARD
MASUDA
HERE!
MY REPORT CARD!!
REPORT CARD...?
AH, THE RECORD OF YOUR SCHOLASTIC ACHIEVEMENTS.
UH-HUH!
?
TODAY WAS THE LAST DAY OF THE SEMESTER.
MAKE SURE TO SHOW IT TO DAD LATER.
...
パラ…
PARA (FLIP)
I'M GONNA GO WASH MY HANDS.
I EXPECTED NOTHING LESS OF SAKURA.
HER GRADES ARE PERFECTLY—
!
...
I'M HOME!
ガチャ
GACHA (KACHAK)
...HIJIRI. DO YOU NOT HAVE SOMETHING TO GIVE ME...?
WHAT!?
NO, I DON'T HAVE ANYTHING TO GIVE YOU! STUPID MORON JERKFACE!
......

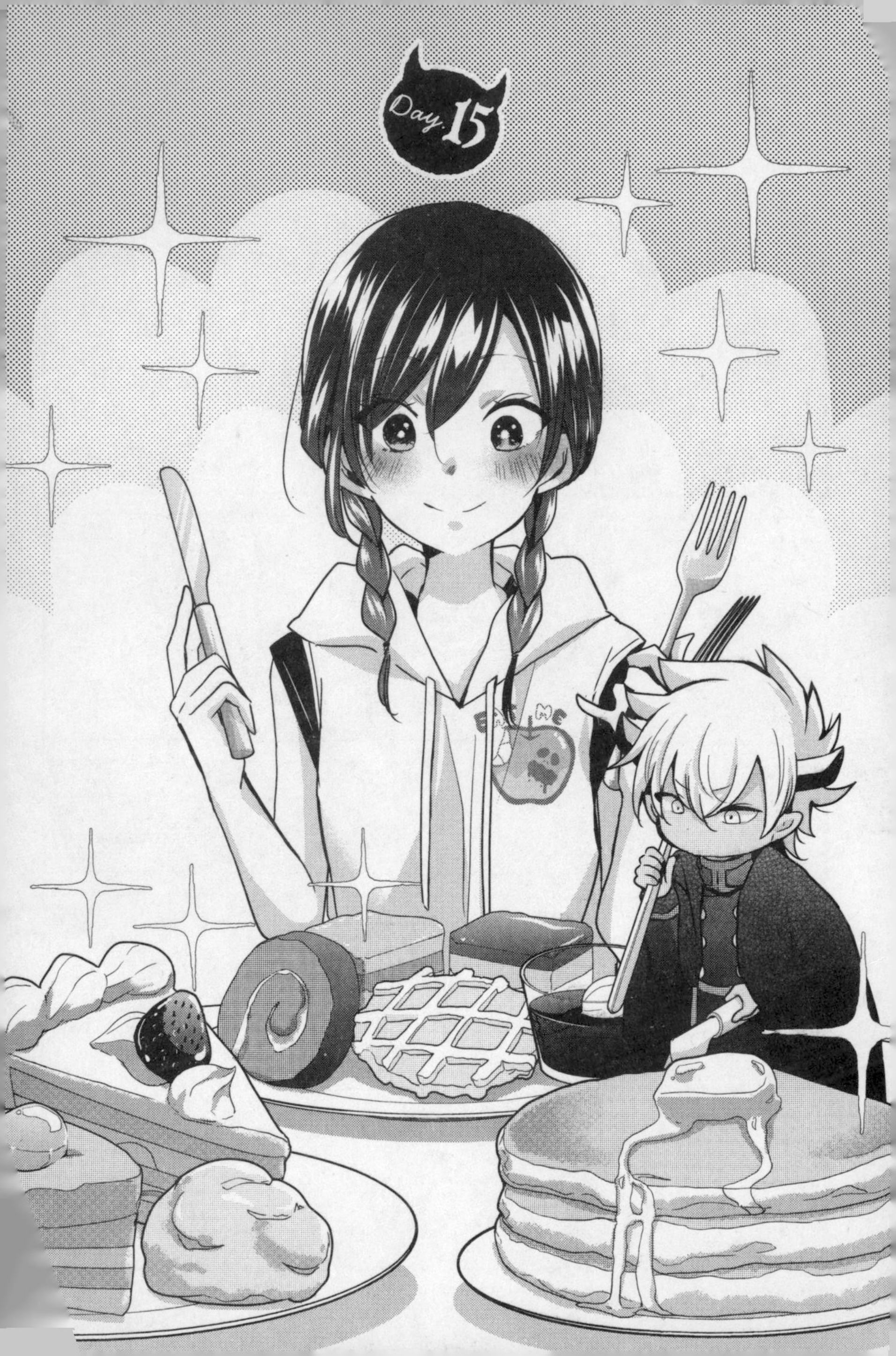
Day. 15

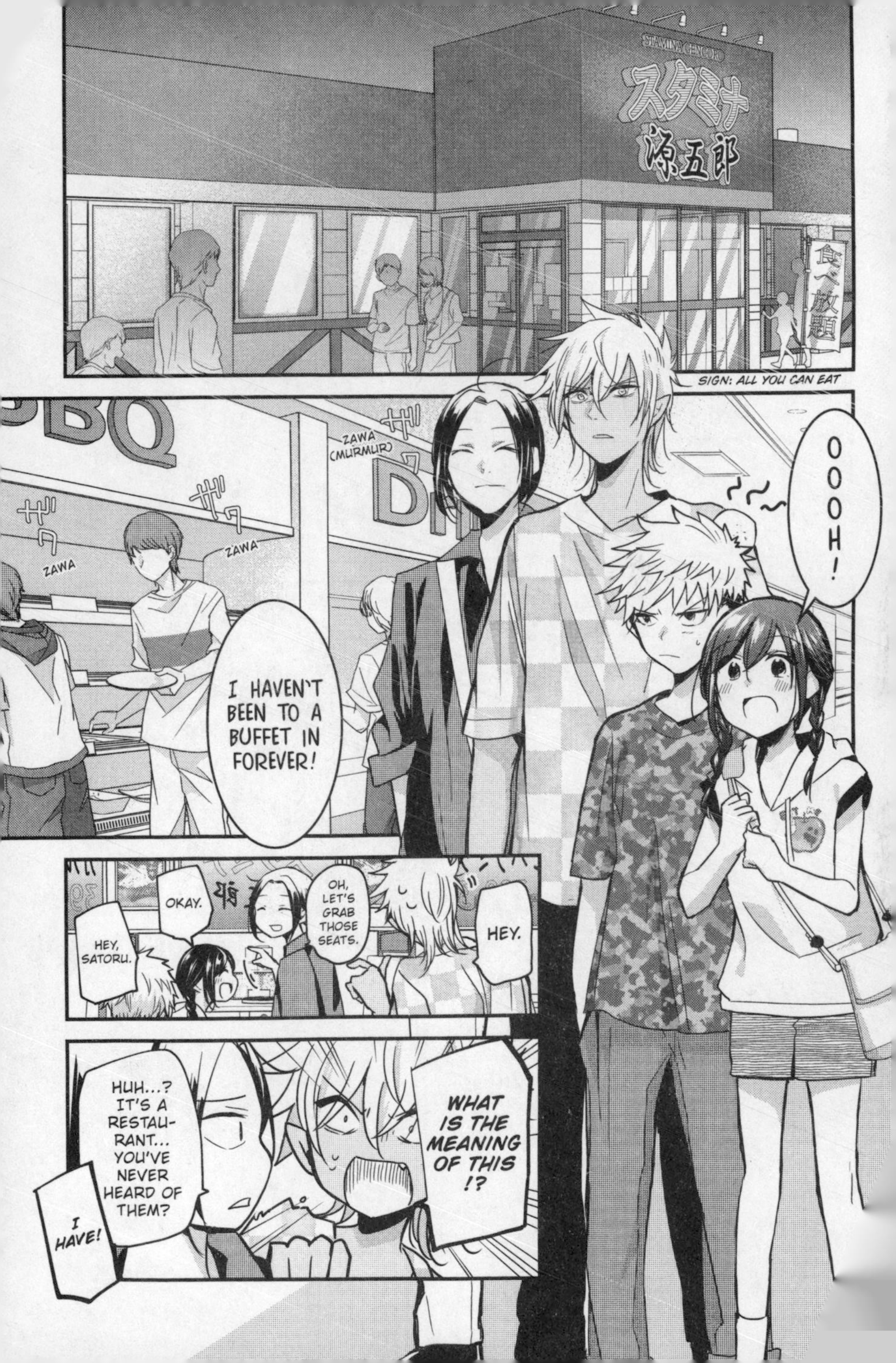
STAMINA GENGORO
スタミナ源五郎
食べ放題
SIGN: ALL YOU CAN EAT
OOOH!
ZAWA (MURMUR)
ザワ
ZAWA
ザワ
ZAWA
ザワ
I HAVEN'T BEEN TO A BUFFET IN FOREVER!
HEY.
OH, LET'S GRAB THOSE SEATS.
OKAY.
HEY, SATORU.
WHAT IS THE MEANING OF THIS!?
HUH...? IT'S A RESTAURANT... YOU'VE NEVER HEARD OF THEM?
I HAVE!

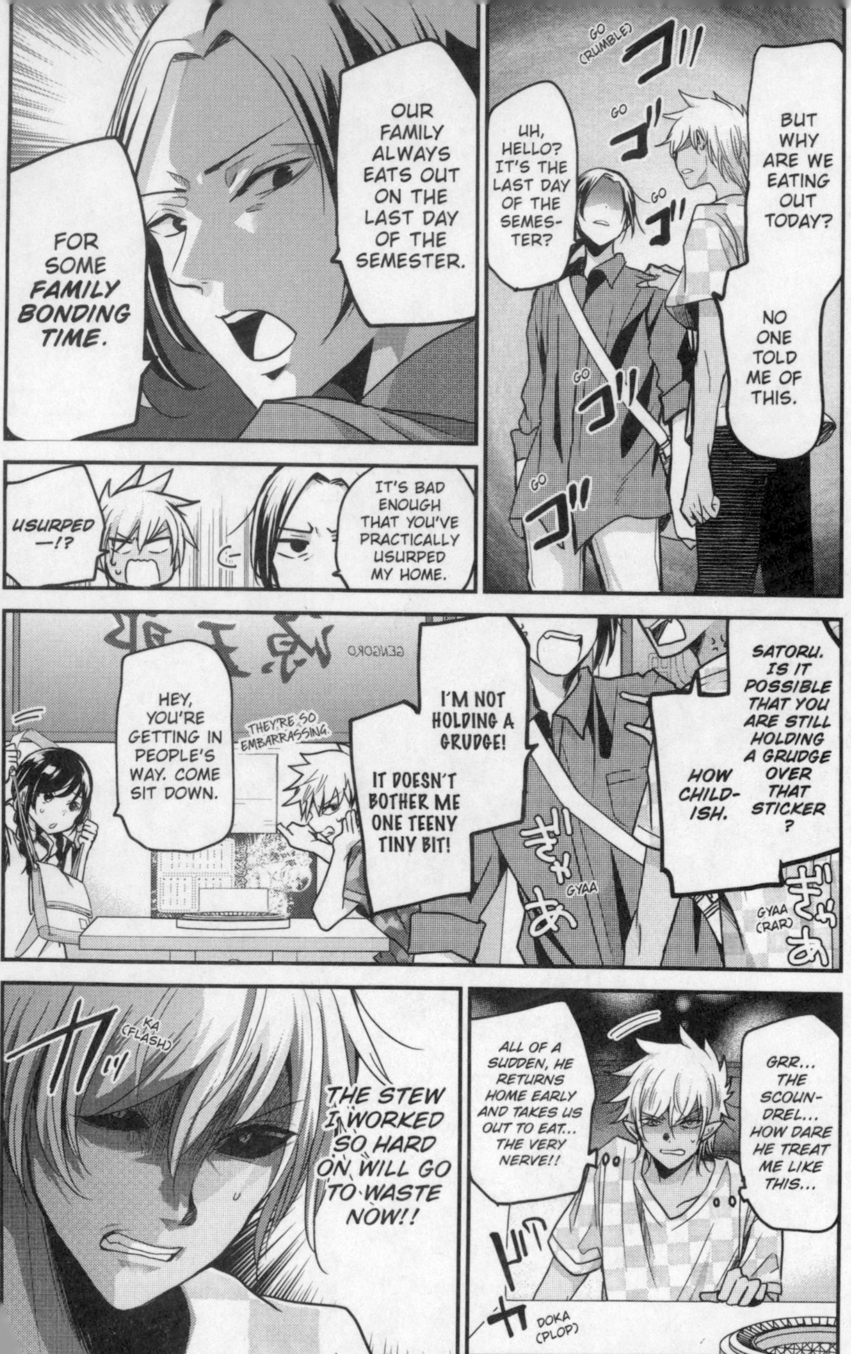

BUT WHY ARE WE EATING OUT TODAY?
GO (RUMBLE)
GO
GO
UH, HELLO? IT'S THE LAST DAY OF THE SEMESTER?
GO
GO
NO ONE TOLD ME OF THIS.
OUR FAMILY ALWAYS EATS OUT ON THE LAST DAY OF THE SEMESTER.
FOR SOME FAMILY BONDING TIME.
IT'S BAD ENOUGH THAT YOU'VE PRACTICALLY USURPED MY HOME.
USURPED—!?
SATORU. IS IT POSSIBLE THAT YOU ARE STILL HOLDING A GRUDGE OVER THAT STICKER?
HOW CHILDISH.
GYAA (RAR)
GYAA
I'M NOT HOLDING A GRUDGE!
IT DOESN'T BOTHER ME ONE TEENY TINY BIT!
THEY'RE SO EMBARRASSING.
HEY, YOU'RE GETTING IN PEOPLE'S WAY. COME SIT DOWN.
GRR... THE SCOUNDREL... HOW DARE HE TREAT ME LIKE THIS...
ALL OF A SUDDEN, HE RETURNS HOME EARLY AND TAKES US OUT TO EAT... THE VERY NERVE!!
DOKA (PLOP)
KA (FLASH)
THE STEW I WORKED SO HARD ON WILL GO TO WASTE NOW!!

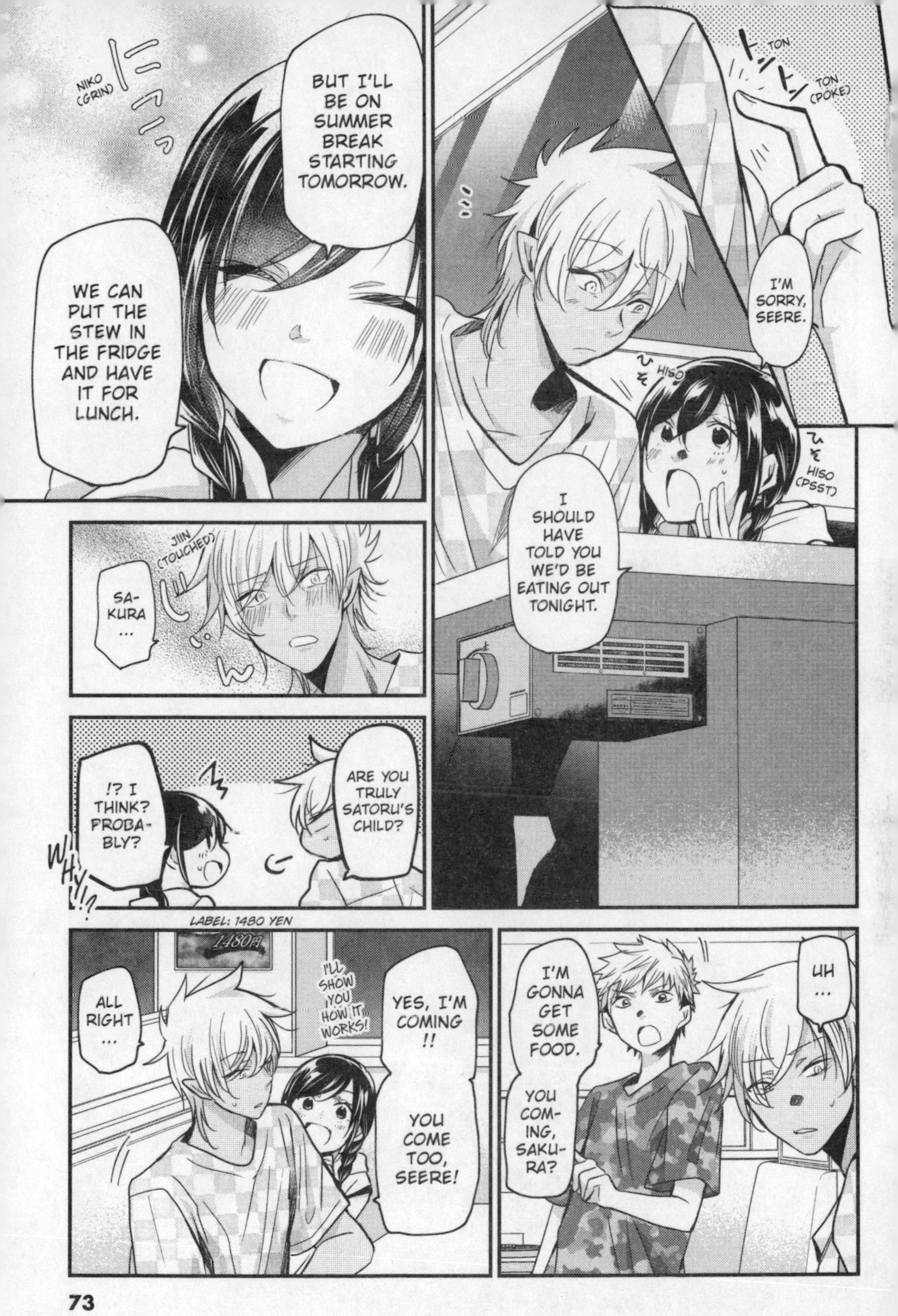
TON
TON (POKE)
I'M SORRY, SEERE.
HISO
HISO (PSST)
I SHOULD HAVE TOLD YOU WE'D BE EATING OUT TONIGHT.
NIKO (GRIN)
BUT I'LL BE ON SUMMER BREAK STARTING TOMORROW.
WE CAN PUT THE STEW IN THE FRIDGE AND HAVE IT FOR LUNCH.
JIIN (TOUCHED)
SA-KURA ...
ARE YOU TRULY SATORU'S CHILD?
!? I THINK? PROBA-BLY?
WHY!!?
LABEL: 1480 YEN
1480円
I'M GONNA GET SOME FOOD.
YOU COM-ING, SAKU-RA?
UH ...
YES, I'M COMING !!
I'LL SHOW YOU HOW IT WORKS!
YOU COME TOO, SEERE!
ALL RIGHT ...

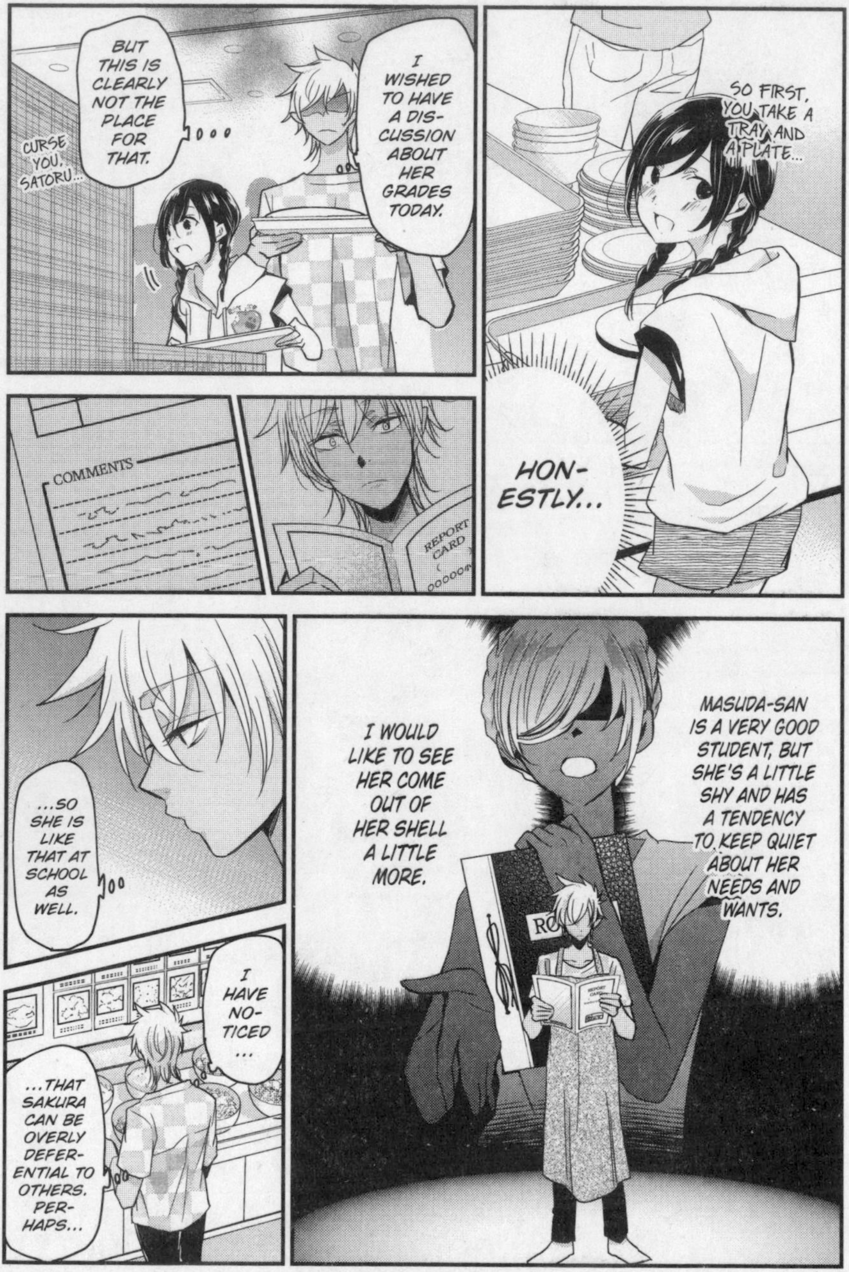
SO FIRST, YOU TAKE A TRAY AND A PLATE...
HON-ESTLY...
I WISHED TO HAVE A DISCUSSION ABOUT HER GRADES TODAY.
BUT THIS IS CLEARLY NOT THE PLACE FOR THAT.
CURSE YOU, SATORU...
REPORT CARD
COMMENTS
MASUDA-SAN IS A VERY GOOD STUDENT, BUT SHE'S A LITTLE SHY AND HAS A TENDENCY TO KEEP QUIET ABOUT HER NEEDS AND WANTS.
I WOULD LIKE TO SEE HER COME OUT OF HER SHELL A LITTLE MORE.
...SO SHE IS LIKE THAT AT SCHOOL AS WELL.
I HAVE NOTICED...
...THAT SAKURA CAN BE OVERLY DEFERENTIAL TO OTHERS. PERHAPS...

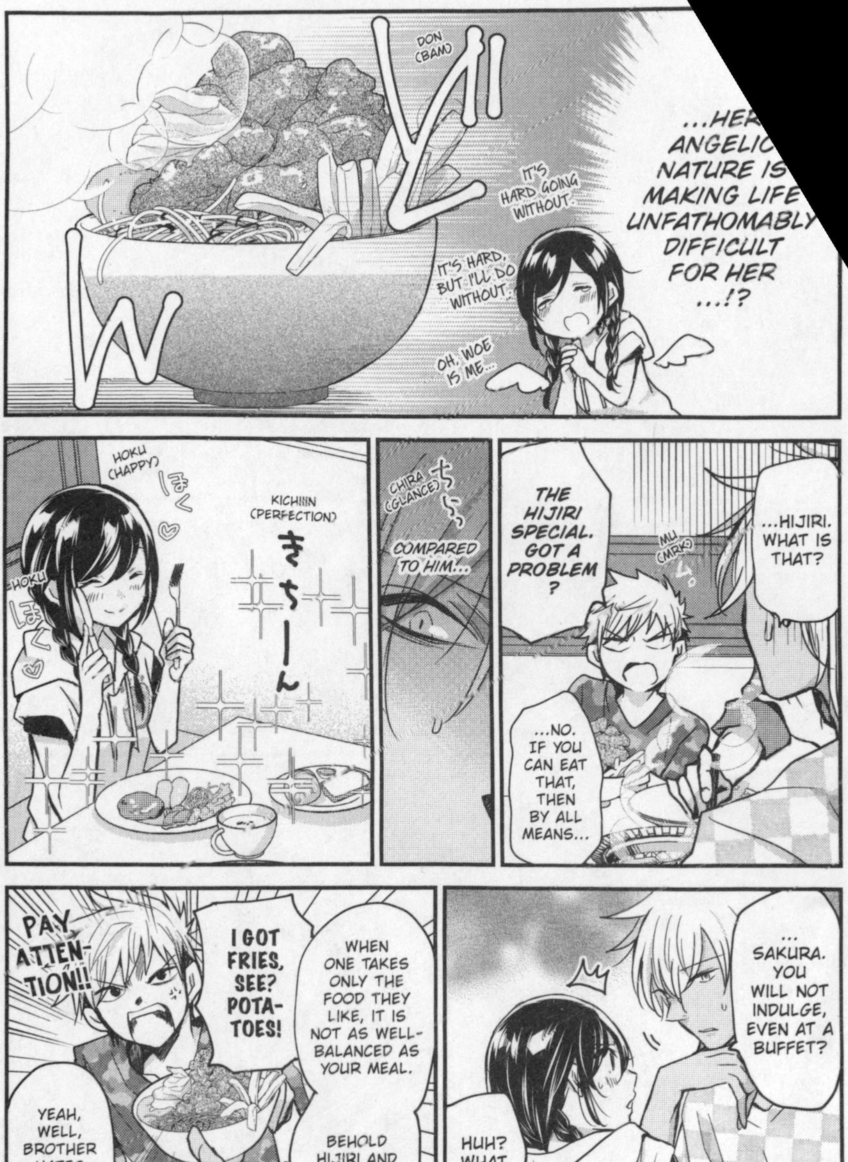
...HER
ANGELIC NATURE IS MAKING LIFE UNFATHOMABLY DIFFICULT FOR HER ...!?
DON (BAM)
IT'S HARD GOING WITHOUT.
IT'S HARD, BUT I'LL DO WITHOUT.
OH, WOE IS ME...
...HIJIRI. WHAT IS THAT?
MU (MRK)
THE HIJIRI SPECIAL. GOT A PROBLEM?
...NO. IF YOU CAN EAT THAT, THEN BY ALL MEANS...
CHIRA (GLANCE)
ちらっ
COMPARED TO HIM...
KICHIIIN (PERFECTION)
きちーん
HOKU (HAPPY)
ほく
HOKU
ほく
...SAKURA. YOU WILL NOT INDULGE, EVEN AT A BUFFET?
HUH? WHAT DO YOU MEAN!?
WHEN ONE TAKES ONLY THE FOOD THEY LIKE, IT IS NOT AS WELL-BALANCED AS YOUR MEAL.
BEHOLD HIJIRI AND HIS BOWL OF ZERO VEGETABLES.
I GOT FRIES, SEE? POTATOES!
PAY ATTENTION!!
YEAH, WELL, BROTHER HATES VEGETABLES.

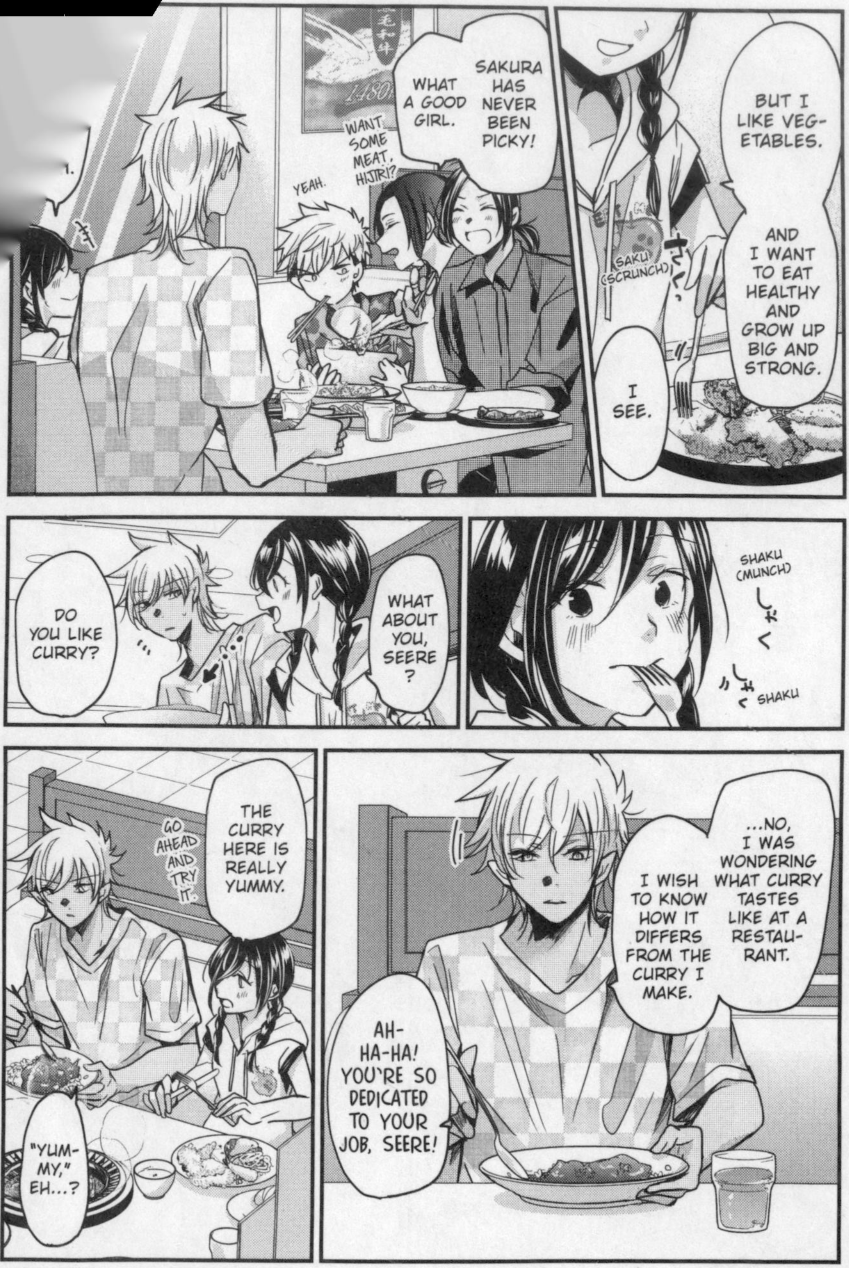
SAKURA HAS NEVER BEEN PICKY!
WHAT A GOOD GIRL.
WANT SOME MEAT, HIJIRI?
YEAH.
BUT I LIKE VEGETABLES.
AND I WANT TO EAT HEALTHY AND GROW UP BIG AND STRONG.
SAKU (SCRUNCH)
I SEE.
SHAKU (MUNCH)
SHAKU
WHAT ABOUT YOU, SEERE?
DO YOU LIKE CURRY?
...NO, I WAS WONDERING WHAT CURRY TASTES LIKE AT A RESTAURANT.
I WISH TO KNOW HOW IT DIFFERS FROM THE CURRY I MAKE.
AH-HA-HA! YOU'RE SO DEDICATED TO YOUR JOB, SEERE!
THE CURRY HERE IS REALLY YUMMY.
GO AHEAD AND TRY IT.
"YUMMY," EH...?

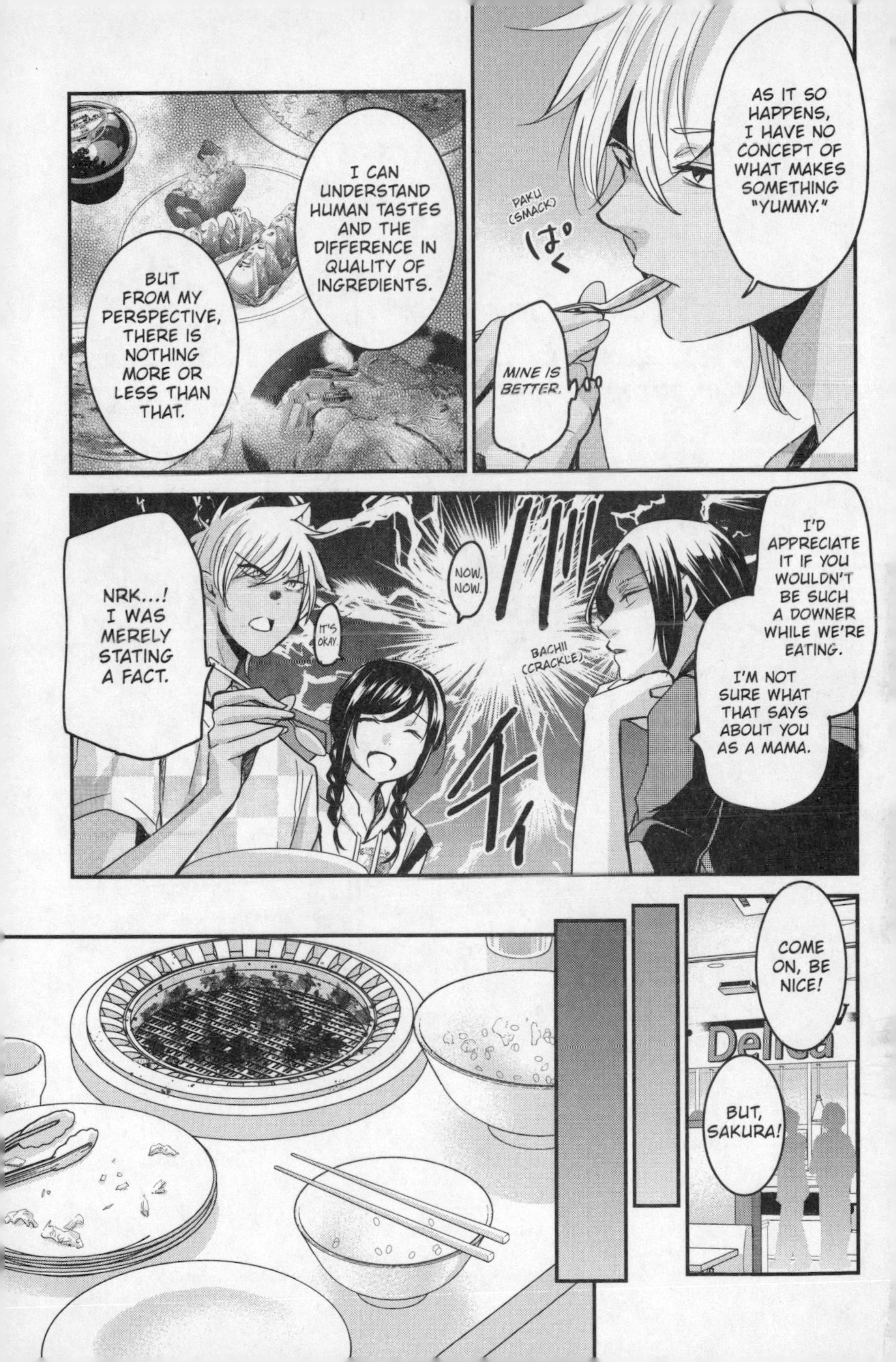
AS IT SO HAPPENS, I HAVE NO CONCEPT OF WHAT MAKES SOMETHING "YUMMY."
PAKU (SMACK)
ぱく
MINE IS BETTER.
I CAN UNDERSTAND HUMAN TASTES AND THE DIFFERENCE IN QUALITY OF INGREDIENTS.
BUT FROM MY PERSPECTIVE, THERE IS NOTHING MORE OR LESS THAN THAT.
I'D APPRECIATE IT IF YOU WOULDN'T BE SUCH A DOWNER WHILE WE'RE EATING.
I'M NOT SURE WHAT THAT SAYS ABOUT YOU AS A MAMA.
BACHII (CRACKLE)
NOW, NOW.
IT'S OKAY.
NRK...! I WAS MERELY STATING A FACT.
COME ON, BE NICE!
BUT, SAKURA!

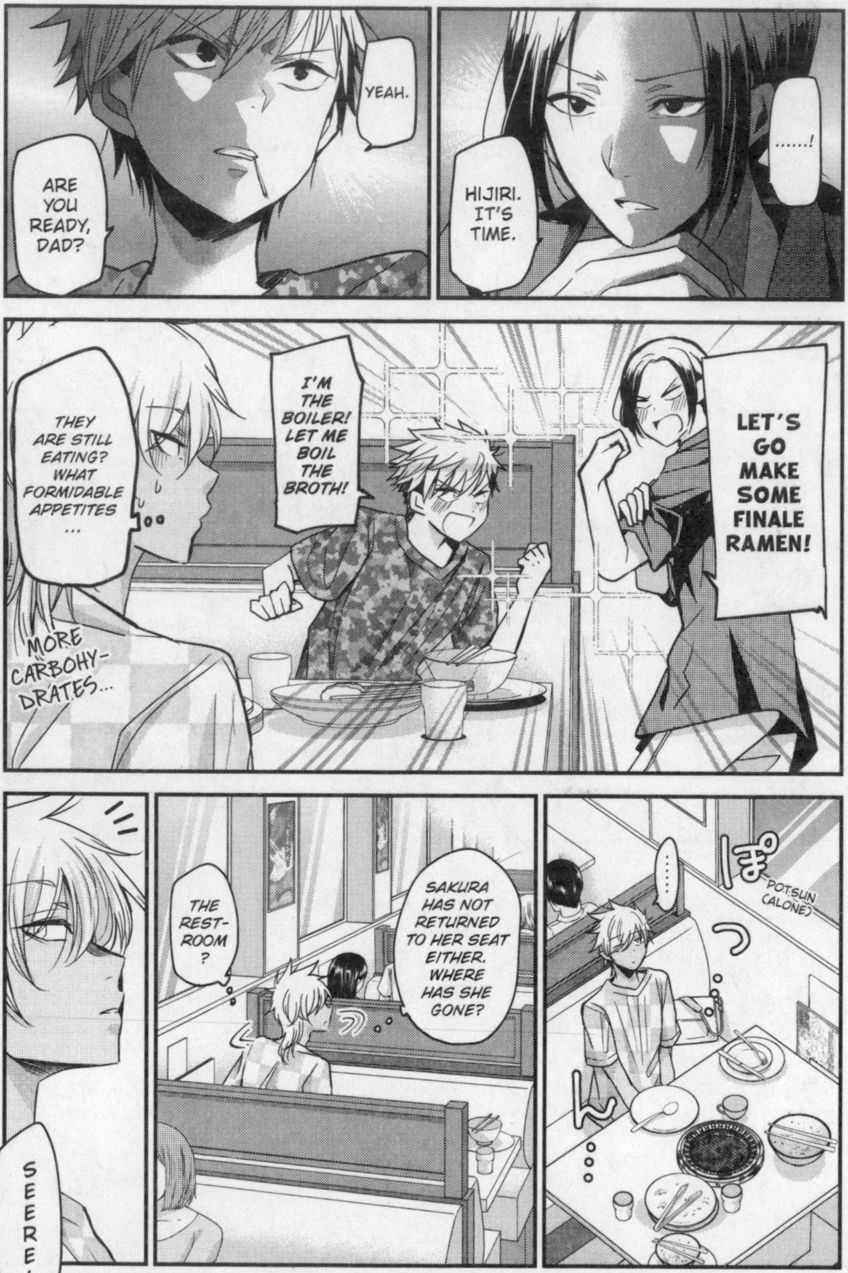
......!
HIJIRI. IT'S TIME.
YEAH.
ARE YOU READY, DAD?
LET'S GO MAKE SOME FINALE RAMEN!
I'M THE BOILER! LET ME BOIL THE BROTH!
THEY ARE STILL EATING? WHAT FORMIDABLE APPETITES...
MORE CARBOHYDRATES...
......
ぽつん
POTSUN (ALONE)
SAKURA HAS NOT RETURNED TO HER SEAT EITHER. WHERE HAS SHE GONE?
THE REST-ROOM?
SEERE.

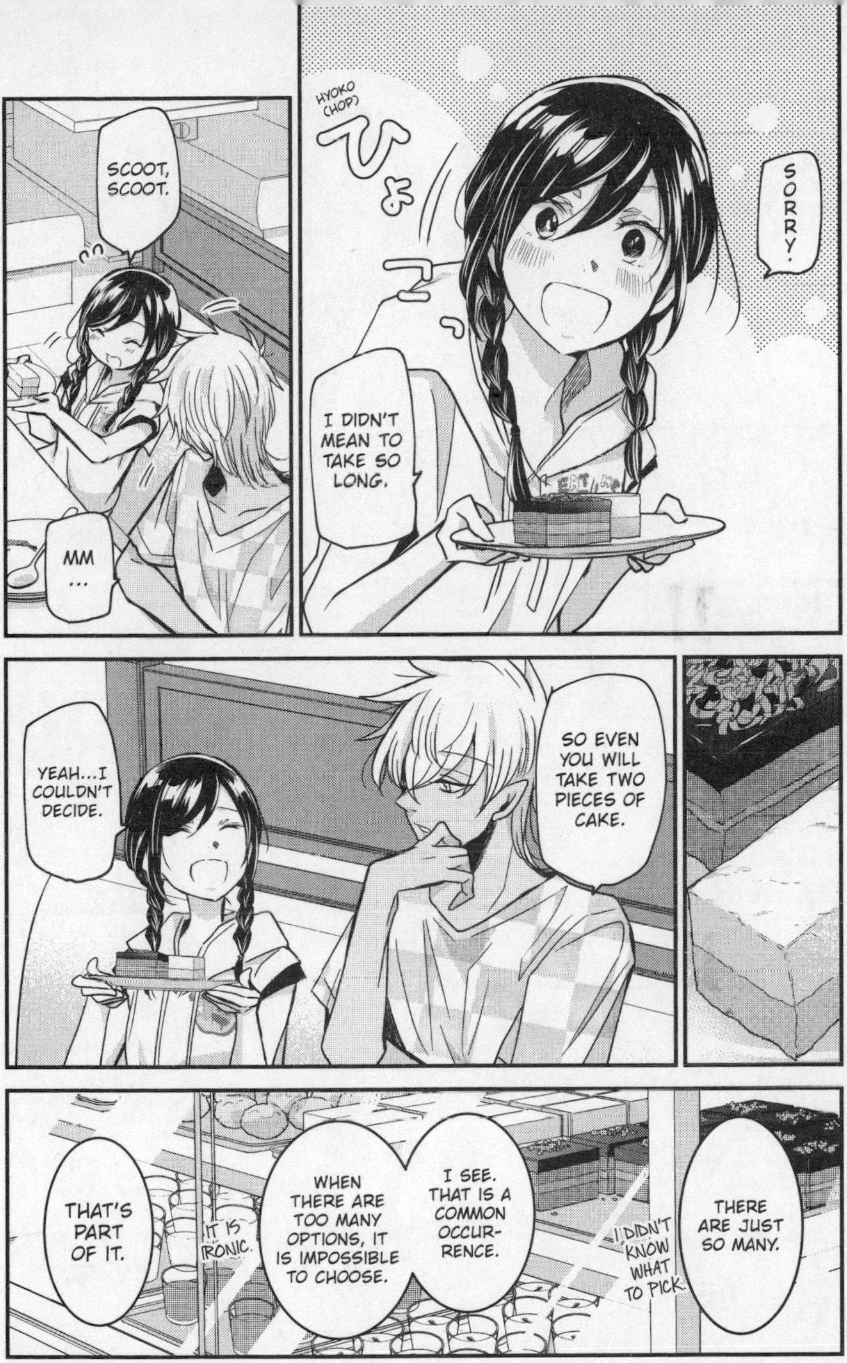
SORRY.
HYOKO (HOP)
I DIDN'T MEAN TO TAKE SO LONG.
SCOOT, SCOOT.
MM ...
SO EVEN YOU WILL TAKE TWO PIECES OF CAKE.
YEAH...I COULDN'T DECIDE.
THERE ARE JUST SO MANY.
I DIDN'T KNOW WHAT TO PICK.
I SEE. THAT IS A COMMON OCCURRENCE.
WHEN THERE ARE TOO MANY OPTIONS, IT IS IMPOSSIBLE TO CHOOSE.
IT IS IRONIC.
THAT'S PART OF IT.

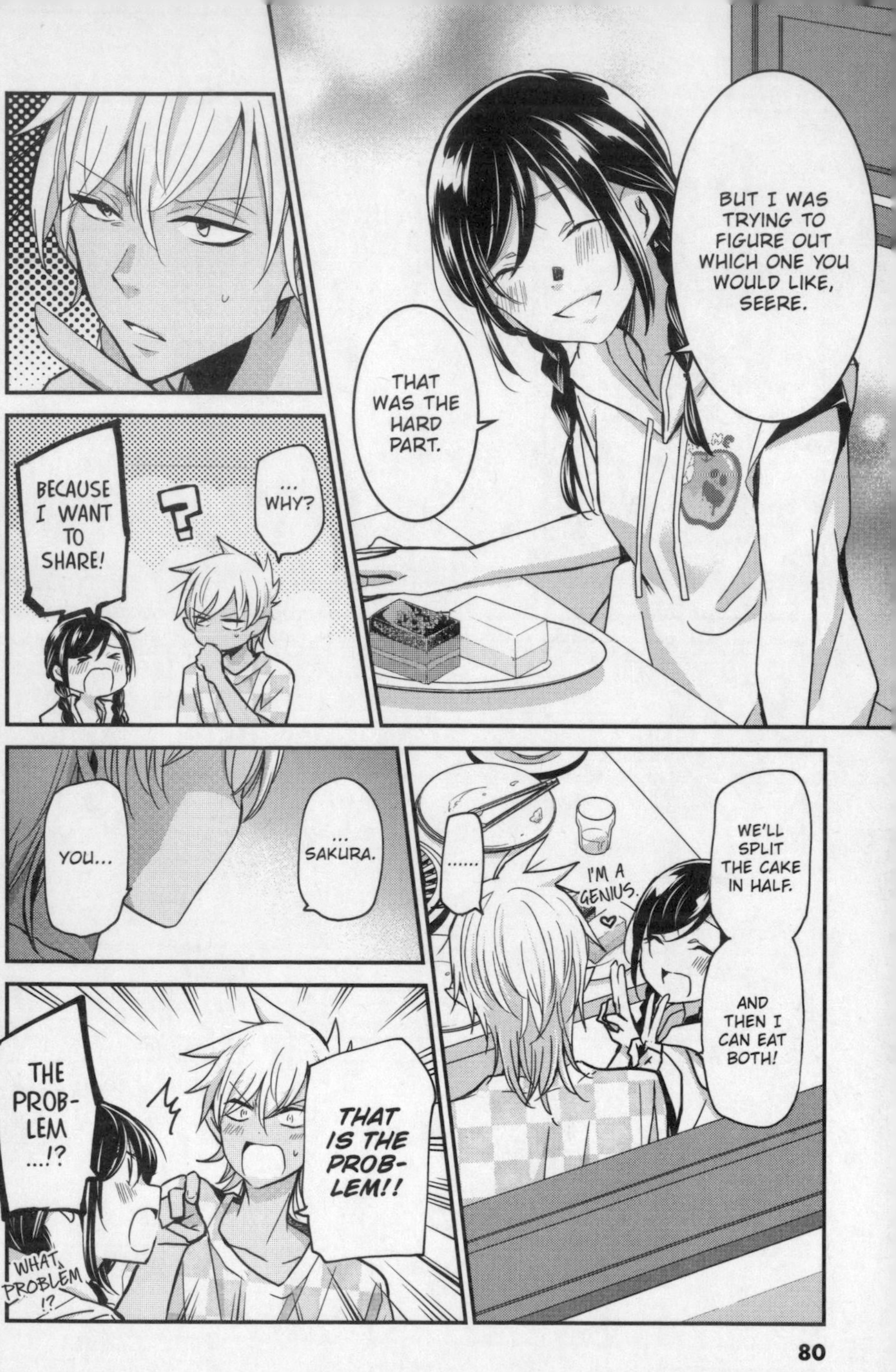
BUT I WAS TRYING TO FIGURE OUT WHICH ONE YOU WOULD LIKE, SEERE.
THAT WAS THE HARD PART.
...WHY?
BECAUSE I WANT TO SHARE!
WE'LL SPLIT THE CAKE IN HALF.
AND THEN I CAN EAT BOTH!
I'M A GENIUS.
......
...SAKURA.
YOU...
THAT IS THE PROB-LEM!!
THE PROB-LEM...!?
WHAT PROBLEM!?

YOU ARE ALLOWED TO CONSIDER YOUR OWN WANTS MORE, YOU KNOW.
IT WAS WRITTEN IN YOUR REPORT CARD AS WELL.
THAT YOU ARE TOO RESERVED.
WHEN IT COMES TO CAKE, YOU NEED NOT CONCERN YOURSELF WITH ME.
YOU MAY EAT AS MUCH AS YOU LIKE OF WHICHEVER CAKE YOU PREFER.
THAT IS HOW THIS RESTAU-RANT WORKS, NO?
......
BUT... YEAH.
...WHEN I EAT ALONE...
...IT'S SO EMPTY.
EMPTY ...!?
I MEAN, YOU KNOW.

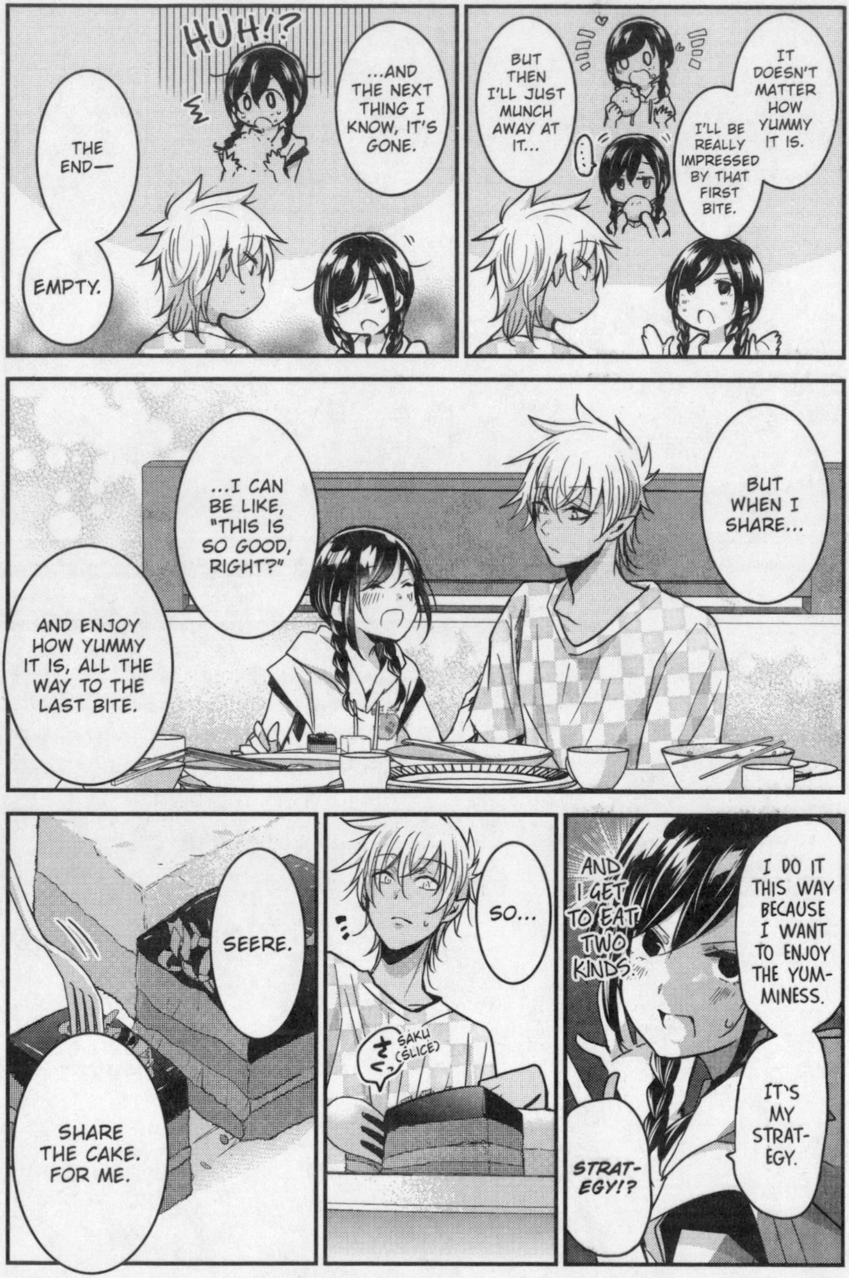
IT DOESN'T MATTER HOW YUMMY IT IS.
I'LL BE REALLY IMPRESSED BY THAT FIRST BITE.
BUT THEN I'LL JUST MUNCH AWAY AT IT...
...
...AND THE NEXT THING I KNOW, IT'S GONE.
HUH!?
THE END—
EMPTY.
BUT WHEN I SHARE...
...I CAN BE LIKE, "THIS IS SO GOOD, RIGHT?"
AND ENJOY HOW YUMMY IT IS, ALL THE WAY TO THE LAST BITE.
I DO IT THIS WAY BECAUSE I WANT TO ENJOY THE YUMMINESS.
IT'S MY STRATEGY.
AND I GET TO EAT TWO KINDS.
STRATEGY!?
SO...
SAKU (SLICE)
SEERE.
SHARE THE CAKE. FOR ME.

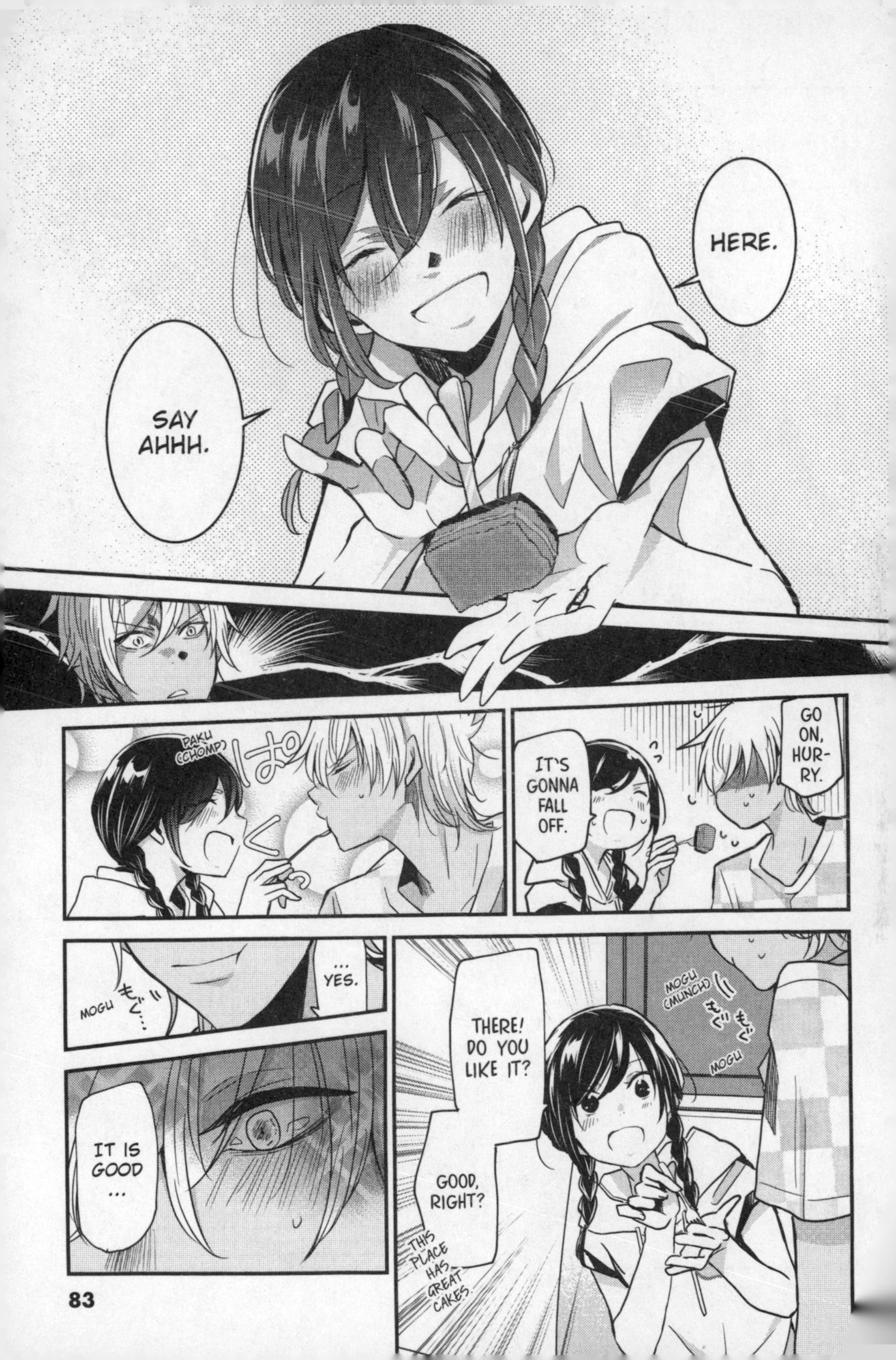
HERE.
SAY AHHH.
GO ON, HURRY.
IT'S GONNA FALL OFF.
PAKU (CHOMP)
THERE! DO YOU LIKE IT?
MOGU (MUNCH)
MOGU
GOOD, RIGHT?
THIS PLACE HAS GREAT CAKES.
... YES.
MOGU
IT IS GOOD ...

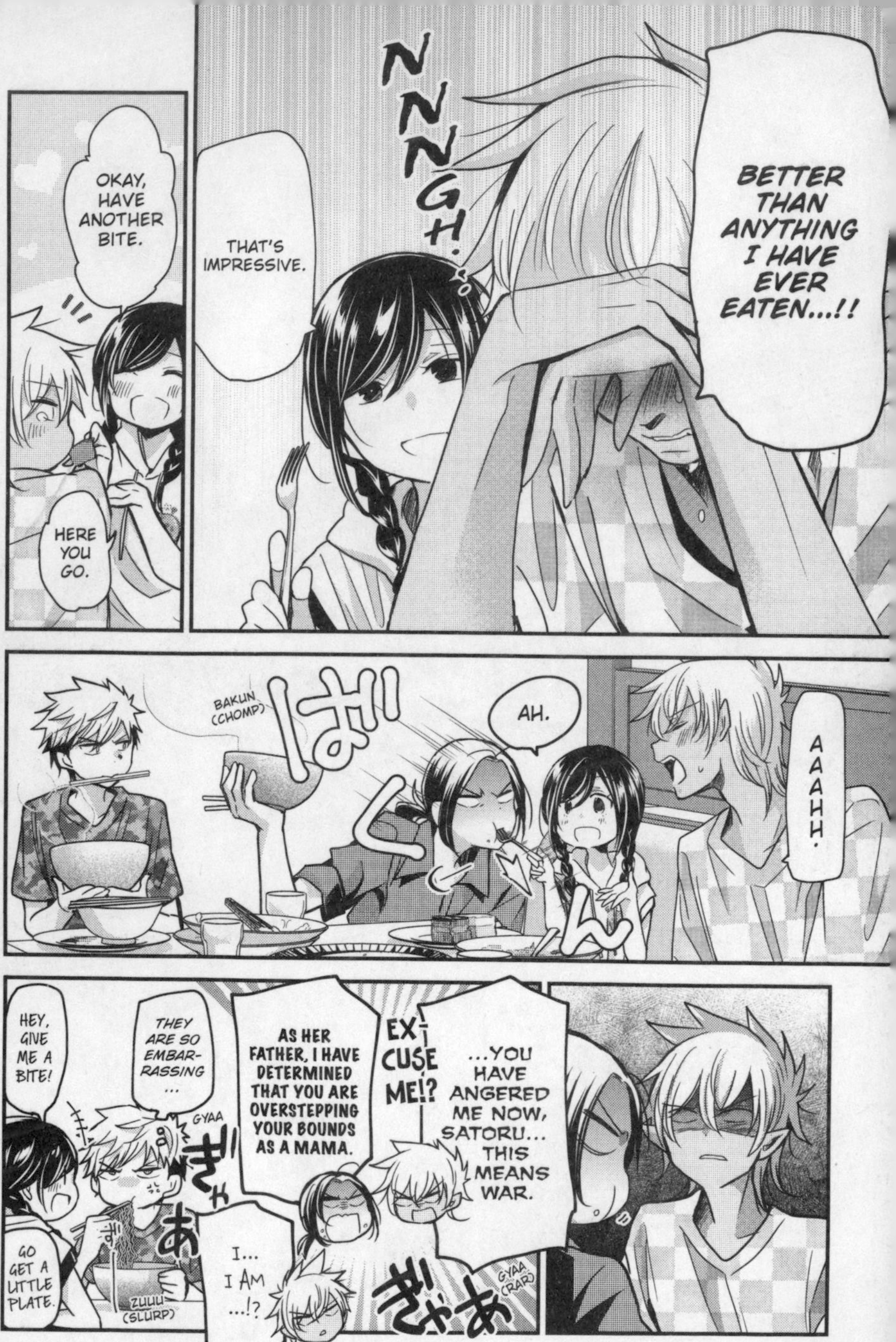
NNNGH!
BETTER THAN ANYTHING I HAVE EVER EATEN...!!
THAT'S IMPRESSIVE.
OKAY, HAVE ANOTHER BITE.
HERE YOU GO.
AAAHH.
AH.
BAKUN (CHOMP)
...YOU HAVE ANGERED ME NOW, SATORU... THIS MEANS WAR.
EX-CUSE ME!?
AS HER FATHER, I HAVE DETERMINED THAT YOU ARE OVERSTEPPING YOUR BOUNDS AS A MAMA.
GYAA (RAR)
I... I AM ...!?
THEY ARE SO EMBARRASSING...
HEY, GIVE ME A BITE!
GYAA
GO GET A LITTLE PLATE.
ZUUUU (SLURP)

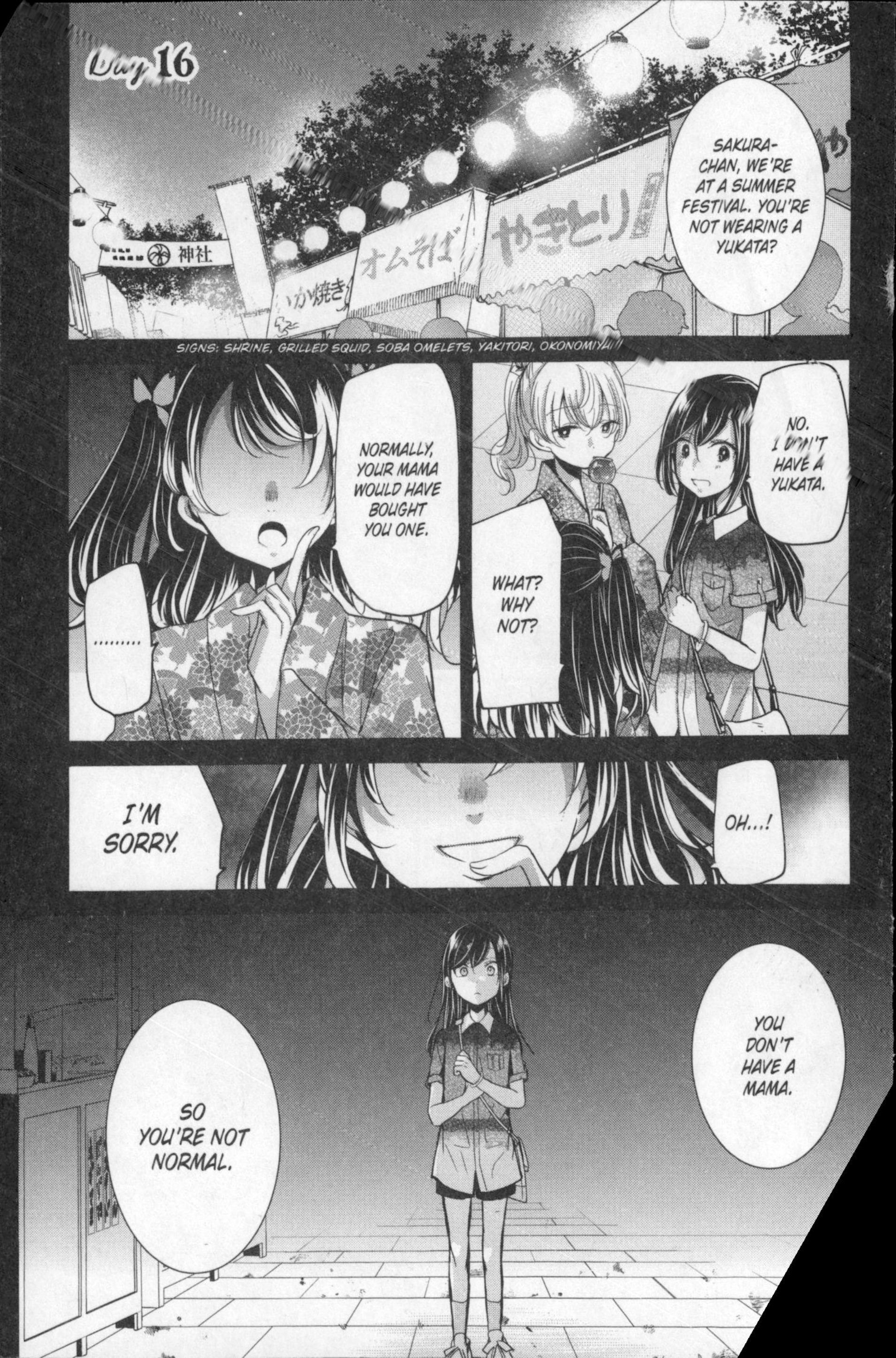
Day 16
神社
いか焼き
オムそば
やきとり
SAKURA-CHAN, WE'RE AT A SUMMER FESTIVAL. YOU'RE NOT WEARING A YUKATA?
SIGNS: SHRINE, GRILLED SQUID, SOBA OMELETS, YAKITORI, OKONOMIYA
NO. I DON'T HAVE A YUKATA.
WHAT? WHY NOT?
NORMALLY, YOUR MAMA WOULD HAVE BOUGHT YOU ONE.
.........
OH...!
I'M SORRY.
YOU DON'T HAVE A MAMA.
SO YOU'RE NOT NORMAL.

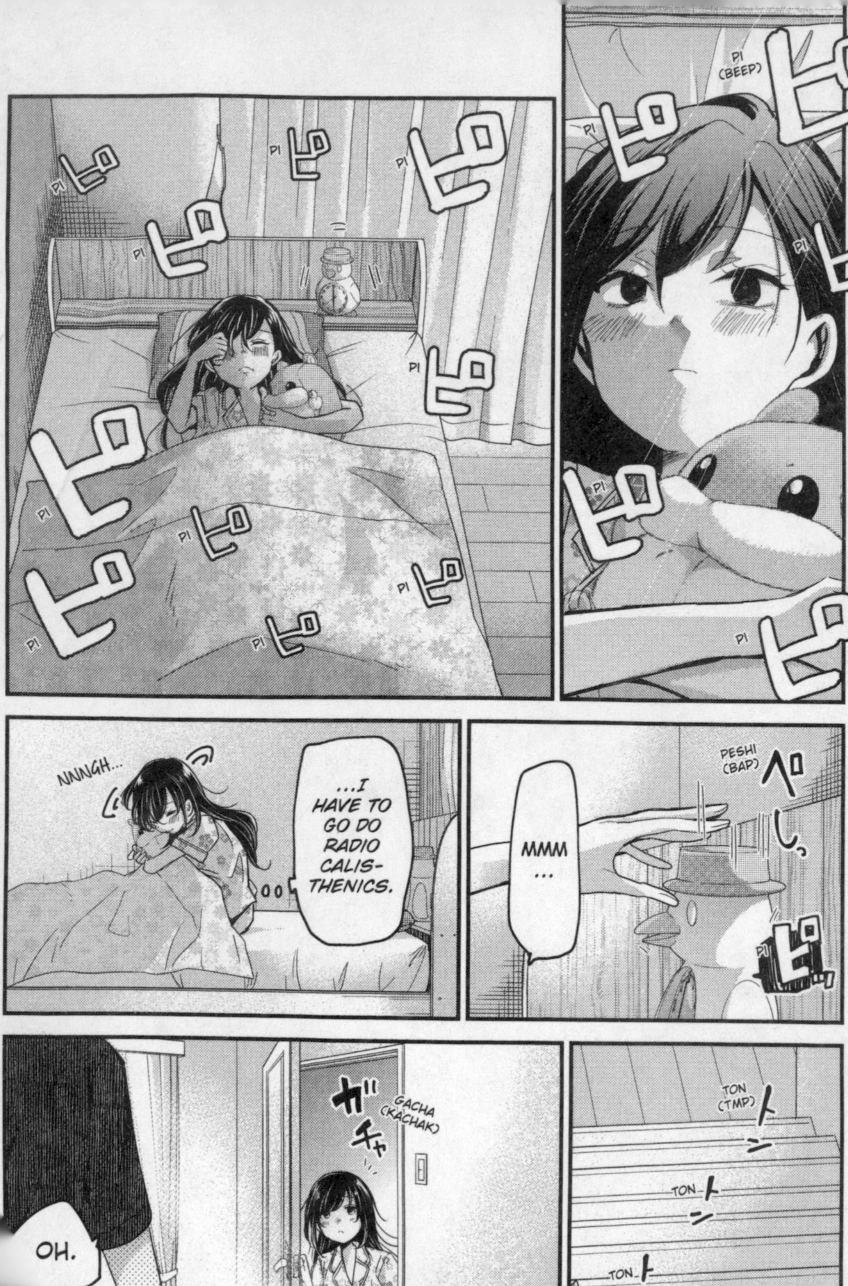

PI (BEEP)
ピ
PI
ピ
PI
ピ
MMM...
PESHI (BAP)
ペしっ
PI
ピ...
NNNGH...
...I HAVE TO GO DO RADIO CALIS-THENICS.
TON (TMP)
トン
TON
トン
TON
トン
GACHA (KACHAK)
ガチャ
OH.

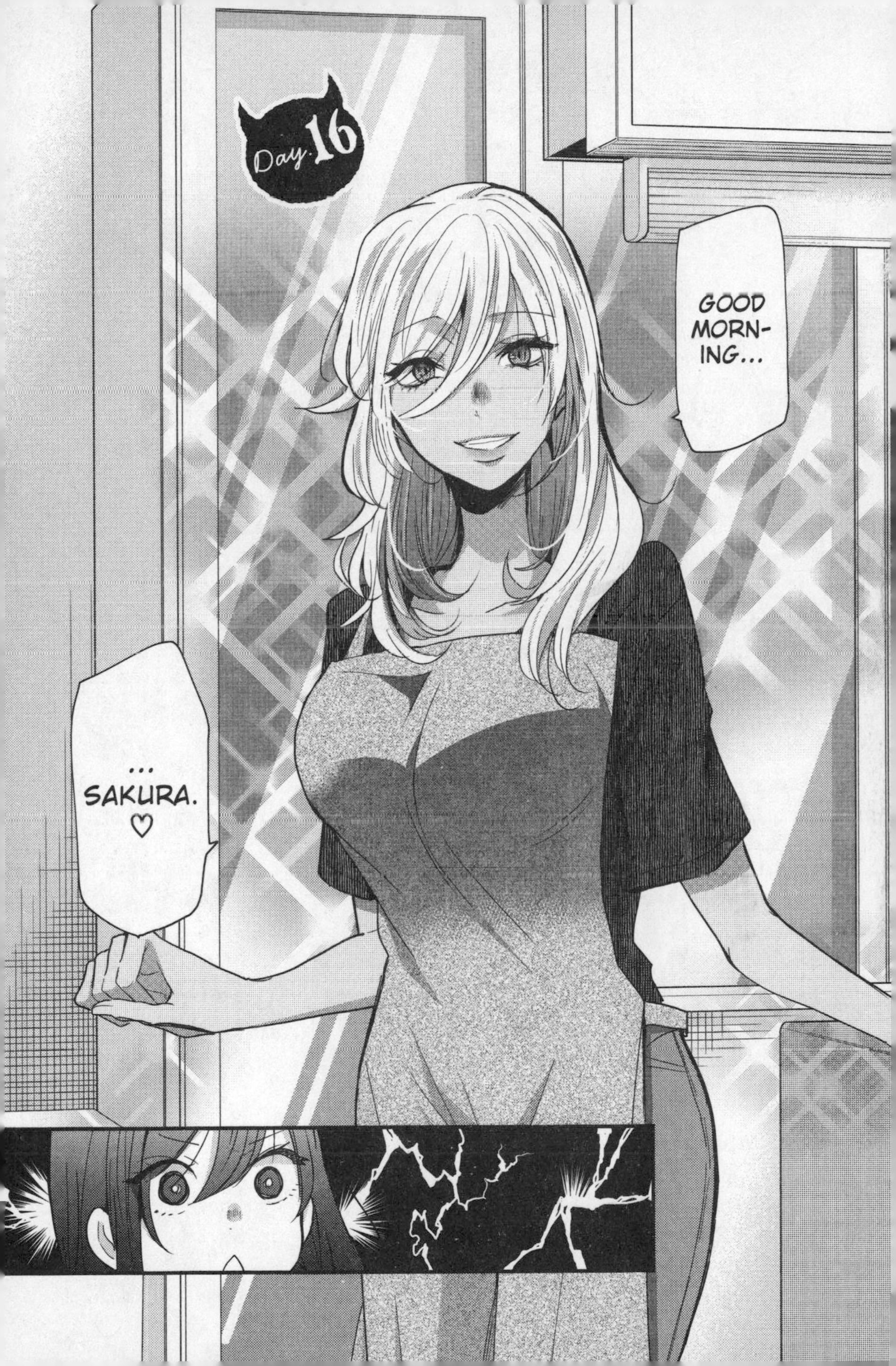
Day. 16
GOOD MORN-ING...
...SAKURA. ♡

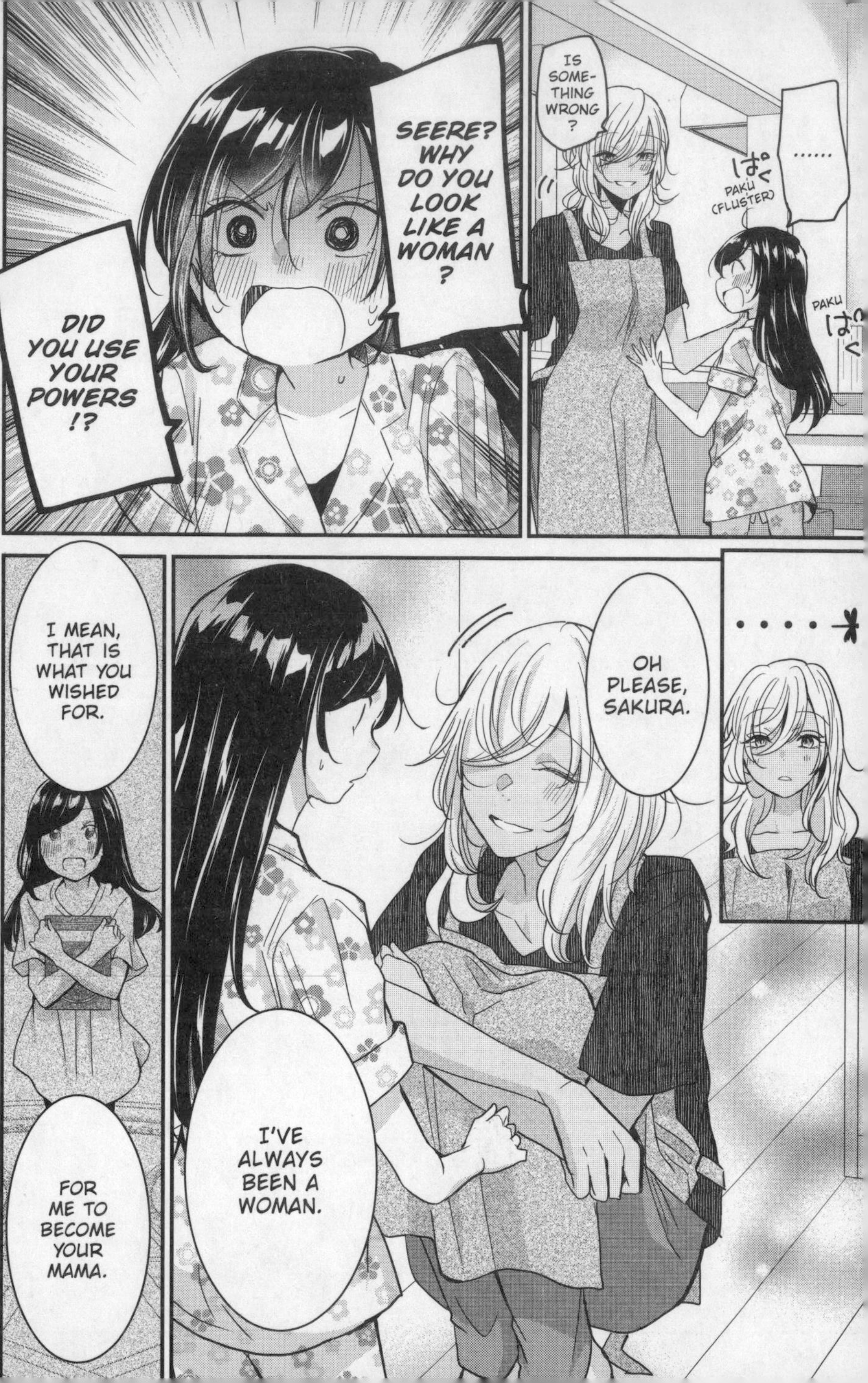
IS SOMETHING WRONG?
......
ぱく
PAKU (FLUSTER)
PAKU
ぱく
SEERE? WHY DO YOU LOOK LIKE A WOMAN?
DID YOU USE YOUR POWERS!?
.....
OH PLEASE, SAKURA.
I'VE ALWAYS BEEN A WOMAN.
I MEAN, THAT IS WHAT YOU WISHED FOR.
FOR ME TO BECOME YOUR MAMA.

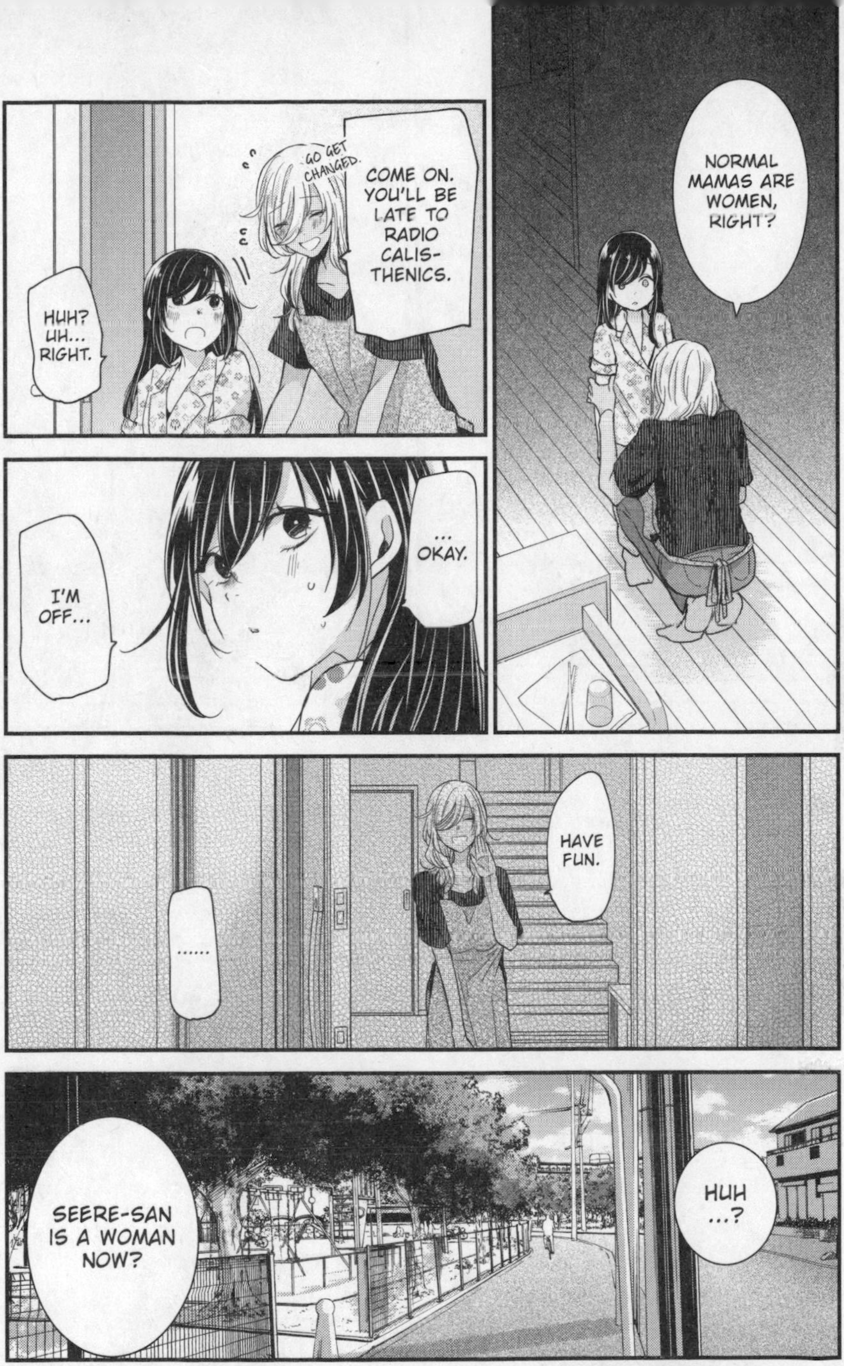
NORMAL MAMAS ARE WOMEN, RIGHT?
COME ON. YOU'LL BE LATE TO RADIO CALIS-THENICS.
GO GET CHANGED.
HUH? UH... RIGHT.
...OKAY.
I'M OFF...
HAVE FUN.
......
HUH ...?
SEERE-SAN IS A WOMAN NOW?

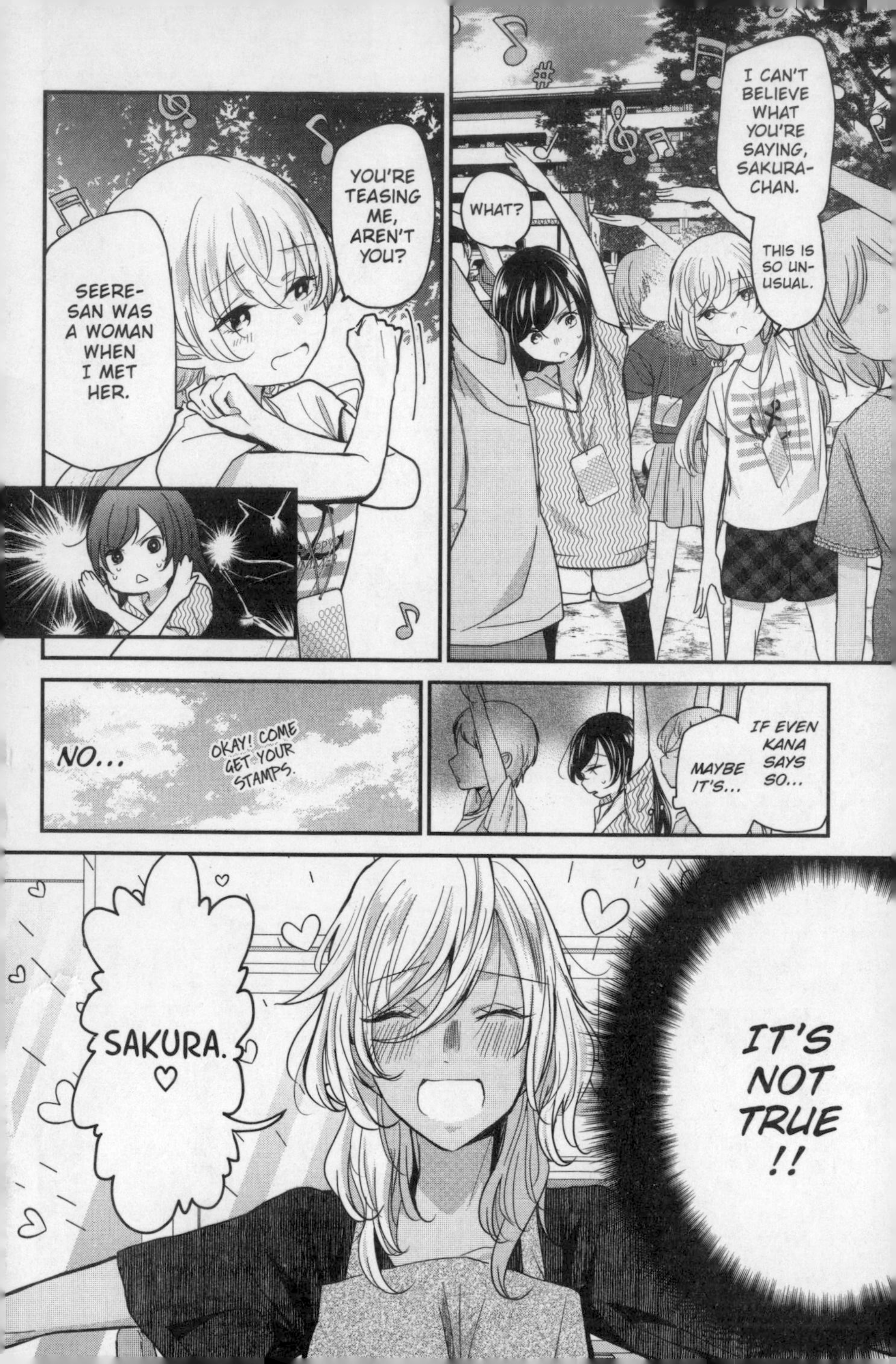
I CAN'T BELIEVE WHAT YOU'RE SAYING, SAKURA-CHAN.
THIS IS SO UN-USUAL.
WHAT?
YOU'RE TEASING ME, AREN'T YOU?
SEERE-SAN WAS A WOMAN WHEN I MET HER.
IF EVEN KANA SAYS SO...
MAYBE IT'S...
NO...
OKAY! COME GET YOUR STAMPS.
IT'S NOT TRUE!!
SAKURA. ♡

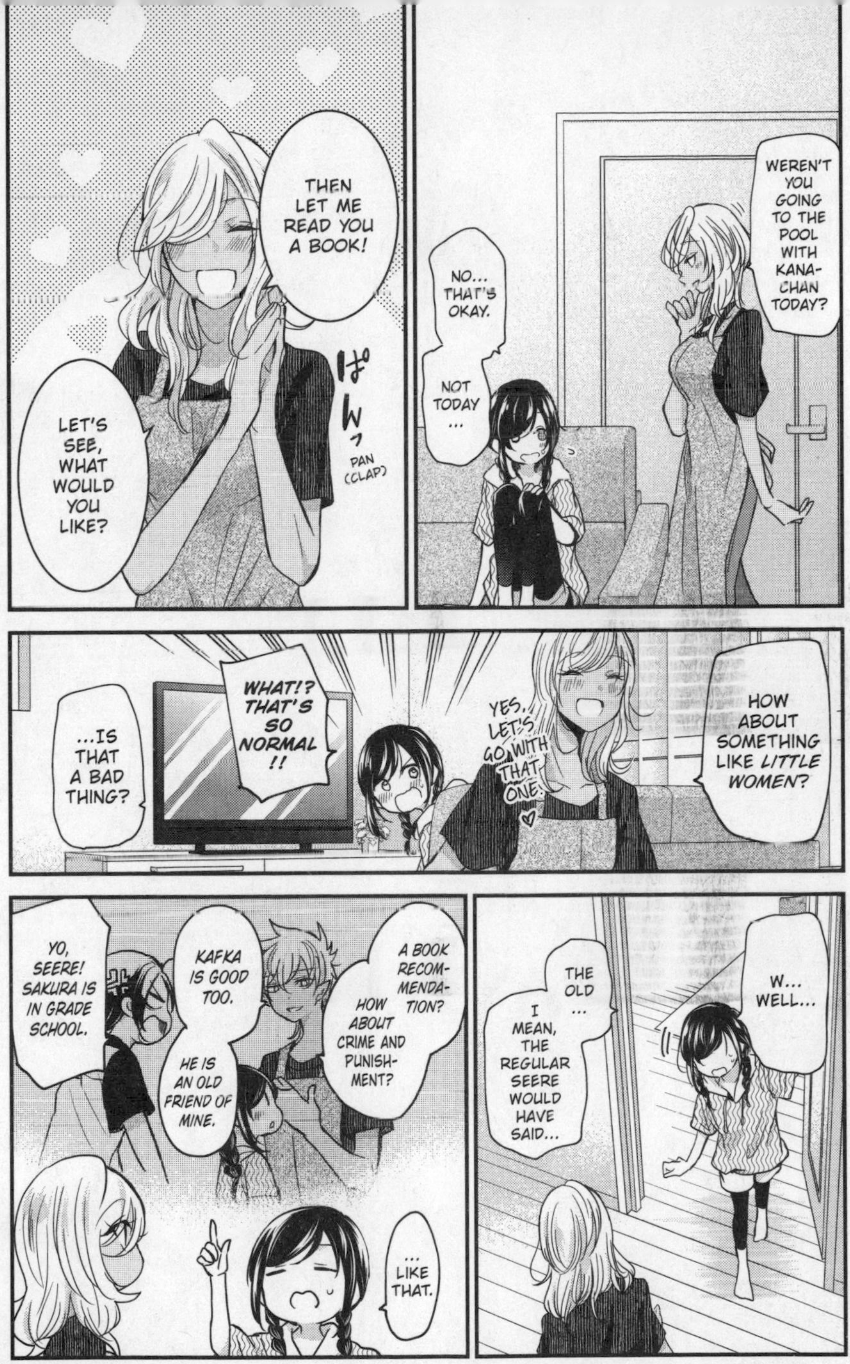
WEREN'T YOU GOING TO THE POOL WITH KANA-CHAN TODAY?
NO... THAT'S OKAY.
NOT TODAY ...
THEN LET ME READ YOU A BOOK!
ぱん
PAN (CLAP)
LET'S SEE, WHAT WOULD YOU LIKE?
HOW ABOUT SOMETHING LIKE *LITTLE WOMEN*?
YES, LET'S GO WITH THAT ONE.
WHAT!? THAT'S SO NORMAL!!
...IS THAT A BAD THING?
W... WELL...
THE OLD ...
I MEAN, THE REGULAR SEERE WOULD HAVE SAID...
A BOOK RECOMMENDATION?
HOW ABOUT CRIME AND PUNISHMENT?
KAFKA IS GOOD TOO.
HE IS AN OLD FRIEND OF MINE.
YO, SEERE! SAKURA IS IN GRADE SCHOOL.
... LIKE THAT.

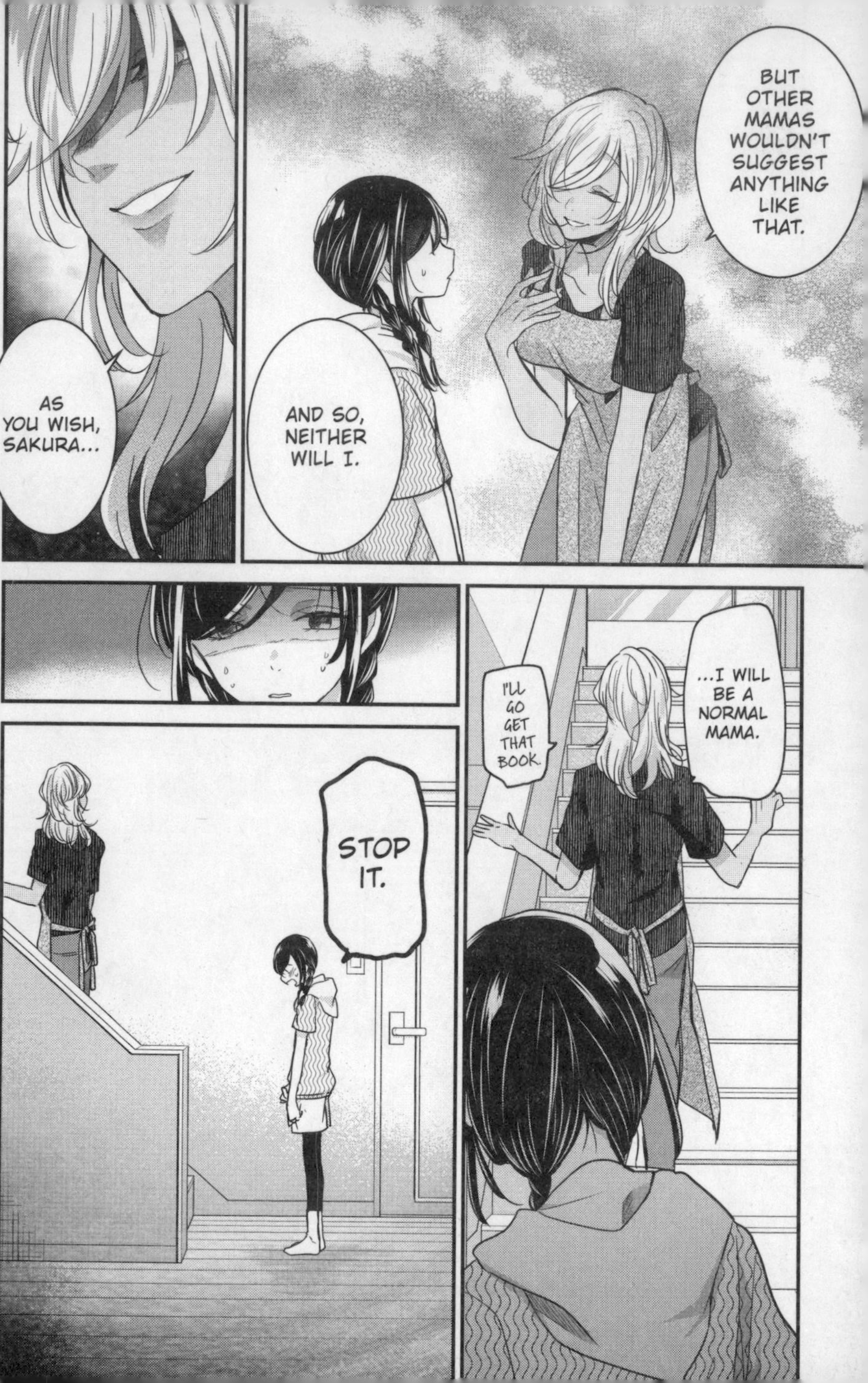
BUT OTHER MAMAS WOULDN'T SUGGEST ANYTHING LIKE THAT.
AND SO, NEITHER WILL I.
AS YOU WISH, SAKURA...
...I WILL BE A NORMAL MAMA.
I'LL GO GET THAT BOOK.
STOP IT.

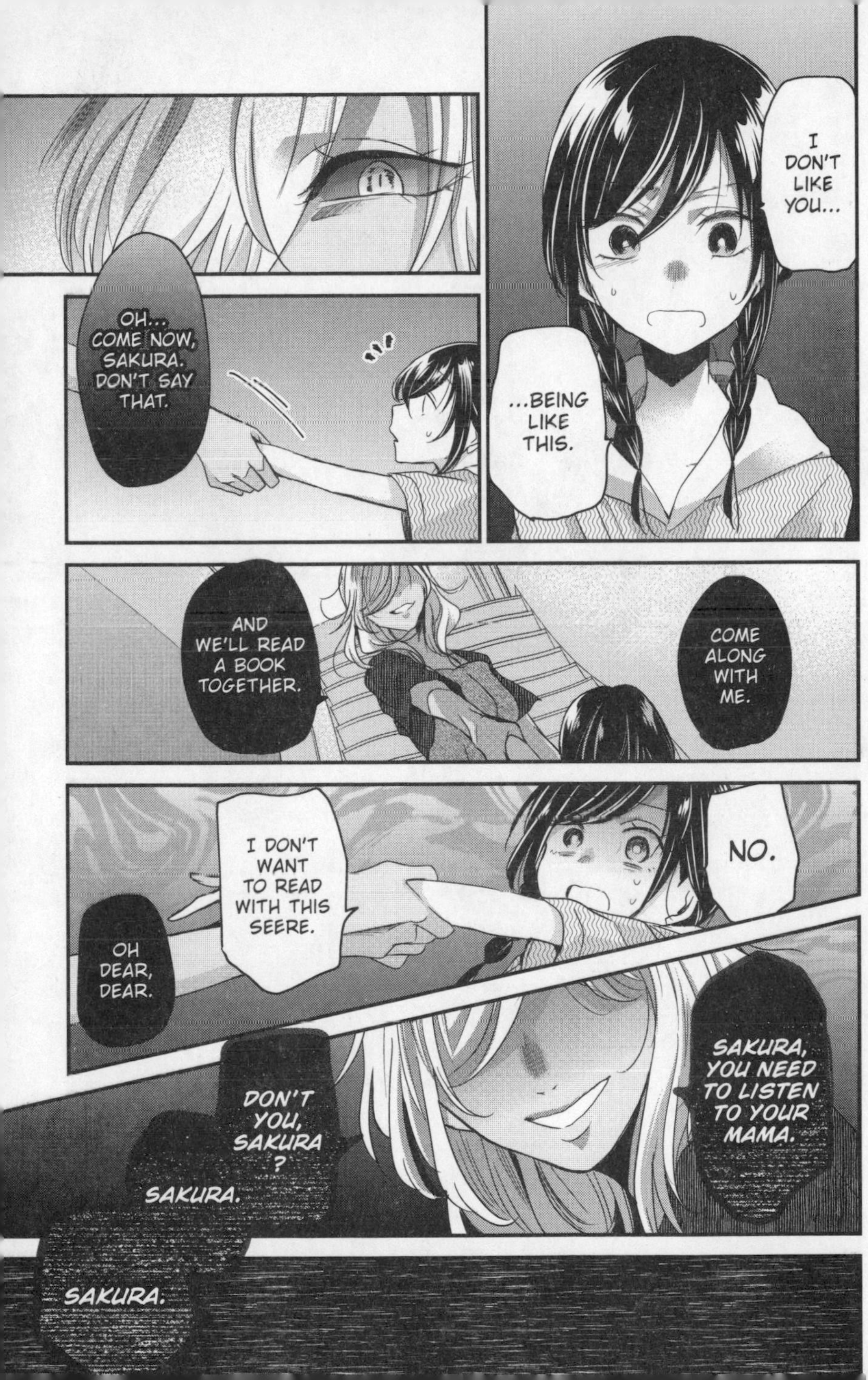
I DON'T LIKE YOU...
...BEING LIKE THIS.
OH... COME NOW, SAKURA. DON'T SAY THAT.
COME ALONG WITH ME.
AND WE'LL READ A BOOK TOGETHER.
NO.
I DON'T WANT TO READ WITH THIS SEERE.
OH DEAR, DEAR.
SAKURA, YOU NEED TO LISTEN TO YOUR MAMA.
DON'T YOU, SAKURA?
SAKURA.
SAKURA.

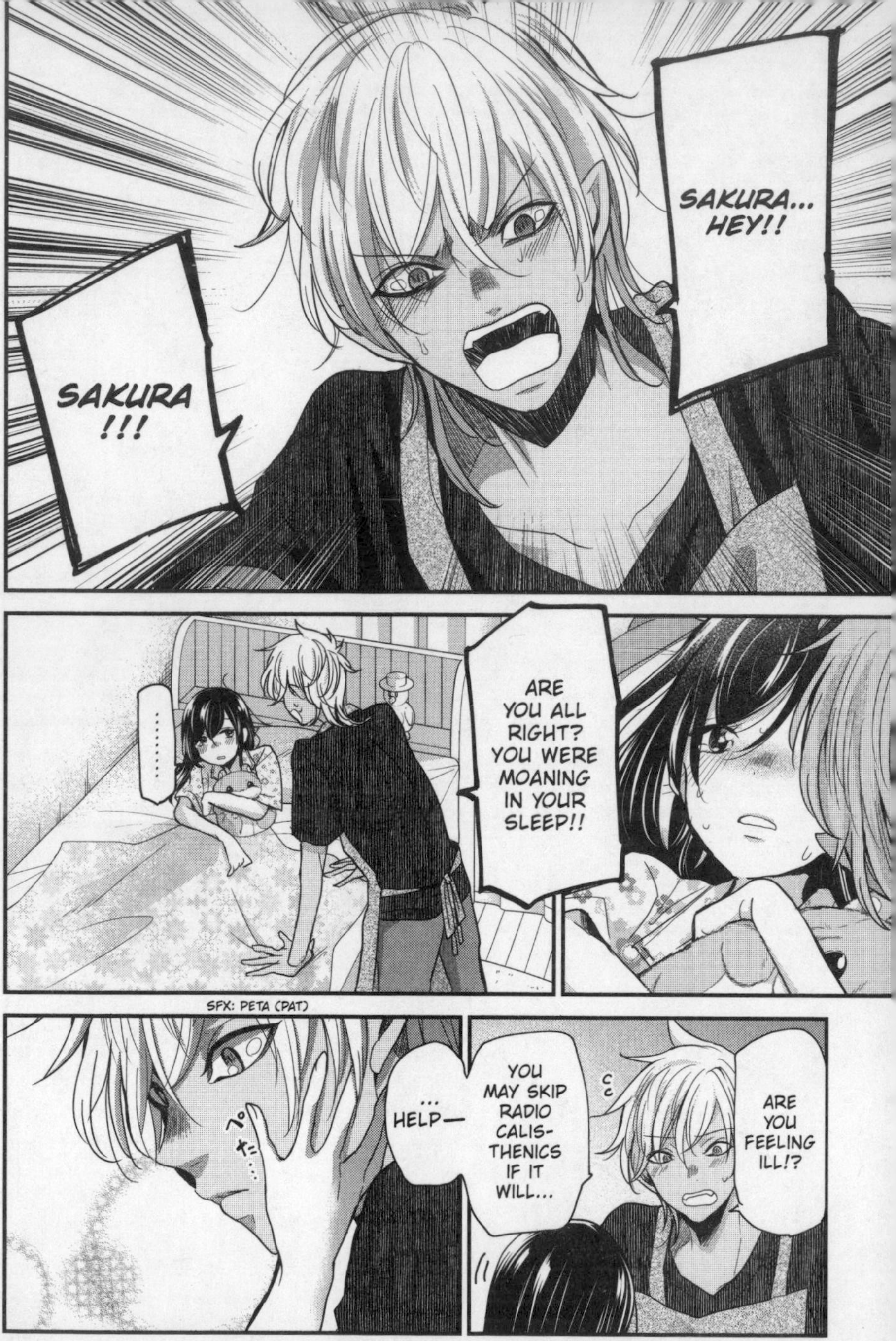
SAKURA... HEY!!
SAKURA !!!
ARE YOU ALL RIGHT? YOU WERE MOANING IN YOUR SLEEP!!
......
SFX: PETA (PAT)
ARE YOU FEELING ILL!?
YOU MAY SKIP RADIO CALIS-THENICS IF IT WILL...
...HELP—

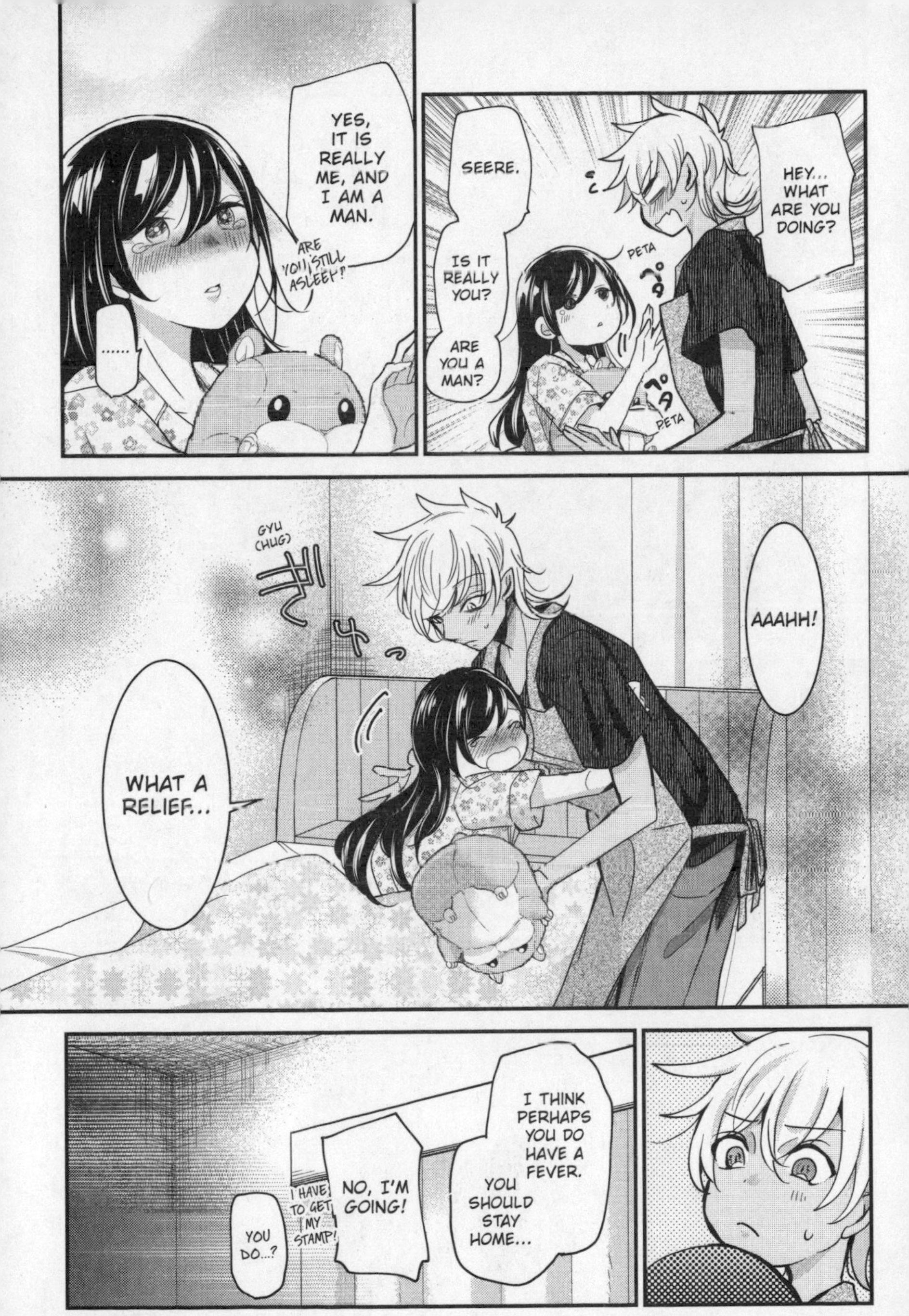
HEY... WHAT ARE YOU DOING?
SEERE.
PETA
IS IT REALLY YOU?
ARE YOU A MAN?
PETA
YES, IT IS REALLY ME, AND I AM A MAN.
ARE YOU STILL ASLEEP!?
......
AAAHH!
GYU (HUG)
WHAT A RELIEF...
I THINK PERHAPS YOU DO HAVE A FEVER.
YOU SHOULD STAY HOME...
NO, I'M GOING!
I HAVE TO GET MY STAMP!
YOU DO...?

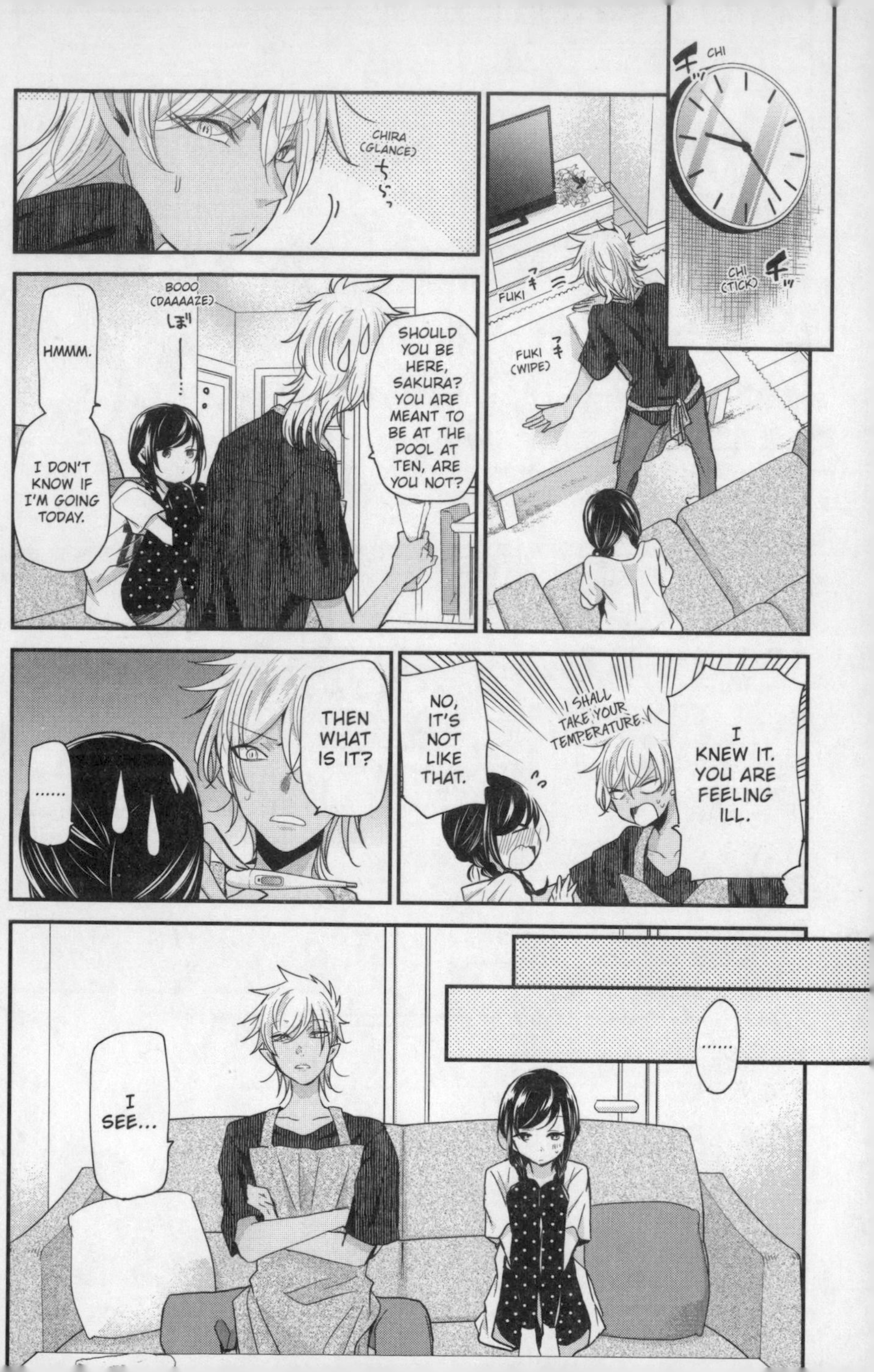
CHI
CHI (TICK)
FUKI
FUKI (WIPE)
CHIRA (GLANCE)
SHOULD YOU BE HERE, SAKURA? YOU ARE MEANT TO BE AT THE POOL AT TEN, ARE YOU NOT?
BOOO (DAAAAZE)
HMMM.
I DON'T KNOW IF I'M GOING TODAY.
I KNEW IT. YOU ARE FEELING ILL.
I SHALL TAKE YOUR TEMPERATURE.
NO, IT'S NOT LIKE THAT.
THEN WHAT IS IT?
......
......
I SEE...

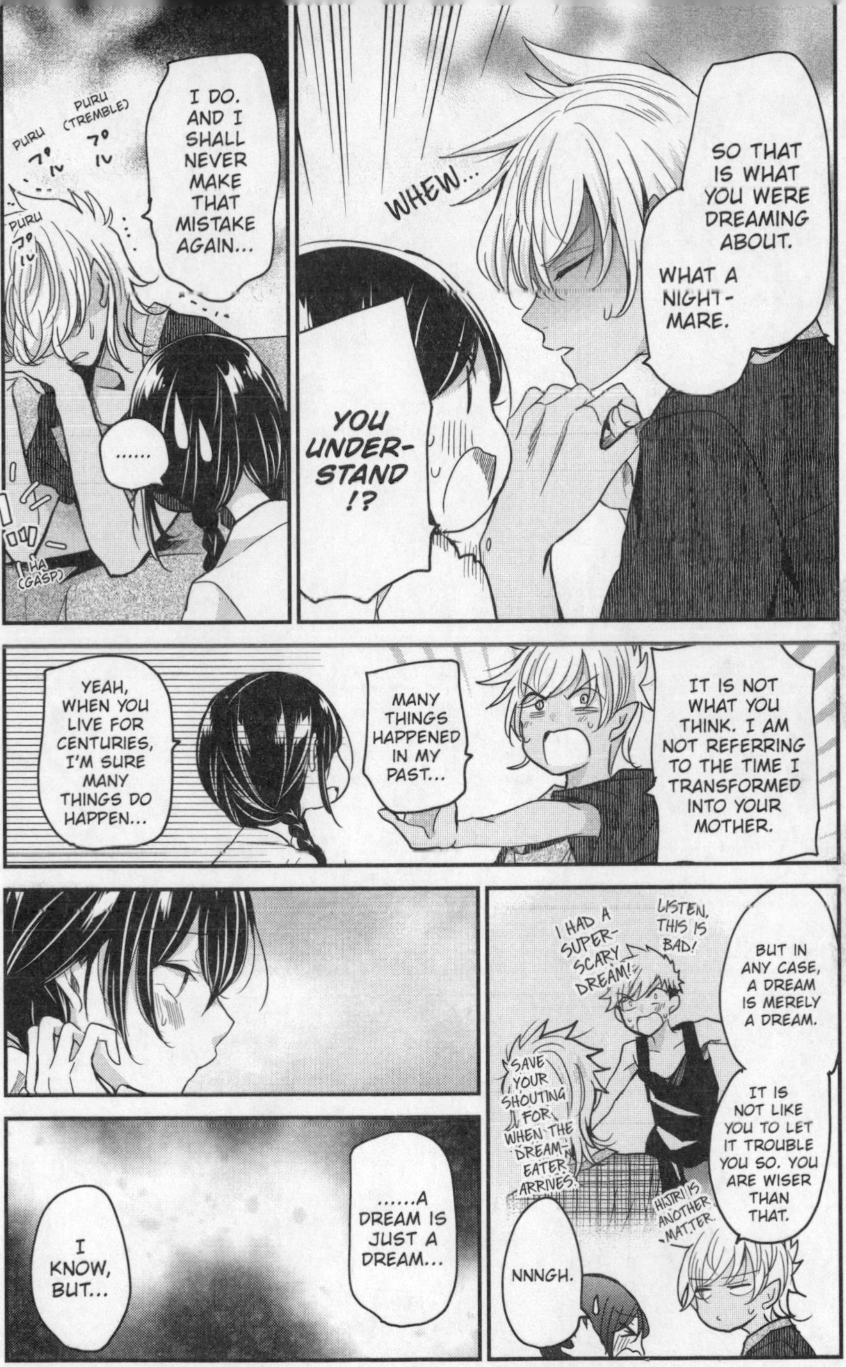
WHEW...
SO THAT IS WHAT YOU WERE DREAMING ABOUT.
WHAT A NIGHT-MARE.
YOU UNDER-STAND!?
I DO. AND I SHALL NEVER MAKE THAT MISTAKE AGAIN...
PURU PURU (TREMBLE)
PURU
......
HA (GASP)
IT IS NOT WHAT YOU THINK. I AM NOT REFERRING TO THE TIME I TRANSFORMED INTO YOUR MOTHER.
MANY THINGS HAPPENED IN MY PAST...
YEAH, WHEN YOU LIVE FOR CENTURIES, I'M SURE MANY THINGS DO HAPPEN...
BUT IN ANY CASE, A DREAM IS MERELY A DREAM.
IT IS NOT LIKE YOU TO LET IT TROUBLE YOU SO. YOU ARE WISER THAN THAT.
LISTEN, THIS IS BAD!
I HAD A SUPER-SCARY DREAM!
SAVE YOUR SHOUTING FOR WHEN THE DREAM-EATER ARRIVES.
HIJIRI IS ANOTHER MATTER.
NNNGH.
......A DREAM IS JUST A DREAM...
I KNOW, BUT...

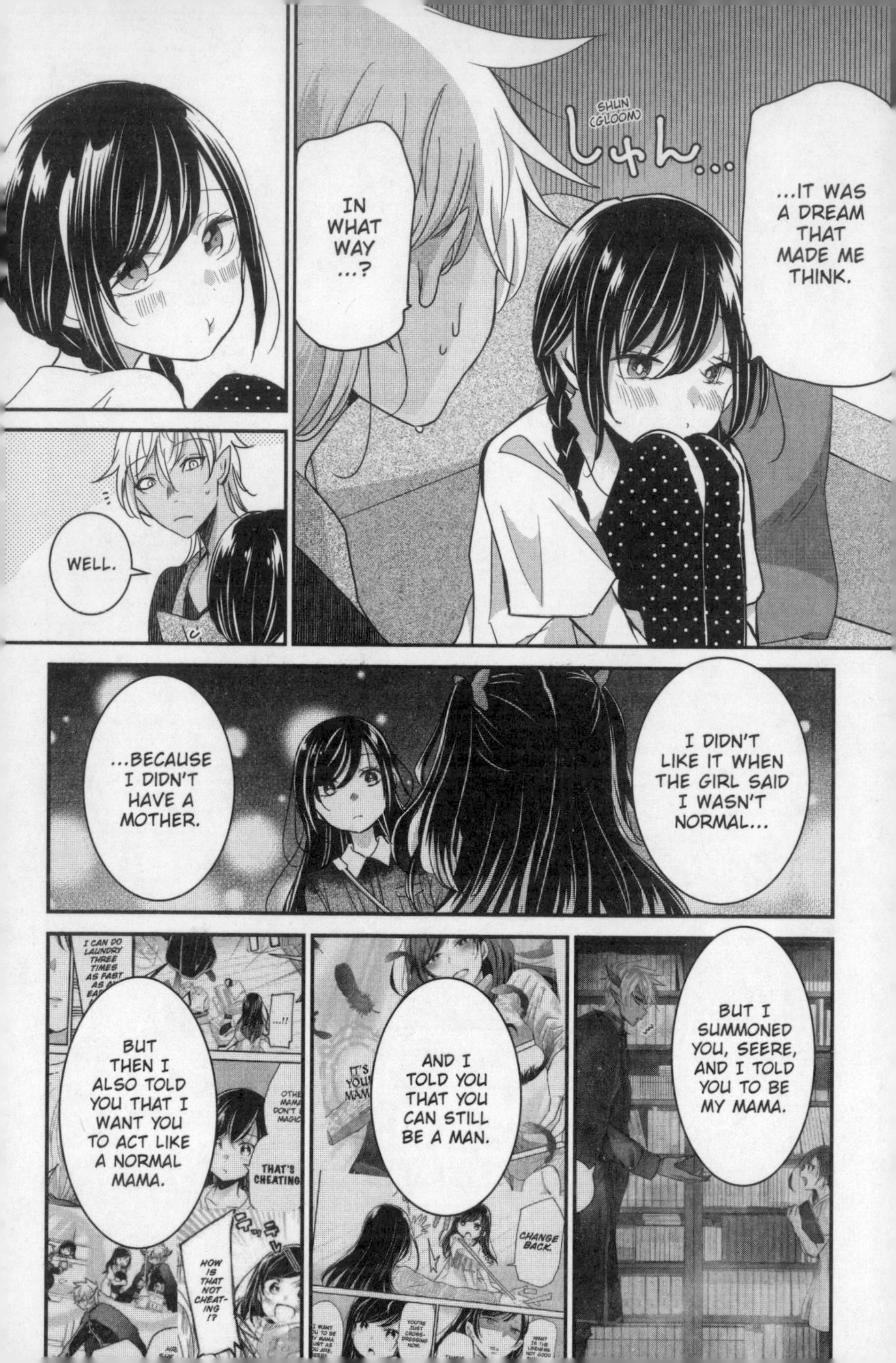
...IT WAS A DREAM THAT MADE ME THINK.
しゅん...
SHUN (GLOOM)
IN WHAT WAY ...?
WELL.
I DIDN'T LIKE IT WHEN THE GIRL SAID I WASN'T NORMAL...
...BECAUSE I DIDN'T HAVE A MOTHER.
BUT I SUMMONED YOU, SEERE, AND I TOLD YOU TO BE MY MAMA.
AND I TOLD YOU THAT YOU CAN STILL BE A MAN.
CHANGE BACK.
YOU'RE JUST CROSS-DRESSING NOW.
BUT THEN I ALSO TOLD YOU THAT I WANT YOU TO ACT LIKE A NORMAL MAMA.
I CAN DO LAUNDRY THREE TIMES AS FAST
...!!
THAT'S CHEATING!
HOW IS THAT NOT CHEATING !?

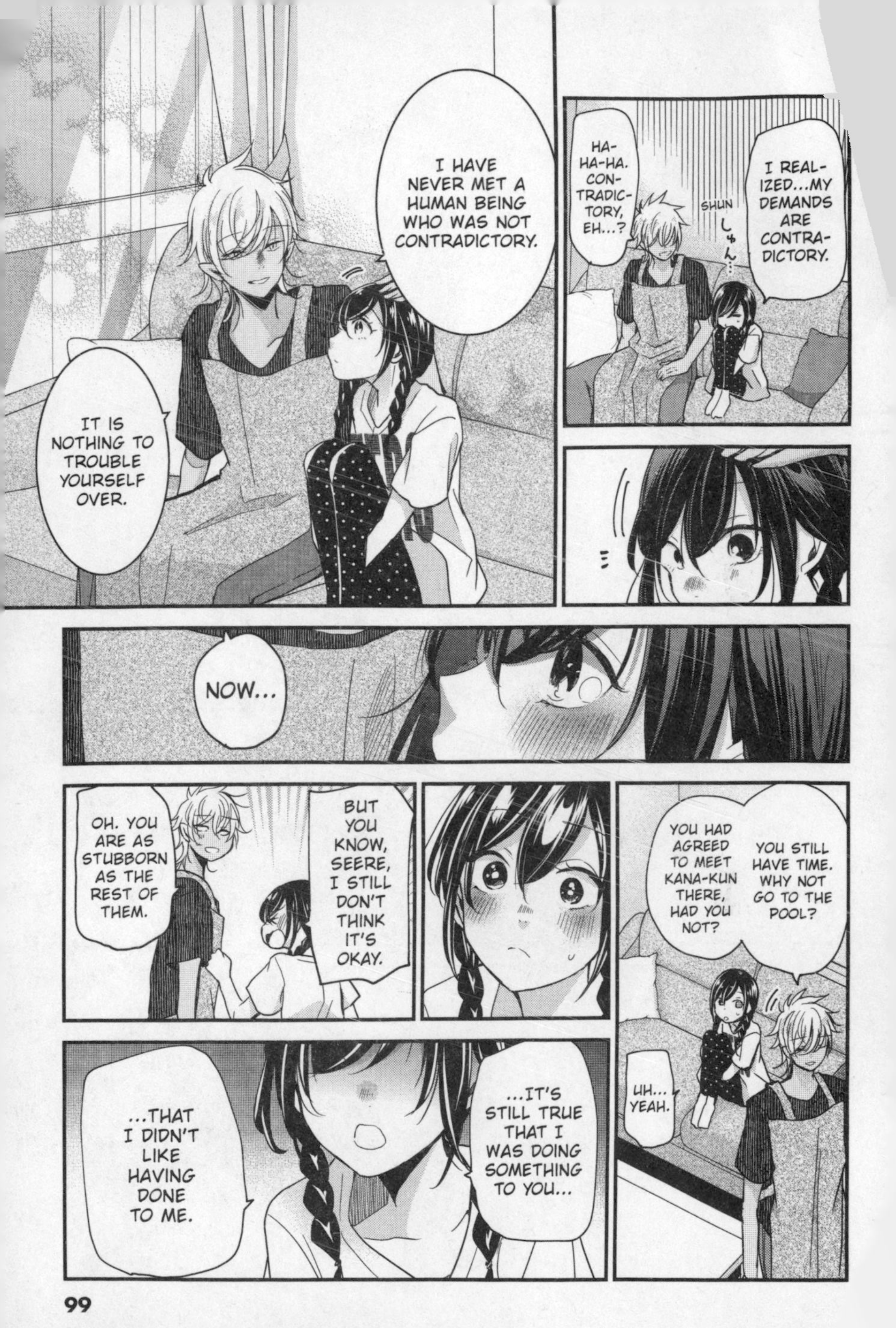
I REALIZED...MY DEMANDS ARE CONTRADICTORY.
SHUN
しゅん…
HA-HA-HA. CONTRADICTORY, EH...?
I HAVE NEVER MET A HUMAN BEING WHO WAS NOT CONTRADICTORY.
IT IS NOTHING TO TROUBLE YOURSELF OVER.
NOW...
YOU STILL HAVE TIME. WHY NOT GO TO THE POOL?
YOU HAD AGREED TO MEET KANA-KUN THERE, HAD YOU NOT?
UH... YEAH.
BUT YOU KNOW, SEERE, I STILL DON'T THINK IT'S OKAY.
OH. YOU ARE AS STUBBORN AS THE REST OF THEM.
...IT'S STILL TRUE THAT I WAS DOING SOMETHING TO YOU...
...THAT I DIDN'T LIKE HAVING DONE TO ME.

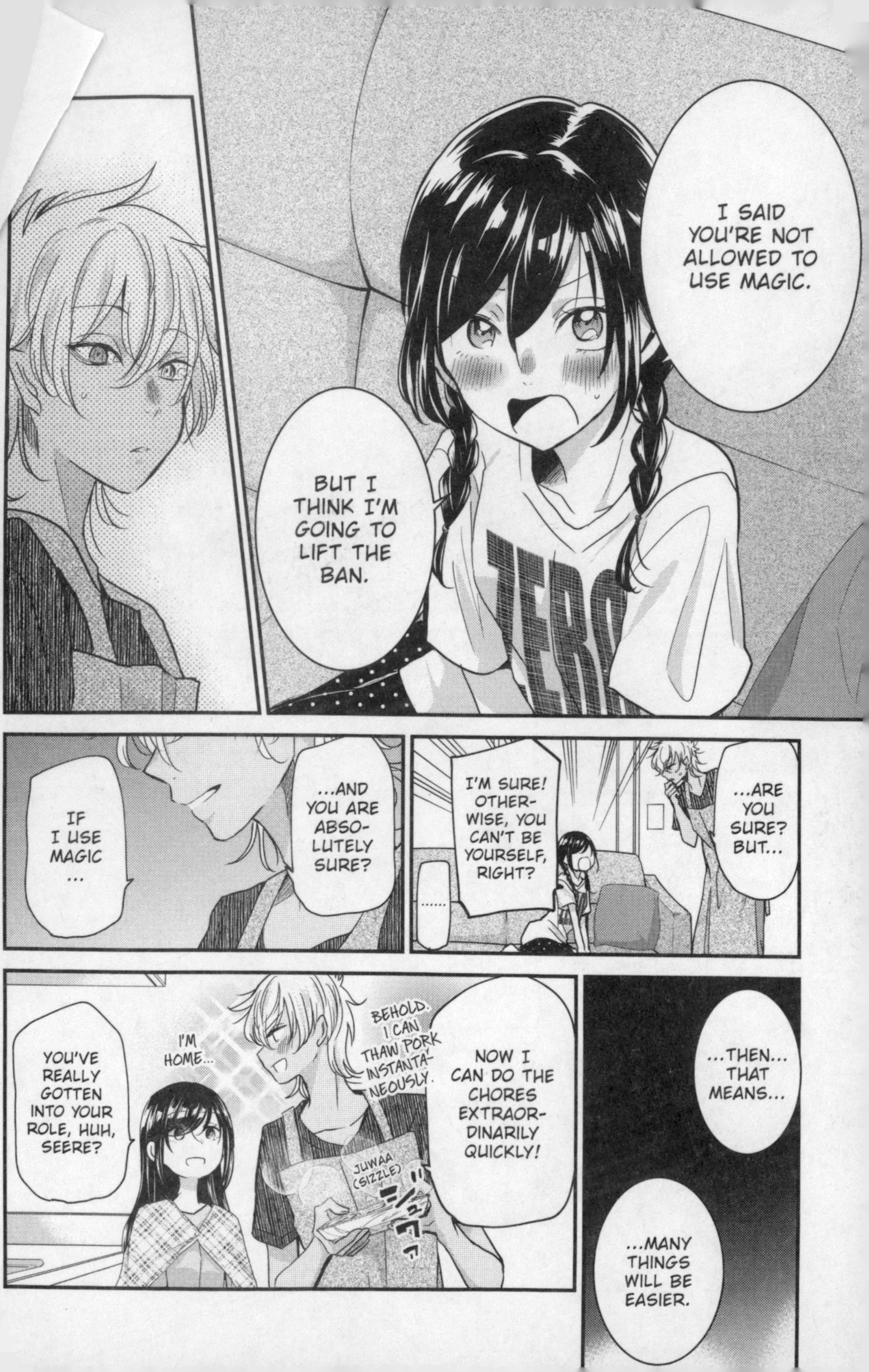
I SAID YOU'RE NOT ALLOWED TO USE MAGIC.
BUT I THINK I'M GOING TO LIFT THE BAN.
...ARE YOU SURE? BUT...
I'M SURE! OTHERWISE, YOU CAN'T BE YOURSELF, RIGHT?
......
...AND YOU ARE ABSOLUTELY SURE?
IF I USE MAGIC...
...THEN... THAT MEANS...
...MANY THINGS WILL BE EASIER.
NOW I CAN DO THE CHORES EXTRAORDINARILY QUICKLY!
BEHOLD. I CAN THAW PORK INSTANTANEOUSLY.
I'M HOME...
YOU'VE REALLY GOTTEN INTO YOUR ROLE, HUH, SEERE?
JUWAA (SIZZLE)

# Day 17

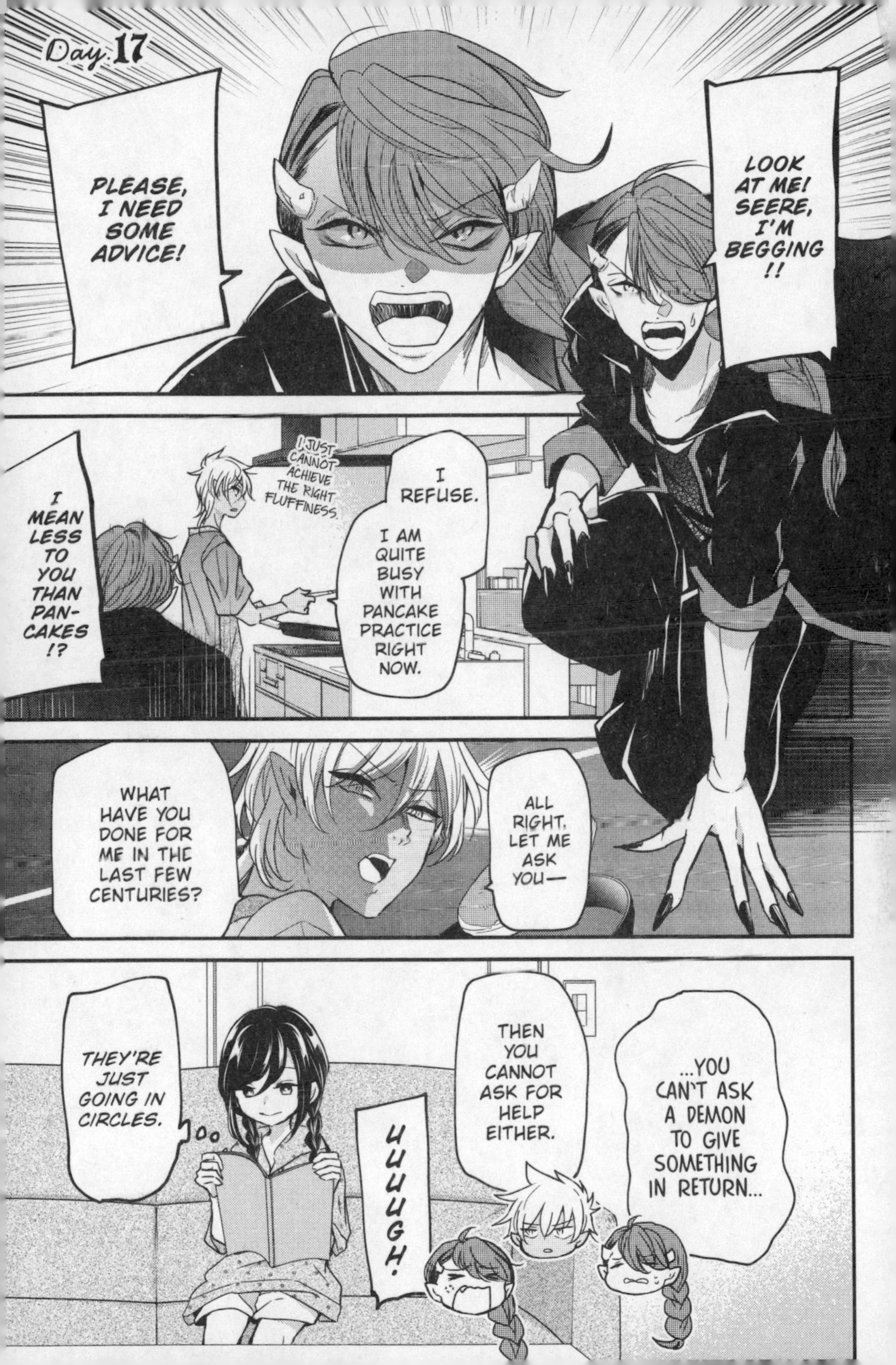
LOOK AT ME! SEERE, I'M BEGGING !!
PLEASE, I NEED SOME ADVICE!
I REFUSE.
I AM QUITE BUSY WITH PANCAKE PRACTICE RIGHT NOW.
I JUST CANNOT ACHIEVE THE RIGHT FLUFFINESS.
I MEAN LESS TO YOU THAN PAN-CAKES !?
ALL RIGHT. LET ME ASK YOU—
WHAT HAVE YOU DONE FOR ME IN THE LAST FEW CENTURIES?
...YOU CAN'T ASK A DEMON TO GIVE SOMETHING IN RETURN...
THEN YOU CANNOT ASK FOR HELP EITHER.
UUUUGH!
THEY'RE JUST GOING IN CIRCLES.

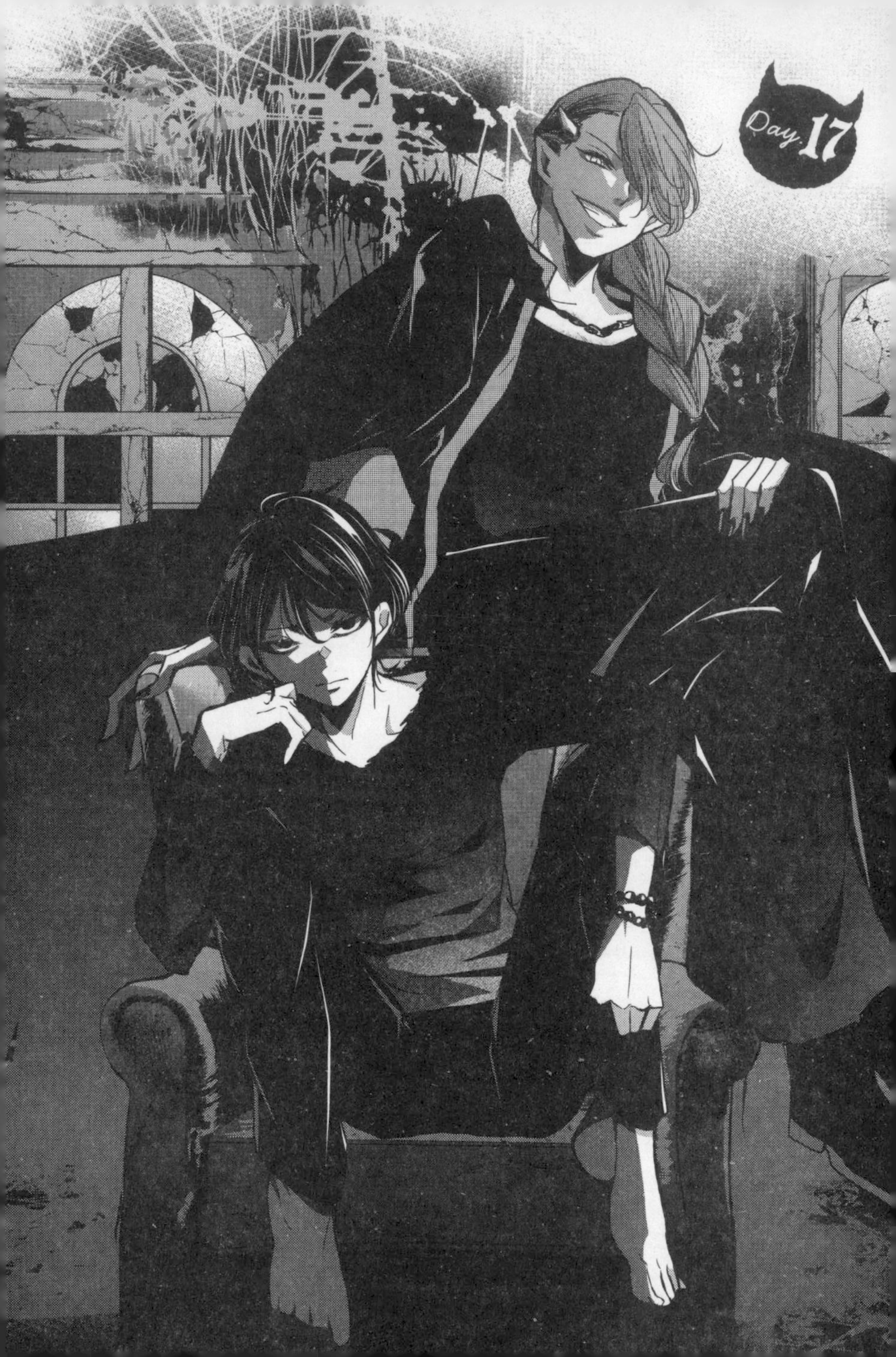
Day 17

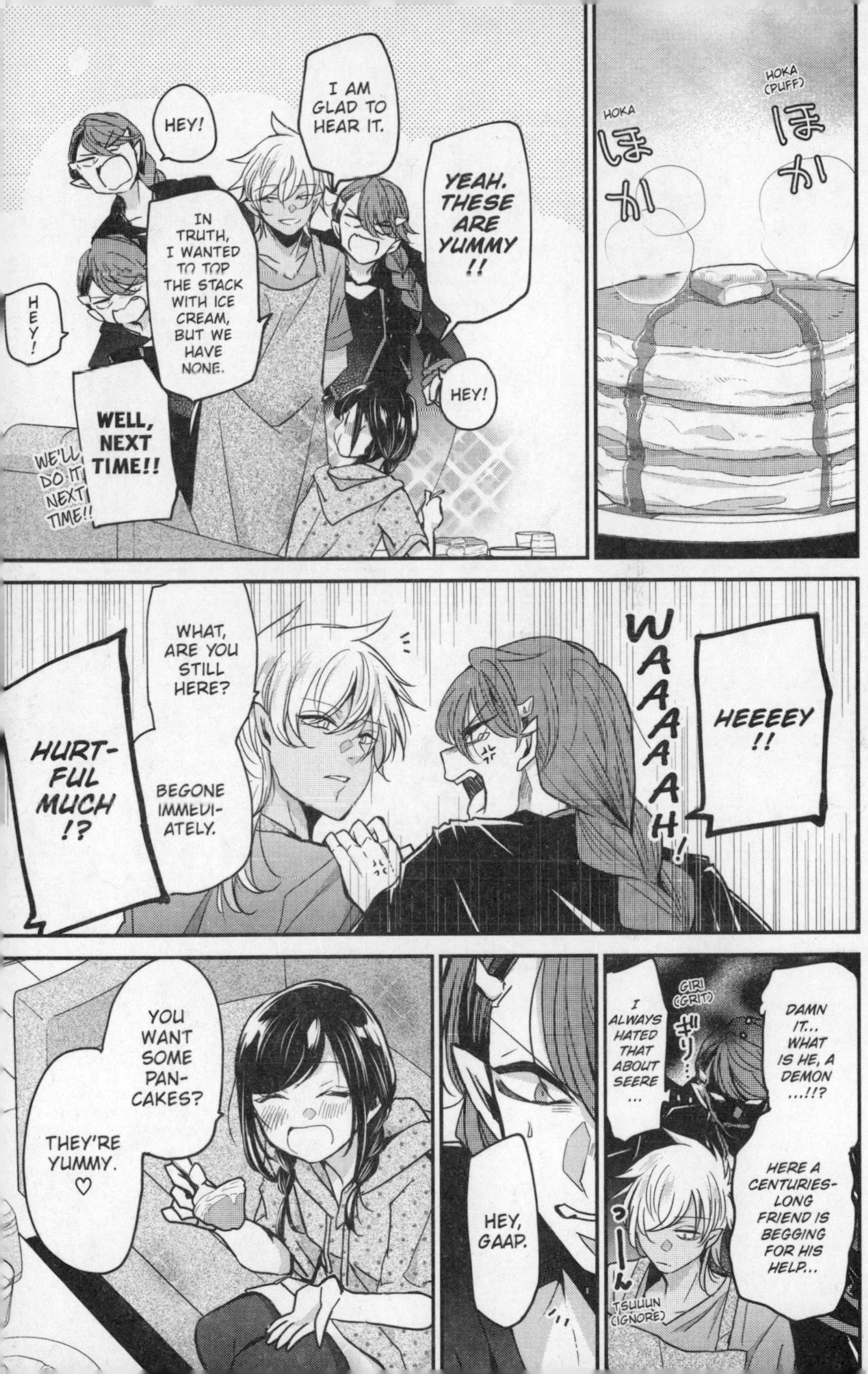
HOKA (PUFF)
ほか
HOKA
ほか
YEAH. THESE ARE YUMMY!!
I AM GLAD TO HEAR IT.
HEY!
IN TRUTH, I WANTED TO TOP THE STACK WITH ICE CREAM, BUT WE HAVE NONE.
HEY!
HEY!
WELL, NEXT TIME!!
WE'LL DO IT NEXT TIME!!
HEEEEY!!
WAAAAAAH!
WHAT, ARE YOU STILL HERE?
BEGONE IMMEDIATELY.
HURTFUL MUCH!?
DAMN IT... WHAT IS HE, A DEMON...!!?
GIRI (GRIT)
I ALWAYS HATED THAT ABOUT SEERE...
HERE A CENTURIES-LONG FRIEND IS BEGGING FOR HIS HELP...
TSUUUN (IGNORE)
HEY, GAAP.
YOU WANT SOME PANCAKES?
THEY'RE YUMMY. ♡

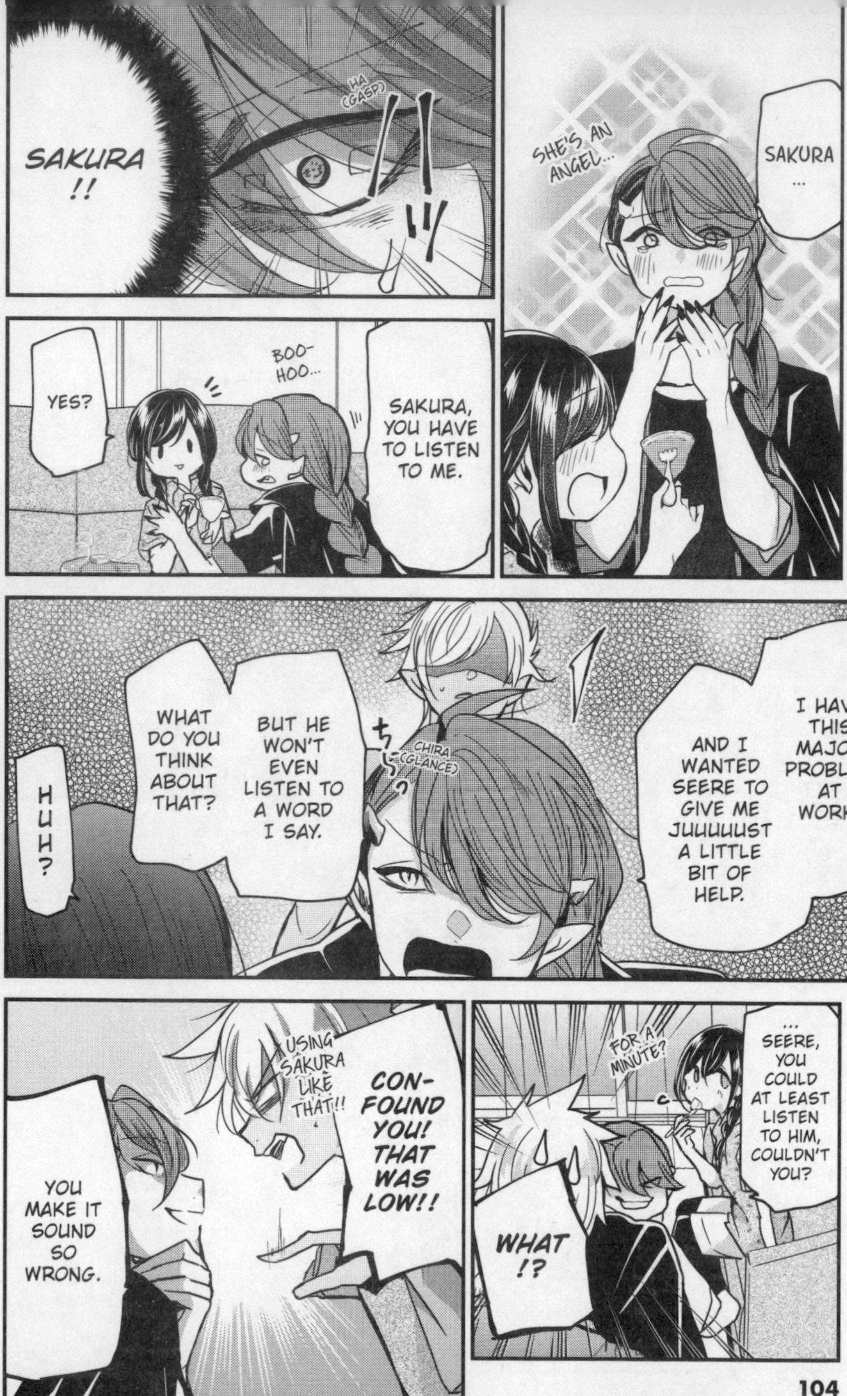
SAKURA ...
SHE'S AN ANGEL...
HA (GASP)
SAKURA !!
SAKURA, YOU HAVE TO LISTEN TO ME.
BOO-HOO...
YES?
I HAVE THIS MAJOR PROBLEM AT WORK.
AND I WANTED SEERE TO GIVE ME JUUUUUST A LITTLE BIT OF HELP.
CHIRA (GLANCE)
BUT HE WON'T EVEN LISTEN TO A WORD I SAY.
WHAT DO YOU THINK ABOUT THAT?
HUH?
... SEERE, YOU COULD AT LEAST LISTEN TO HIM, COULDN'T YOU?
FOR A MINUTE?
WHAT !?
CON-FOUND YOU! THAT WAS LOW!!
USING SAKURA LIKE THAT!!
YOU MAKE IT SOUND SO WRONG.

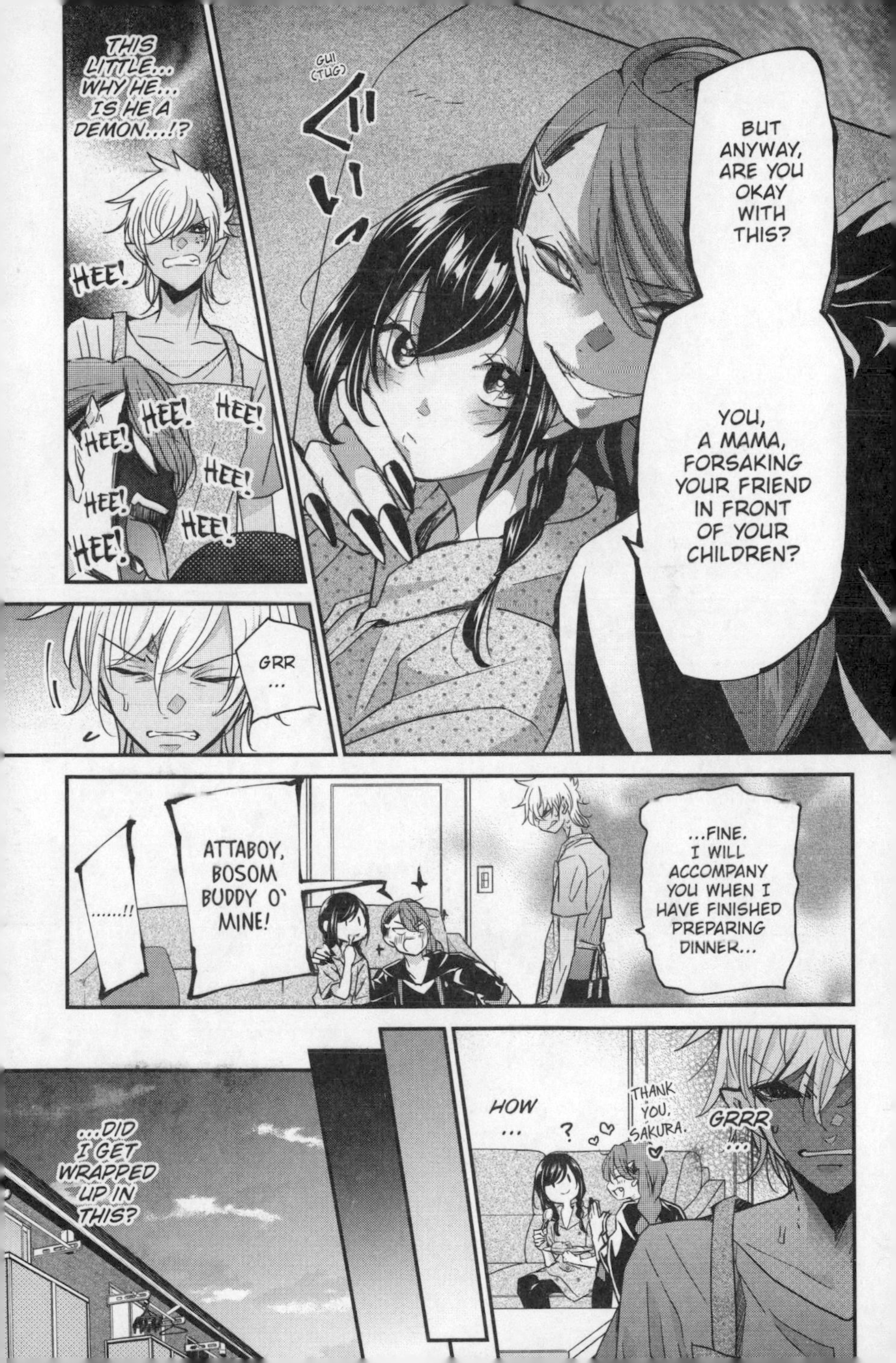
BUT ANYWAY, ARE YOU OKAY WITH THIS?
YOU, A MAMA, FORSAKING YOUR FRIEND IN FRONT OF YOUR CHILDREN?
GUI (TUG)
THIS LITTLE... WHY HE... IS HE A DEMON...!?
HEE! HEE! HEE! HEE! HEE! HEE! HEE! HEE!
GRR ...
...FINE. I WILL ACCOMPANY YOU WHEN I HAVE FINISHED PREPARING DINNER...
ATTABOY, BOSOM BUDDY O' MINE!
......!!
THANK YOU, SAKURA.
GRRR ...
HOW ...
?
...DID I GET WRAPPED UP IN THIS?

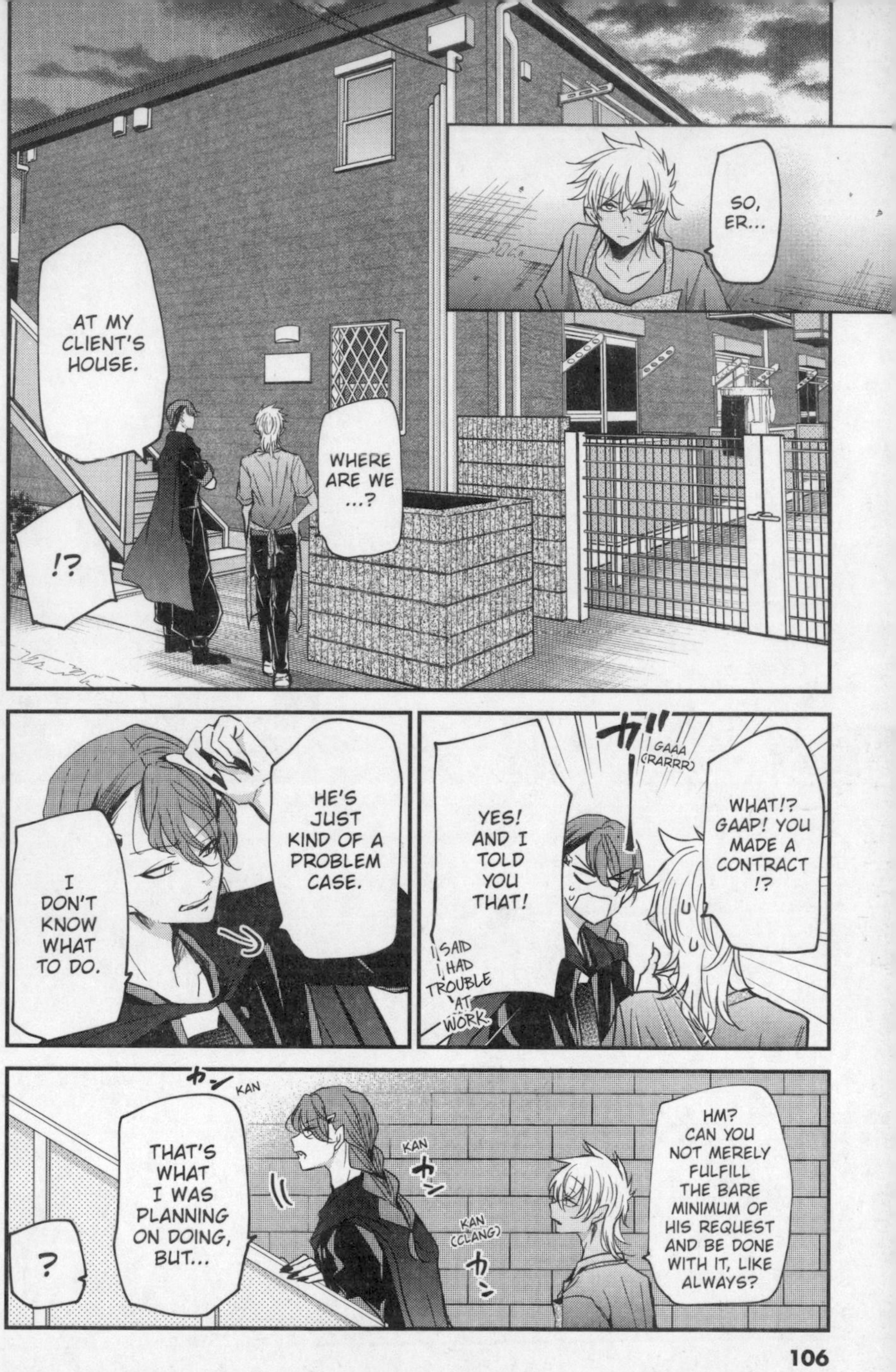
SO, ER...
WHERE ARE WE ...?
AT MY CLIENT'S HOUSE.
!?
GAAA (RARRR)
WHAT!? GAAP! YOU MADE A CONTRACT !?
YES! AND I TOLD YOU THAT!
I SAID I HAD TROUBLE AT WORK.
HE'S JUST KIND OF A PROBLEM CASE.
I DON'T KNOW WHAT TO DO.
HM? CAN YOU NOT MERELY FULFILL THE BARE MINIMUM OF HIS REQUEST AND BE DONE WITH IT, LIKE ALWAYS?
KAN (CLANG)
KAN
KAN
THAT'S WHAT I WAS PLANNING ON DOING, BUT...
?

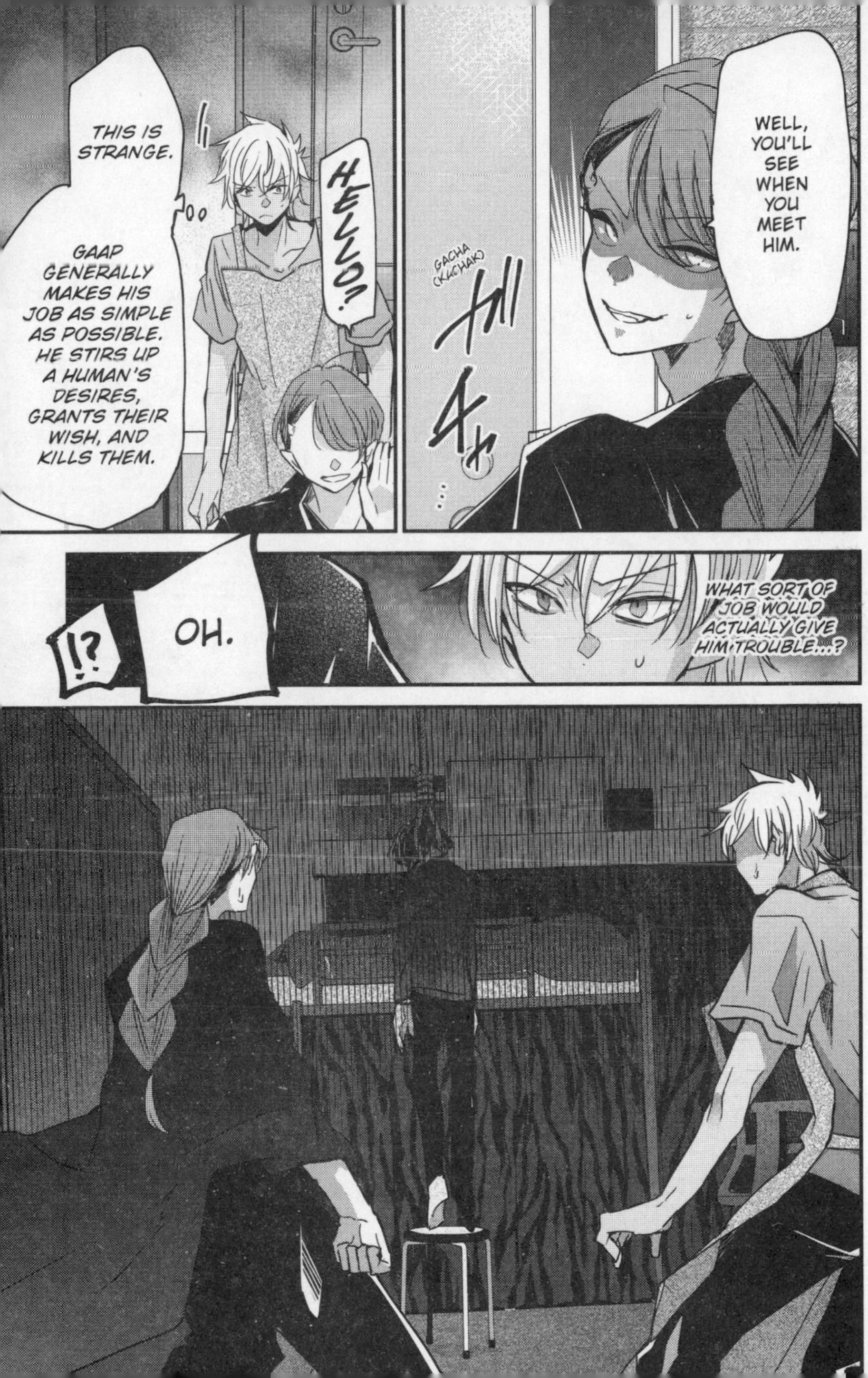
WELL, YOU'LL SEE WHEN YOU MEET HIM.
GACHA (KACHAK)
HELLO?
THIS IS STRANGE.
GAAP GENERALLY MAKES HIS JOB AS SIMPLE AS POSSIBLE. HE STIRS UP A HUMAN'S DESIRES, GRANTS THEIR WISH, AND KILLS THEM.
WHAT SORT OF JOB WOULD ACTUALLY GIVE HIM TROUBLE...?
OH.
!?

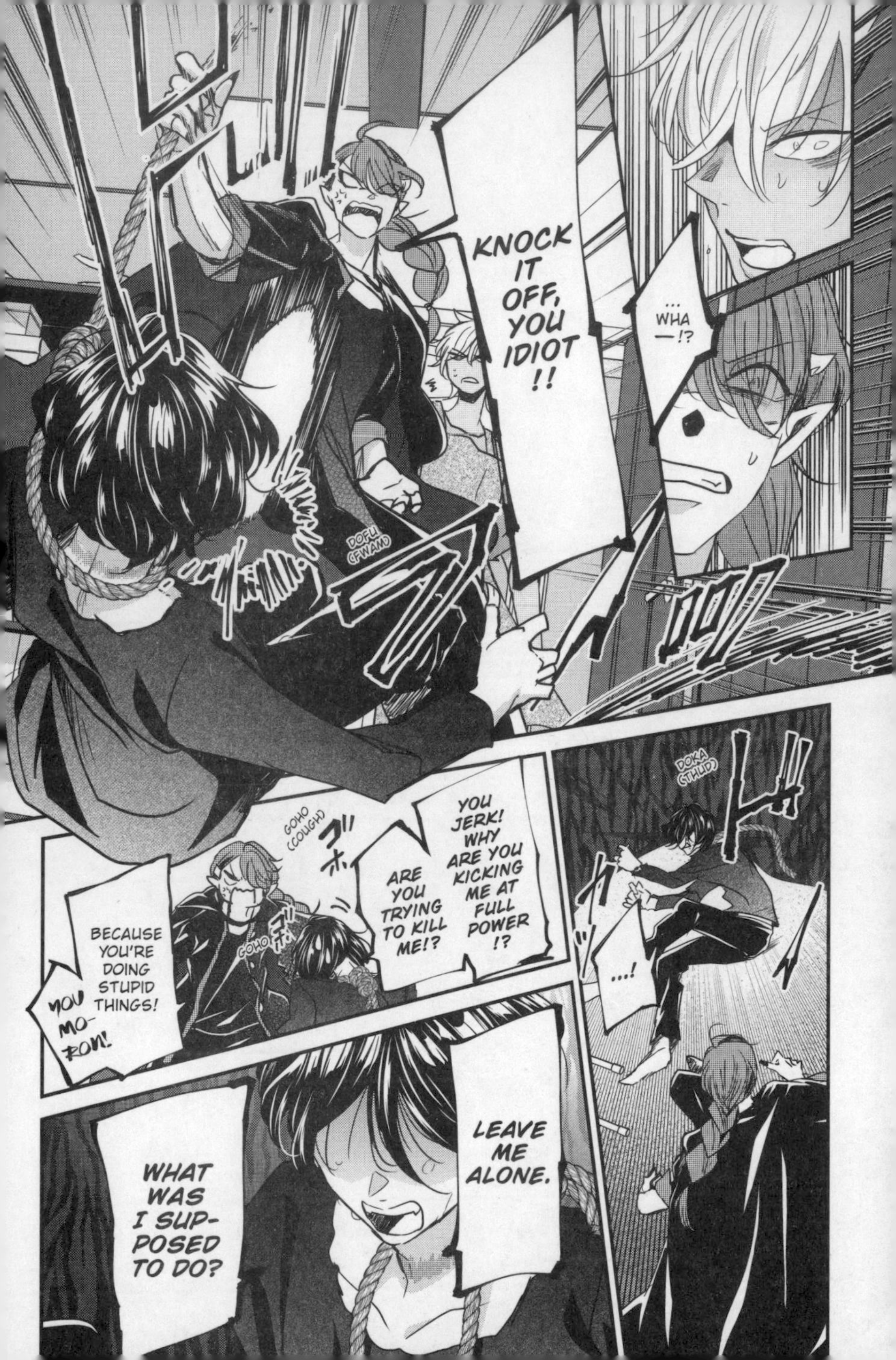

... WHA—!?
KNOCK IT OFF, YOU IDIOT!!
DOFU (FWAM)
DOKA (THUD)
...!
YOU JERK! WHY ARE YOU KICKING ME AT FULL POWER!?
ARE YOU TRYING TO KILL ME!?
GOHO (COUGH)
GOHO
BECAUSE YOU'RE DOING STUPID THINGS!
YOU MORON!
LEAVE ME ALONE.
WHAT WAS I SUPPOSED TO DO?

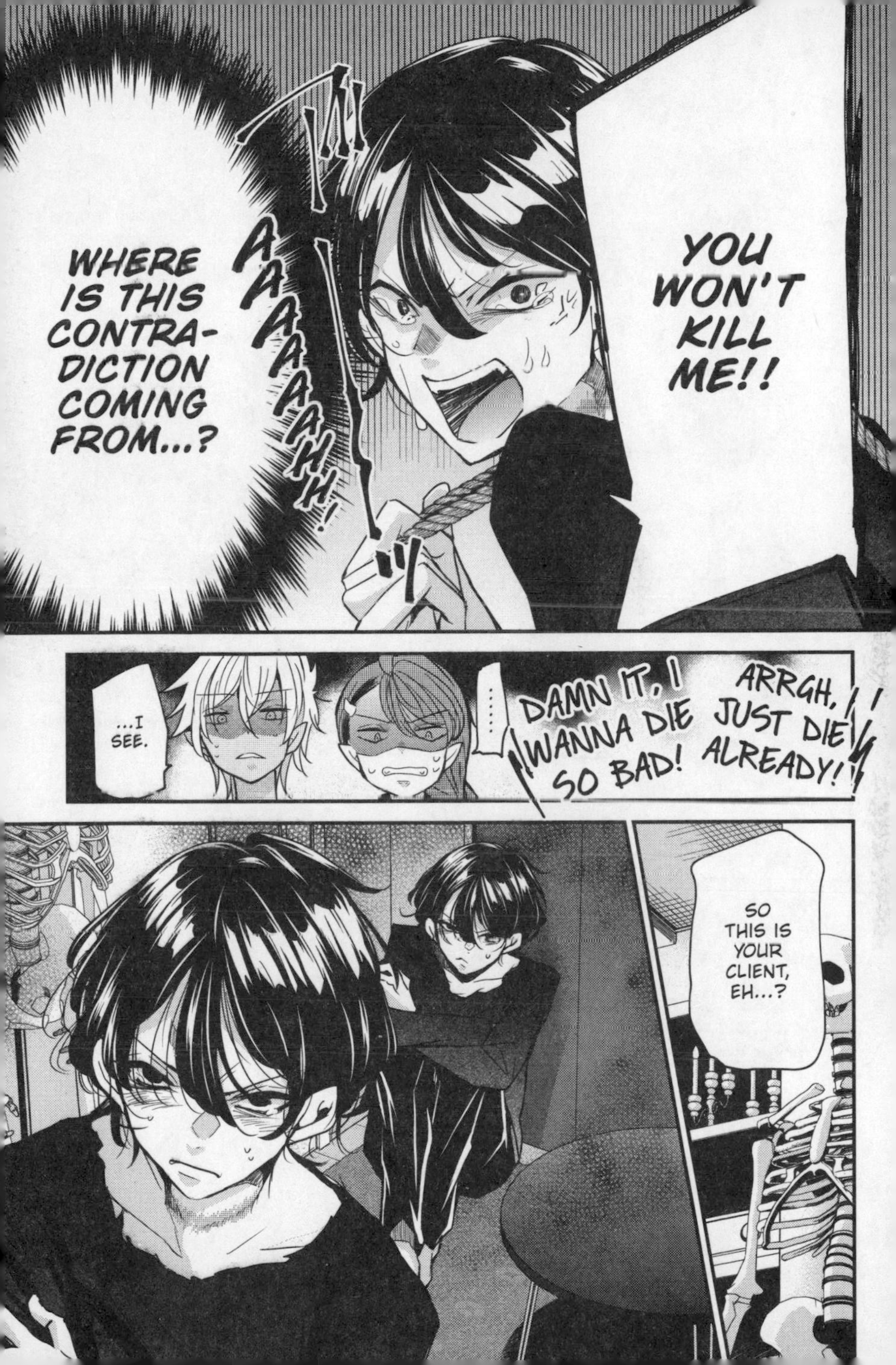
YOU WON'T KILL ME!!
AAAAAAHH!
WHERE IS THIS CONTRA-DICTION COMING FROM...?
ARRGH, JUST DIE ALREADY!
DAMN IT, I WANNA DIE SO BAD!
...
...I SEE.
SO THIS IS YOUR CLIENT, EH...?

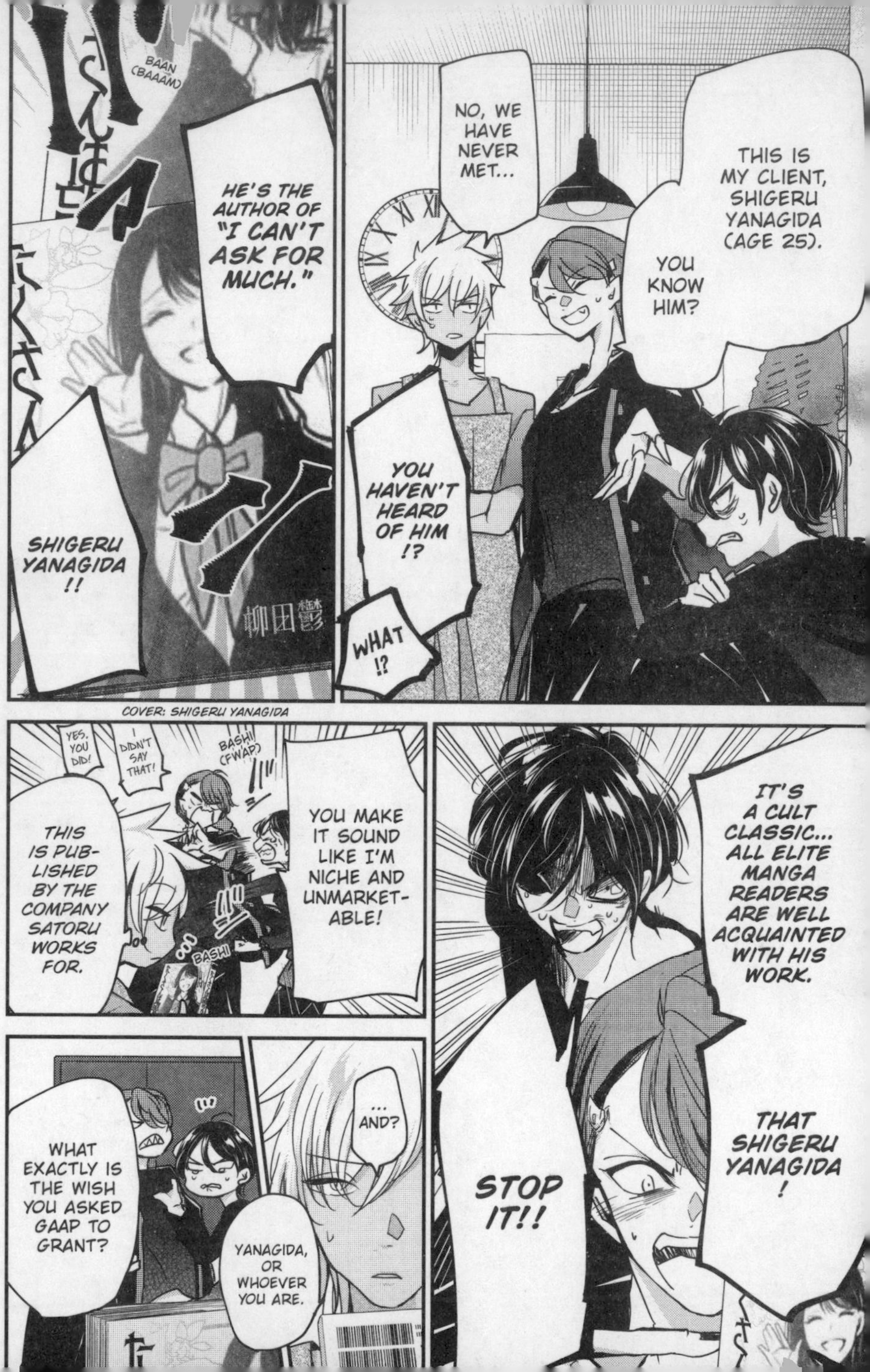
THIS IS MY CLIENT, SHIGERU YANAGIDA (AGE 25).
YOU KNOW HIM?
NO, WE HAVE NEVER MET...
YOU HAVEN'T HEARD OF HIM!?
WHAT!?
BAAN (BAAAM)
HE'S THE AUTHOR OF "I CAN'T ASK FOR MUCH."
SHIGERU YANAGIDA!!
柳田鬱
COVER: SHIGERU YANAGIDA
IT'S A CULT CLASSIC... ALL ELITE MANGA READERS ARE WELL ACQUAINTED WITH HIS WORK.
THAT SHIGERU YANAGIDA!
STOP IT!!
YOU MAKE IT SOUND LIKE I'M NICHE AND UNMARKETABLE!
BASHI (FWAP)
I DIDN'T SAY THAT!
YES, YOU DID!
THIS IS PUBLISHED BY THE COMPANY SATORU WORKS FOR.
BASHI
...AND?
YANAGIDA, OR WHOEVER YOU ARE.
WHAT EXACTLY IS THE WISH YOU ASKED GAAP TO GRANT?

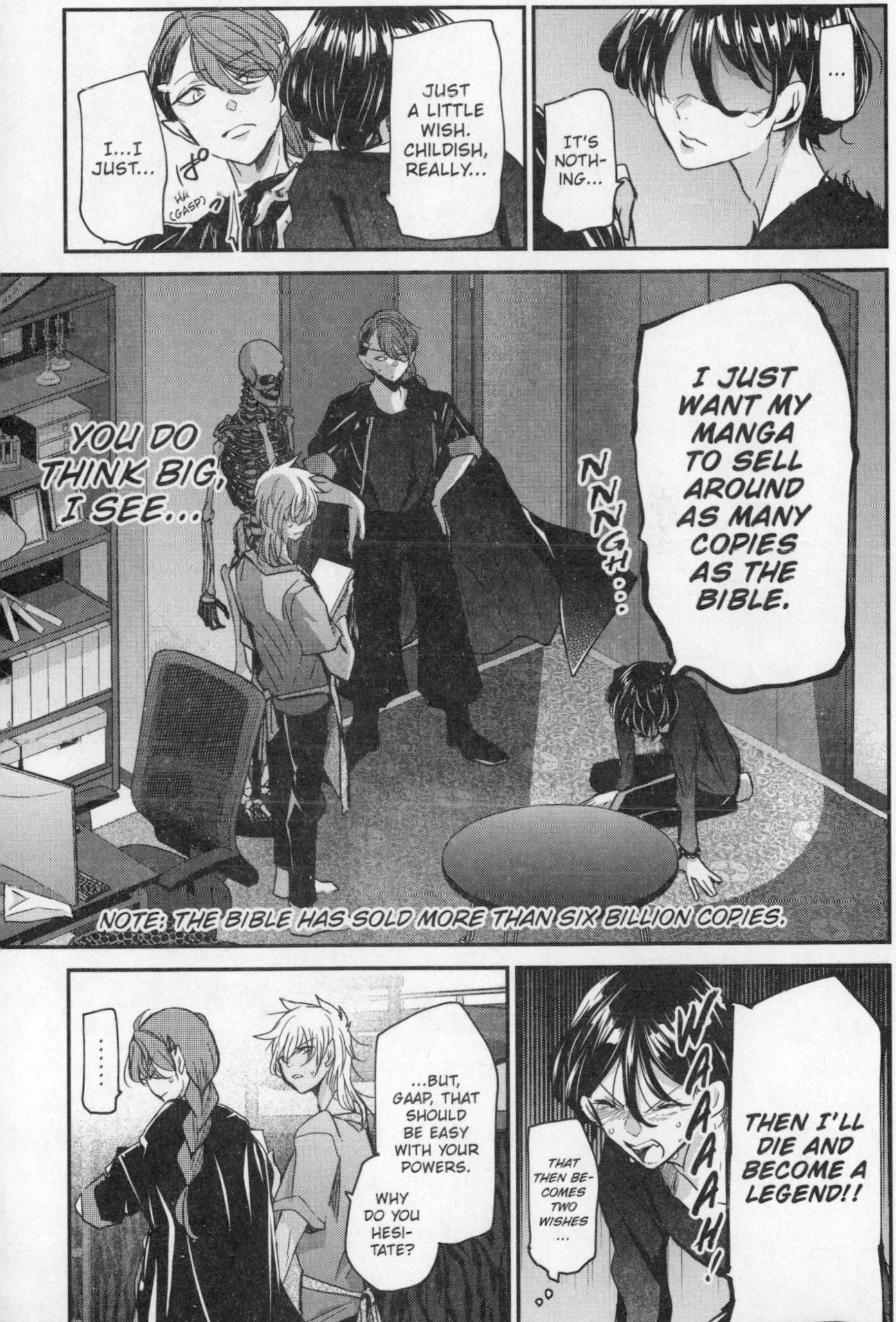
...
IT'S NOTHING...
JUST A LITTLE WISH. CHILDISH, REALLY...
I...I JUST...
ぱ
HA (GASP)
I JUST WANT MY MANGA TO SELL AROUND AS MANY COPIES AS THE BIBLE.
NNNGH...
YOU DO THINK BIG, I SEE...
NOTE: THE BIBLE HAS SOLD MORE THAN SIX BILLION COPIES.
THEN I'LL DIE AND BECOME A LEGEND!!
WAAAAAH!
THAT THEN BECOMES TWO WISHES...
...BUT, GAAP, THAT SHOULD BE EASY WITH YOUR POWERS.
WHY DO YOU HESITATE?
......

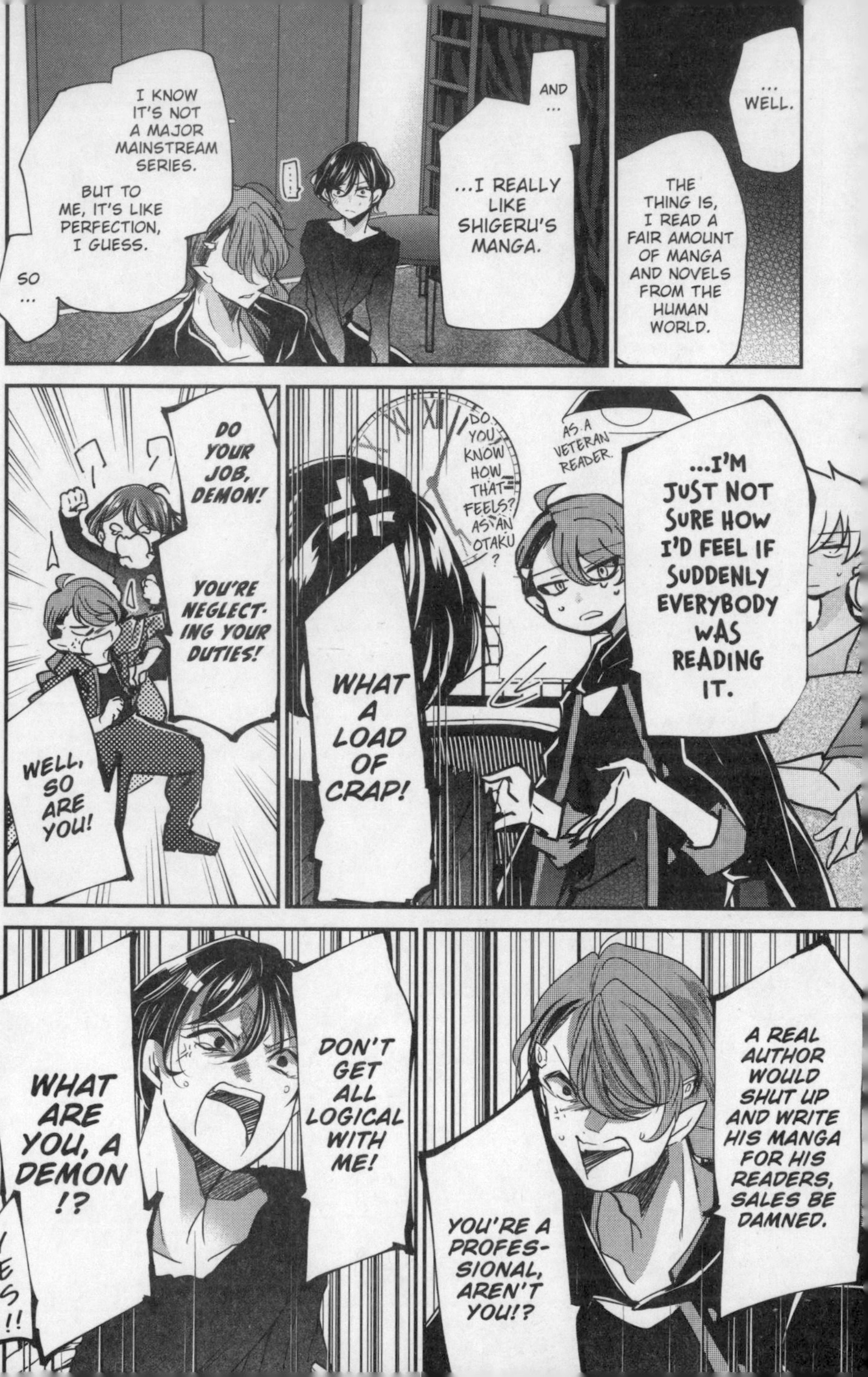
... WELL.
THE THING IS, I READ A FAIR AMOUNT OF MANGA AND NOVELS FROM THE HUMAN WORLD.
AND ...
...I REALLY LIKE SHIGERU'S MANGA.
I KNOW IT'S NOT A MAJOR MAINSTREAM SERIES.
BUT TO ME, IT'S LIKE PERFECTION, I GUESS.
SO ...
...I'M JUST NOT SURE HOW I'D FEEL IF SUDDENLY EVERYBODY WAS READING IT.
AS A VETERAN READER.
DO YOU KNOW HOW THAT FEELS? AS AN OTAKU?
WHAT A LOAD OF CRAP!
DO YOUR JOB, DEMON!
YOU'RE NEGLECTING YOUR DUTIES!
WELL, SO ARE YOU!
A REAL AUTHOR WOULD SHUT UP AND WRITE HIS MANGA FOR HIS READERS, SALES BE DAMNED.
YOU'RE A PROFESSIONAL, AREN'T YOU!?
DON'T GET ALL LOGICAL WITH ME!
WHAT ARE YOU, A DEMON!?
YES!!

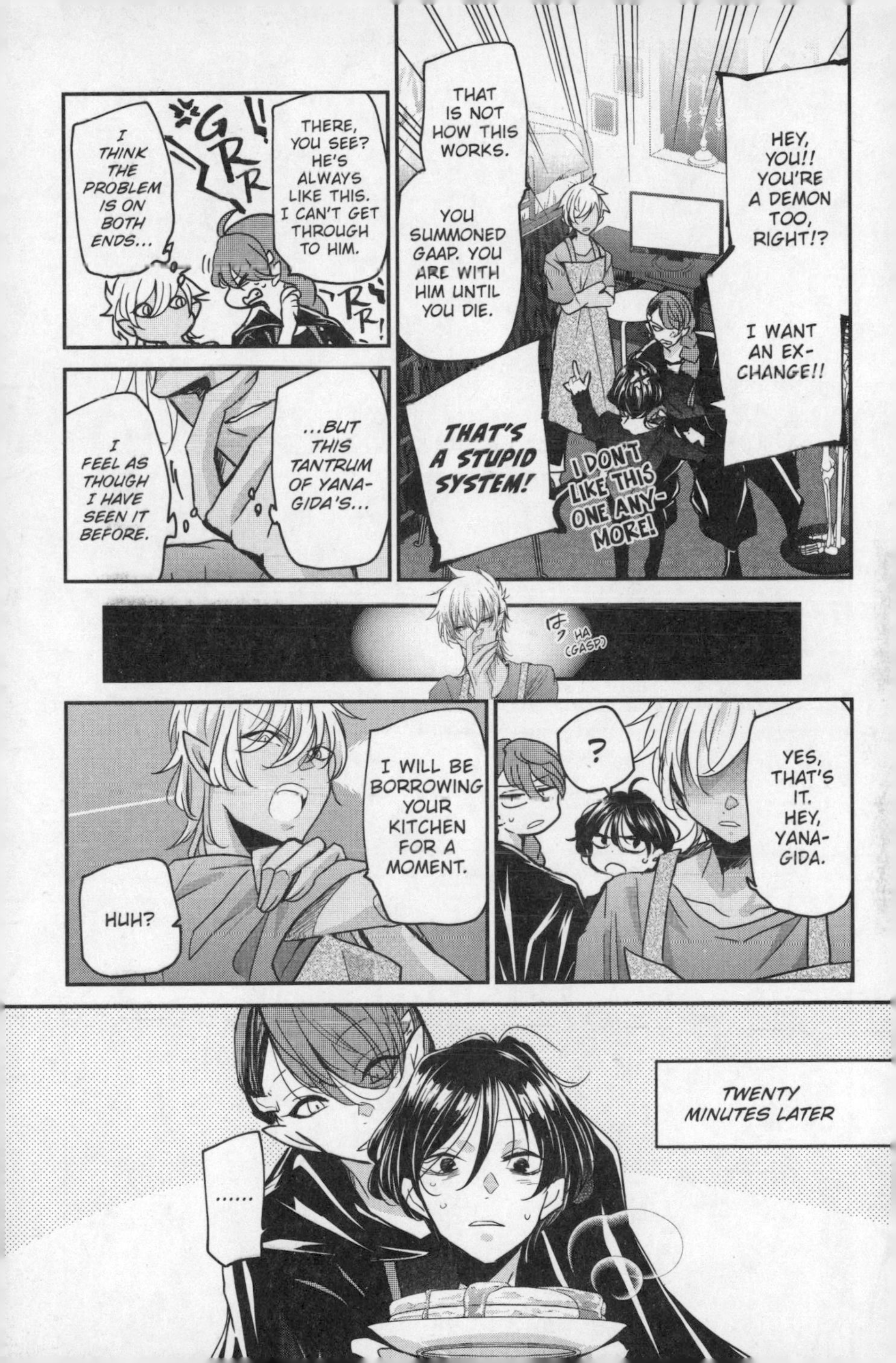
HEY, YOU!! YOU'RE A DEMON TOO, RIGHT!?
I WANT AN EX-CHANGE!!
THAT IS NOT HOW THIS WORKS.
YOU SUMMONED GAAP. YOU ARE WITH HIM UNTIL YOU DIE.
I DON'T LIKE THIS ONE ANY-MORE!
THAT'S A STUPID SYSTEM!
THERE, YOU SEE? HE'S ALWAYS LIKE THIS. I CAN'T GET THROUGH TO HIM.
GRR
RR
I THINK THE PROBLEM IS ON BOTH ENDS...
...BUT THIS TANTRUM OF YANA-GIDA'S...
I FEEL AS THOUGH I HAVE SEEN IT BEFORE.
HA (GASP)
YES, THAT'S IT. HEY, YANA-GIDA.
?
I WILL BE BORROWING YOUR KITCHEN FOR A MOMENT.
HUH?
TWENTY MINUTES LATER
......

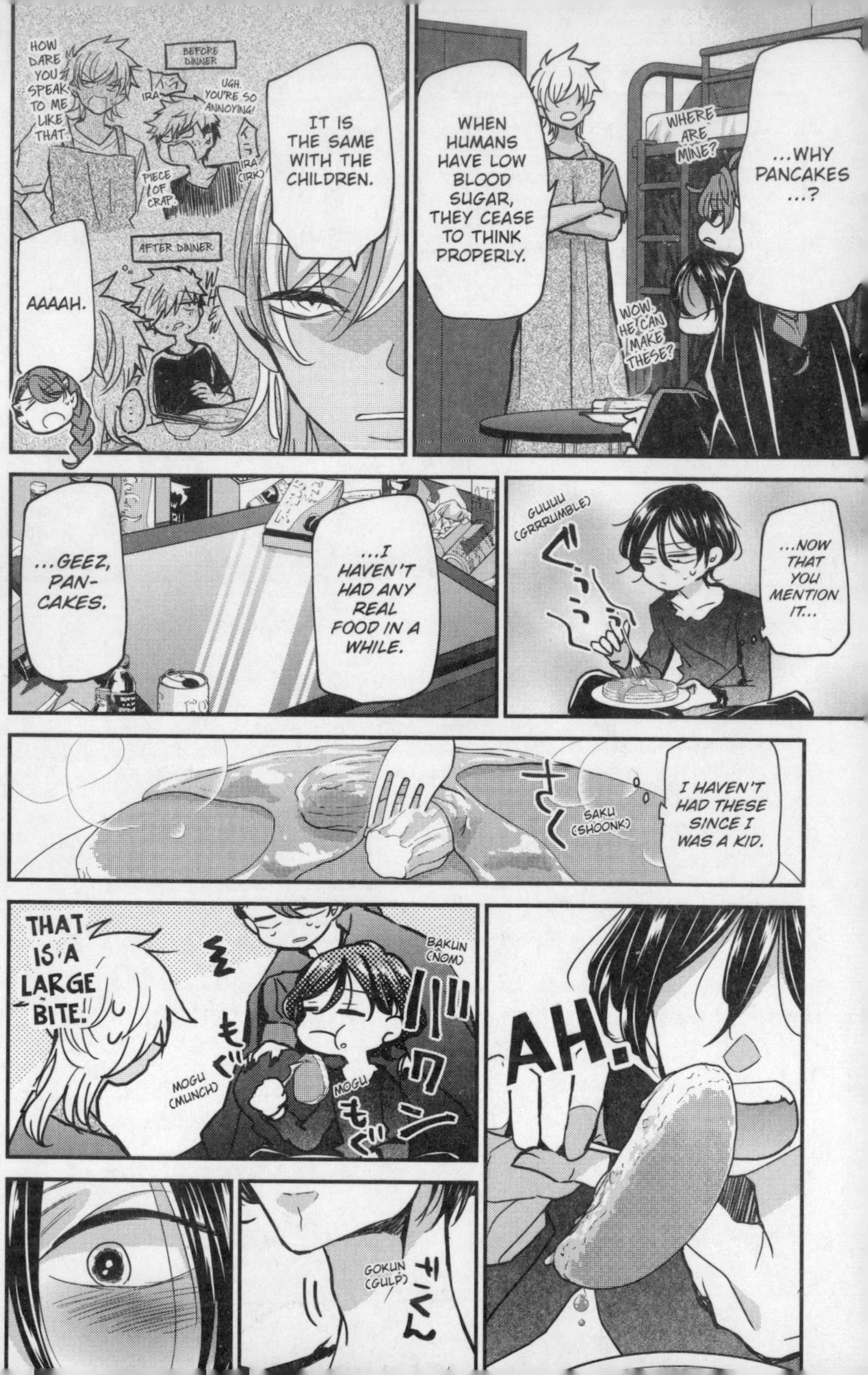
...WHY PANCAKES ...?
WHERE ARE MINE?
WOW. HE CAN MAKE THESE?
WHEN HUMANS HAVE LOW BLOOD SUGAR, THEY CEASE TO THINK PROPERLY.
IT IS THE SAME WITH THE CHILDREN.
BEFORE DINNER
UGH. YOU'RE SO ANNOYING!
IRA
HOW DARE YOU SPEAK TO ME LIKE THAT.
IRA (IRK)
PIECE OF CRAP.
AFTER DINNER
AAAAH.
...NOW THAT YOU MENTION IT...
GUUUU (GRRRUMBLE)
...I HAVEN'T HAD ANY REAL FOOD IN A WHILE.
...GEEZ, PAN-CAKES.
I HAVEN'T HAD THESE SINCE I WAS A KID.
SAKU (SHOONK)
AH.
BAKUN (NOM)
THAT IS A LARGE BITE!
MOGU (MUNCH)
MOGU
GOKUN (GULP)

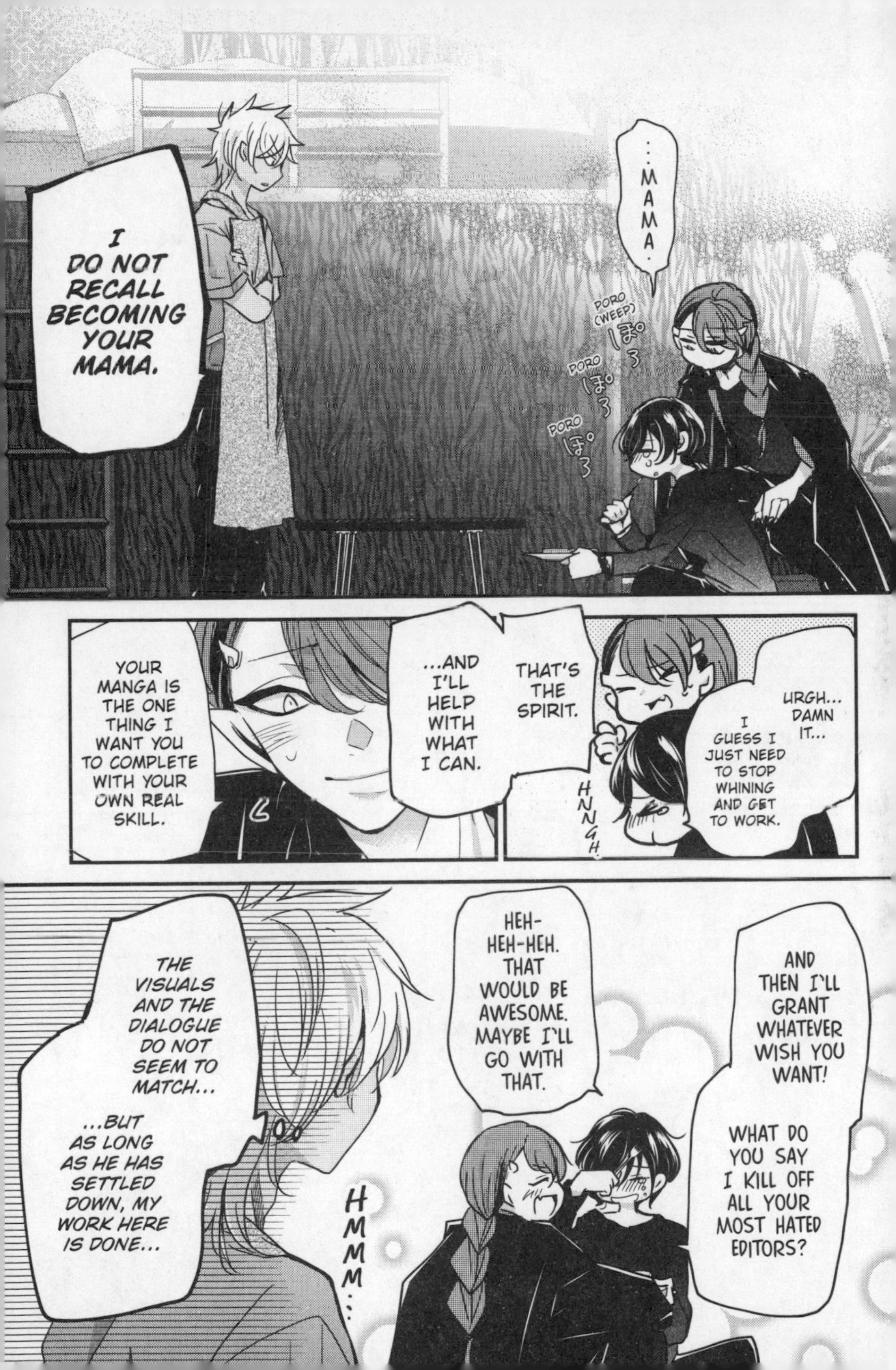
...MAMA...
PORO (WEEP) ぽろ
PORO ぽろ
PORO ぽろ
I DO NOT RECALL BECOMING YOUR MAMA.
URGH... DAMN IT...
I GUESS I JUST NEED TO STOP WHINING AND GET TO WORK.
HNNGH.
THAT'S THE SPIRIT.
YOUR MANGA IS THE ONE THING I WANT YOU TO COMPLETE WITH YOUR OWN REAL SKILL.
...AND I'LL HELP WITH WHAT I CAN.
AND THEN I'LL GRANT WHATEVER WISH YOU WANT!
WHAT DO YOU SAY I KILL OFF ALL YOUR MOST HATED EDITORS?
HEH-HEH-HEH. THAT WOULD BE AWESOME. MAYBE I'LL GO WITH THAT.
HMMM...
THE VISUALS AND THE DIALOGUE DO NOT SEEM TO MATCH...
...BUT AS LONG AS HE HAS SETTLED DOWN, MY WORK HERE IS DONE...

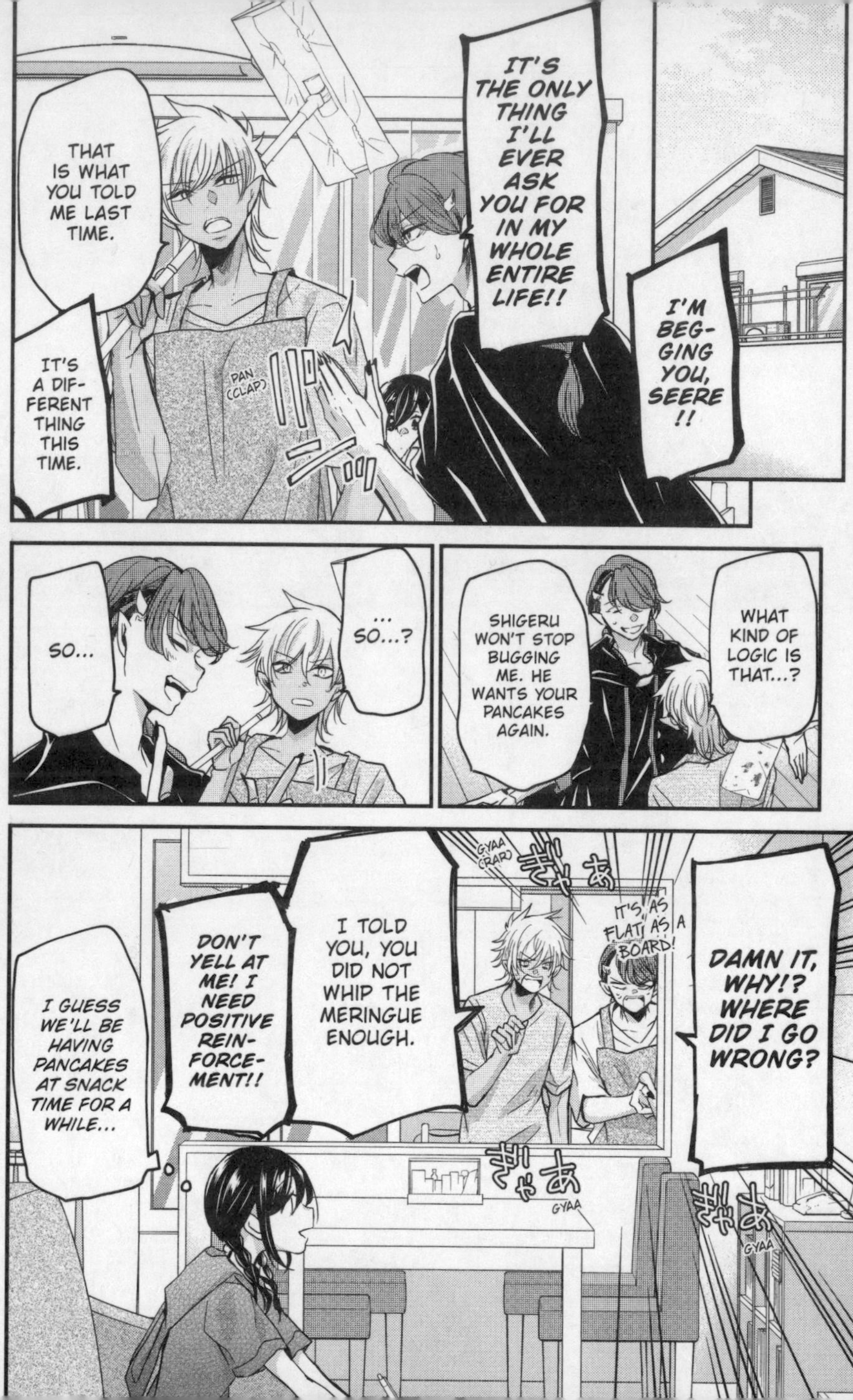
I'M BEGGING YOU, SEERE!!
IT'S THE ONLY THING I'LL EVER ASK YOU FOR IN MY WHOLE ENTIRE LIFE!!
PAN (CLAP)
THAT IS WHAT YOU TOLD ME LAST TIME.
IT'S A DIFFERENT THING THIS TIME.
SO...
... SO...?
SHIGERU WON'T STOP BUGGING ME. HE WANTS YOUR PANCAKES AGAIN.
WHAT KIND OF LOGIC IS THAT...?
DAMN IT, WHY!? WHERE DID I GO WRONG?
GYAA (RAR)
IT'S AS FLAT AS A BOARD!
I TOLD YOU, YOU DID NOT WHIP THE MERINGUE ENOUGH.
DON'T YELL AT ME! I NEED POSITIVE REINFORCEMENT!!
I GUESS WE'LL BE HAVING PANCAKES AT SNACK TIME FOR A WHILE...
GYAA
GYAA

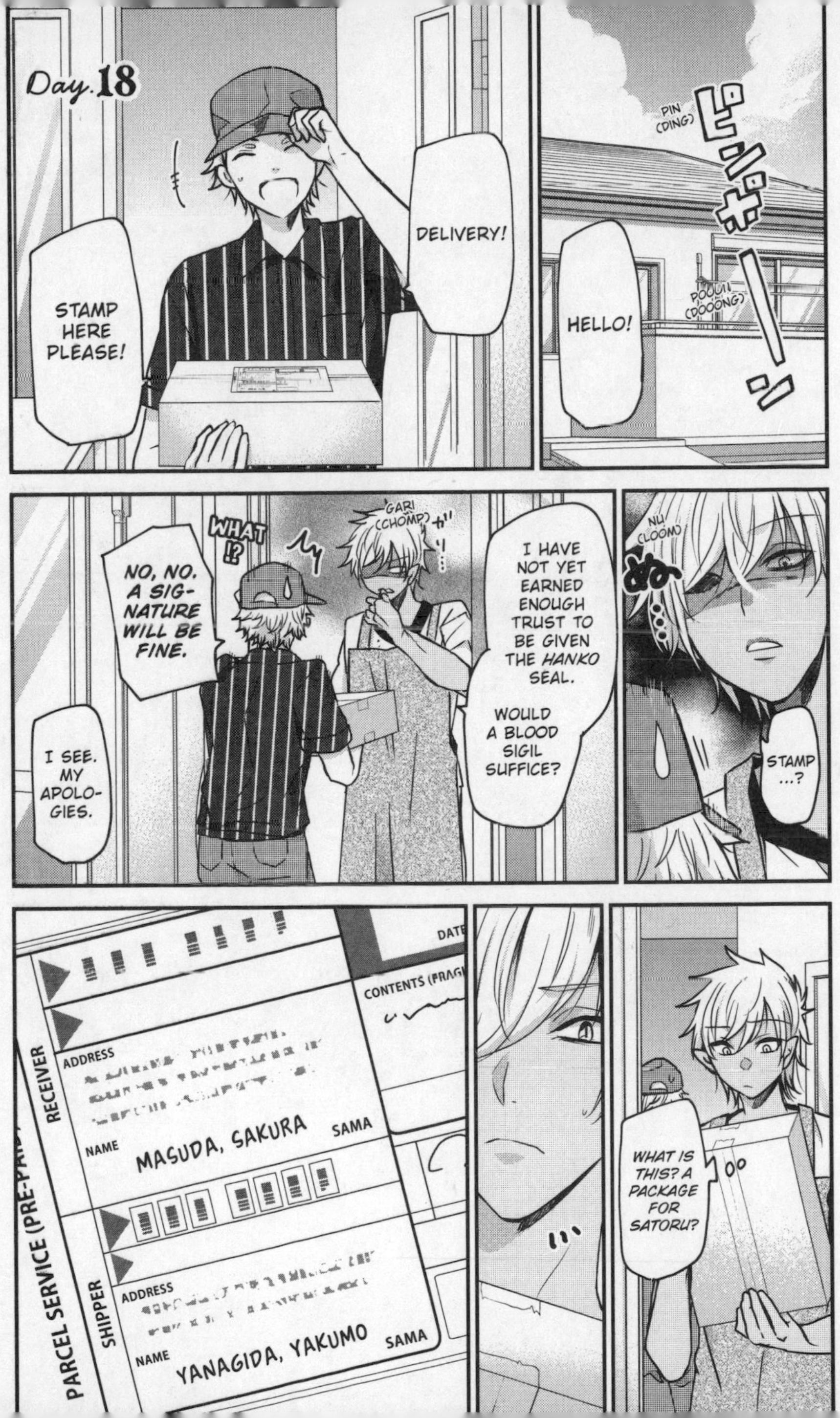
Day. 18
PIN (DING)
ピンポーン
POOUN (DOOONG)
HELLO!
DELIVERY!
STAMP HERE PLEASE!
NU (LOOM)
STAMP ...?
GARI (CHOMP)
I HAVE NOT YET EARNED ENOUGH TRUST TO BE GIVEN THE HANKO SEAL.
WOULD A BLOOD SIGIL SUFFICE?
WHAT !?
NO, NO. A SIGNATURE WILL BE FINE.
I SEE. MY APOLOGIES.
WHAT IS THIS? A PACKAGE FOR SATORU?
PARCEL SERVICE (PRE-PAID)
DATE
CONTENTS (FRAG
RECEIVER
ADDRESS
NAME MASUDA, SAKURA SAMA
SHIPPER
ADDRESS
NAME YANAGIDA, YAKUMO SAMA

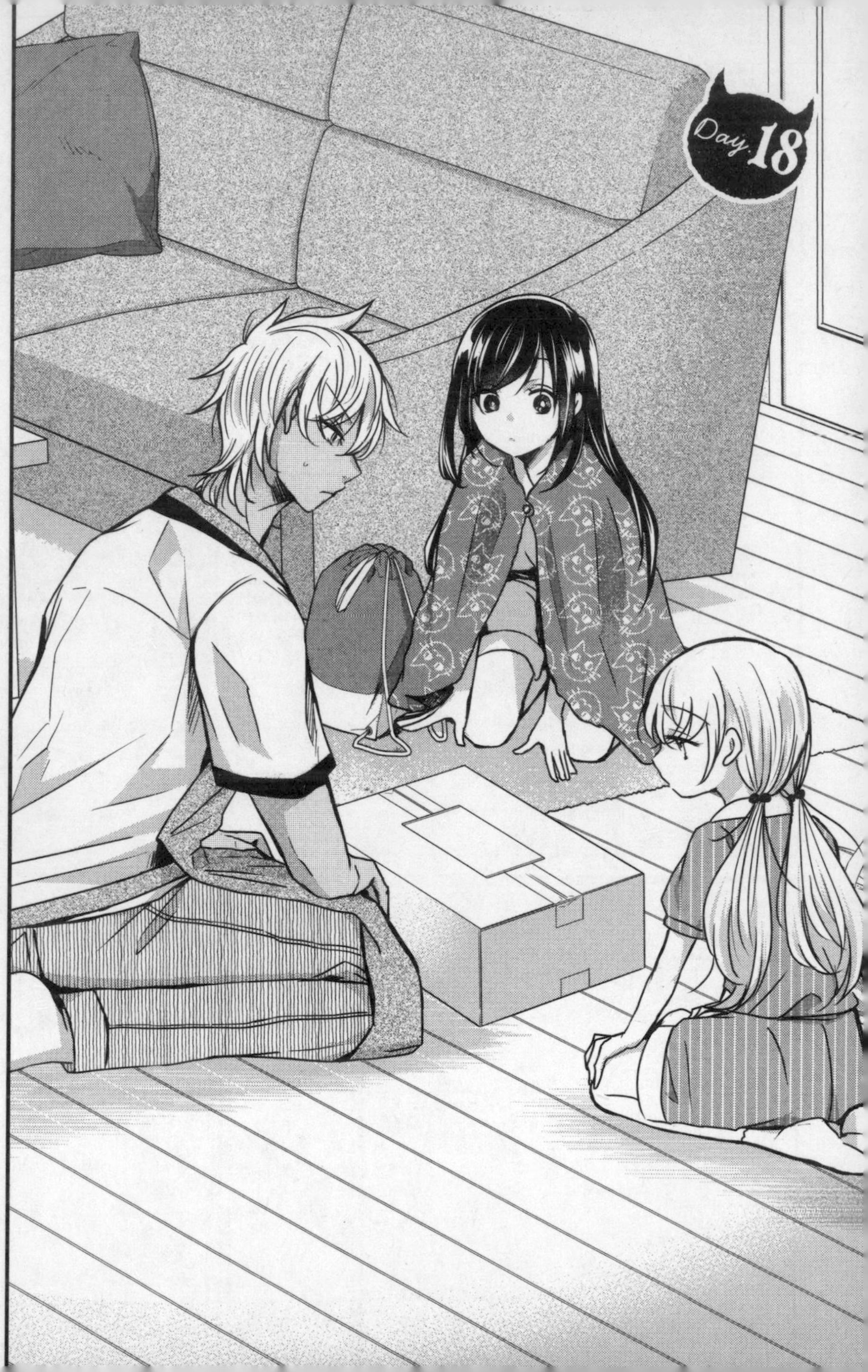
Day. 18

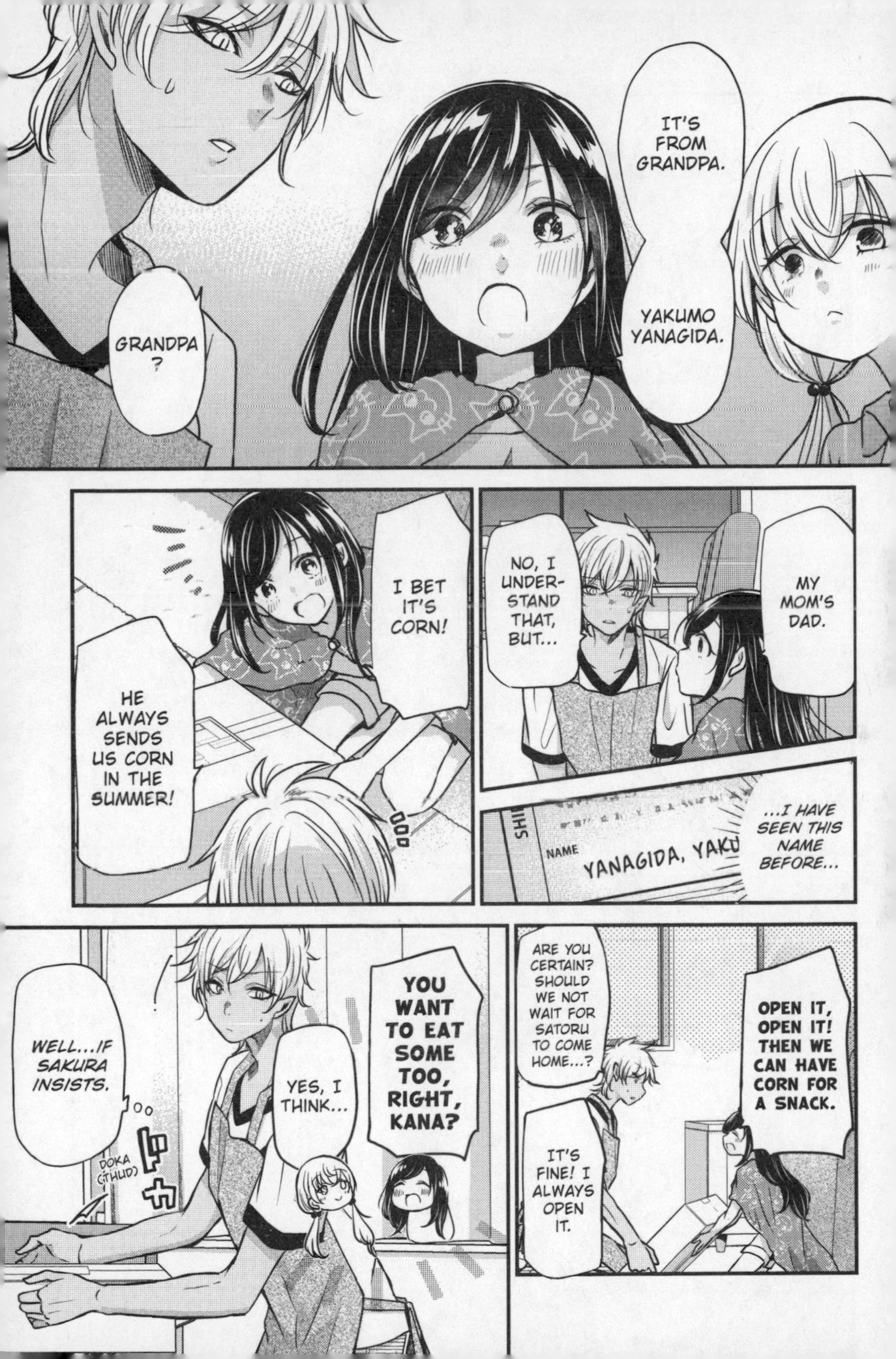
IT'S FROM GRANDPA.
YAKUMO YANAGIDA.
GRANDPA?
MY MOM'S DAD.
NO, I UNDERSTAND THAT, BUT...
...I HAVE SEEN THIS NAME BEFORE...
NAME
YANAGIDA, YAKU
I BET IT'S CORN!
HE ALWAYS SENDS US CORN IN THE SUMMER!
OPEN IT, OPEN IT! THEN WE CAN HAVE CORN FOR A SNACK.
ARE YOU CERTAIN? SHOULD WE NOT WAIT FOR SATORU TO COME HOME...?
IT'S FINE! I ALWAYS OPEN IT.
YOU WANT TO EAT SOME TOO, RIGHT, KANA?
YES, I THINK...
WELL...IF SAKURA INSISTS.
DOKA (THUD)

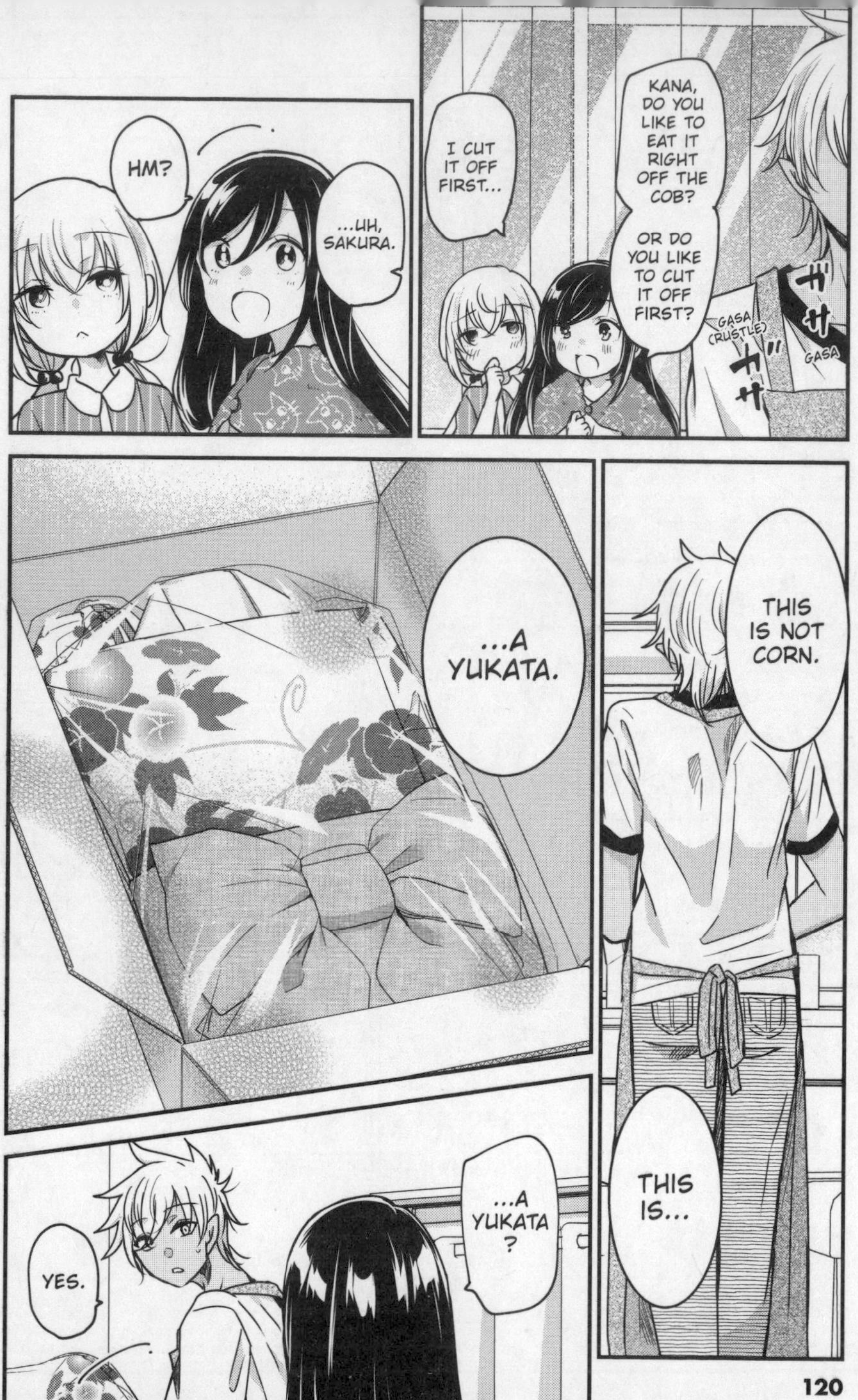
KANA, DO YOU LIKE TO EAT IT RIGHT OFF THE COB?
OR DO YOU LIKE TO CUT IT OFF FIRST?
GASA (RUSTLE)
GASA
I CUT IT OFF FIRST...
...UH, SAKURA.
HM?
THIS IS NOT CORN.
THIS IS...
...A YUKATA.
...A YUKATA?
YES.

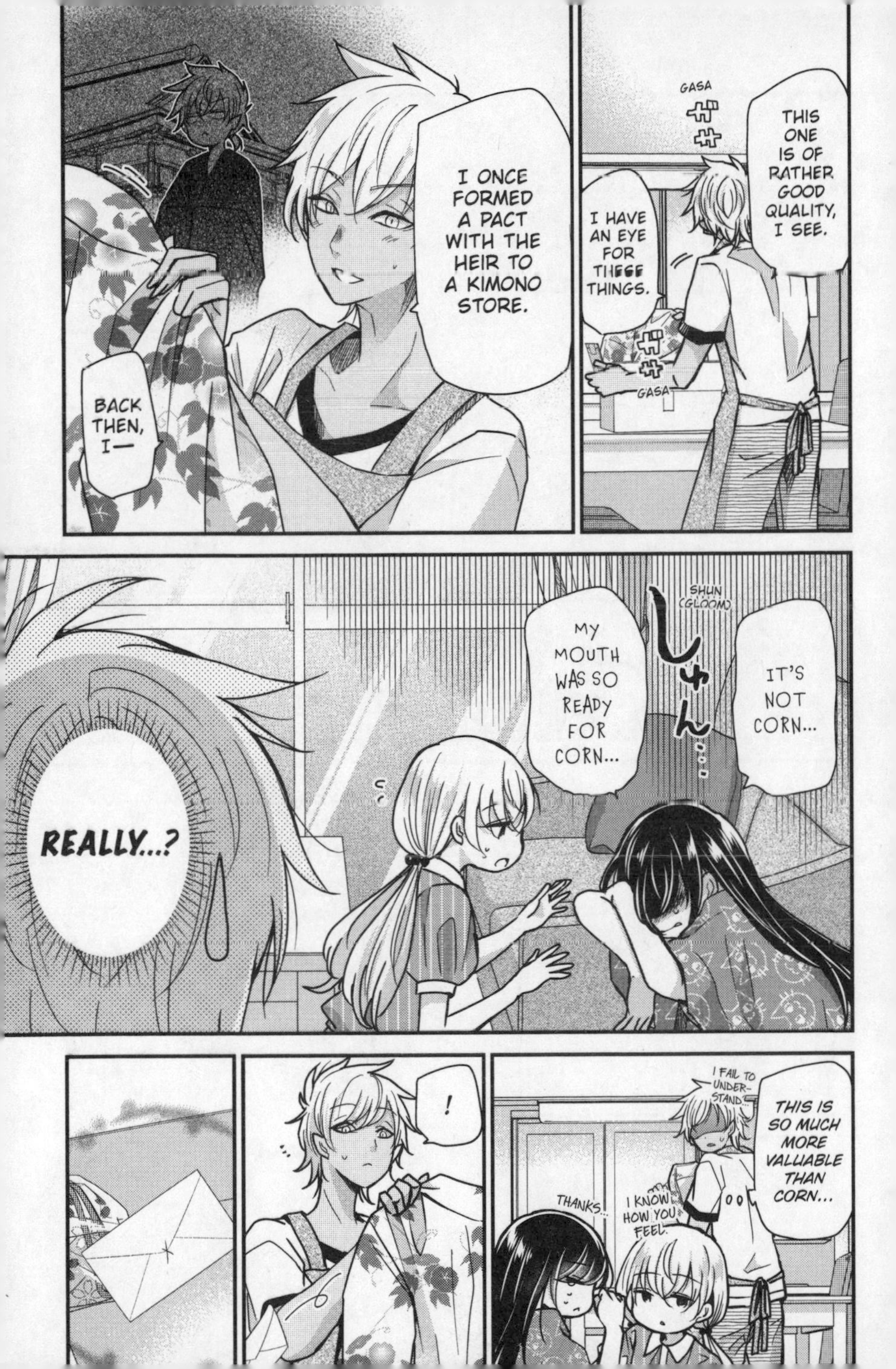
GASA
THIS ONE IS OF RATHER GOOD QUALITY, I SEE.
I HAVE AN EYE FOR THESE THINGS.
GASA
I ONCE FORMED A PACT WITH THE HEIR TO A KIMONO STORE.
BACK THEN, I—
SHUN (GLOOM)
IT'S NOT CORN...
MY MOUTH WAS SO READY FOR CORN...
REALLY...?
THIS IS SO MUCH MORE VALUABLE THAN CORN...
I FAIL TO UNDERSTAND...
I KNOW HOW YOU FEEL.
THANKS...
!

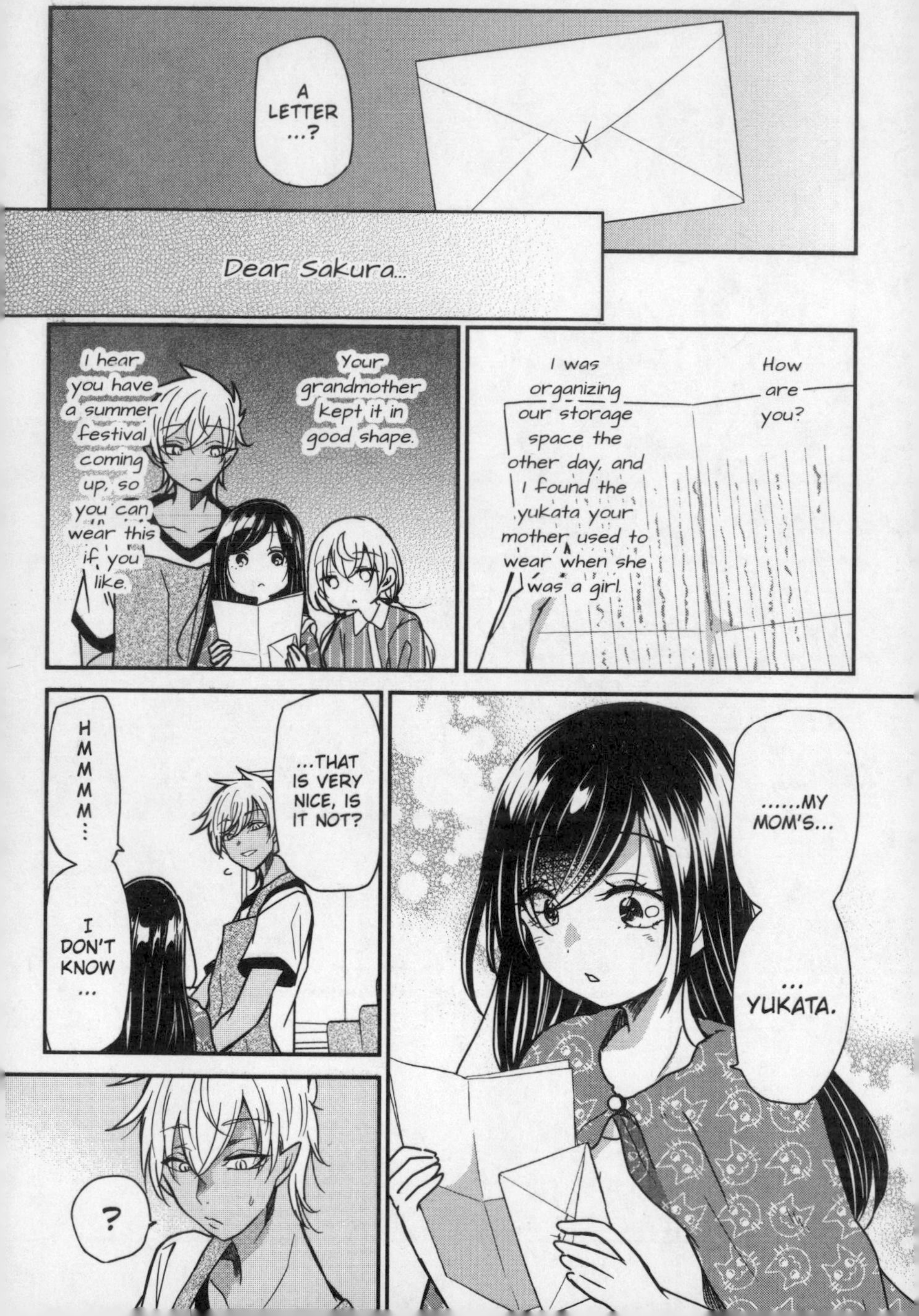
A LETTER ...?
Dear Sakura...
How are you?
I was organizing our storage space the other day, and I found the yukata your mother used to wear when she was a girl.
Your grandmother kept it in good shape.
I hear you have a summer festival coming up, so you can wear this if you like.
......MY MOM'S...
... YUKATA.
...THAT IS VERY NICE, IS IT NOT?
HMMMM...
I DON'T KNOW ...
?

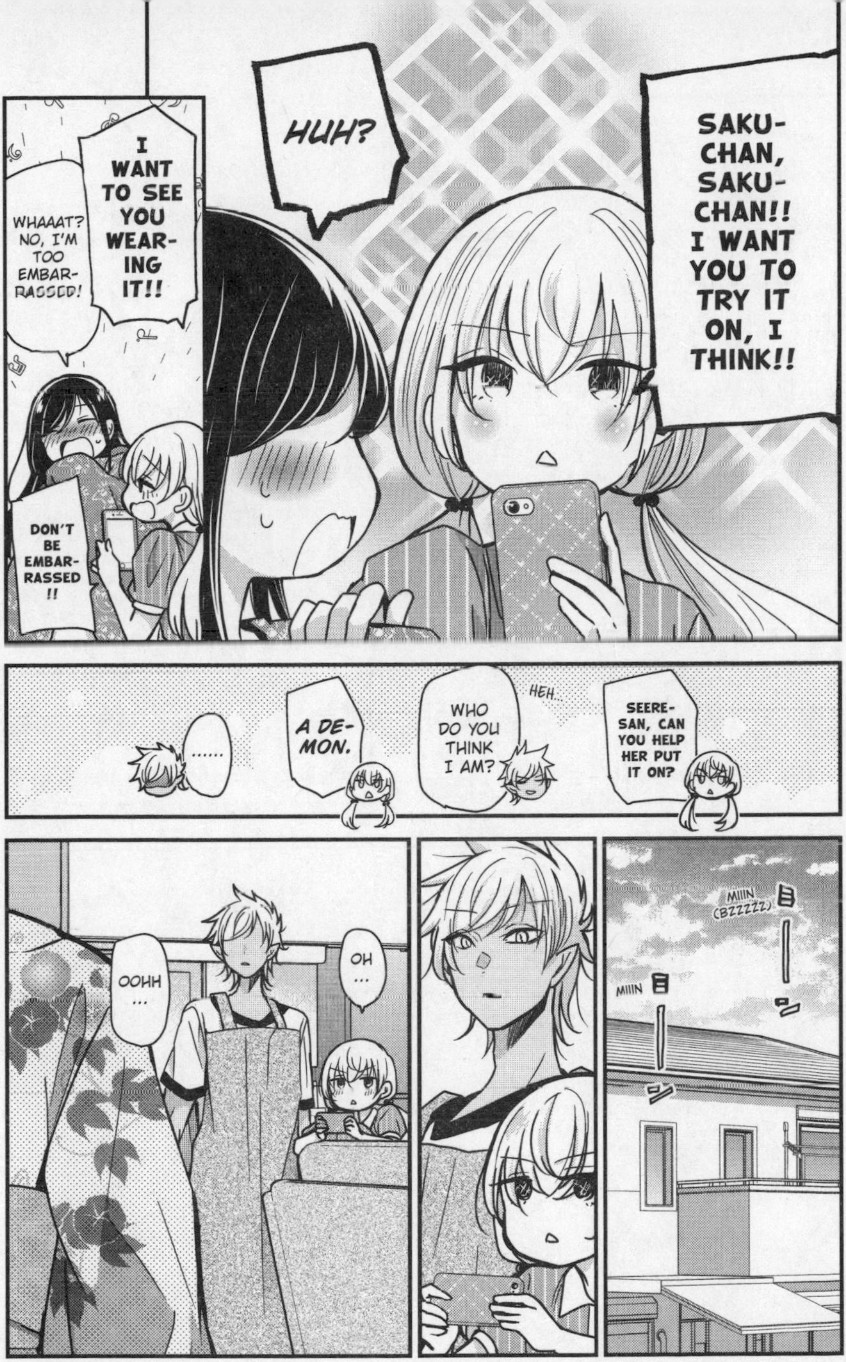
SAKU-CHAN, SAKU-CHAN!! I WANT YOU TO TRY IT ON, I THINK!!
HUH?
I WANT TO SEE YOU WEAR-ING IT!!
WHAAAT? NO, I'M TOO EMBAR-RASSED!
DON'T BE EMBAR-RASSED !!
SEERE-SAN, CAN YOU HELP HER PUT IT ON?
HEH...
WHO DO YOU THINK I AM?
A DE-MON.
......
MIIN (BZZZZZ)
MIIN
OH ...
OOHH ...

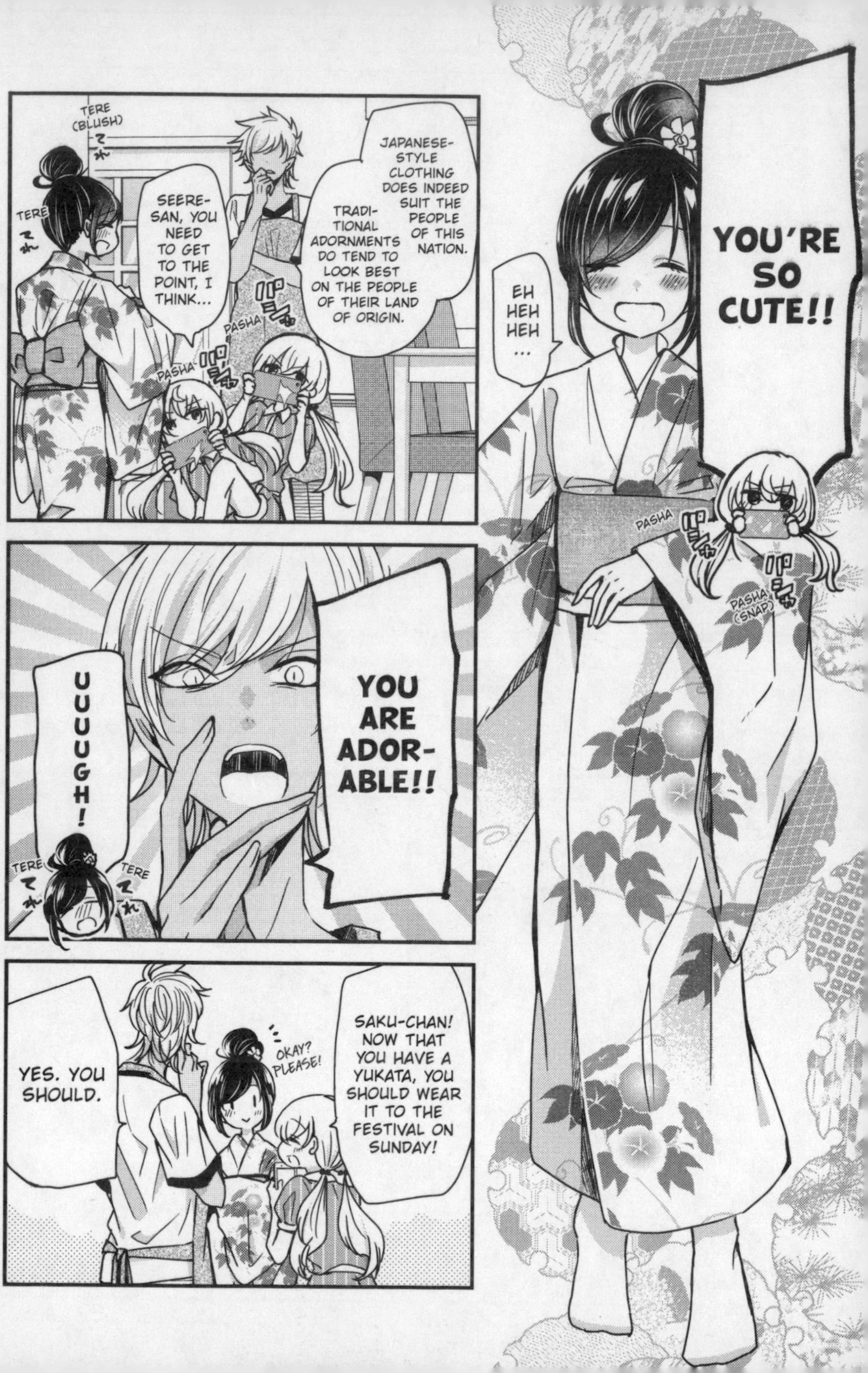
YOU'RE SO CUTE!!
EH HEH HEH...
PASHA
PASHA (SNAP)
TERE (BLUSH)
TERE
JAPANESE-STYLE CLOTHING DOES INDEED SUIT THE PEOPLE OF THIS NATION.
TRADITIONAL ADORNMENTS DO TEND TO LOOK BEST ON THE PEOPLE OF THEIR LAND OF ORIGIN.
SEERE-SAN, YOU NEED TO GET TO THE POINT, I THINK...
PASHA
PASHA
YOU ARE ADORABLE!!
UUUUGH!
TERE
TERE
SAKU-CHAN! NOW THAT YOU HAVE A YUKATA, YOU SHOULD WEAR IT TO THE FESTIVAL ON SUNDAY!
OKAY? PLEASE!
YES. YOU SHOULD.

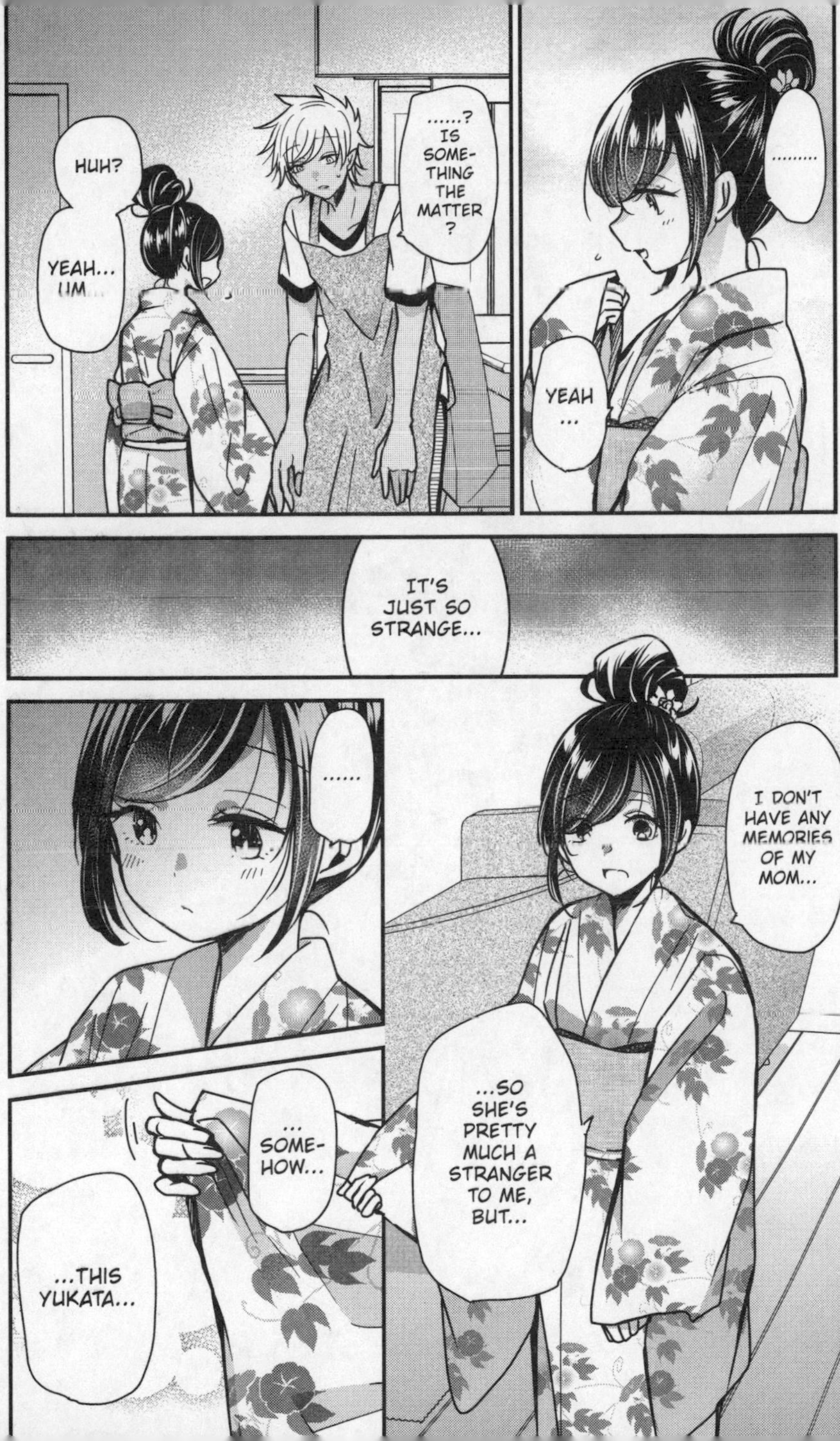
......? IS SOMETHING THE MATTER ?
HUH?
YEAH... UM...
.........
YEAH ...
IT'S JUST SO STRANGE...
I DON'T HAVE ANY MEMORIES OF MY MOM...
...SO SHE'S PRETTY MUCH A STRANGER TO ME, BUT...
......
... SOME-HOW...
...THIS YUKATA...

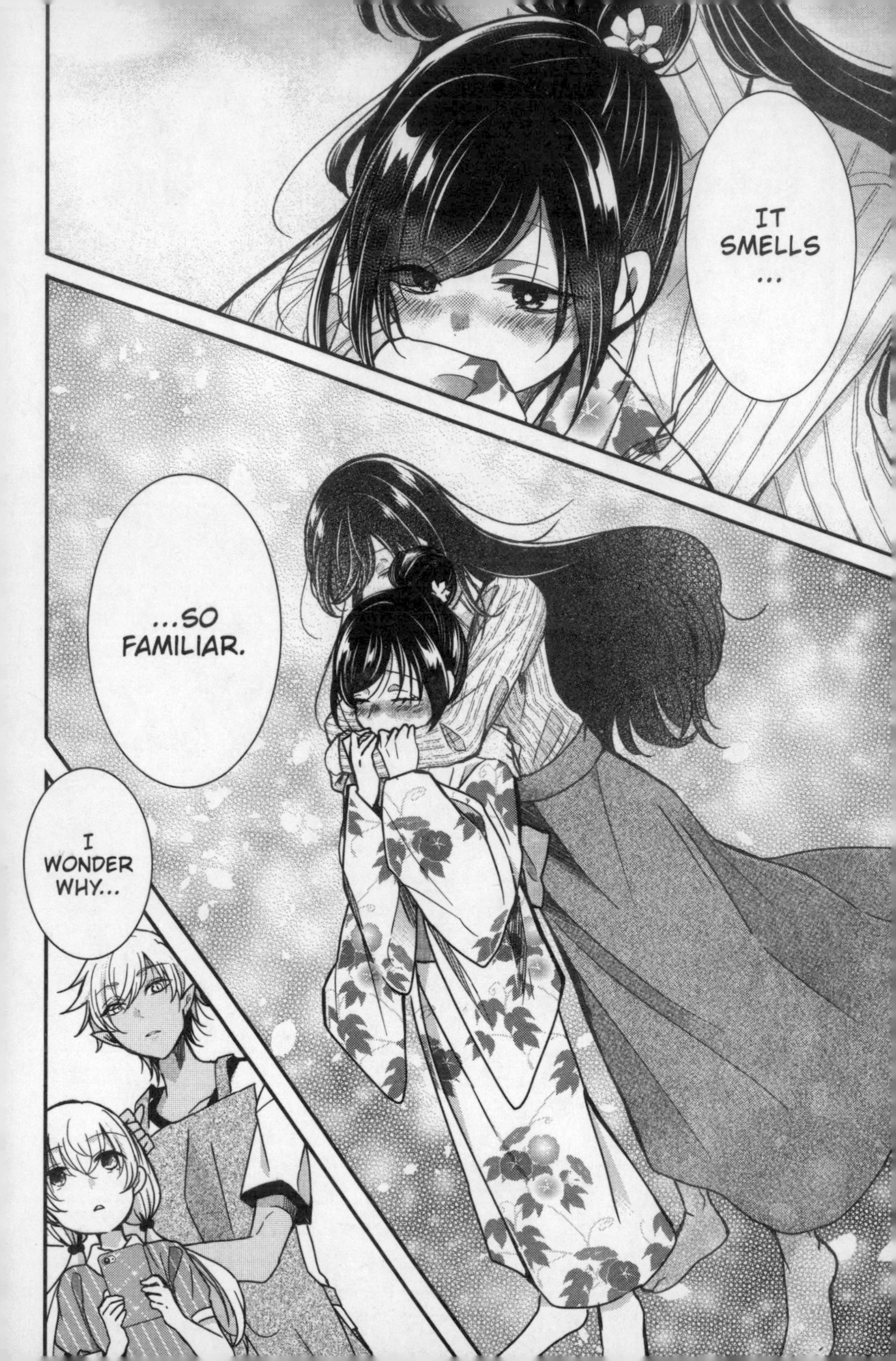
IT SMELLS ...
...SO FAMILIAR.
I WONDER WHY...

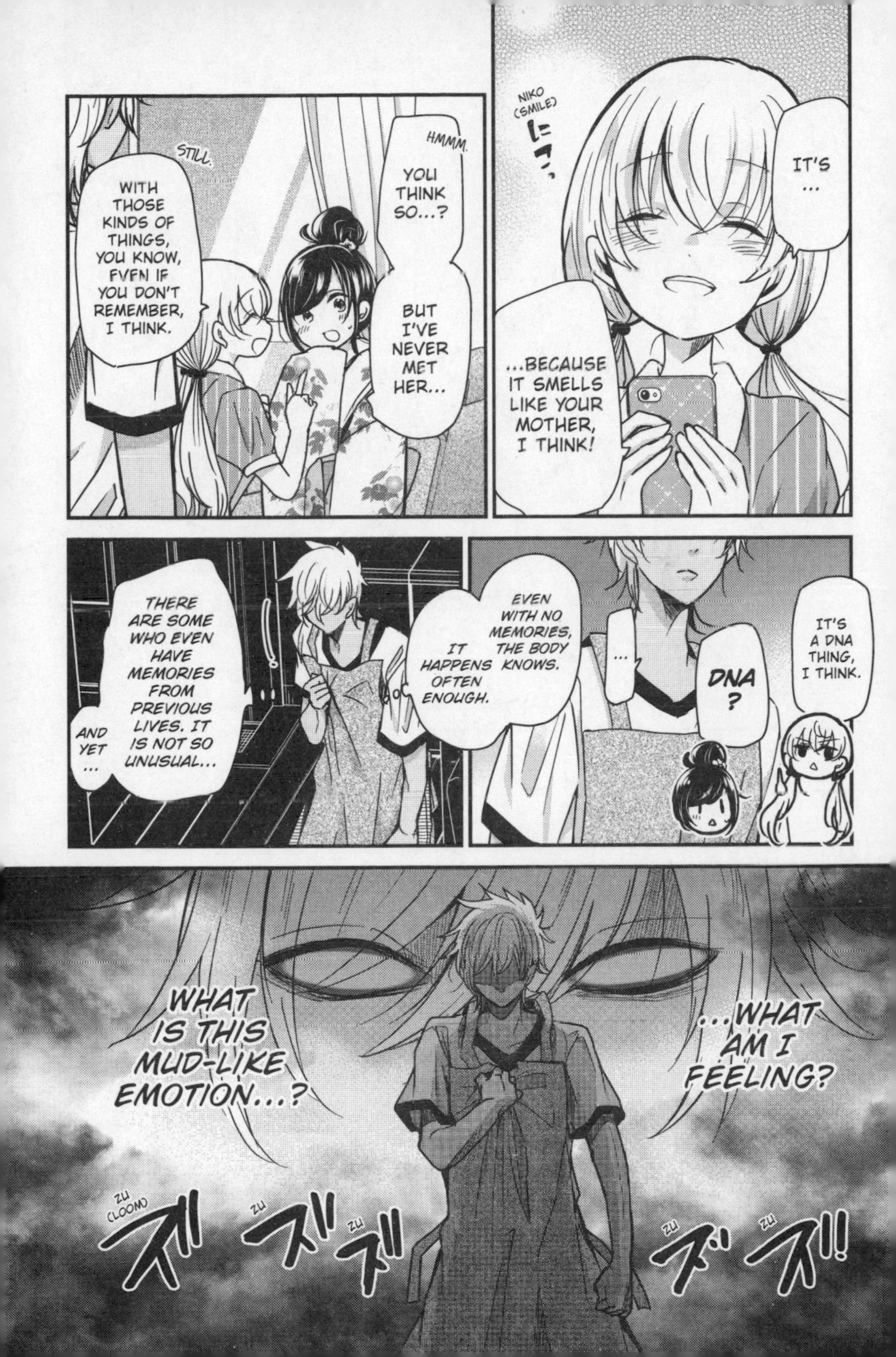
NIKO (SMILE)
IT'S ...
...BECAUSE IT SMELLS LIKE YOUR MOTHER, I THINK!
HMMM.
YOU THINK SO...?
BUT I'VE NEVER MET HER...
STILL.
WITH THOSE KINDS OF THINGS, YOU KNOW, EVEN IF YOU DON'T REMEMBER, I THINK.
IT'S A DNA THING, I THINK.
DNA ?
...
EVEN WITH NO MEMORIES, THE BODY KNOWS.
IT HAPPENS OFTEN ENOUGH.
THERE ARE SOME WHO EVEN HAVE MEMORIES FROM PREVIOUS LIVES. IT IS NOT SO UNUSUAL...
AND YET ...
...WHAT AM I FEELING?
WHAT IS THIS MUD-LIKE EMOTION...?
ZU (LOOM) ZU ZU ZU ZU

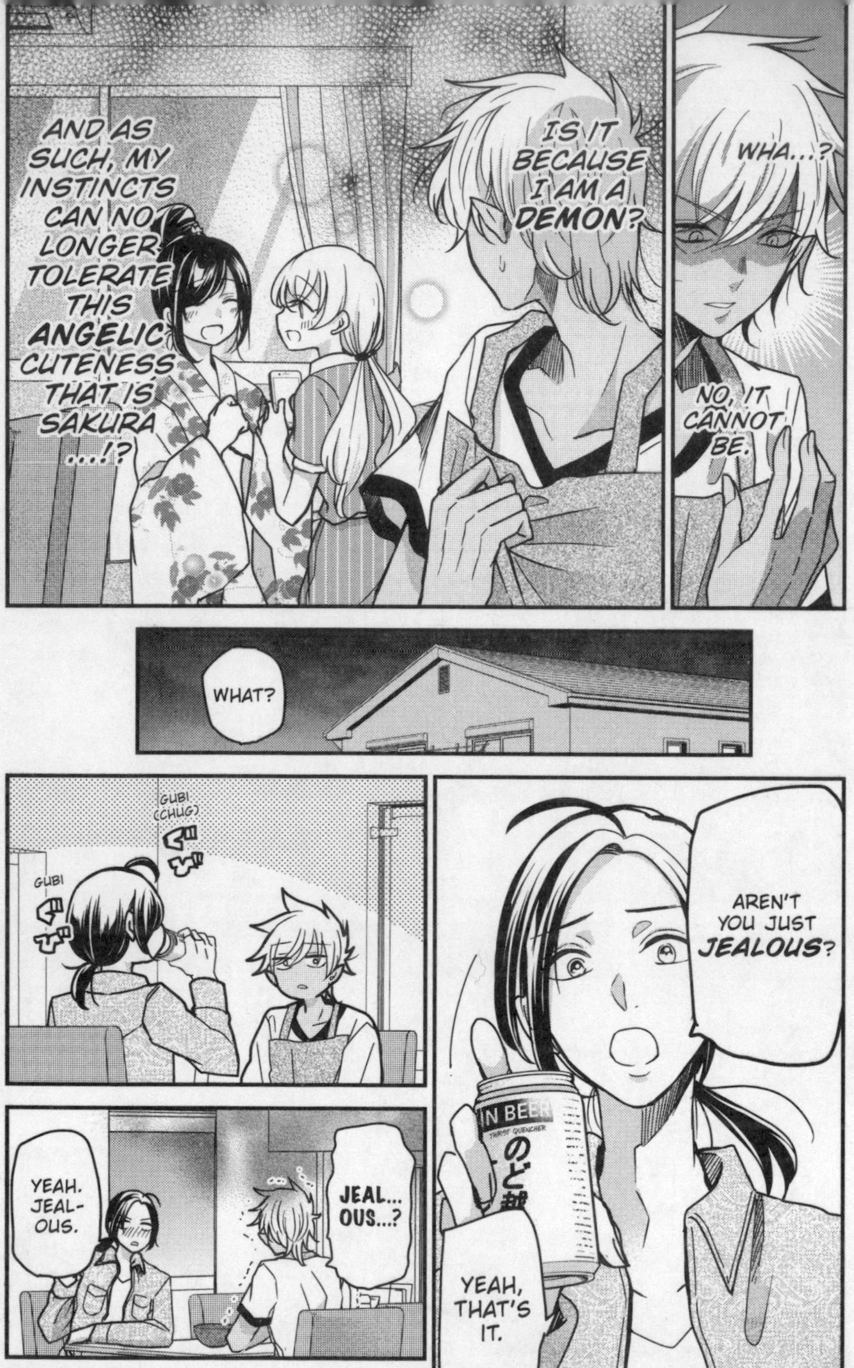
AND AS SUCH, MY INSTINCTS CAN NO LONGER TOLERATE THIS ANGELIC CUTENESS THAT IS SAKURA ...!?
IS IT BECAUSE I AM A DEMON?
WHA...?
NO, IT CANNOT BE.
WHAT?
GUBI (CHUG)
GUBI
AREN'T YOU JUST JEALOUS?
IN BEER
THIRST QUENCHER
JEAL... OUS...?
YEAH. JEAL-OUS.
YEAH, THAT'S IT.

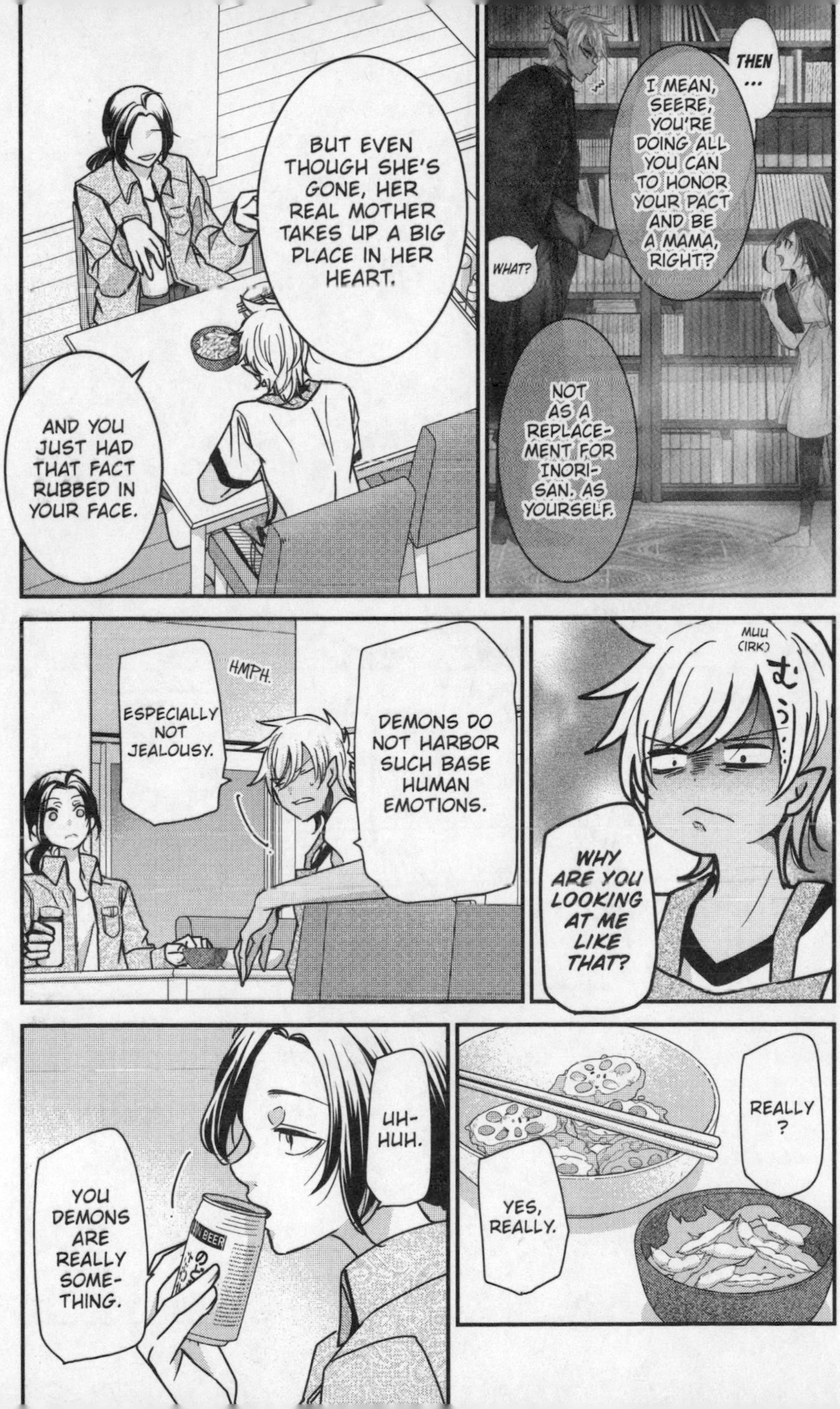
THEN...
I MEAN, SEERE, YOU'RE DOING ALL YOU CAN TO HONOR YOUR PACT AND BE A MAMA, RIGHT?
WHAT?
NOT AS A REPLACEMENT FOR INORI-SAN. AS YOURSELF.
BUT EVEN THOUGH SHE'S GONE, HER REAL MOTHER TAKES UP A BIG PLACE IN HER HEART.
AND YOU JUST HAD THAT FACT RUBBED IN YOUR FACE.
MUU (IRK)
WHY ARE YOU LOOKING AT ME LIKE THAT?
DEMONS DO NOT HARBOR SUCH BASE HUMAN EMOTIONS.
ESPECIALLY NOT JEALOUSY.
HMPH.
REALLY?
YES, REALLY.
UH-HUH.
YOU DEMONS ARE REALLY SOMETHING.

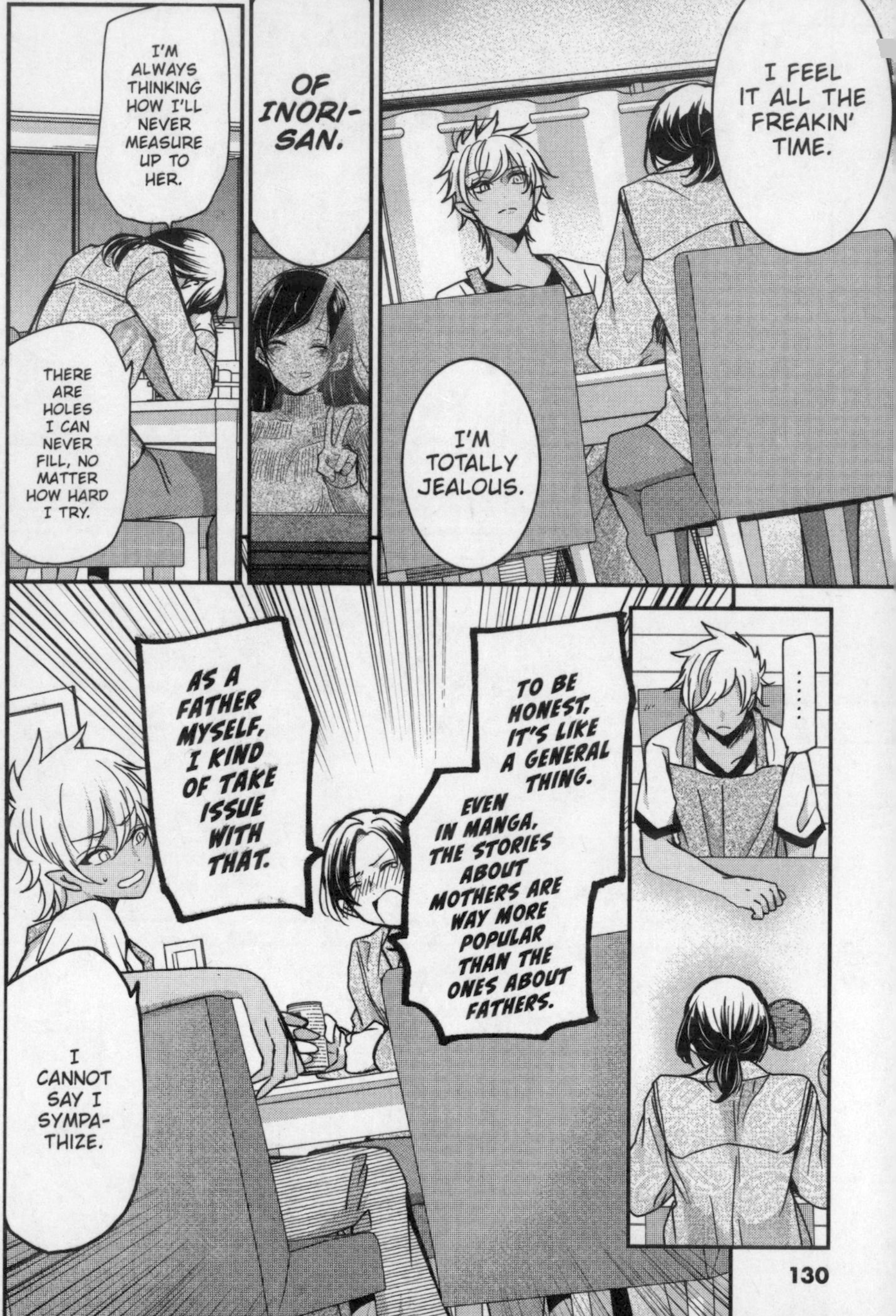
I FEEL IT ALL THE FREAKIN' TIME.
I'M TOTALLY JEALOUS.
OF INORI-SAN.
I'M ALWAYS THINKING HOW I'LL NEVER MEASURE UP TO HER.
THERE ARE HOLES I CAN NEVER FILL, NO MATTER HOW HARD I TRY.
......
TO BE HONEST, IT'S LIKE A GENERAL THING.
EVEN IN MANGA, THE STORIES ABOUT MOTHERS ARE WAY MORE POPULAR THAN THE ONES ABOUT FATHERS.
AS A FATHER MYSELF, I KIND OF TAKE ISSUE WITH THAT.
I CANNOT SAY I SYMPATHIZE.

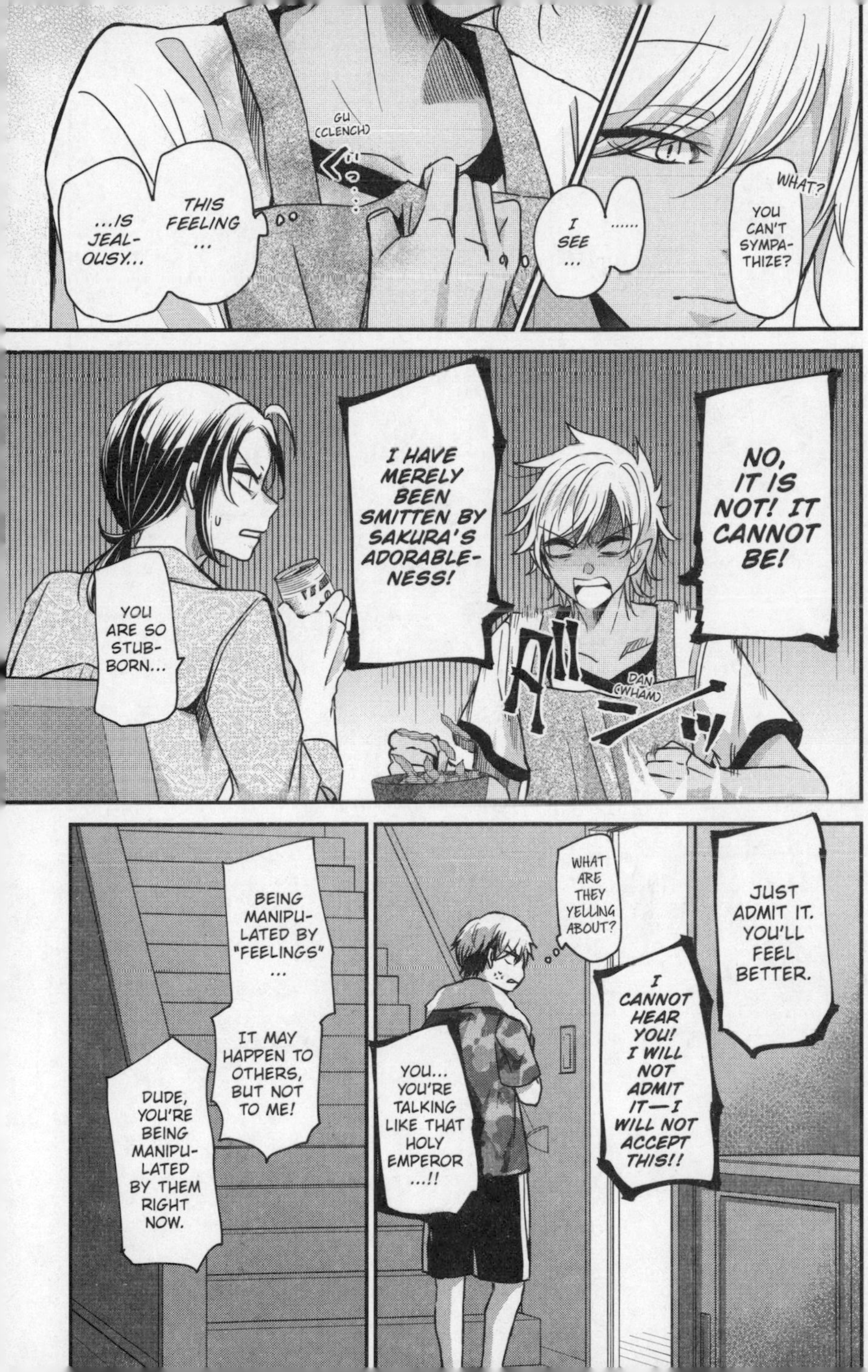
WHAT? YOU CAN'T SYMPATHIZE?
......
I SEE...
THIS FEELING...
...IS JEALOUSY...
GU (CLENCH)
NO, IT IS NOT! IT CANNOT BE!
I HAVE MERELY BEEN SMITTEN BY SAKURA'S ADORABLENESS!
DAN (WHAM)
YOU ARE SO STUBBORN...
JUST ADMIT IT. YOU'LL FEEL BETTER.
I CANNOT HEAR YOU! I WILL NOT ADMIT IT—I WILL NOT ACCEPT THIS!!
WHAT ARE THEY YELLING ABOUT?
YOU... YOU'RE TALKING LIKE THAT HOLY EMPEROR...!!
BEING MANIPULATED BY "FEELINGS"...
IT MAY HAPPEN TO OTHERS, BUT NOT TO ME!
DUDE, YOU'RE BEING MANIPULATED BY THEM RIGHT NOW.

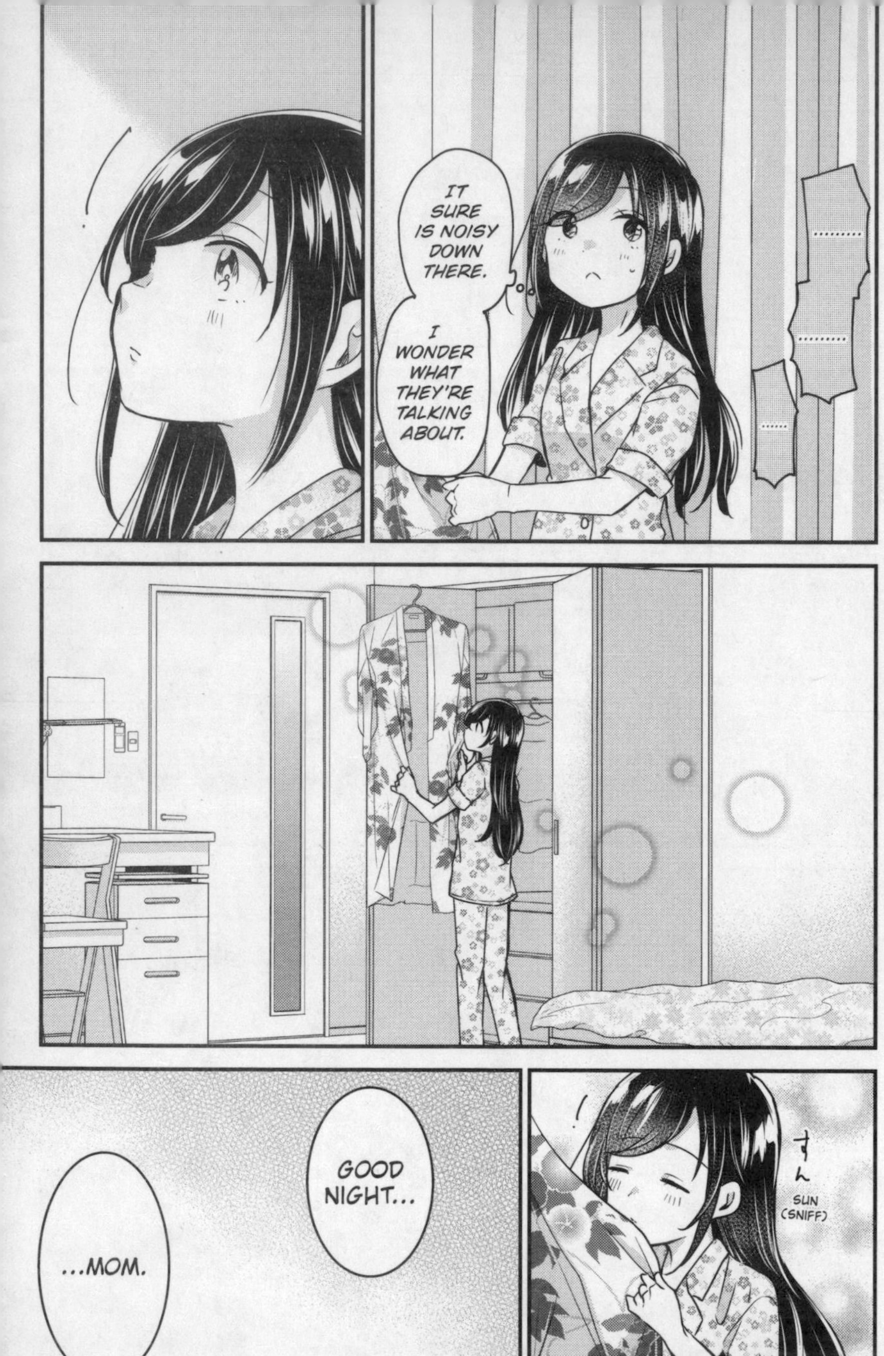
IT SURE IS NOISY DOWN THERE.
I WONDER WHAT THEY'RE TALKING ABOUT.
すん
SUN (SNIFF)
GOOD NIGHT...
...MOM.

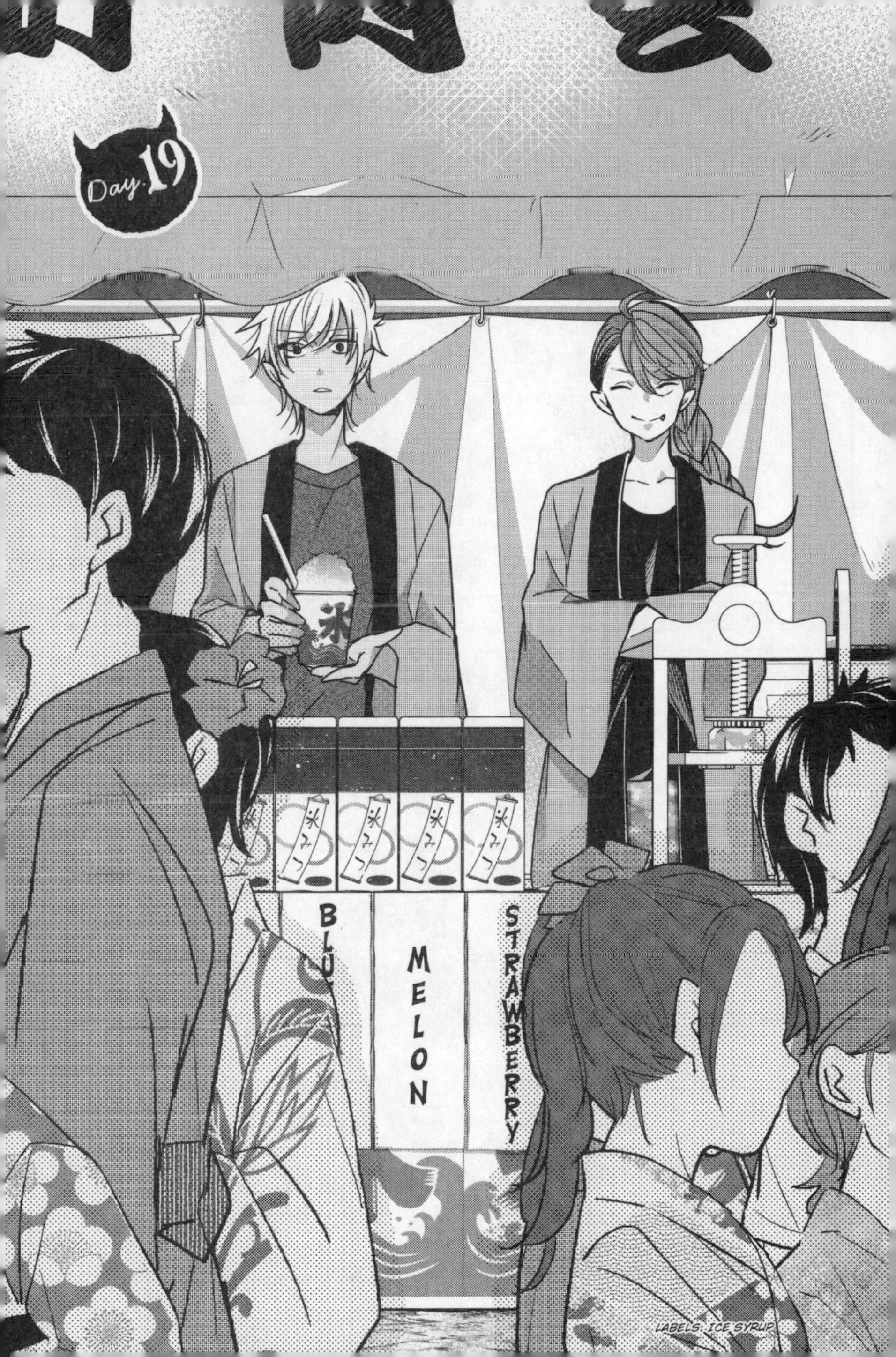
Day.19
氷みつ
氷みつ
氷みつ
氷みつ
BLU
MELON
STRAWBERRY
LABELS: ICE SYRUP

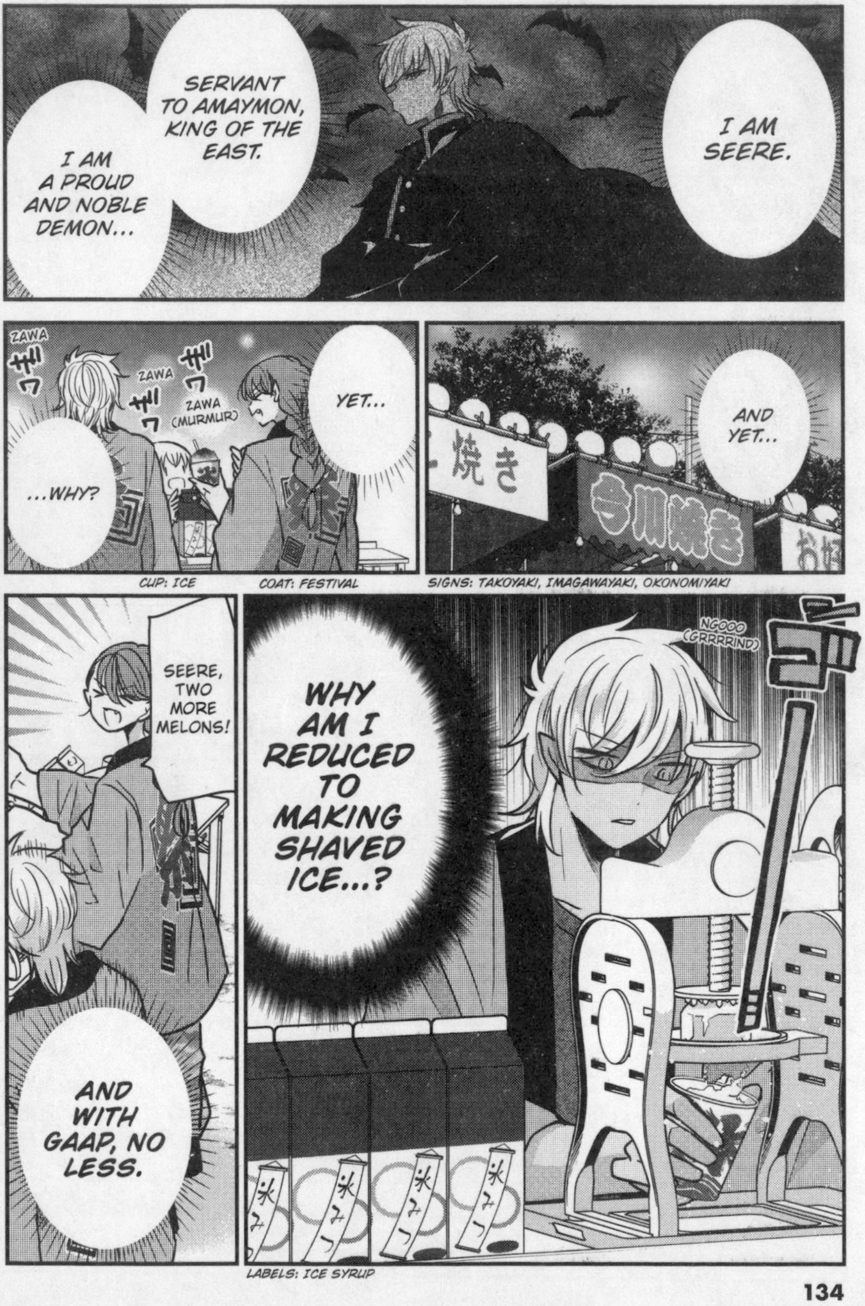
I AM SEERE.
SERVANT TO AMAYMON, KING OF THE EAST.
I AM A PROUD AND NOBLE DEMON...
AND YET...
焼き
今川焼き
お好
YET...
ZAWA
ザワ
ZAWA
ザワ
ZAWA (MURMUR)
...WHY?
NGOOO (GRRRRIND)
WHY AM I REDUCED TO MAKING SHAVED ICE...?
氷みつ
氷みつ
氷みつ
氷み
SEERE, TWO MORE MELONS!
AND WITH GAAP, NO LESS.

CUP: ICE COAT: FESTIVAL SIGNS: TAKOYAKI, IMAGAWAYAKI, OKONOMIYAKI

LABELS: ICE SYRUP

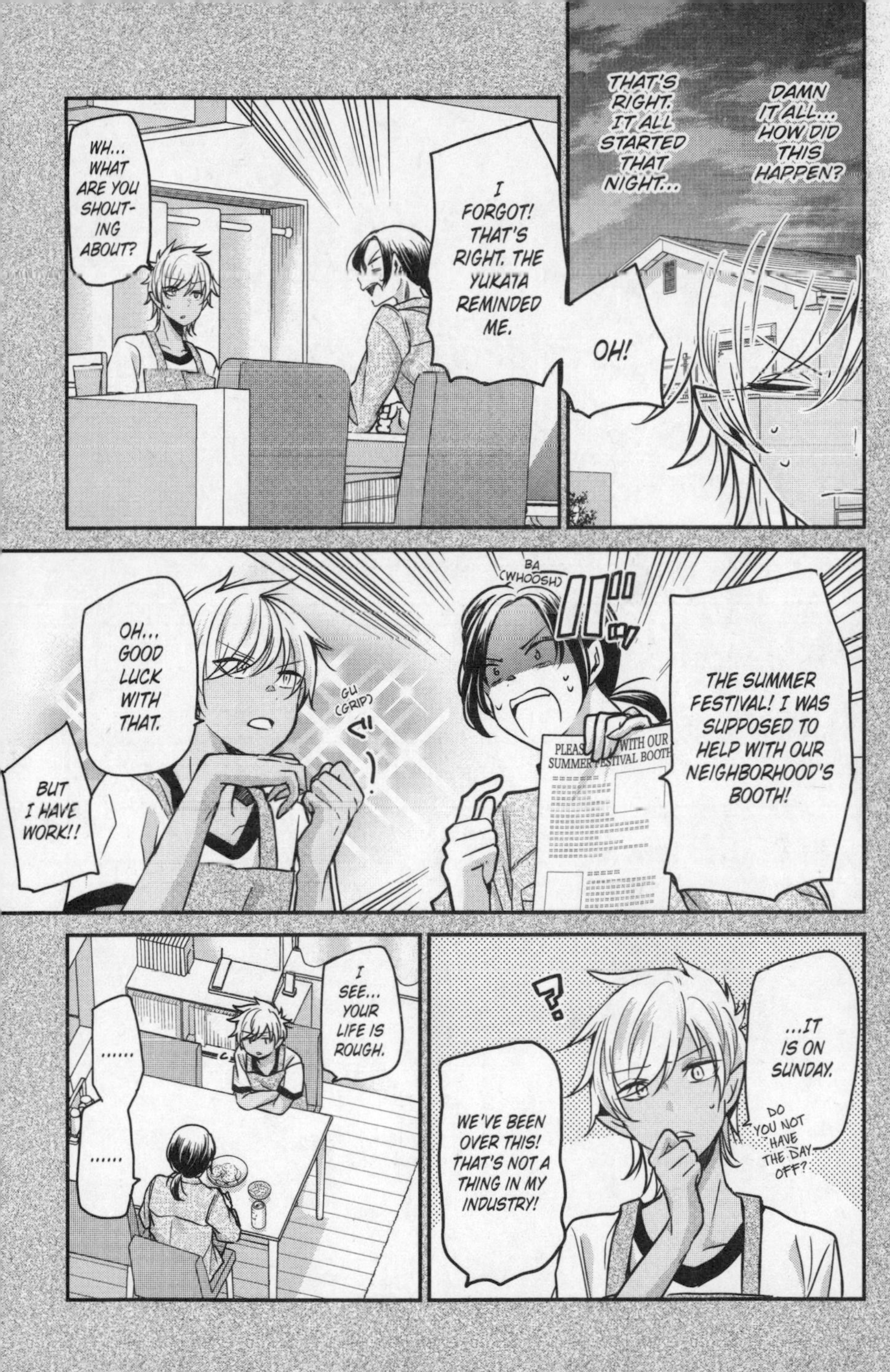
DAMN IT ALL... HOW DID THIS HAPPEN?
THAT'S RIGHT. IT ALL STARTED THAT NIGHT...
OH!
I FORGOT! THAT'S RIGHT. THE YUKATA REMINDED ME.
WH... WHAT ARE YOU SHOUT-ING ABOUT?
BA (WHOOSH)
THE SUMMER FESTIVAL! I WAS SUPPOSED TO HELP WITH OUR NEIGHBORHOOD'S BOOTH!
PLEAS WITH OUR SUMMER FESTIVAL BOOTH
GU (GRIP)
OH... GOOD LUCK WITH THAT.
BUT I HAVE WORK!!
...IT IS ON SUNDAY.
DO YOU NOT HAVE THE DAY OFF?
WE'VE BEEN OVER THIS! THAT'S NOT A THING IN MY INDUSTRY!
I SEE... YOUR LIFE IS ROUGH.
......
......

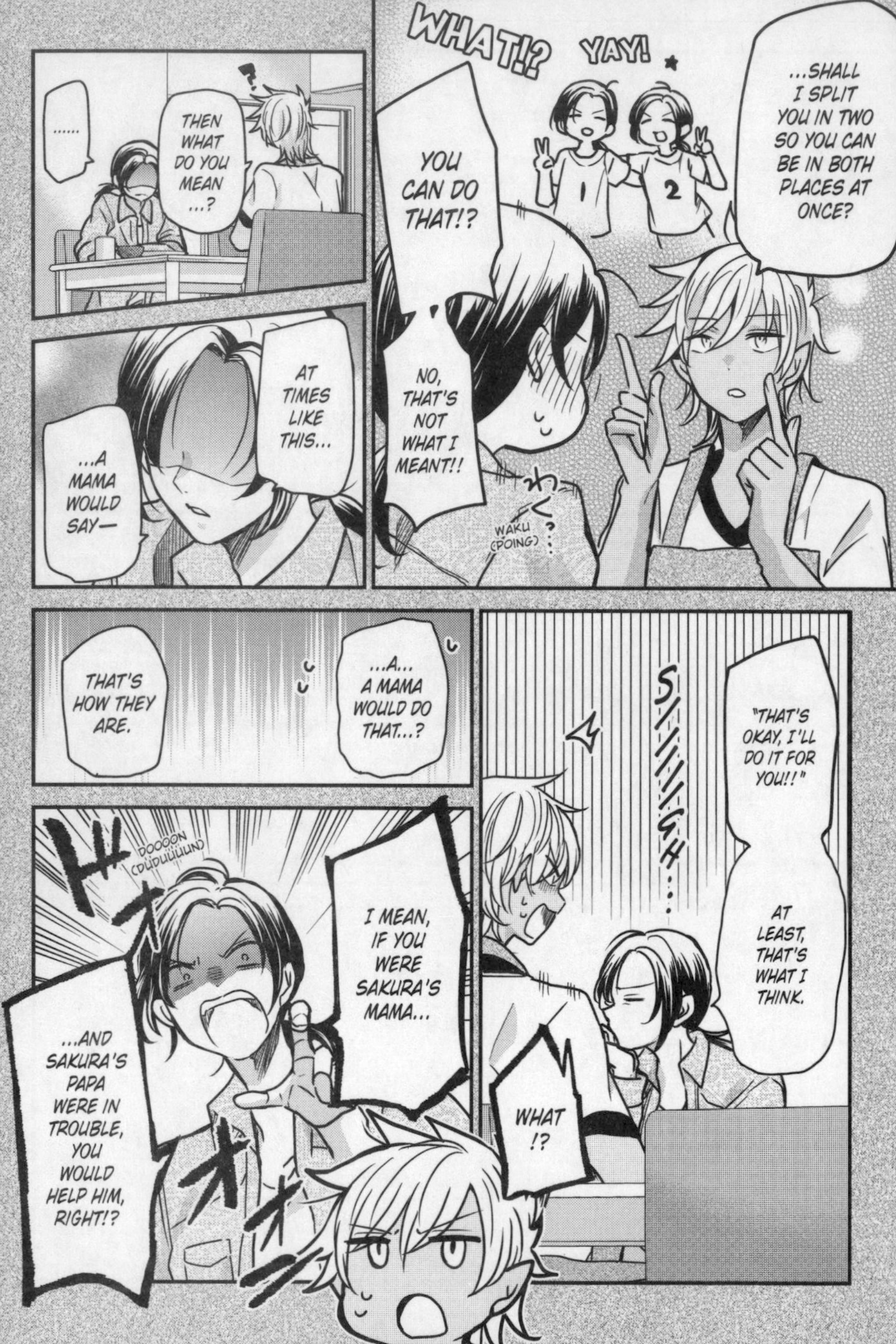
...SHALL I SPLIT YOU IN TWO SO YOU CAN BE IN BOTH PLACES AT ONCE?
YAY!
WHAT!?
YOU CAN DO THAT!?
NO, THAT'S NOT WHAT I MEANT!!
WAKU (POING)
THEN WHAT DO YOU MEAN ...?
......
AT TIMES LIKE THIS...
...A MAMA WOULD SAY—
"THAT'S OKAY, I'LL DO IT FOR YOU!!"
AT LEAST, THAT'S WHAT I THINK.
SIIIIIGH...
WHAT !?
...A... A MAMA WOULD DO THAT...?
THAT'S HOW THEY ARE.
DOOOON (DUDUUUUUN)
I MEAN, IF YOU WERE SAKURA'S MAMA...
...AND SAKURA'S PAPA WERE IN TROUBLE, YOU WOULD HELP HIM, RIGHT!?

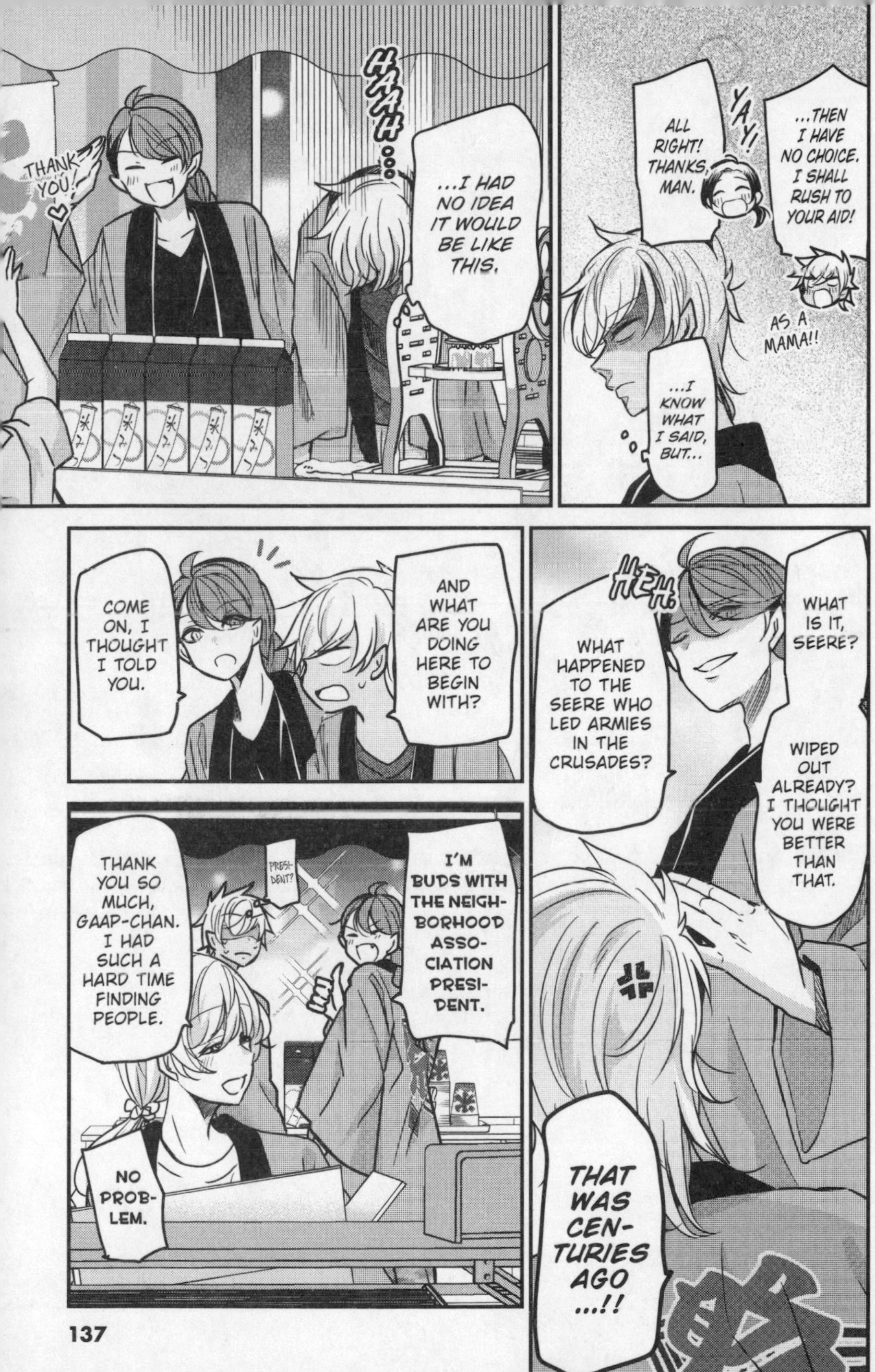
...THEN I HAVE NO CHOICE. I SHALL RUSH TO YOUR AID!
YAY!
ALL RIGHT! THANKS, MAN.
AS A MAMA!!
...I KNOW WHAT I SAID, BUT...
HAAAH...
...I HAD NO IDEA IT WOULD BE LIKE THIS.
THANK YOU! ♡
WHAT IS IT, SEERE?
HEH.
WHAT HAPPENED TO THE SEERE WHO LED ARMIES IN THE CRUSADES?
WIPED OUT ALREADY? I THOUGHT YOU WERE BETTER THAN THAT.
THAT WAS CENTURIES AGO...!!
AND WHAT ARE YOU DOING HERE TO BEGIN WITH?
COME ON, I THOUGHT I TOLD YOU.
I'M BUDS WITH THE NEIGHBORHOOD ASSOCIATION PRESIDENT.
PRESIDENT?
THANK YOU SO MUCH, GAAP-CHAN. I HAD SUCH A HARD TIME FINDING PEOPLE.
NO PROBLEM.

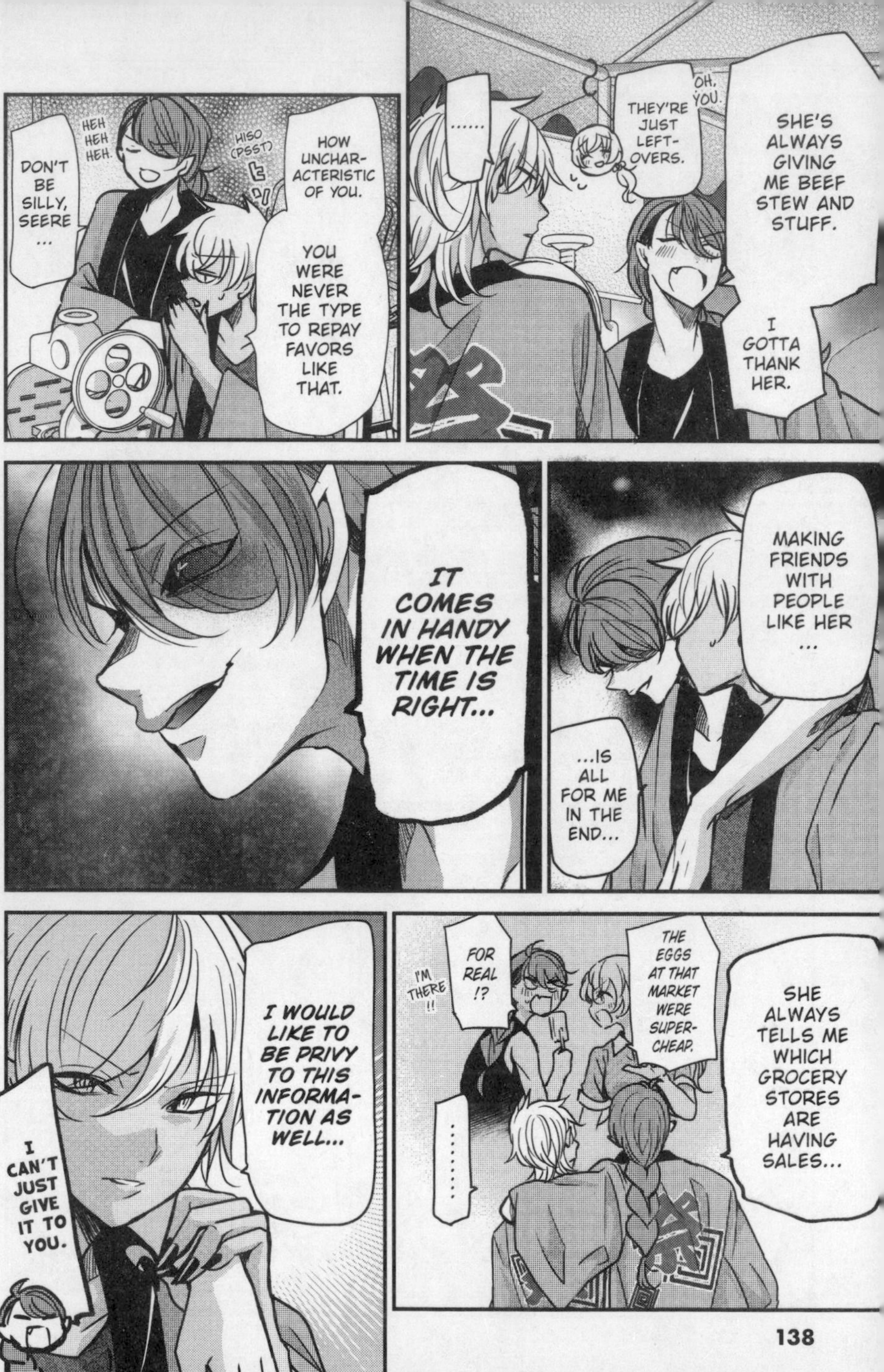
SHE'S ALWAYS GIVING ME BEEF STEW AND STUFF.
OH, YOU.
THEY'RE JUST LEFT-OVERS.
......
I GOTTA THANK HER.
HOW UNCHARACTERISTIC OF YOU.
HISO (PSST)
YOU WERE NEVER THE TYPE TO REPAY FAVORS LIKE THAT.
HEH HEH HEH.
DON'T BE SILLY, SEERE...
MAKING FRIENDS WITH PEOPLE LIKE HER...
...IS ALL FOR ME IN THE END...
IT COMES IN HANDY WHEN THE TIME IS RIGHT...
SHE ALWAYS TELLS ME WHICH GROCERY STORES ARE HAVING SALES...
THE EGGS AT THAT MARKET WERE SUPER-CHEAP.
FOR REAL!?
I'M THERE!!
......
I WOULD LIKE TO BE PRIVY TO THIS INFORMATION AS WELL...
I CAN'T JUST GIVE IT TO YOU.

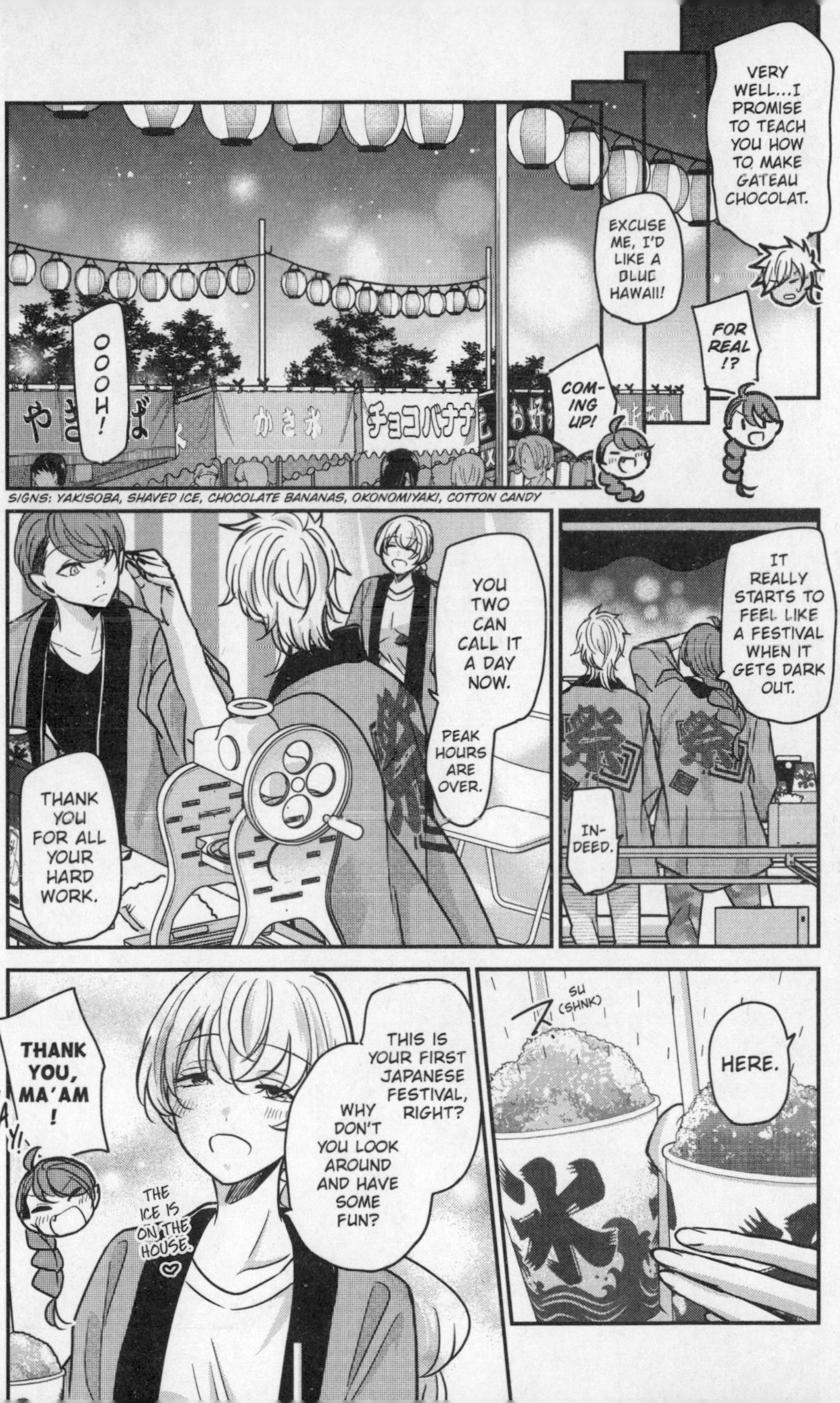
VERY WELL...I PROMISE TO TEACH YOU HOW TO MAKE GATEAU CHOCOLAT.
FOR REAL!?
EXCUSE ME, I'D LIKE A BLUE HAWAII!
COMING UP!
OOOH!
かき氷
チョコバナナ
SIGNS: YAKISOBA, SHAVED ICE, CHOCOLATE BANANAS, OKONOMIYAKI, COTTON CANDY
IT REALLY STARTS TO FEEL LIKE A FESTIVAL WHEN IT GETS DARK OUT.
INDEED.
YOU TWO CAN CALL IT A DAY NOW.
PEAK HOURS ARE OVER.
THANK YOU FOR ALL YOUR HARD WORK.
SU (SHNK)
HERE.
THIS IS YOUR FIRST JAPANESE FESTIVAL, RIGHT?
WHY DON'T YOU LOOK AROUND AND HAVE SOME FUN?
THE ICE IS ON THE HOUSE.
THANK YOU, MA'AM!
YAY!!

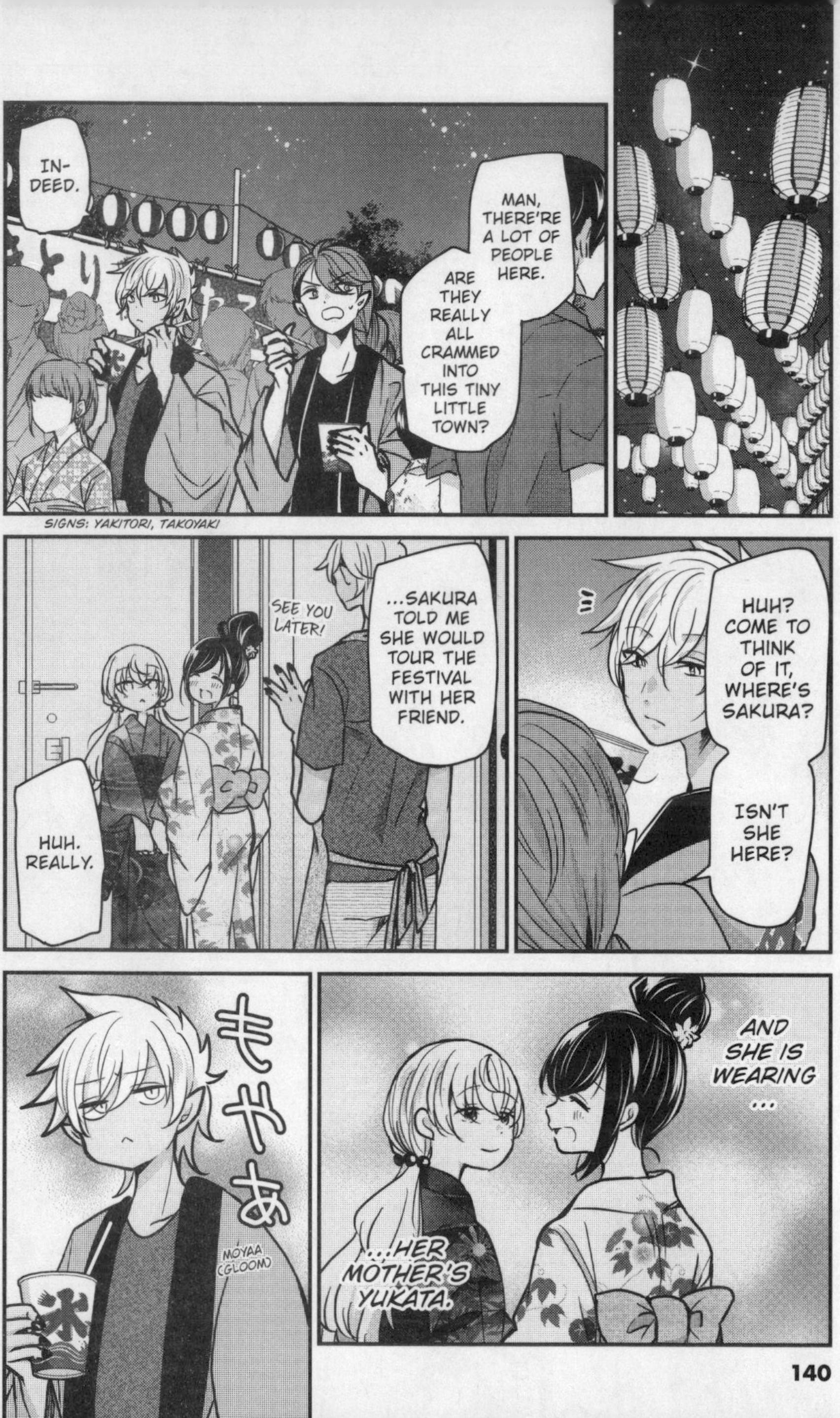
MAN, THERE'RE A LOT OF PEOPLE HERE.
ARE THEY REALLY ALL CRAMMED INTO THIS TINY LITTLE TOWN?
IN-DEED.
SIGNS: YAKITORI, TAKOYAKI
HUH? COME TO THINK OF IT, WHERE'S SAKURA?
ISN'T SHE HERE?
...SAKURA TOLD ME SHE WOULD TOUR THE FESTIVAL WITH HER FRIEND.
SEE YOU LATER!
HUH. REALLY.
AND SHE IS WEARING...
...HER MOTHER'S YUKATA.
もやぁ
MOYAA (GLOOM)

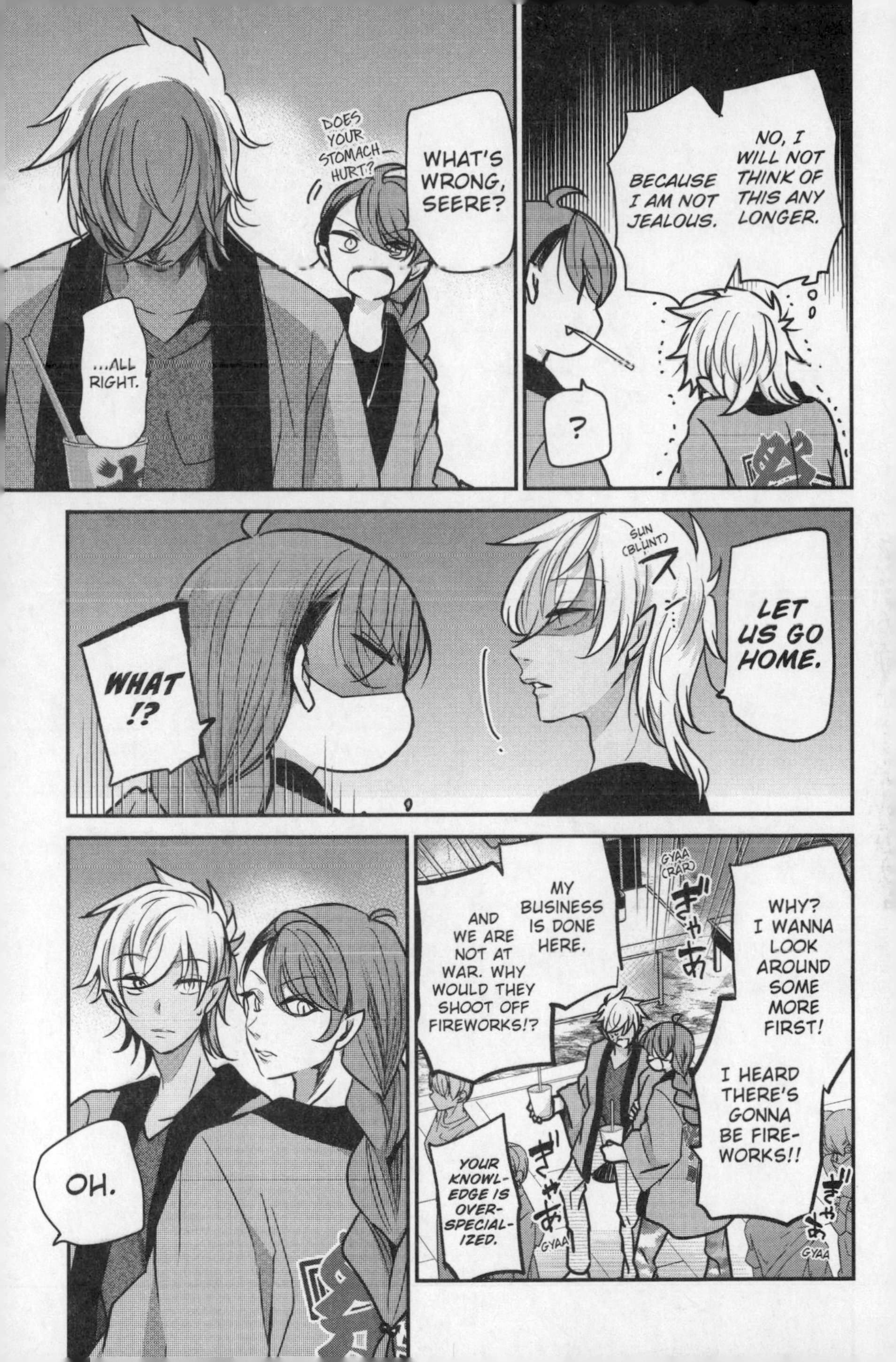
NO, I WILL NOT THINK OF THIS ANY LONGER.
BECAUSE I AM NOT JEALOUS.
?
WHAT'S WRONG, SEERE?
DOES YOUR STOMACH HURT?
...ALL RIGHT.
SUN (BLUNT)
LET US GO HOME.
WHAT!?
WHY? I WANNA LOOK AROUND SOME MORE FIRST!
I HEARD THERE'S GONNA BE FIRE-WORKS!!
ぎゃあ GYAA (RAR)
MY BUSINESS IS DONE HERE.
AND WE ARE NOT AT WAR. WHY WOULD THEY SHOOT OFF FIREWORKS!?
YOUR KNOWL-EDGE IS OVER-SPECIAL-IZED.
ぎゃあ GYAA
ぎゃあ GYAA
OH.

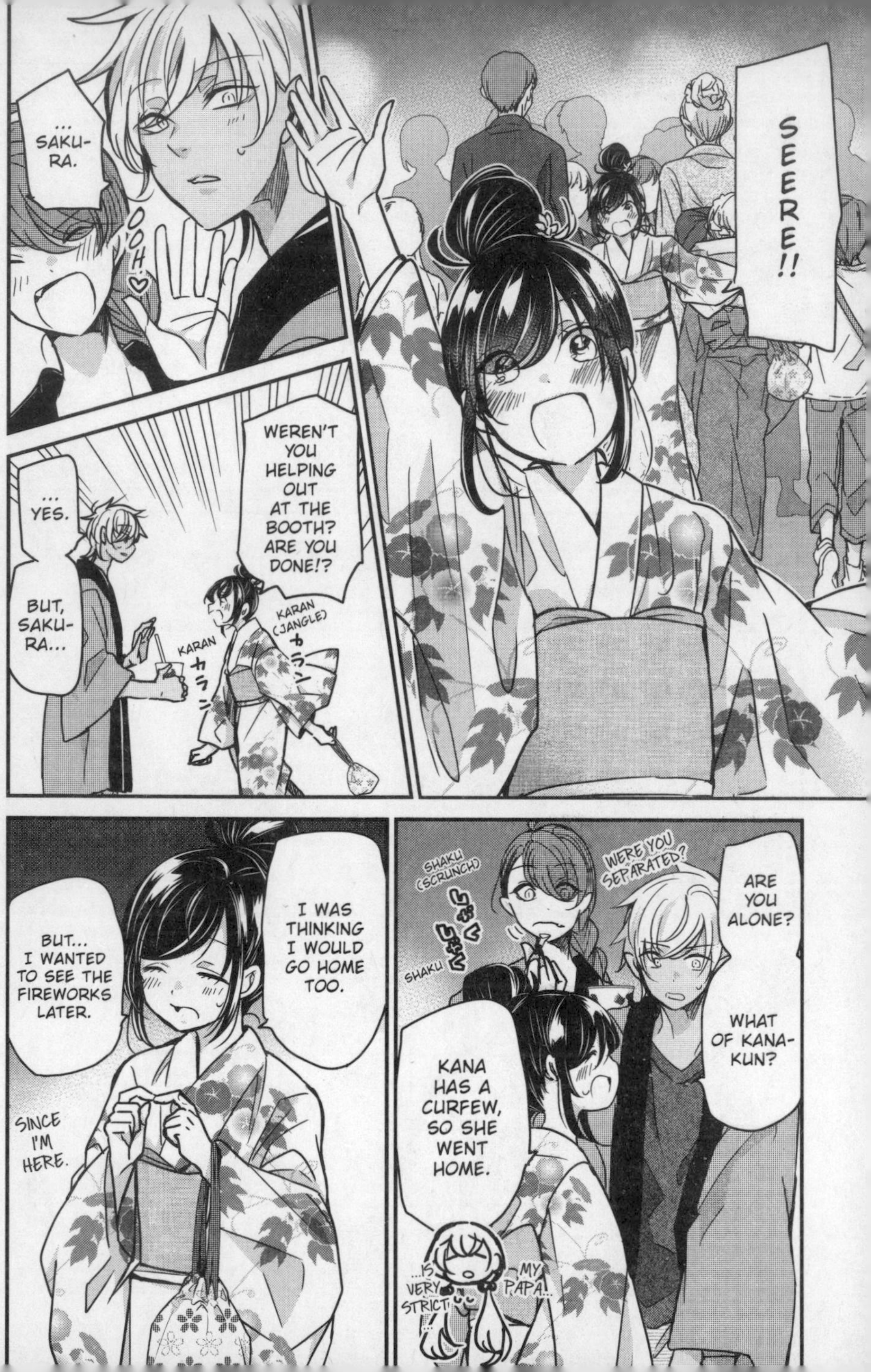
SEERE!!
... SAKURA.
OOH ♥
WEREN'T YOU HELPING OUT AT THE BOOTH? ARE YOU DONE!?
... YES.
BUT, SAKURA...
KARAN (JANGLE) カラン
KARAN カラン
ARE YOU ALONE?
WERE YOU SEPARATED?
SHAKU (SCRUNCH) しゃく
SHAKU しゃく
WHAT OF KANA-KUN?
KANA HAS A CURFEW, SO SHE WENT HOME.
MY PAPA...
...IS VERY STRICT...
I WAS THINKING I WOULD GO HOME TOO.
BUT... I WANTED TO SEE THE FIREWORKS LATER.
SINCE I'M HERE.

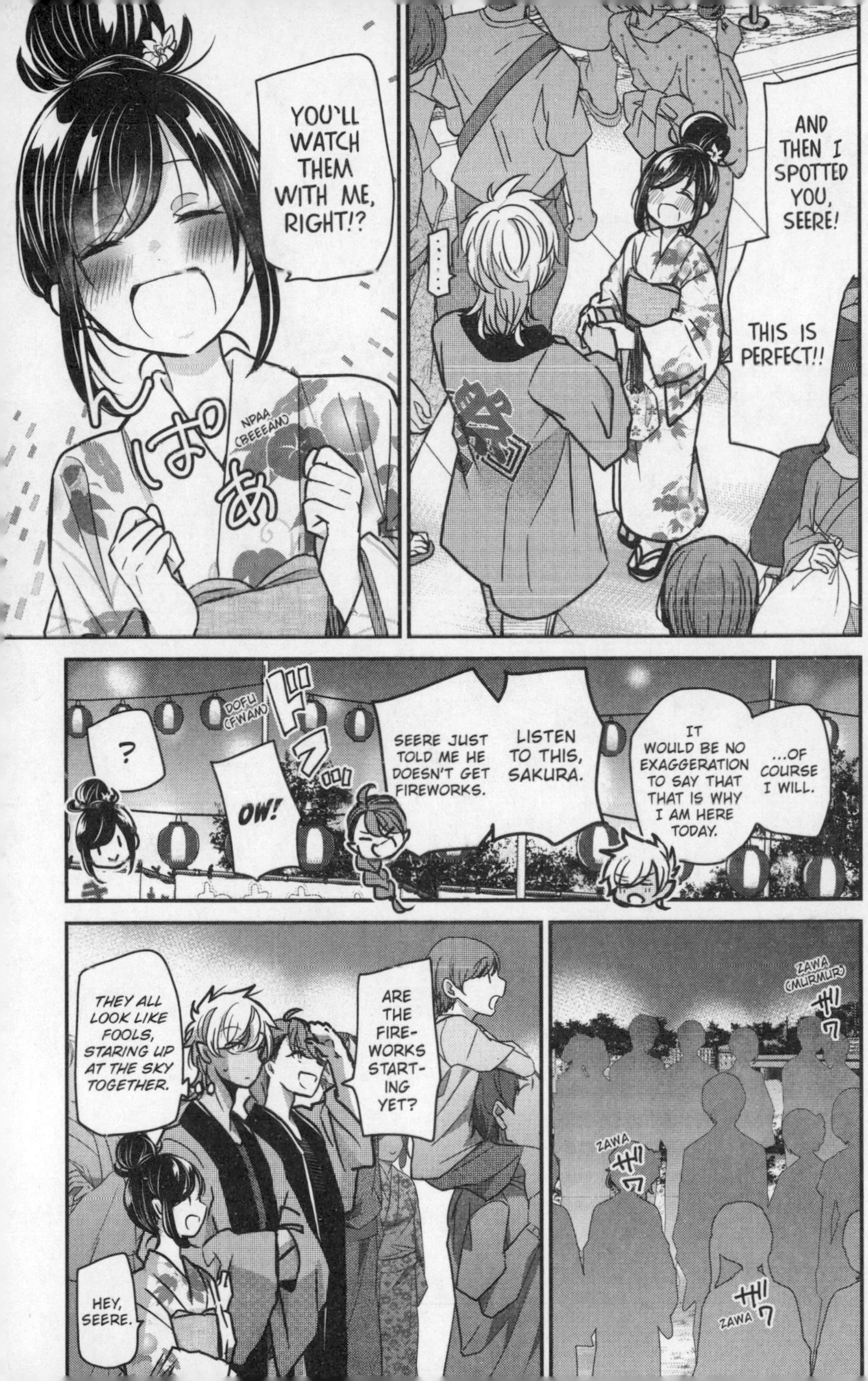
AND THEN I SPOTTED YOU, SEERE!
THIS IS PERFECT!!
......
YOU'LL WATCH THEM WITH ME, RIGHT!?
NPAA (BEEEAM)
...OF COURSE I WILL.
IT WOULD BE NO EXAGGERATION TO SAY THAT THAT IS WHY I AM HERE TODAY.
LISTEN TO THIS, SAKURA.
SEERE JUST TOLD ME HE DOESN'T GET FIREWORKS.
DOFU (FWAM)
OW!
?
ZAWA (MURMUR)
ZAWA
ZAWA
ARE THE FIRE-WORKS START-ING YET?
THEY ALL LOOK LIKE FOOLS, STARING UP AT THE SKY TOGETHER.
HEY, SEERE.

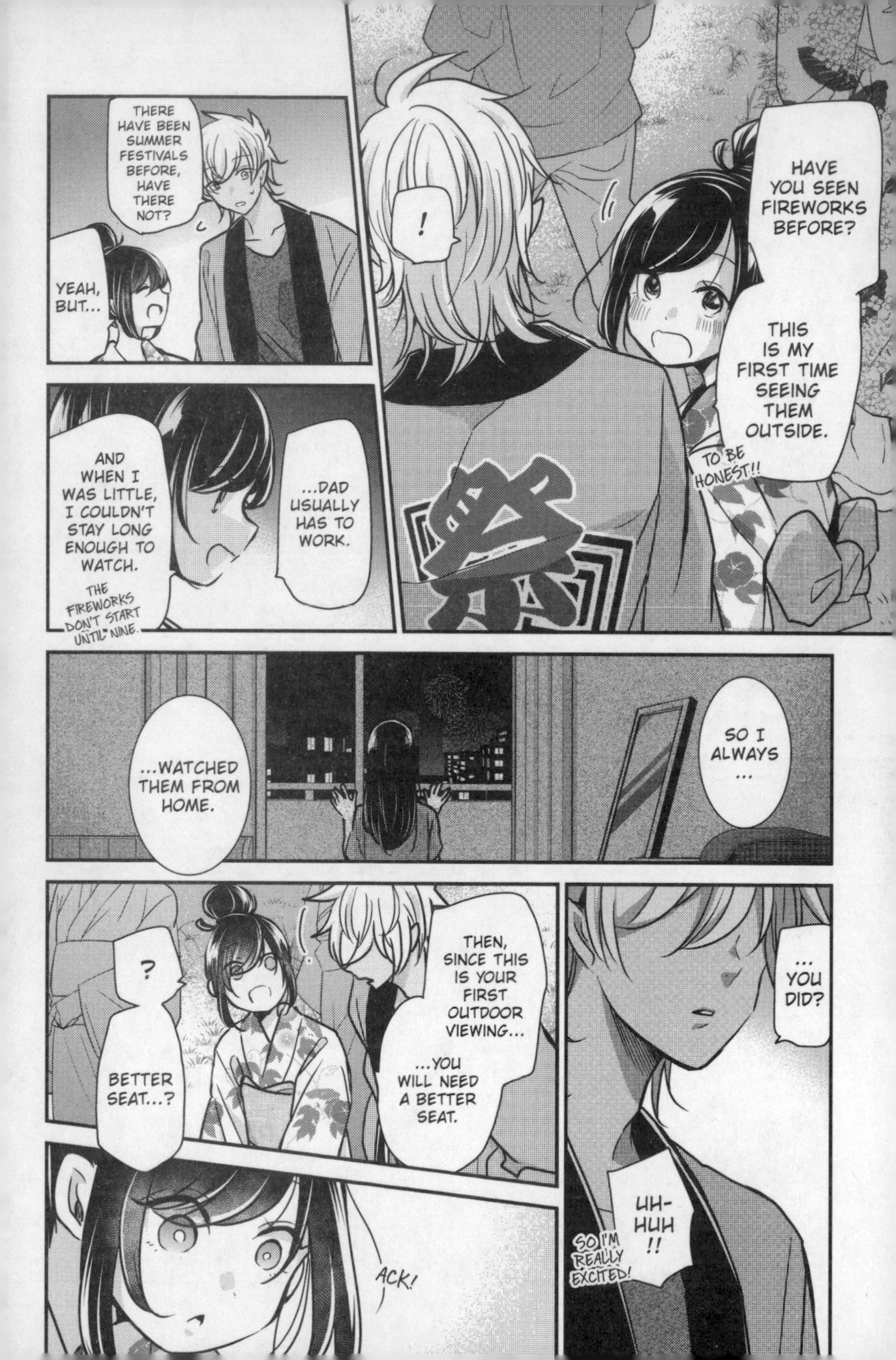
HAVE YOU SEEN FIREWORKS BEFORE?
THIS IS MY FIRST TIME SEEING THEM OUTSIDE.
TO BE HONEST!!
!
THERE HAVE BEEN SUMMER FESTIVALS BEFORE, HAVE THERE NOT?
YEAH, BUT...
...DAD USUALLY HAS TO WORK.
AND WHEN I WAS LITTLE, I COULDN'T STAY LONG ENOUGH TO WATCH.
THE FIREWORKS DON'T START UNTIL NINE.
SO I ALWAYS...
...WATCHED THEM FROM HOME.
...YOU DID?
UH-HUH!!
SO I'M REALLY EXCITED!
THEN, SINCE THIS IS YOUR FIRST OUTDOOR VIEWING...
...YOU WILL NEED A BETTER SEAT.
?
BETTER SEAT...?
ACK!

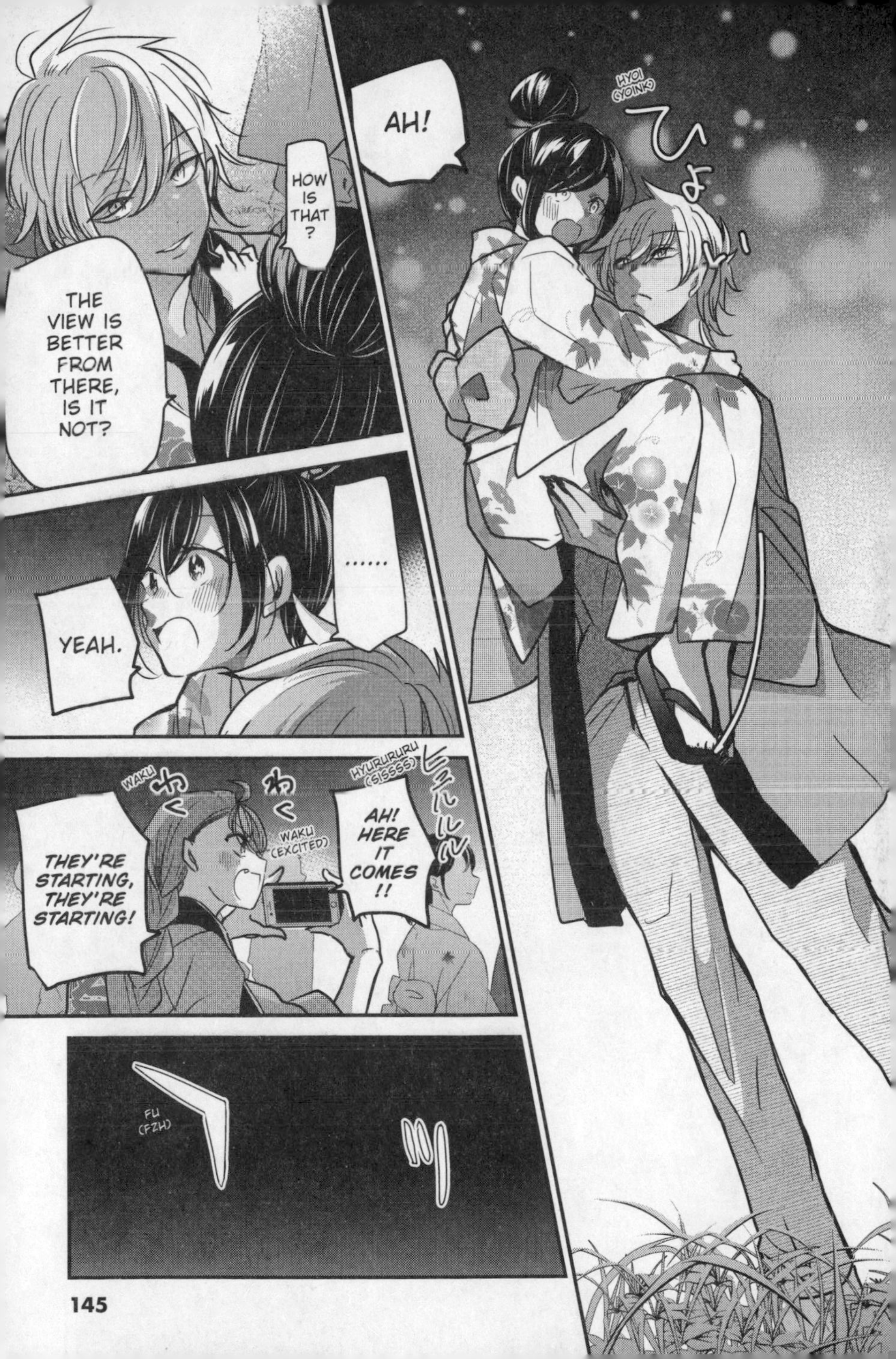
HYOI (YOINK)
AH!
HOW IS THAT?
THE VIEW IS BETTER FROM THERE, IS IT NOT?
......
YEAH.
HYURURURU (SISSSS)
AH! HERE IT COMES!!
WAKU
WAKU (EXCITED)
THEY'RE STARTING, THEY'RE STARTING!
FU (FZH)

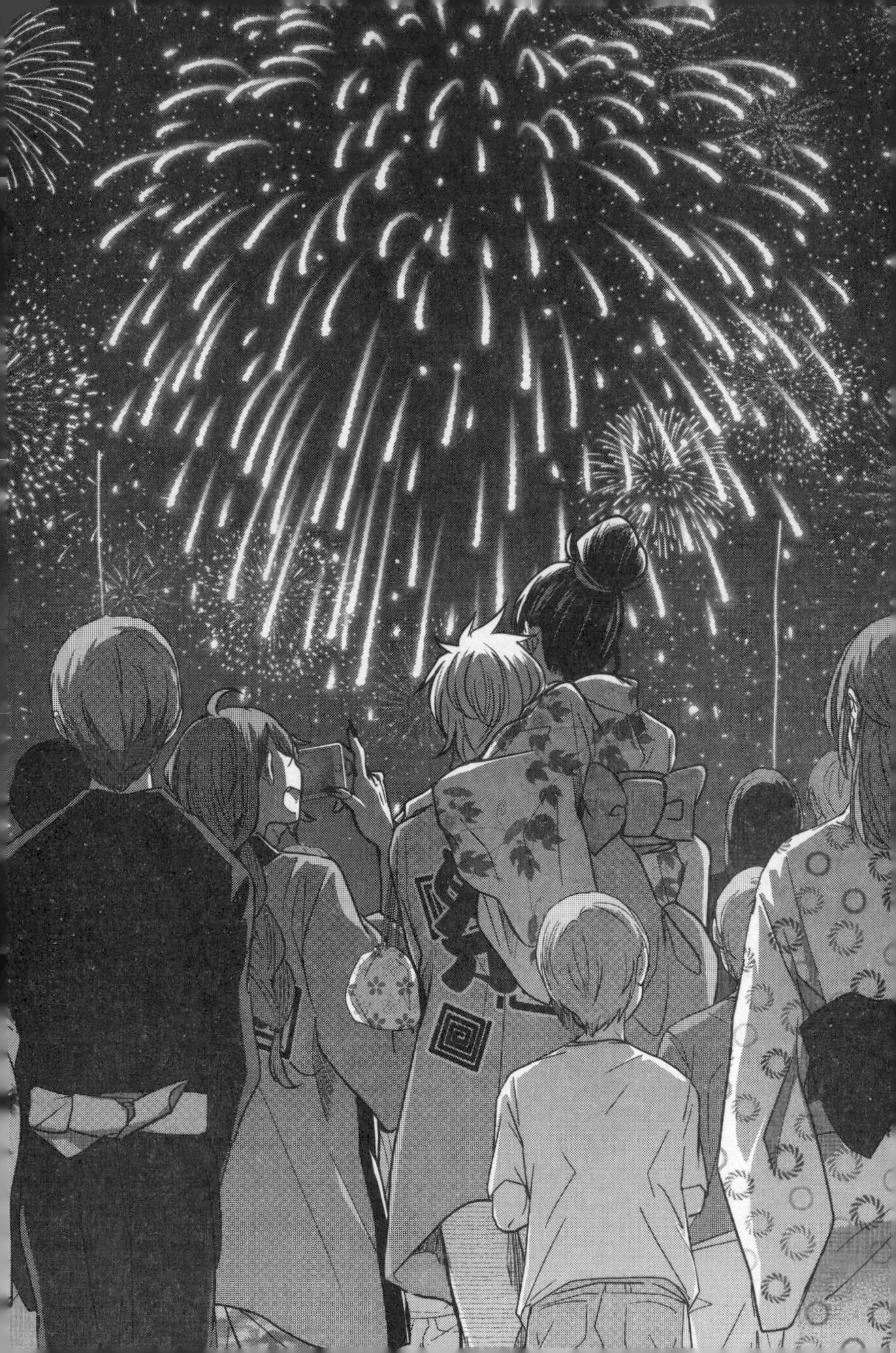

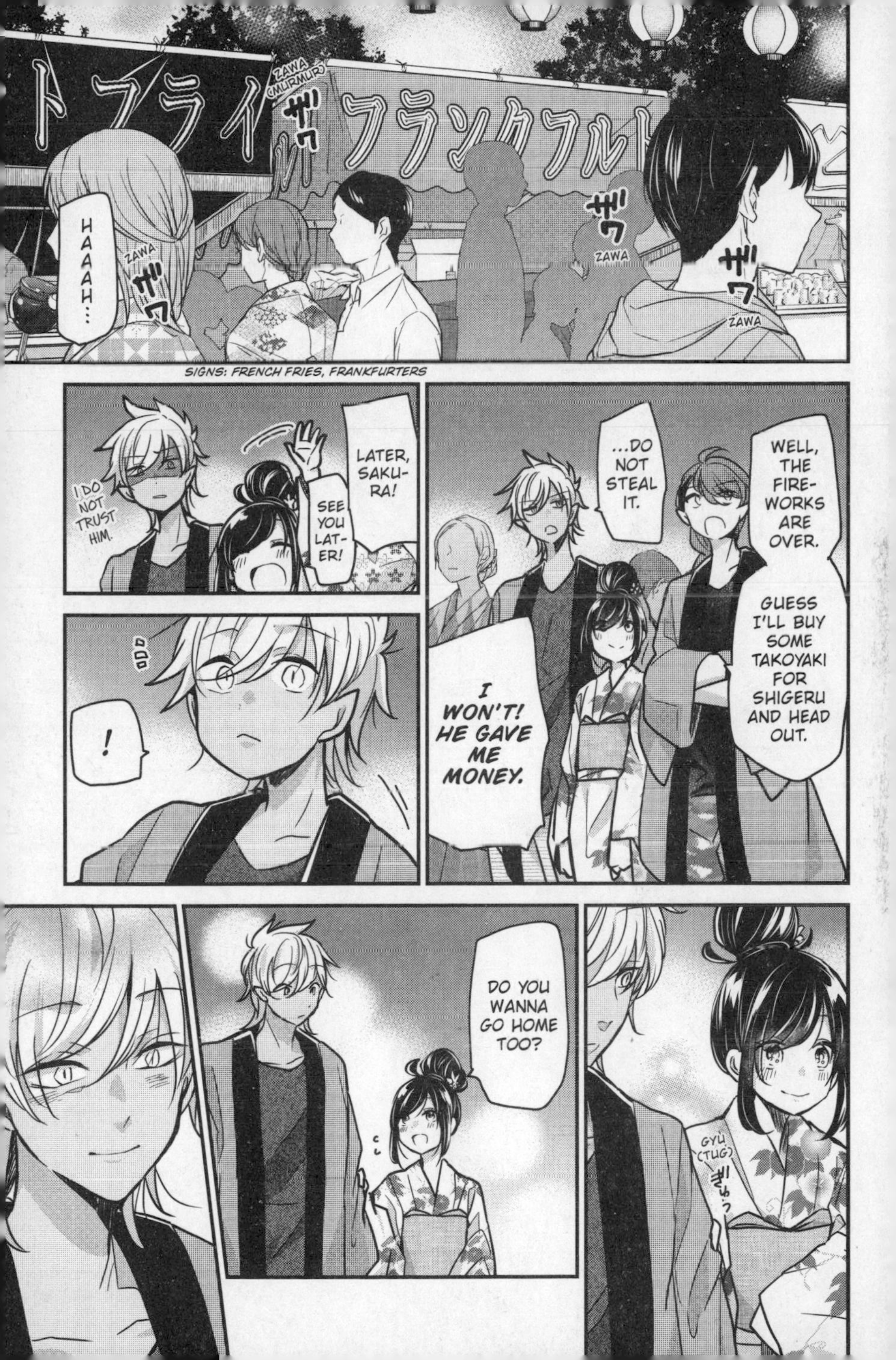
ZAWA
ZAWA
ZAWA (MURMUR)
ZAWA
HAAAAH...
SIGNS: FRENCH FRIES, FRANKFURTERS
WELL, THE FIRE-WORKS ARE OVER.
GUESS I'LL BUY SOME TAKOYAKI FOR SHIGERU AND HEAD OUT.
...DO NOT STEAL IT.
I WON'T! HE GAVE ME MONEY.
LATER, SAKU-RA!
SEE YOU LAT-ER!
I DO NOT TRUST HIM.
!
GYU (TUG)
DO YOU WANNA GO HOME TOO?

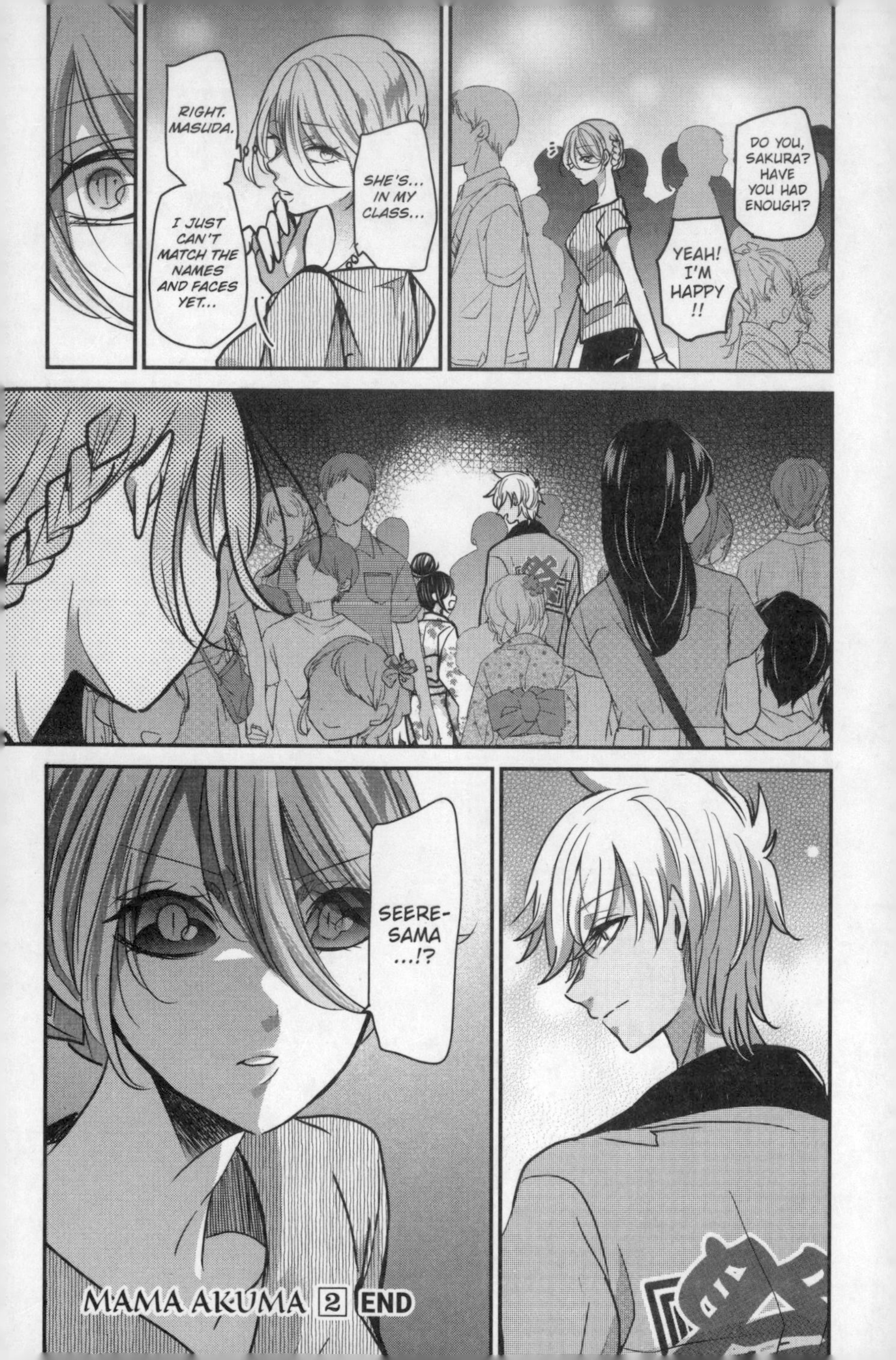
DO YOU, SAKURA? HAVE YOU HAD ENOUGH?
YEAH! I'M HAPPY !!
SHE'S... IN MY CLASS...
RIGHT. MASUDA.
I JUST CAN'T MATCH THE NAMES AND FACES YET...
SEERE-SAMA ...!?
MAMA AKUMA 2 END

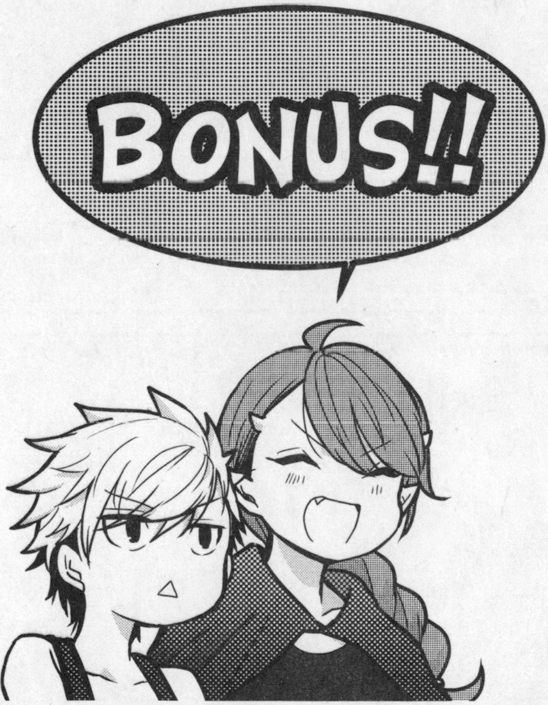
BONUS!!

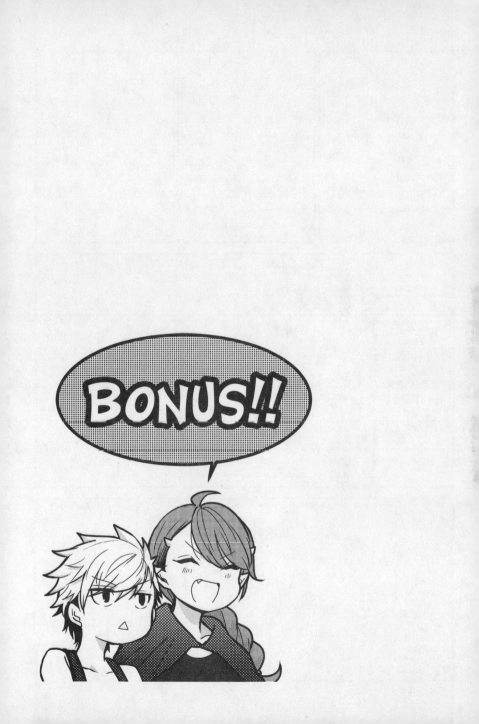

# Demon Pancakes

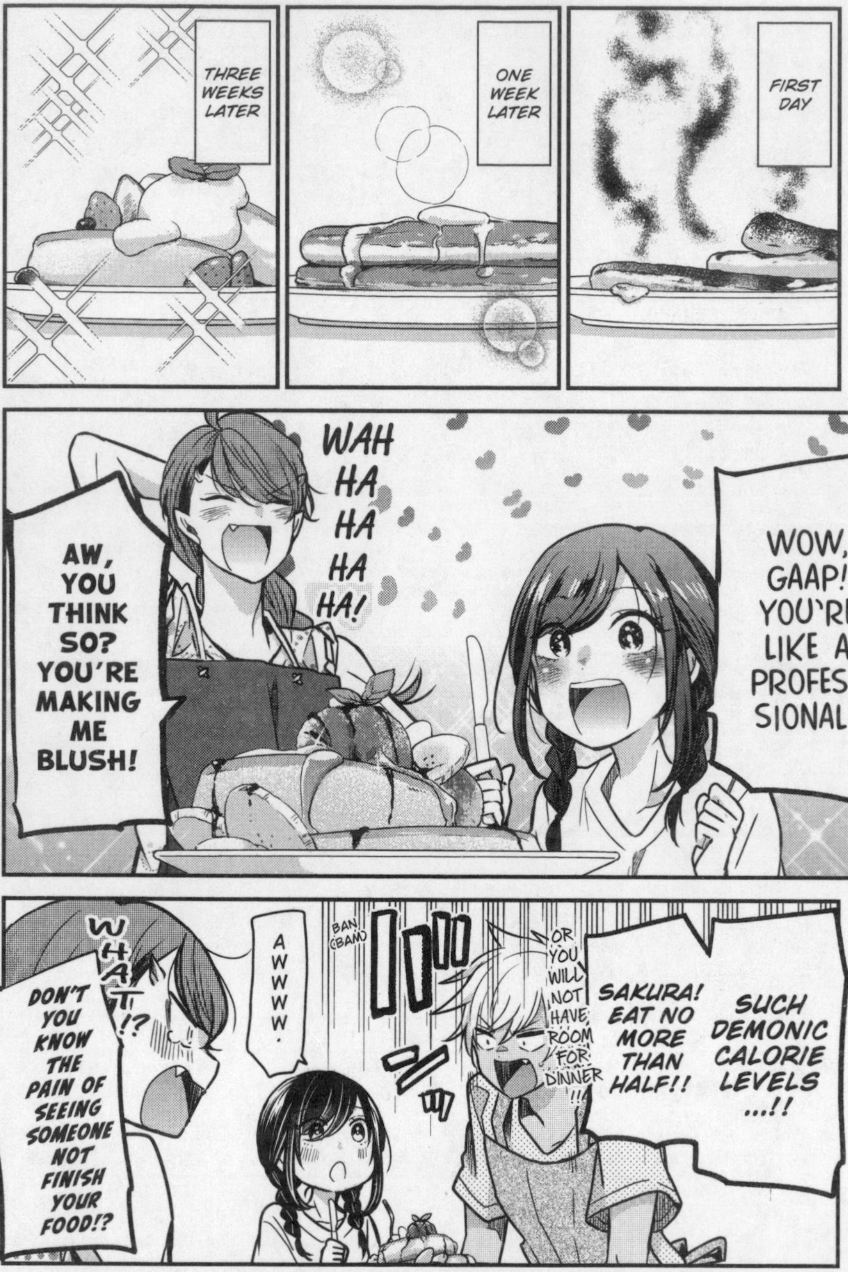
FIRST DAY
ONE WEEK LATER
THREE WEEKS LATER
WOW, GAAP! YOU'RE LIKE A PROFES-SIONAL!
WAH HA HA HA HA!
AW, YOU THINK SO? YOU'RE MAKING ME BLUSH!
SUCH DEMONIC CALORIE LEVELS ...!!
SAKURA! EAT NO MORE THAN HALF!!
OR YOU WILL NOT HAVE ROOM FOR DINNER!!
BAN BAM
AWWWW.
WHAT!?
DON'T YOU KNOW THE PAIN OF SEEING SOMEONE NOT FINISH YOUR FOOD!?

# Demon Conflicted

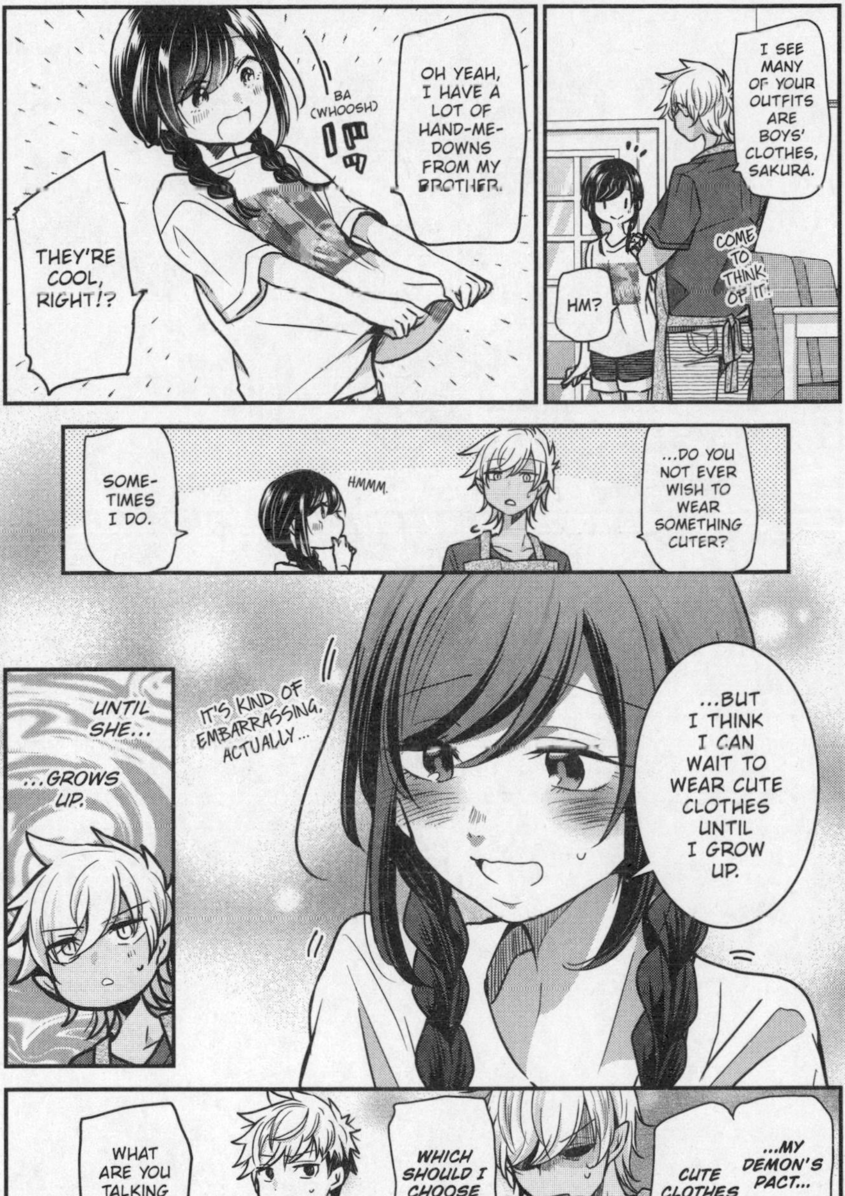
I SEE MANY OF YOUR OUTFITS ARE BOYS' CLOTHES, SAKURA.
COME TO THINK OF IT.
HM?
BA (WHOOSH)
OH YEAH, I HAVE A LOT OF HAND-ME-DOWNS FROM MY BROTHER.
THEY'RE COOL, RIGHT!?
...DO YOU NOT EVER WISH TO WEAR SOMETHING CUTER?
HMMM.
SOME-TIMES I DO.
...BUT I THINK I CAN WAIT TO WEAR CUTE CLOTHES UNTIL I GROW UP.
IT'S KIND OF EMBARRASSING, ACTUALLY...
UNTIL SHE...
...GROWS UP.
...MY DEMON'S PACT...
CUTE CLOTHES ...
WHICH SHOULD I CHOOSE ...?
WHAT ARE YOU TALKING ABOUT?

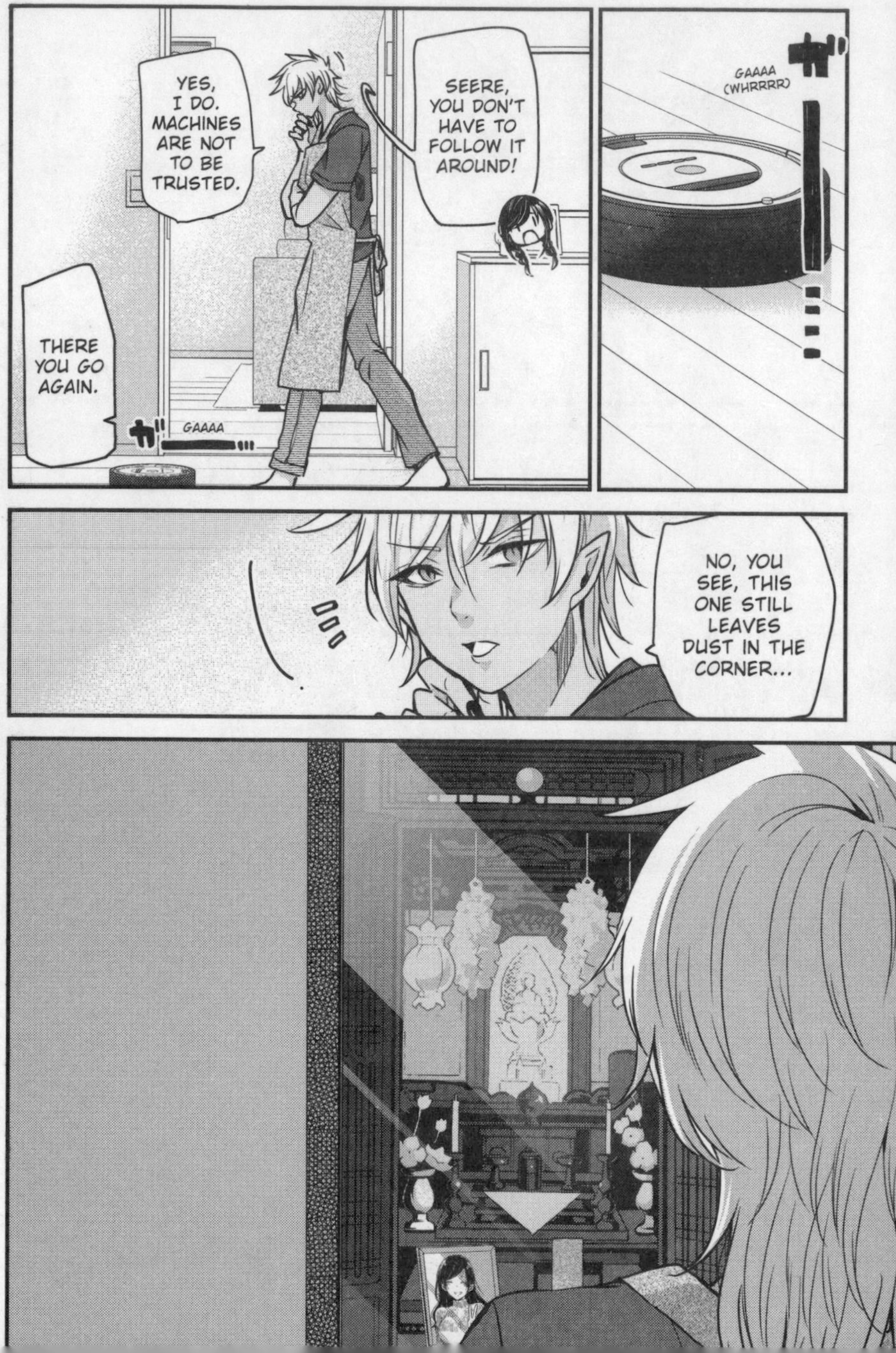
GAAAA (WHRRRR)
SEERE, YOU DON'T HAVE TO FOLLOW IT AROUND!
YES, I DO. MACHINES ARE NOT TO BE TRUSTED.
THERE YOU GO AGAIN.
GAAAA
NO, YOU SEE, THIS ONE STILL LEAVES DUST IN THE CORNER...

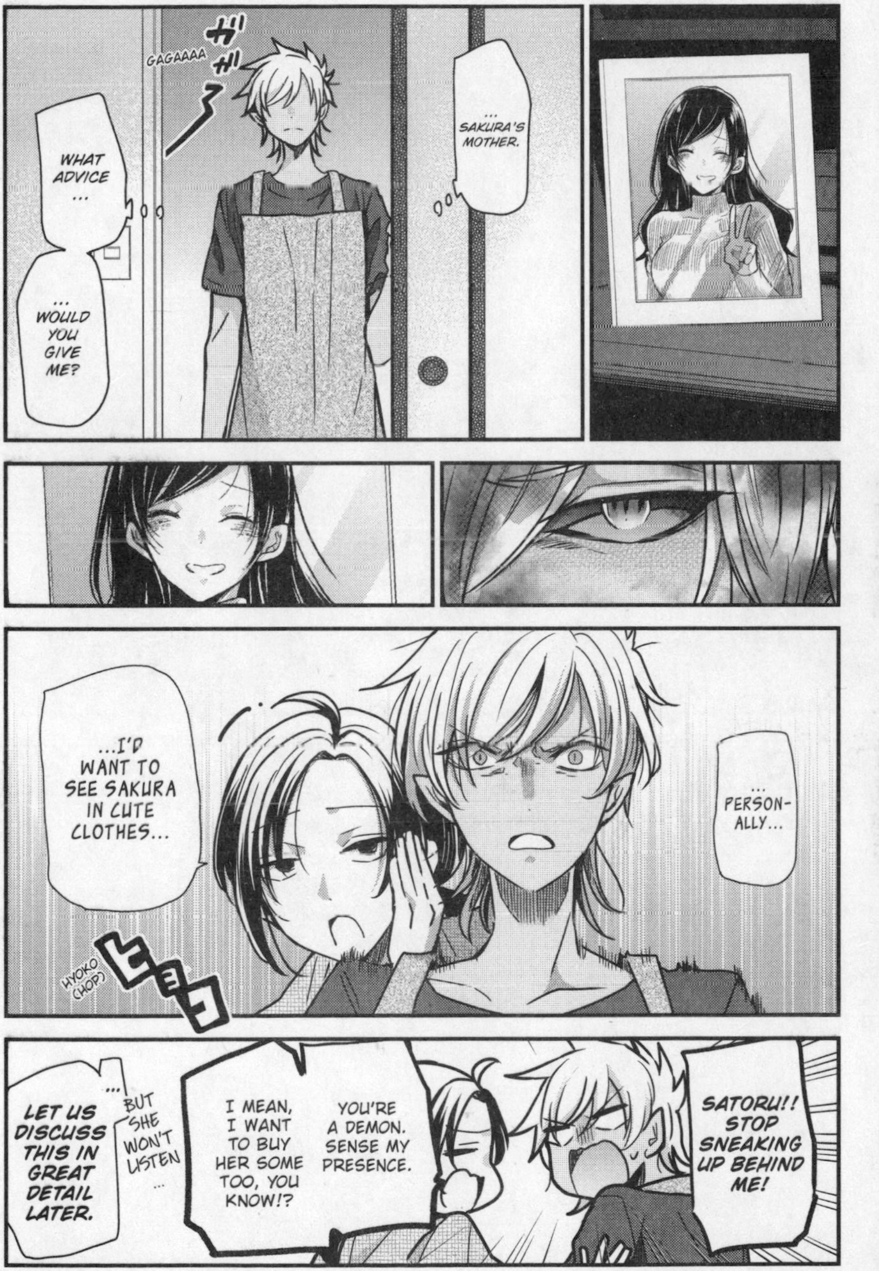
GAGAAAA
... SAKURA'S MOTHER.
WHAT ADVICE ...
... WOULD YOU GIVE ME?
... PERSON-ALLY...
...I'D WANT TO SEE SAKURA IN CUTE CLOTHES...
HYOKO (HOP)
SATORU!! STOP SNEAKING UP BEHIND ME!
YOU'RE A DEMON. SENSE MY PRESENCE.
I MEAN, I WANT TO BUY HER SOME TOO, YOU KNOW!?
... BUT SHE WON'T LISTEN ...
LET US DISCUSS THIS IN GREAT DETAIL LATER.

# Day.16.9

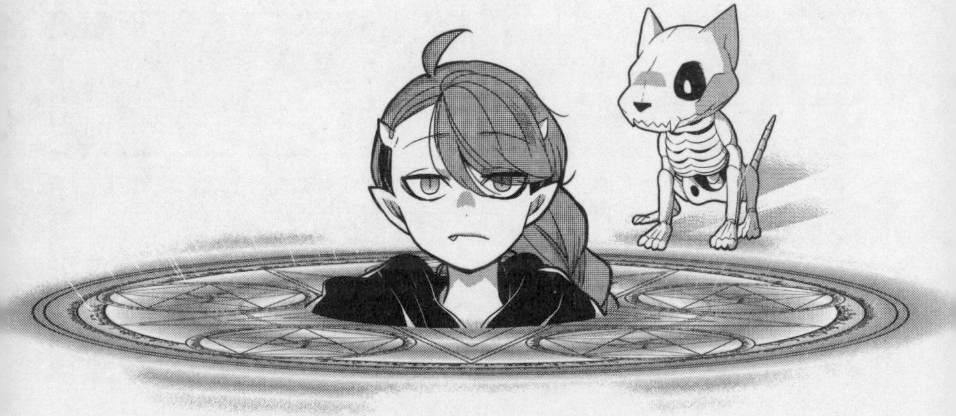

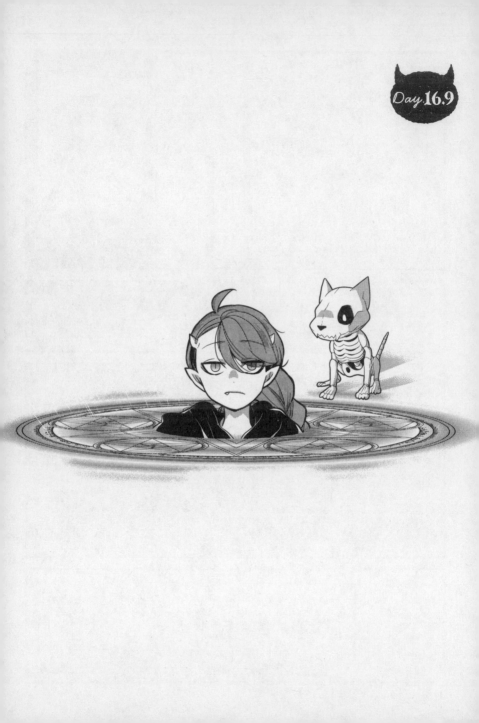

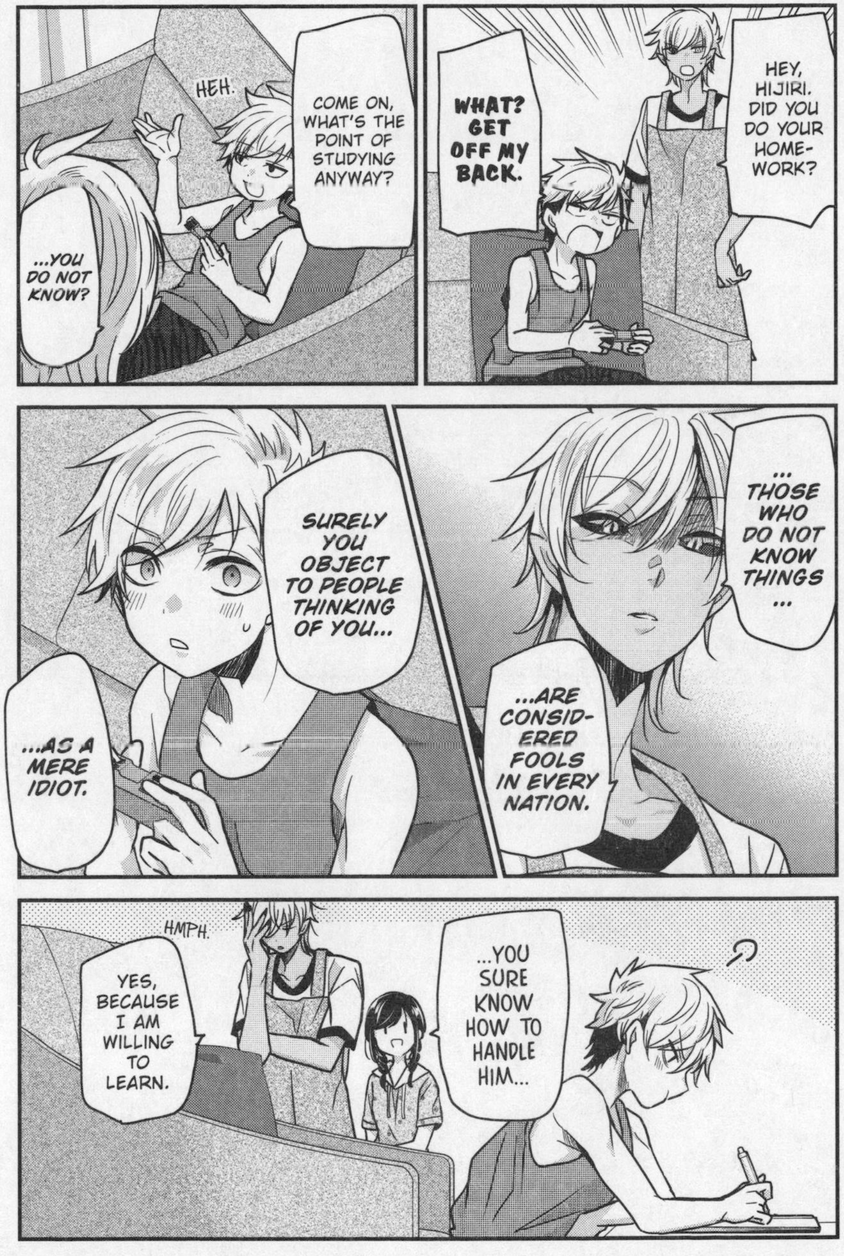
HEY, HIJIRI. DID YOU DO YOUR HOME-WORK?
WHAT? GET OFF MY BACK.
HEH.
COME ON, WHAT'S THE POINT OF STUDYING ANYWAY?
...YOU DO NOT KNOW?
... THOSE WHO DO NOT KNOW THINGS ...
...ARE CONSID-ERED FOOLS IN EVERY NATION.
SURELY YOU OBJECT TO PEOPLE THINKING OF YOU...
...AS A MERE IDIOT.
...YOU SURE KNOW HOW TO HANDLE HIM...
HMPH.
YES, BECAUSE I AM WILLING TO LEARN.

# Translation Notes

**Common Honorifics**

**no honorific:** Indicates familiarity or closeness; if used without permission or reason, addressing someone in this manner would constitute an insult.

**-san:** The Japanese equivalent of Mr./Mrs./Miss. If a situation calls for politeness, this is the fail-safe honorific.

**-kun:** Used most often when referring to boys, this indicates affection or familiarity. Occasionally used by older men among their peers, but it may also be used by anyone referring to a person of lower standing.

**-chan:** An affectionate honorific indicating familiarity used mostly in reference to girls; also used in reference to cute persons or animals of either gender.

**-sama:** Extremely formal and conveys an enormous amount of respect for the addressee.

**-sensei:** Used to refer to teachers, doctors, and respected artistic talents like manga authors.

## Page 11
**Anzai-sensei** is the beloved coach from the hit manga and anime series about basketball, *Slam Dunk*.

## Page 22
Contrary to Gaap's guess, **nasi goreng** is a dish popular in Indonesia, consisting of rice, meat, and vegetables.

## Page 28
**Happosai** is the Japanese name of the Chinese dish *babaocai*, consisting of a number of ingredients, mostly vegetables. It comes in many varieties, including some with meat, but clearly, Seere did not make one of those varieties.

## Page 36
**Kamiyui** is a catchall term for hairdressers in Japan during the Edo and Meiji periods. Despite Seere's boasting of his experience, women were generally only attended to by female *kamiyui*. As a man, he would likely have spent most of his time shaving heads and trimming beards.

## Page 66
This is a reference to a famous scene in *Neon Genesis Evangelion*, where Rei tells Shinji, **"You won't die, because I will protect you."**

**Page 85**
A **yukata** is a sort of summer kimono, made of lighter, cooler fabric. It is common to wear them at traditional Japanese events, such as summer festivals.

**Page 86**
Over the summer in Japan, there are exercise programs for children to attend called **radio calisthenics**. As part of the program, the children get an attendance card with a calendar on it, and they get a stamp on the card for each day they attend.

**Page 97**
In Japanese folklore, there is a creature that is said to devour nightmares called a *baku*. Presumably, in Seere's mind, this creature is much more frightening than a mere dream.

**Page 117**
In Japan, it is common practice to use a **hanko**, or signature seal, instead of signing one's name on official documents, package delivery forms, etc.

**Page 123**
There is an art to properly wearing a kimono or yukata, and an unpracticed wearer may need help from someone with more experience and/or the proper training. The art of dressing another in kimono is called *kitsuke*.

**Page 131**
This is a reference to Souther from the post-apocalyptic martial arts manga, *Fist of the North Star*. Souther takes the title of **Holy Emperor** and claims to have renounced all emotion.

©Aidalro/SQUARE ENIX

# Toilet-bound Hanako-Kun

At Kamome Academy, rumors abound about the school's Seven Mysteries, one of which is Hanako-san. Said to occupy the third stall of the third floor girls' bathroom in the old school building, Hanako-san grants any wish when summoned. Nene Yashiro, an occult-loving high school girl who dreams of romance, ventures into this haunted bathroom...but the Hanako-san she meets there is nothing like she imagined! Kamome Academy's Hanako-san...is a boy!

Yen Press

For more information
visit www.yenpress.com

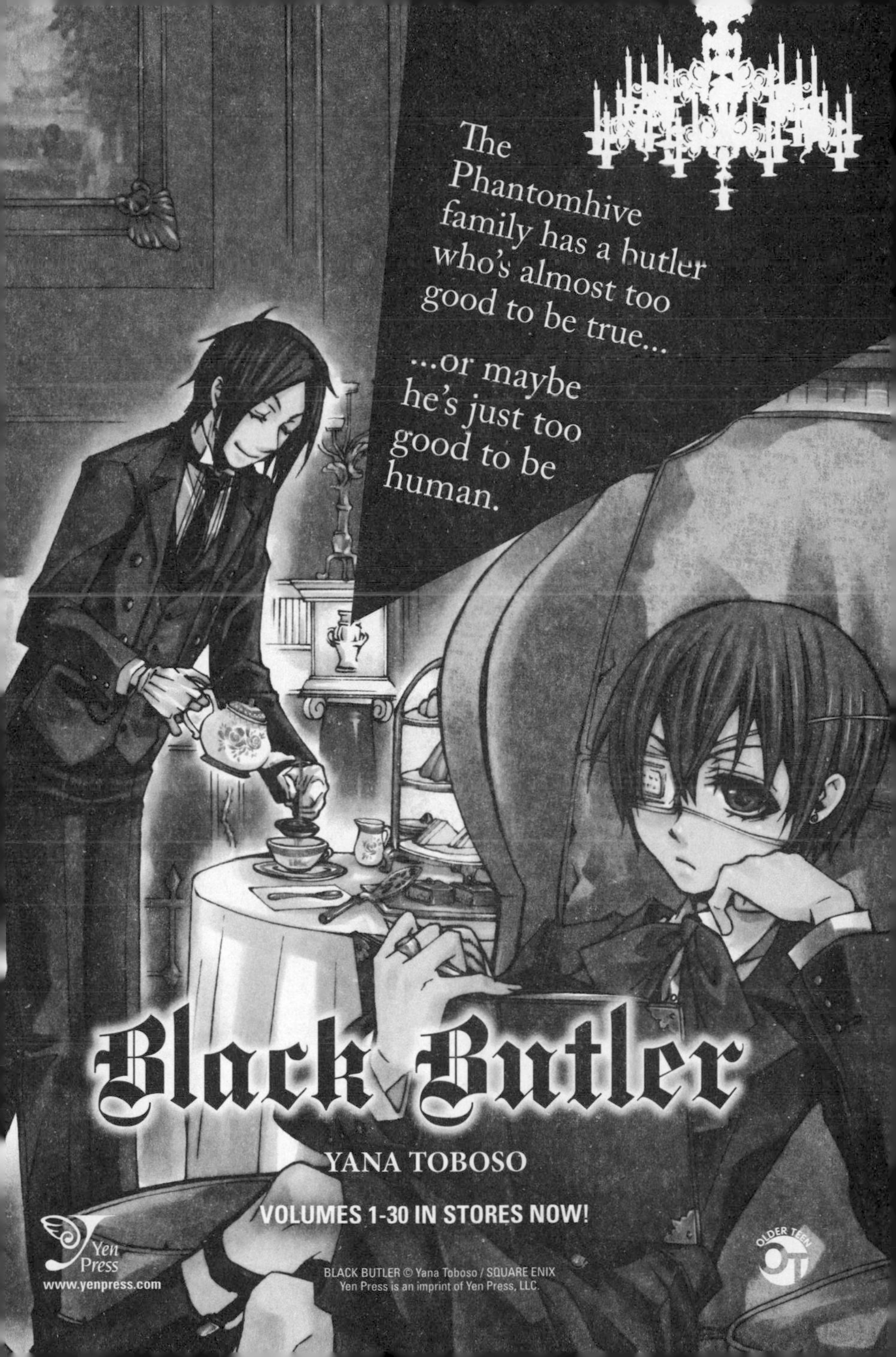
The Phantomhive family has a butler who's almost too good to be true...
...or maybe he's just too good to be human.
Black Butler
YANA TOBOSO
VOLUMES 1-30 IN STORES NOW!
Yen Press
www.yenpress.com
OLDER TEEN
BLACK BUTLER © Yana Toboso / SQUARE ENIX
Yen Press is an imprint of Yen Press, LLC.

# There's something really strange about the maid I just hired!

No normal person could be so beautiful, or cook such amazingly delicious food, or know exactly what I want before I even ask. She must be using magic—right, a spell is the only thing that can explain why my chest feels so tight whenever I look at her. I swear, I'm going to get to the bottom of what makes this maid so...mysterious!

## Volume 2 Now Available!

The **Maid** I **Hired Recently** is **Mysterious**

# MAMA AKUMA 2

## Kuzushiro

Translation: Alethea and Athena Nibley
Lettering: Bianca Pistillo

AKUMA NO MAMA Vol. 2
© 2020 Kuzushiro
First published in Japan in 2020 by SQUARE ENIX CO., LTD.
English translation rights arranged with SQUARE ENIX CO., LTD.
and Yen Press, LLC through Tuttle-Mori Agency, Inc.

English translation © 2022 by SQUARE ENIX CO., LTD.

Yen Press
150 West 30th Street, 19th Floor
New York, NY 10001

Visit us at yenpress.com
facebook.com/yenpress
twitter.com/yenpress
yenpress.tumblr.com
instagram.com/yenpress

First Yen Press Edition: February 2022

Yen Press is an imprint of Yen Press, LLC. The Yen Press name and logo are trademarks of Yen Press, LLC.

Library of Congress Control Number: 2020949563

ISBNs:
978-1-9753-3639-4 (paperback)
978-1-9753-3640-0 (ebook)

10 9 8 7 6 5 4 3 2 1

WOR

Printed in the United States of America